ESTIMATING MARKET POWER AND STRATEGIES

This book presents, compares, and develops various techniques for estimating market power – the ability to set price profitably above marginal cost – and strategies – the game-theoretic plans used by firms to compete with rivals. The authors start by examining static model approaches to estimating market power. They extend the analysis to dynamic models. Finally, they develop methods to estimate firms' strategies directly and examine how these strategies determine market power. A detailed technical appendix reviews the relevant information-theoretic and other econometric models that are used throughout. Questions and detailed answers for students and researchers are provided in the book for easy use.

Jeffrey M. Perloff is a professor in and Chair of the Department of Agricultural and Resource Economics at the University of California, Berkeley. He has written the textbooks *Modern Industrial Organization* (coauthored with Dennis Carlton) and *Microeconomics*. Professor Perloff has been an editor of *Industrial Relations* and an associate editor of the *American Journal of Agricultural Economics*. He is currently an associate editor of the *Journal of Productivity Analysis* and edits the *Journal of Industrial Organization Education*. A Fellow of the American Agricultural Economics Association, his economic research covers industrial organization, marketing, labor, trade, and econometrics. He has consulted with a number of nonprofit organizations and government agencies, including the Federal Trade Commission and the Departments of Commerce, Justice, and Agriculture.

Larry S. Karp is a professor in the Department of Agricultural and Resource Economics at the University of California, Berkeley. Professor Karp has served on the editorial boards of *Journal of Environmental Economics and Management*, *Journal of Economic Dynamics and Control*, *American Journal of Agricultural Economics*, and *Review of International Economics*. His research emphasis is environmental and resource economics, trade policy, and industrial organization, and he has consulted for federal and state agencies and private litigation on antitrust and environmental issues.

Amos Golan is a professor in the Department of Economics at American University. He cowrote *Maximum Entropy Econometrics: Robust Elimination with Limited Data* (with George Judge and Douglas Miller). Professor Golan has been a guest editor of the *Journal of Econometrics* and *Econometric Reviews*, and he is an associate editor of *Econometric Reviews* and *Entropy* and serves on the editorial board of *Foundations and Trends in Econometrics*. He has consulted for nonprofit organizations and government agencies including the Departments of Treasury and Agriculture, as well as the U.S. Navy and U.S. Air Force. Professor Golan's main research covers theoretical and applied econometrics and statistics, with specialties in the new field of information-theoretic and entropy econometrics.

Estimating Market Power and Strategies

JEFFREY M. PERLOFF
University of California, Berkeley

LARRY S. KARP
University of California, Berkeley

AMOS GOLAN
American University

CAMBRIDGE
UNIVERSITY PRESS

CAMBRIDGE
UNIVERSITY PRESS

University Printing House, Cambridge CB2 8BS, United Kingdom

One Liberty Plaza, 20th Floor, New York, NY 10006, USA

477 Williamstown Road, Port Melbourne, VIC 3207, Australia

314-321, 3rd Floor, Plot 3, Splendor Forum, Jasola District Centre, New Delhi - 110025, India

79 Anson Road, #06-04/06, Singapore 079906

Cambridge University Press is part of the University of Cambridge.

It furthers the University's mission by disseminating knowledge in the pursuit of education, learning and research at the highest international levels of excellence.

www.cambridge.org
Information on this title: www.cambridge.org/9780521011143

First published 2007

A catalogue record for this publication is available from the British Library

Library of Congress Cataloging in Publication data
Perloff , Jeffrey M.
Estimating market power and strategies / Jeffrey M. Perloff , Larry S. Karp, Amos Golan.
p. cm.
Includes bibliographical references and index.
ISBN 978-0-521-80440-0 (hardback) – ISBN 978-0-521-0111-4 (pbk)
1. Business enterprises – Finance. 2. Corporation – Finance. 3. Accounting. 4. Strategic planning. 5. Oraganizational effectiveness. I. Karp, Larry. II. Golan, Amos. Title.
HG4026.P4494 2007
338.4′301 – dc22 2007000000

ISBN 978-0-521-80440-0 Hardback
ISBN 978-0-521-01114-3 Paperback

For our parents

Mimi and Harvey Perloff

Rachel and Samuel Karp

Shulamith Katz and Nachum Golan

Contents

Foreword *page* xi

1 Introduction and Overview 1

Three Main Questions 1
Structure–Conduct–Performance 3
Static Models 5
Dynamics 7
Strategies 11

2 Structure–Conduct–Performance 13

Measures of Market Performance 14
Rate of Return 14
Price–Cost Margins 18
Tobin's q 19
Measures of Market Structure 19
Firm Size Distribution 20
Concentration Measures 20
Concentration Statistics 20
Problems with Using Concentration Measures 22
Summary Statistic Biases 23
Barriers to Entry 24
Unionization 25
The Relationship of Structure to Performance 25
Rates of Return and Industry Structure 25
Price–Cost Margins and Industry Structure 27
Price–Average Cost Margins 27
Price–Marginal Cost Margins 28
Other Explanatory Variables 30
International Studies of Performance and Structure 30

Performance and Structure in Individual Industries 31
Measurement and Statistical Problems 31
Conceptual Problems 32
A Modern Structure–Conduct–Performance Approach 34
Theory 34
Exogenous Sunk Cost 35
Endogenous Sunk Costs 37
Empirical Research 39
Summary 40
Problems 40

3 Industry Models of Market Power 42

Structural Approach 43
Interpretations of λ 45
Identification 47
Estimation and Hypothesis Tests 50
Taxes: An Application 51
Nonparametric and Reduced-Form Models 53
Comparative Statics 53
Hall's Reduced-Form Approach 55
Oligopsony 58
Structural Oligopsony Model 58
Hall's Reduced-Form Oligopsony Model 59
How Well These Methods Work 59
Tests Based on Cost Evidence 60
Oligopoly Simulations 60
Structural Model 62
Hall's Reduced-Form Model 65
Empirical Comparisons 69
Summary 70
Problems 72

4 Differentiated-Product Structural Models 74

Residual Demand 75
Neoclassical Demand System 77
Multilevel Demand Specifications 77
An Almost Ideal Demand System Example 78
Estimation 80
Identification 80
Instruments 81
Hypothesis Tests 82
Random Parameter Model 83
Linear Random Utility Model 83

Estimating the Random-Parameter Model 86
Market Power 89
Summary 91
Problems 91

5 Strategic Reasons for a Dynamic Estimation Model 93
Supergames 94
Empirical Implications 98
Models of Repeated Games with Trigger Strategies 99
Models of Repeated Games with Continuous Strategies 104
Summary 108
Problems 109

6 Dynamic Games Involving Economic Fundamentals 113
Fundamental Reasons for Dynamics 114
Production Fundamentals 114
Demand Fundamentals 116
A Dynamic Game with a Quasi-Fixed Input 117
Open-Loop Rules 121
Time Consistency of Open-Loop Rules 122
Different Approaches to Obtaining Necessary Conditions 123
Subgame Perfection and Markov Strategies 125
Differentiable Markov Perfect Strategies 127
A Sticky Price Model 128
Multiplicity of Equilibria 130
Selecting a Particular Equilibrium 132
Comparing Open-Loop and Markov Equilibria 132
Markov Perfect Equilibria and Conjectural Variations 135
Empirical Implications 136
Different Ways to Interpret Open-Loop Equilibrium 140
Summary 141
Problems 142

7 Estimation of Dynamic Games Involving Economic Fundamentals 147
Overview of Two Examples 147
The Sticky Price Model 149
The Dynamic Programming Equation 151
The Euler Equation for a Special Case 152
Other Approaches to Deriving the Euler Equation 153
The Estimation Model 154
The General Model 155
An Additional Assumption about Demand 156
Random Demand Shifters 157

Estimation Using the Dynamic Programming Equation 158
A Related Dynamic Oligopoly Model 162
A Dynamic Model with Advertising 163
The Open-Loop Equilibrium to the Advertising Model 164
The Markov Perfect Equilibrium to the Advertising Model 166
The Hybrid Model 168
Estimation of Markov Perfect Equilibria 170
Summary 178
Problems 179

8 Estimation of Market Power Using a Linear-Quadratic Model 181
Assumptions and Definitions 182
The Static Analog 183
The Dynamic Model 184
Implications of the Linear-Quadratic Structure 185
The Recursive Structure of the Solution 186
The Principle of Certainty Equivalence 187
Properties of the Equilibria 189
Equilibrium Conditions Used for Estimation 192
Necessary Conditions for the Open-Loop Equilibrium 193
Necessary Conditions for the Markov Perfect Equilibrium 195
Additional Restrictions and Testing 197
Empirical Applications 198
Coffee 198
Rice 199
Estimation Results 200
Classical Estimates 200
Bayesian Estimates 202
Simulations 204
Summary 205
Appendix 8A: Derivation of Restrictions 206
The Open-Loop Restrictions 206
The Markov Perfect Restrictions 207
Problems 208

9 Estimating Strategies: Theory 211
Related Studies 213
Mixed Strategies 217
Oligopoly Game 219
The Strategies and the Game 219
Econometric Adjustments for the Game 220
The Estimation Model 221

Classical Maximum Entropy Formulation for the Multinomial Problem 222
Incorporating the Sample Information 223
Incorporating the Nonsample, Game-Theoretic Information 227
Properties of the Estimators 229
The GME-Nash Estimator: Hypothesis Testing 229
Summary 232
Appendix 9A: Proof that the GME-Nash Estimator Is Consistent 233
Problems 234

10 Estimating Strategies: Case Studies 235
Airlines Game 235
Airlines Model 236
Estimates 237
Comparing Estimators 241
Hypothesis Tests 243
Sampling and Sensitivity Experiments 245
Airlines Summary 246
Cola Game 247
Cola Model 247
Estimates 249
Basic Statistics and Tests of the Cola Market 252
Lerner Measures of Market Power 257
Effects of the Exogenous Variables 257
Cola Summary 259
Summary 259
Appendix 10A: Expected Lerner Measure 260
Problems 261

Statistical Appendix 263
Bibliography 289
Answers 303
Index 325

Foreword

The purpose of this book is to show how to estimate a variety of traditional and new empirical industrial organization models of market power: the ability to raise price above marginal cost. We review the literature and methods to date, and focus on our work, particularly on dynamic models and estimating firms' strategies.

The book is appropriate for graduate students and researchers who have at least a basic understanding of theoretical industrial organization and standard econometric techniques. The chapters on dynamic models require a basic knowledge of dynamic optimization. A technical appendix at the end of the book reviews basic econometric techniques and covers in detail information-theoretic techniques, which we use in the last two chapters of the book.

We believe that it is crucial that economists be able to estimate and explain market power and determine firms' strategies. Economic theory alone cannot tell us how much market power firms exercise or which strategies they use. Thus, empirical work is critical if we are to understand how markets function. This work is also of importance for many policy purposes such as writing and enforcing antitrust and merger laws, regulating markets, facilitating entry, encouraging or discouraging product differentiation or advertising, or predicting the effects of taxes and other policies.

We are grateful to Scott Parris, the world's most patient editor; Dennis Carlton for permission to use the material in Chapter 2; four anonymous referees for many useful suggestions; Hugo Salgado for thoughtful advice; Alastair Hall for reviewing the Statistical Appendix; Glenn Woroch for comments on an early version; and our many colleagues who helped with much of the underlying research.

JP, LK, and AG

ONE

Introduction and Overview

We present and compare various techniques for estimating *market power* – the ability to set price profitably above marginal cost – and *strategies* – game-theoretic plans used by firms to compete with rivals. We start by examining static model approaches to estimating market power. Then, we extend our market power analysis to dynamic models. Finally, we develop methods to estimate firms' strategies directly and examine how these strategies determine market power. Throughout, we emphasize that the type of study we undertake depends crucially on which variables are observed and on the unobserved strategies of firms.

Research on market power and strategies is important for both policy makers and academics. It provides evidence that policy makers can use to improve antitrust and merger laws. It is used in court cases – and presumably will be increasingly employed in the future. It also allows academics to test theoretical models that were previously accepted on faith.

THREE MAIN QUESTIONS

Throughout this book, we focus on three major questions:

(1) How much market power does a firm or industry exercise?
(2) What are the major factors that determine this market power?
(3) How do firms' strategies determine market power?

Whether one can observe a reliable measure of market power often determines how researchers proceed. For example, in a one-period market, if we can observe the price, p, charged and can observe or estimate the marginal cost, MC, we can provide a direct answer to the first question – how much market power is exercised – by measuring the gap between price and marginal cost. To make this answer independent of the units of measurement of price, p, and marginal cost, MC, it is traditional to use the Lerner's (1934) index,

$$L \equiv \frac{p - MC}{p}. \tag{1.1}$$

Lerner's index is the percentage markup of price over marginal cost. This construct answers the question "How much market power does a firm exercise?" and not the question "How much market power does a firm (in theory) possess?" In a competitive market, price equals marginal cost, so any gap – a positive Lerner's index – shows that firms are exercising market power.

As we discuss in Chapter 2, most *structure–conduct–performance* (SCP) studies implicitly treat Question 1 as moot by assuming that an available measure reflects the degree of market power in an industry.[1] SCP researchers focus on answering our second question by explaining variations in market power across industries based on the structure of the industry and other factors.

In Chapters 3 and 4, we discuss the static model approach that starts by rejecting the assumption of the SCP studies that we have reliable measures of Lerner's index or other measures of market power. These studies answer Question 1 – the degree of market power – and Question 2 – the cause of market power – simultaneously using formal models that reflect exogenous institutional features of a particular industry.

In dynamic models, even if we observe current price and some measure of short-run marginal cost, we generally cannot determine the degree of market power, which may depend on unobserved opportunity costs or option values. In Chapters 5 through 8, we examine the answers to Questions 1 and 2 using dynamic structural models. In these chapters, we discuss how the cause of the dynamics plays a critical role in determining the appropriate model. In many dynamic studies, the single-period models are generalized to allow firms to have multiperiod strategies.

Finally, in Chapters 9 and 10, we discuss methods to estimate firms' strategies directly, Question 3, along with demand and cost functions. We show how to use these estimated strategies to solve for the market equilibrium, which allows us to estimate market power.

We now provide a detailed overview of the book. The book is divided into four parts. We start by providing a basic background chapter on the traditional structure–conduct–performance (SCP) approach. We then show how to estimate static models, dynamic models, and strategies. The SCP, static, and dynamic analyses focus on our first two questions: measuring and explaining market power. In the final section, where we estimate firm strategies – answer our third question – we show how to use those estimated strategies to provide good answers to the first two questions as well. The end of the book contains a detailed statistical appendix, which provides a background on all the traditional estimation methods we use,

[1] In contrast to legal discussions, we use the terms "industry" and "market" interchangeably.

and a relatively complete presentation of information theoretic methods that we use in the strategy section.

STRUCTURE–CONDUCT–PERFORMANCE

The traditional approach to empirical studies of market power, Mason's (1939, 1949) SCP approach, has been in use for two-thirds of a century.[2] It holds that an industry's performance (the success of an industry in producing benefits for consumers or profits for firms) depends on the conduct (behavior) of sellers and buyers, which depends on the structure of the market. The structure is often summarized by the number of firms or some other measure of the distribution of firms, such as the relative market shares of the largest firms.

Mason and his colleagues initially conducted case studies of individual industries. Eventually, Bain (1951, 1956) and others introduced comparisons across industries. Since Bain's early work, a typical SCP study regresses a measure of market power such as profit or the gap between price and a cost measure on a structural variable such as the market shares of the four largest firms and other variables. That is, these studies presume that the answer to our first question – how much market power is exercised – is known, and concentrate on the second question – what causes this market power.

This literature has been criticized as being descriptive rather than theoretical. A more generous way to view it is that SCP researchers are estimating a reduced-form regression in which performance is linked to market structure. Although these researchers rarely use formal theoretical models to justify their empirical research, many such models exist.

For simplicity, suppose that the n firms in a market produce a homogeneous product, so that industry output, Q, equals sum of the output of the n firms: $Q = q_1 + q_2 + \cdots + q_n$. Given full information and no other distortions, there is a single market price, p, determined by the inverse market demand curve, $p(Q)$. The single-period profit of Firm i is

$$\pi_i = p(Q)q_i - mq_i,$$

where m is a constant marginal cost that is common to all firms.

The firms engage in a one-period game. Each firm has a strategy determining its actions. A set of strategies is a Nash equilibrium if, holding the strategies of all other players (firms) constant, no player (firm) can obtain a higher payoff (profit) by choosing a different strategy. In particular, suppose that the firms choose quantities. We call the outcome of this game a Nash-in-quantities, Cournot, or Nash-Cournot equilibrium.

[2] Schmalensee (1989) thoroughly analyzed the SCP literature through the 1980s.

Each firm's first-order condition, given the Nash-in-quantities assumption that other firms do not change their outputs, is obtained by setting the derivative of profit with respect to the firm's output equation to zero: $\mathrm{d}\pi_i/\mathrm{d}q_i = p + q_i(\mathrm{d}p/\mathrm{d}Q) - m = 0$. Rearranging terms, we obtain the optimality condition that

$$MR = p + q_i \frac{\mathrm{d}p}{\mathrm{d}Q} = m = MC, \tag{1.2}$$

where MR is the marginal revenue.

We obtain the Nash-Cournot equilibrium quantities by solving the n optimality equations for $q_1, q_2, \ldots, q_n$. Because the firms face the same marginal cost, they produce identical quantities, $q_1 = \cdots = q_n \equiv q$, in equilibrium so that industry output is $Q \equiv nq$. By substituting these identities into Equation (1.2), we can rewrite this expression as

$$L \equiv \frac{p - m}{p} = -\frac{1}{n\varepsilon} = -\frac{s}{\varepsilon}, \tag{1.3}$$

where $\varepsilon = (\mathrm{d}Q/\mathrm{d}p)(p/Q)$ is the market demand elasticity and $s \equiv q/Q = 1/n$ is the share of each firm. According to Equation (1.3), in the degenerate case in which $n = 1$, we find the usual result that a monopoly price–cost markup equals the negative of one over the market elasticity. Where n is greater than or equal to two, we learn that the markup equals the negative of one over $n\varepsilon$ or s/ε, which is the elasticity of demand facing each firm in equilibrium. As the number of firms grows without bound, we obtain the competitive result that the markup is zero.

Now, suppose that we generalize the optimality condition to allow the marginal cost to vary across firms, m_i. By summing with respect to i, Cowling and Waterson (1976) observed that the weighted average price–cost margin for the industry is

$$L = \sum_i s_i \frac{p - m_i}{p} = -\sum_i \frac{s_i^2}{\varepsilon} = -\frac{HHI}{\varepsilon}, \tag{1.4}$$

where $s_i = q_i/Q$ and HHI is the Herfindahl-Hirschman Index, the sum of the square of the share of each firm in the market is a measure of industry concentration. Thus, at least for these Cournot models, we obtain a clear relationship between Lerner's index, a measure of performance, and the structure of the market as captured by the number of firms, the share of each firm, or the HHI.

If the industry is monopolistically competitive and firms enter until the marginal firm earns zero profits, then n depends on the average cost function of the firms as well as the elasticity of demand. That is, both fixed and variable costs matter. Actions by governments or others that prevent firms from entering the industry (e.g., licensing laws, taxi medallions) similarly affect a firm's market power. Actions by a firm to differentiate physically its product or to convince consumers that its product is different through advertising, raise the elasticity of demand the firm faces and hence its market power. Thus, these "explanations" for market power can be built directly into the demand curve, the cost curve, or a market equilibrium equation in a structural model.

STATIC MODELS

All the subsequent studies that we discuss throughout the book make use of these basic ideas to model the optimizing behavior of firms conditional on the demand, cost, and other explanations for market power. The modern static approach, which has been used for a third of a century, attempts to estimate the unobserved degree of market power and to determine its causes by estimating optimality and other equations simultaneously.[3]

There are three major types of modern static models, which are based on a single-period oligopoly model. In Chapter 3, we examine the first two types of studies, which examine industries that (are assumed to) produce homogeneous products. One set of studies uses structural models whereas the other uses comparative statics to estimate or test for market power with reduced-form or nonparametric models. In Chapter 4, we show how more recent studies extend the structural models to examine differentiated goods markets.

In Chapter 3, we discuss studies based on industry-level data. The first step is to construct each firm's first-order, or optimality, conditions via a profit maximization procedure similar to Equation (1.2). However, these models do not assume that the industry necessarily has a Cournot equilibrium. Rather, they use a more flexible approach that permits a large family of possible equilibria including monopoly, Cournot oligopoly, other oligopoly, and competitive outcomes. Typically, researchers use a single parameter to index the various possible outcomes. For example, they may introduce a "conjectural variation" parameter v that characterizes how Firm i believes its rivals will respond to a change in its output: $v = \mathrm{d}Q_{-i}/\mathrm{d}q_i$, where Q_{-i} is the collective output of all the firms except for Firm i. Depending on the value of v, firms could behave competitively, oligopolistically, or collusively, and hence v is a measure of market power.

Because the researchers do not know marginal cost, they usually express marginal cost as a function of output and possibly other variables such as factor prices. Researchers then aggregate these optimality conditions to get a market-level condition. Next, they simultaneously estimate that equation and other equations describing the market, such as the market demand equation. Their purpose is to simultaneously identify the market-power parameter and the marginal cost.

[3] Bresnahan (1989) summarized most of the modern static approaches through the 1980s. The June 1987 issue of the *Journal of Industrial Economics*, entitled "The Empirical Renaissance in Industrial Economics," edited by Bresnahan and Schmalensee, contains a number of the most important papers as of that time and a brief summary of the literature by the editors (Bresnahan and Schmalensee, 1987). See also Geroski, Phlips, and Ulph (1985), which surveys the literature on measuring conjectural variations and monopoly power.

This approach makes heavy use of assumptions about the exact specification of structural equations and may introduce constructs like conjectural variations. Consequently, other researchers prefer to use an approach than makes fewer assumptions. They employ reduced-form or nonparametric models to measure market power, bound it, or test whether the data are consistent with one market structure versus another. Because they relax the assumptions in the structural model, these researchers may not be able to estimate the degree of market power, but they can test the null hypothesis that the market is competitive. Typically, underlying the reduced-form approach is a comparative statics analysis. One might choose this simpler approach rather than the richer structural models because of limits on data or as a way to avoid the danger of specification bias caused by incorrect choice of functional form.

In Chapter 4, we turn to more recent static models in which researchers focus on individual firms rather than markets and relax the assumption that all firms produce identical products. The emphasis in most of these generalized models is on the role of factors that affect demand in determining market power. Most studies use one of two approaches to estimating market power with multiple firms with differentiated products. The first approach is based on estimating the firms' residual demand functions. In the second approach, researchers simultaneous estimate the complete demand system and the set of optimality conditions. Both approaches are based on a structural model and generalize the homogeneous good, one-sector model. Several of the earliest studies derive residual demand functions for individual firms from the full structural model. For example, the inverse residual demand curve facing Firm i, $d_i(q_i)$, is the inverse market demand curve, $p(Q)$, less the supply curve, $S_o(p)$, of all other firms (where it is defined):

$$d_i(q_i) = p(Q) - S_o(p). \tag{1.5}$$

Regardless of market structure, we again find that Firm i maximizes its profit by equating its marginal revenue (corresponding to its residual demand curve) to its marginal cost,

$$MR_i = p_i\left(1 + \frac{1}{\varepsilon_i}\right) = MC_i, \tag{1.6}$$

where ε_i is the elasticity of its residual demand curve, Equation (1.5). By rearranging this expression in the usual way, we obtain the Lerner index expression:

$$L_i = \frac{p_i - MC_i}{p_i} = -\frac{1}{\varepsilon_i}. \tag{1.7}$$

The markup depends solely on the elasticity of residual demand. From Equation (1.7), it appears that we can calculate the degree of market power, L_i, without using cost information; however, we need to use information about at least other firms' costs to determine the residual demand curve properly. Thus, these studies take into account both demand and cost factors, and estimate a market-power or conjectural variation parameter directly.

More recent studies estimate full systems of demand and optimality equations. Most of these studies use one of two approaches to specify and estimate the demand system. In the neoclassical demand-system approach, a demand model is estimated based on market-level data using a flexible functional form and imposing restrictions from economic theory such as adding up, symmetry, and homogeneity properties.

In the most recent work, researchers use market share or consumer-level data to estimate the consumer demand system, typically without imposing restrictions from economic theory. The best-known studies using this approach employ a random utility model. Combining these more sophisticated demand estimates with optimality conditions, researchers determine market power using similar methods to those used in the earlier static structural models.

DYNAMICS

In Chapters 5 through 8, we study the generalization of the early static structural models to dynamic models. Although in these dynamic models the emphasis is on estimating market power, they can also provide an answer to the second question on the determinants of market power.

In these models, firms interact over many periods – they play a dynamic game. Each firm maximizes its expected present discounted value of the stream of its future profits. We want to use observations on firms' behavior to measure the extent of competition in a dynamic game. The estimation problem depends on the reason for the dynamics, the type of game that firms play, and on the data observed by the researcher. We distinguish between *strategic* and *fundamental* reasons why firms might play a dynamic game rather than engage in a sequence of static games.

It is possible that firms interact in a market repeatedly over time, where a firm's decision this period does not affect demand, costs, or other variables that affect profit in subsequent periods. Nevertheless, a firm's current decision might alter its rivals' beliefs about how that firm will behave in the future, thus altering the rivals' equilibrium future behavior. If dynamic interactions arise because firms think that their rivals will respond in the future to their current action, because of a change in beliefs, we say that the reason for the dynamics is strategic.

In contrast, a firm's decision about advertising, capital investment, or other long-lasting factors in the current period might directly affect future demand or cost. In these cases, current decisions alter a payoff-relevant state variable such as the stock of loyal customers, or the stock of capital. The change in this market "fundamental" alters future decisions by all firms. In this case, we describe the source of dynamics as fundamental.

With both strategic and fundamental dynamics, current actions affect future actions, but the mechanism that creates this dynamic relation is different, and it calls for different estimation methods. Although dynamics may be important for both strategic and fundamental reasons, we discuss them separately. Chapter 5 considers the estimation problem when the only source of dynamics is strategic. Chapters 6 through 8 discuss models used when there is a fundamental source of dynamics.

Chapter 5 reviews basic concepts from game theory, including subgame perfection and the Folk theorem of supergames, and explains their role in the estimation problem. A supergame is a static one-shot game that (with positive probability) is repeated infinitely often. The simplest way to think of a subgame is to envision a game tree with infinitely many nodes. In each period, players begin at a particular node. Their collective decisions in that period send them to a new node in the next period. The game beginning at each node is referred to as a "subgame." A strategy is a mapping from a player's information set to the player's set of actions; in this sense, a strategy "instructs" each agent how to behave in every subgame. An equilibrium strategy is a collection of strategies; one for each player, for which each player's strategy is a best response to the rivals' strategies. An equilibrium is "subgame perfect" if and only if the set of strategies is an equilibrium for each possible subgame (i.e., at each node) – not just at the subgames that are actually visited along the equilibrium trajectory. The Folk theorem shows that there are (typically) infinitely many subgame perfect equilibria. This result is empirically important because it means that we (typically) cannot rely on economic theory to identify a unique equilibrium in dynamic settings.

Chapter 5 considers two classes of models, using either punishment strategies or continuous strategies. The equilibrium strategy involving punishments typically requires that players use one action (such as choosing a price or a quantity) in the cooperative phase, and a different action in the punishment phase. The outcome in the cooperative phase leads to a higher payoff than in the noncooperative equilibrium to the one-shot game, but it need not produce the cartel solution.

The use of the term "cooperative" is potentially confusing because the underlying game is noncooperative. The noncooperative equilibrium consists of a set of strategies, where each firm's strategy is a best response to other firms' equilibrium strategies. The (credible) threat of punishment causes firms to resist the temptation to deviate from their cooperative action. Actions in the cooperative phase might look approximately or even exactly like cooperation, but these actions are sustained as part of a noncooperative equilibrium. In this setting, even if the cooperative phase produces the cartel solution, firms have not colluded. In other words, noncooperative behavior in a supergame is consistent with a wide range of outcomes, sometimes extending from the one-shot noncooperative equilibrium to the cartel solution. The econometric objective is to determine where the outcome lies on this continuum of possible equilibria.

Models with continuous strategies assume that agents use a decision rule that depends continuously on their rivals' previous actions. In contrast, with the punishment strategies described earlier, the observed actions (in most models) take one of two values, the cooperative and the noncooperative levels. The two types of models are similar, however, in that both assume that current actions affect rivals' future actions, even though current actions do not alter an economic fundamental (such as demand or costs).

Chapter 6 provides an overview of the concepts needed to estimate dynamic models based on fundamental rather than purely strategic considerations. We illustrate the role of fundamentals using both production-driven and demand-driven scenarios. For example, current investment in physical capital affects future production costs, and current advertising affects the level of future demand. In these kinds of models, firms make decisions that may affect their current profit only (a "static decision") in addition to decisions that affect their future stream of profit (a "dynamic decision"). The level of output in the current period (the static decision) affects current profits, but need have no direct effect on future profit; in contrast, the current level of investment (the dynamic decision) does have a direct effect on future profits. Empirical estimates of market power attempt to measure how close an industry is to cartel or cooperative behavior. However, firms might have different degrees of cooperation regarding their static and dynamic decisions. If the game is misspecified, estimates of a measure of the degree of cooperation with respect to one type of decision may be biased. In addition, increased cooperation with respect to one type of decision can have ambiguous effects on firms' profits and on social welfare. Thus, the coexistence of static and dynamic decisions complicates both the problem of obtaining reasonable estimates of market power, and also interpreting the welfare implications of those measures.

There are many types of dynamic strategies. We explain the difference between two important types of strategies, *open-loop* and *Markov Perfect*, using a deterministic setting in which firms incur convex adjustment costs to change the level of their capital stock. With Markov strategies, firms understand that their current actions affect a state variable (e.g., a level of capital or a stock of loyal customers) that affects rivals' future actions. Firms take their rivals' strategies (i.e., their decision rules) as given, and understand that by altering the state variable they can affect rivals' future actions. In contrast, with open-loop strategies, firms believe that their rivals' strategies do not depend on these state variables. Firms therefore behave as if their actions have no effect on their rivals' future actions. The open-loop equilibrium can be obtained by solving a one-agent optimal control problem, but finding the Markov Perfect equilibrium requires the solution to a game.

When agents have symmetric power (as distinct from a leader–follower role), both the open-loop and the Markov Perfect equilibria are "time-consistent." To understand time consistency, suppose that we compute the equilibrium at an arbitrary time – for example, time 0 – and assume that firms follow their equilibrium strategies until a future time, t. Because (by assumption) firms have followed the equilibrium strategies up to time t, the game is "on the equilibrium trajectory" at time t. Time consistency of the equilibrium means that the equilibrium computed at time t equals the continuation of the equilibrium that was computed at time 0.

Subgame perfection is a stronger condition; it requires that the continuation of the initial equilibrium is an equilibrium starting at *any* subgame, not just the subgames that are visited in equilibrium. That is, the equilibrium decision rules computed at time 0 are also equilibrium decision rules at time t even if one (or more) firm deviated from its equilibrium rule between the two points in time (thus causing the state variable to be "off the equilibrium path"). The Markov Perfect equilibrium is a particular member of the set of subgame perfect equilibria. The open-loop equilibrium is, in general, not subgame perfect. For this reason, the Markov Perfect equilibrium is usually considered to be a more plausible solution concept than the open-loop equilibrium.

There typically are many Markov Perfect equilibria. In some cases, a "good" outcome can be supported by credible threats to adopt punitive strategies following "bad" behavior. This kind of strategy is reminiscent of the punishment strategies that are used in supergames; however, in supergame models, the current actions are explicit functions of past actions, whereas in a Markov equilibrium, the current action depends only on a directly payoff-relevant variable, such as current capital stocks. Non-uniqueness of Markov equilibria also arises for a more subtle reason; the necessary (equilibrium) conditions do not pin down agents' beliefs about how rivals will respond to deviations from equilibrium in a steady state. This reason for non-uniqueness is similar to the reason why there are multiple consistent conjectural variation equilibria in static games.

Chapter 7 discusses the estimation of dynamic models under different assumptions about the equilibrium: open-loop, Markov Perfect, or a hybrid. The chapter describes in detail two models that differ in the fundamental reasons for dynamics. These models are used to address different empirical questions. The first of these, the sticky price model, provides a straightforward dynamic generalization of the static conjectural variation models used in the first part of this book. We discuss the estimation of this model under the assumption that firms use open-loop strategies. A conjectural variations parameter provides an index that measures the extent to which the observed outcome is closer to a competitive or collusive equilibrium. The necessary condition for optimality, the Euler Equation, is the basic estimation equation, just as the first-order conditions to static optimization problems are the basis for estimating static models.

The second model in Chapter 7 studies firms' advertising decisions. Here we assume that the equilibrium is Nash-in-advertising. We compare the necessary conditions (the Euler equations) when firms use either an open-loop rule or a Markov Perfect rule, and we consider a hybrid that lies "between" these two types of equilibria. By estimating this hybrid model, it is possible to determine whether firms use a naïve (open-loop) or a more sophisticated strategy in which they recognize that rivals may respond to changes in the endogenous state variable.

The final section of this chapter discusses a relatively new technique for estimating the parameters of the objective function in a game in which firms use Markov Perfect strategies. Using an example, we show how this estimation strategy can be modified so that the researcher can identify the industry's structure – for example, test whether firms are playing a noncooperative game, acting collusively, or behaving as price takers.

Chapter 8 presents the theory for the linear-quadratic model and provides examples. In this model, demand is linear in output so revenue is quadratic in output. Firms incur quadratic costs of changing their output (or sales). The endogenous state variable (those variables whose values firms jointly determine) is the lagged level of output. Thus, the single-period payoff is a linear-quadratic function of the endogenous state variable and the control variable (the change in output) and the equation of motion for the endogenous state is linear in these variables, resulting in a linear-quadratic game.

The linear-quadratic specification makes it possible to compare, in a simple manner, equilibria under the open-loop and Markov Perfect assumptions. For a given measure of market power, we can determine the magnitude of the difference in these two models in the price trajectory and steady state. We can also see how the estimate of market power depends on whether we assume that firms use open-loop or Markov policies, by comparing the estimated indices of market structure and the corresponding steady-state prices under the two equilibrium assumptions. This comparison indicates whether the Markov assumption really matters for empirical work. We present empirical work based on this model in Chapter 8.

STRATEGIES

Only a small number of studies have tried to estimate strategies directly. By doing so, they can answer all three of our questions. In Chapters 9 and 10, we summarize some recent approaches to estimating strategies, but we concentrate on our previous joint work.

In Chapter 9, we derive two methods for estimating oligopoly strategies directly. The first allows strategies to depend on variables that affect demand and cost. The second adds restrictions from game theory. Both methods build on the information-theoretic, general maximum entropy (GME) formulation discussed in the Statistical Appendix to this book.[4] The second method is just a generalization of the first one.

Unlike most previous empirical studies of oligopoly behavior, we do not assume that firms use a single pure strategy, nor do we make the sort of ad hoc assumptions used in most static models (e.g., conjectural variations – see Chapter 3). We introduce into the estimation procedure the game-theoretic equations. Both our

[4] The Appendix provides a detailed discussion of recently developed econometric methods. The Appendix is a self-contained discussion of the econometric methods necessary to estimate and analyze applied industrial organization analyses. Each method is developed and summarized in enough detail so that the user can apply these methods without searching through other texts.

approaches recognize that firms may use either pure or mixed strategies. In our approach, we use both the hard data reflecting prices, quantities, and other relevant information and soft data representing our beliefs about the strategies used by the firms. Specifically, we start by constructing the hypothesized game. We then solve that game to obtain the equilibrium conditions. We incorporate these conditions within the estimation method so that we can simultaneously estimate the strategy and all the other parameters (demand, cost, etc.) based on the observed data.

Firms may use a single decision variable (say, price) or multiple decision variables (such as price and advertising). We divide each firm's continuous strategy action space into a grid over these strategies. The upper and lower bounds on the possible actions are constructed based on observed data. Then, we estimate the vector of probabilities – the mixed or pure strategies – that reflects the different actions the firm may choose. For example, in the two-decision-variables case, we estimate the probabilities over a price–advertising rectangular grid.

In Chapter 10, we apply these techniques to two markets. First we examine the pricing strategies of American and United Airlines in a number of city-pair routes. After estimating each firm's vector of mixed (probabilities) or pure strategies for various routes, we use our estimates to calculate the Lerner index of market structure and examine how changes in exogenous variables affect strategies.

In addition to presenting estimates of the strategies and demand estimates of United and American Airlines, we also provide a detailed set of hypothesis tests concerning the firms' behavior, as well as a number of sampling experiments illustrating the small sample properties of our information-theoretic estimators.

Next, we generalize the airline example to higher dimensional strategy spaces. Using data corresponding to demand cost and advertising, we estimate the joint pricing and advertising strategies of Coca-Cola and Pepsi-Cola for various time periods. This application is more general than the airlines example: firms have two decision variables rather than just one and their strategies are explicit functions of exogenous variables that affect demand and cost.

As in the airlines study, we use our estimates to analyze the market structure, calculate the expected Lerner index, and examine how changes in exogenous variables affect strategies. We also provide detailed tests showing that the game-theoretic behavior formulated here is consistent with the empirical data.

TWO

Structure–Conduct–Performance

Edward S. Mason's (1939, 1949) structure–conduct–performance (SCP) approach revolutionized the study of industrial organization by introducing the use of inferences from microeconomic analysis.[1] In the SCP paradigm,[2] an industry's *performance* – the success of an industry in producing benefits for consumers – depends on the *conduct* – behavior – of sellers and buyers, which depends on the *structure* of the market. The structure, in turn, depends on basic conditions such as technology and demand for a product. Typically, researchers summarize the structure by the number of firms or some other measure of the distribution of firms, such as the relative market shares of the largest firms.

Because the nature of these connections is usually not explained in detail, many economists criticize the SCP approach for being descriptive rather than analytic. George J. Stigler (1968) and others urged economists to use price-theory models based on explicit, maximizing behavior by firms and governments rather than the SCP method. Others suggested replacing the SCP paradigm with analyses that emphasized monopolistic competition (Chamberlin 1933, Hotelling 1929), game theory (von Neumann and Morgenstern 1944), or transaction costs (Williamson 1975). Indeed, the rest of this book concerns modern empirical alternatives to the SCP approach.

Mason and his colleagues at Harvard initially conducted case studies of individual industries (e.g., Wallace 1937). The first empirical applications of the SCP theory were by Mason's colleagues and students, such as Joe S. Bain (1951, 1956). In contrast to the case studies, these studies made comparisons across industries.

A typical SCP study has two main stages. First, one obtains a measure of performance – through direct measurement rather than through estimation – and several measures of industry structure for many industries. Second, the economist uses

[1] The following discussion of structure–conduct–performance studies draws heavily on Carlton and Perloff (2005), Chapter 8. We are very grateful to Dennis Carlton for his permission to use this material.

[2] In all books on industrial organization, SCP is the only acceptable modifier for "paradigm."

the cross-industry observations to regress the performance measure on the various structure measures to explain the difference in market performance across industries. We first discuss the measurement of performance and structure variables and then examine the evidence relating performance to structure.

MEASURES OF MARKET PERFORMANCE

Measures of market performance provide an answer to our first key question as to whether market power is exercised in an industry. Measures that directly or indirectly reflect profit or the relationship of price to costs are commonly used to gauge how close an industry's performance is to a competitive benchmark:

- The *rate of return* is the profit per dollar of investment.
- The *price–cost margin* reflects the difference between price and marginal cost, although, in practice, SCP researchers often use some average cost in place of marginal cost. A few studies use just the price based on the assumption that marginal cost is equal across industries or time.
- *Tobin's q* is the ratio of the market value of a firm to its value based upon the replacement cost of its assets.

RATE OF RETURN

Determining whether a firm or industry's rate of return differs from the competitive level is difficult. We start by discussing the conceptual approach and then point out the pitfalls.

A firm's profit is revenue less labor, material, and capital costs,

$$\pi = R - \text{labor costs} - \text{material costs} - (r + \delta) p_k K,$$

where R is revenue, r is the earned rate of return, δ is the depreciation rate, p_k is the price of capital, $[r + \delta]p_k$ is the rental rate of capital, and K is the quantity of capital. The competitive earned rate of return is r such that economic profit is zero:

$$r = \frac{R - \text{labor costs} - \text{material costs} - \delta p_k K}{p_k K}. \tag{2.1}$$

To illustrate how excess rates of return translate into price overcharges, we suppose that a firm earns a rate of return, r^*, that is 5% above the normal rate: $r^* = r + 0.05$. That is, the firm's invested capital earns excess revenues of 5% times the value of its capital above what it would earn if it were in a competitive industry. If the firm's revenue is R^*, then its rate of return is

$$r^* = \frac{R^* - \text{labor costs} - \text{material costs} - \delta p_k K}{p_k K} = r + 0.05.$$

Let R^* be the revenue that would yield a normal rate of return, r^*. The amount by which revenues (or price) must decline to yield the normal returns is $R - R^*$. Using Equation (2.1) for r and the expression for r^*, we know that $r - r^* = -0.05 = (R - R^*)/(p_k K)$. Multiplying both sides by $p_k K$, we find that $R - R^* = -0.05\, p_k K$. Thus, to get the normal rate of return, price (and hence the revenue) would have to fall by 5% of the value of capital.

Suppose that in some manufacturing industries the ratio of the value of capital to the value of annual revenue is roughly one. Therefore, if a firm is earning a real rate of return 5% higher than the normal rate of return (which was roughly between 5% and 10% over the period 1948-1976), the competitive price is roughly 95% ($= 1 - 0.05$) of its current value. That is, industries that earn a rate of return 1.5 times higher than the return earned by competitive industries (say, 15% instead of 10%) have prices that are only 5% above the competitive level.[3] In other words, in industries with low values of capital, even large differences in rates of return between concentrated and unconcentrated industries do not necessarily imply prices that are much above the competitive level.

Because a conceptually valid calculation of rates of return is difficult, reported rates of return are often based on compromises that introduce biases. The first, and key concern, is whether the rate of return captures economic profit (which takes account of opportunity costs) or accounting profit.

There are eight major problems in calculating rates of return correctly (Fisher and McGowan 1983, Carlton and Perloff 2005). First, capital is usually not valued appropriately because accounting definitions are used instead of the economic definitions. An economist measures annual capital cost flows as the annual rental fees if all the capital assets were rented. When rental rates are not readily available, the economist implicitly calculates a rental rate at replacement cost, which is the long-run cost of buying a comparable-quality asset. At least in the past, the accounting value of capital, or *book value*, has been based on the historical cost of the capital combined with accounting assumptions about depreciation. Because historical cost is often very different from the actual replacement cost of the capital, using the book value of capital rather than the economic value can severely bias the measurement of rate of return.

Second, depreciation is usually measured improperly. The economic rental rate on capital must provide an owner of capital with a certain rate of return *after* depreciation has been deducted on the equipment. Accountants use several fixed formulas to measure the depreciation of an asset. One common formula, called *straight-line depreciation,* assumes that the asset's value declines in equal annual amounts over some fixed period (the *useful life* of the asset). For example, a machine that costs $1,000 and is assigned a useful life of ten years would incur $100 of

[3] According to Equation (1.4), $(p - MC)/p = -1/\varepsilon$, so a price about 5% above marginal cost is consistent with an elasticity of demand of $\varepsilon = -21$: $p = MC/(1 + 1/\varepsilon) = MC/(1 - 1/21) \approx 1.05MC$.

depreciation annually for its first ten years of life. If it lasts more than ten years, it incurs no additional depreciation. The fixed formula's predictions of the amount of depreciation may be unrelated to the asset's decline in economic value, which is the measure of its economic depreciation. As a result, the estimate of the rate of return may be biased.

Third, valuing problems arise for advertising and research and development (R&D) because, as with capital, they have lasting impacts. The money a firm spends on advertising this year may generate benefits next year, just as a plant built this year provides a benefit next year. If consumers forget an advertisement's message slowly over time, the advertisement's effect on demand may last for several years. If a firm expensed (initially deducted its entire cost of) annual advertising expenditures and then made no deductions in subsequent years, its earned rate of return would be misleadingly low in the initial year and too high in later years. A better approach is to base the advertising expenses on the interest rate and the annual decline in the economic value of the advertising as the annual cost. Unfortunately, it is difficult to determine the correct rates of depreciation to use for advertising expenses.

Fourth, rates of return may not be properly adjusted for risk. To determine whether a firm is earning an excess rate of return, the proper comparison is between the rate of return actually earned and the competitive risk-adjusted rate of return, which is the rate of return earned by competitive firms engaged in projects with the same level of risk as that of the firm under analysis. Investors dislike risk and must be compensated for bearing it: the greater the risk, the higher the expected rate of return. For example, suppose a firm's research to discover new products is successful one time in five. If the firm's expected profit is zero, then the profit on the successful product must be high enough to offset the losses on the four failures. It is misleading to conclude that there are excessively high profits based on an examination of the profit of the one successful product.

Fifth, a related point concerning uncertainty is that some rates of return do not take debt into account properly. Researchers often use the rate of return to the stockholders as a measure of the firm's profitability. If a firm issues debt in addition to equity, both debt holders and equity holders (stockholders) have claims on the firm's income. Because the assets of the firm are paid for by both debt holders and stockholders, the rate of return on the firm's assets equals a weighted average of the rate of return to the debt holders and the stockholders. The rate of return to debt holders is typically lower than the rate of return to stockholders, because debt is less risky than stock and debt holders get paid before stockholders when a firm is in financial distress. The return to stockholders increases with debt because the income received by stockholders in a *highly leveraged* firm (one with a high ratio of debt to equity) is risky, so stockholders in such firms demand high rates of return.[4]

[4] Suppose, first, that a firm has no debt and finances an investment with $1,000 raised through sale of stock. Next year, the investment returns the $1,000 plus either $80 or $200 with equal probability, so that the stockholders' rate of return is either 8% or 20% for an average return of

Therefore, it is improper to compare the rates of return to stockholders in two firms in order to measure differences in the degree of competition if the two firms have very different ratios of debt to equity. The debt–equity ratio has nothing to do with whether the firm is earning excess rates of return on its assets. Differences among firms in their rates of return to stockholders could reflect differences in competition facing firms or differences in their debt–equity ratios. However, even though the rate of return calculated by dividing net income by assets differs from the rate of return from dividing income to stockholders by the value of stockholder's equity, they tend to be highly correlated (Liebowitz 1982).

Sixth, proper adjustments must be made for inflation. The earned rate of return can be calculated as either a *real* rate of return (a rate of return adjusted to eliminate the effects of inflation) or as a *nominal* rate (which includes the effects of inflation). One should be careful to compare rates that are all real or all nominal.

If one uses a real rate, income in the numerator of the rate of return should not include the price appreciation on assets from inflation – it should only include the gain in the value of assets beyond that due to general price inflation. For example, if capital is initially worth \$100, annual income before depreciation is \$20, and the annual depreciation rate is 10% (so depreciation is \$10), then the earned rate of return is 10% [= (20 − 10)/100]. If inflation was 20% during the year, the value of the capital at the end of the year is \$90 (= \$100 − depreciation) times 1.2 (to adjust for inflation), or \$108. The firm has incurred a *gain* of \$18 on its capital, but it is illusory; it does not represent an increase in purchasing power because all prices have risen as a result of the inflation.

Seventh, monopoly profit may be inappropriately included in the calculated rate of return by using book value in the calculation. Book value sometimes includes *capitalized* (the present value of future) monopoly profits. Suppose the monopoly earns excess annual economic profits of \$100 above the competitive rate of return and the annual interest rate is 10%. The owner of the monopoly sells the firm (and its future stream of monopoly profits) for \$1,000 more than the replacement cost of its assets. The owner willingly sells the firm because that extra \$1,000 will earn \$100, or 10%, a year in a bank. The new owner only makes a competitive rate of return because the monopoly profits per year are exactly offset by the foregone interest payments from the extra \$1,000. The extra \$1,000 paid for the monopoly is the capitalized value of the monopoly profits, *not* the replacement

14%. Suppose, instead, that the firm raises the \$1,000 for the investment by issuing debt of \$500 that pays 10% interest and selling stock worth \$500. The debt holders must receive payment of interest before the stockholders receive any income. Therefore, whether the firm earns \$80 or \$200, the debt holders receive \$500 plus \$50 of interest. The stockholders receive \$500 plus either \$30 or \$150, so that the total amount paid to both debt holders and stockholders is \$1,000 plus either \$80 or \$200. The stockholders therefore earn either 6% (= 30/500) or 30% (= 150/500), for an average return of 18%, whereas the debt holders earn 10%. The stockholders now earn a higher average rate of return and face a wider range of outcomes, even though the income potential of the firm is unchanged.

cost to society of replacing the monopoly's capital. Thus, if the reported value of capital inappropriately includes capitalized monopoly profits, the calculated rate of return is misleadingly low if one wants to determine whether an industry is restricting output and is thereby earning an above normal rate of return.

Eighth, pre-tax rates of return may have been calculated instead of the appropriate after-tax rates of return. Corporations pay taxes to the government, and only what is left is of interest to individual investors. That is, after-tax rates of return govern entry and exit decisions. Competition among investors causes after-tax rates of return to be equated on different assets. If assets are taxed at different rates, the before-tax rate of return could vary widely even if all markets are competitive. For that reason, we should use after-tax rates of return and after-tax measures of profit, especially when comparisons are made across industries that are subject to different tax rates.

Price–Cost Margins

In order to avoid the problems associated with calculating rates of return, many economists prefer a different measure of performance, the Lerner index or price–cost margin, $L \equiv (p - MC)/p$, which is the difference between price, p, and marginal cost, MC, as a fraction of the price. That is, the Lerner index is the percentage markup of price over marginal cost. Because the correlation between accounting rates of return and the price–cost margin can be relatively low (Liebowitz 1982), it makes a difference which of these two performance measures is used.

A competitive firm sets $p = MC$ because its residual demand price elasticity is negative infinity (it faces a horizontal demand curve). As a consequence, $L = 0$.

Unfortunately, because a marginal cost measure is rarely available, many SCP researchers use the price–average variable cost (AVC) margin instead of the appropriate price–marginal cost margin. Their approximation to the price–average variable cost margins is typically calculated as revenue minus payroll minus material cost divided by revenue. (Some researchers commit an even more serious error by using average total cost instead of average variable cost.)

Substituting average variable cost for marginal cost may cause a serious bias (see Fisher 1987). Suppose that marginal cost is constant and is given as

$$MC = AVC + (r + \delta)\frac{p_k K}{q}, \tag{2.2}$$

where r is the competitive rate of return, δ is the depreciation rate, and AVC is the (constant) average variable cost of the labor and materials needed to produce one unit of output, q. Equation (2.2) describes a technology that requires K/q units of capital (at a cost of p_K per unit of capital) to produce one unit of output.

To show the bias from using *AVC* in place of *MC*, we substitute *MC* from Equation (2.2) into Equation (1.4), $(p - MC)/p = -1/\varepsilon$ (where we suppress the *i* subscript), to obtain:

$$\frac{p - AVC}{p} = -\frac{1}{\varepsilon} + (r + \delta)\frac{p_K K}{pq}. \tag{2.3}$$

Thus, $(p - AVC)/p$ differs from the price–cost margin, $(p - MC)/p = -1/\varepsilon$, by the last term in Equation (2.3), $(r + \delta)p_K K/(pq)$, which is the rental value of capital divided by the value of output.

Tobin's *q*

Tobin's *q* is less commonly used as a measure of performance than either a rate of return or a price–cost margin. Tobin's *q* is the ratio of the market value of a firm (as measured by the market value of its outstanding stock and debt) to the replacement cost of the firm's assets (Tobin 1969). If a firm is worth more than what it would cost to rebuild it, then it is earning an *excess profit*: a profit that is greater than the level necessary to keep the firm in the industry.

By using Tobin's *q*, researchers avoid the difficult problems associated with estimating rates of return or marginal costs. On the other hand, for *q* to be meaningful, one needs accurate measures of both the market value and replacement cost of a firm's assets.

It is usually possible to get an accurate estimate for the market value of a firm's assets by summing the values of the securities that a firm has issued, such as stocks and bonds. It is much more difficult to obtain an estimate of the replacement costs of its assets unless markets for used equipment exist. Moreover, expenditures on advertising and R&D create intangible assets that may be hard to value. Typically, researchers who construct Tobin's *q* ignore the replacement costs of these intangible assets in their calculations. For that reason, *q* typically exceeds 1. Accordingly, it can be misleading to use *q* as a measure of market power without further adjustment.

It is possible to determine the degree of monopoly overcharge if Tobin's *q* is measured accurately. To do so, one must calculate how much earnings (excluding the return to capital) would have to fall for *q* to equal one. For example, let e_m be the constant annual earnings of a monopoly and e_c be the constant annual earnings of a firm under competition. The ratio of the market value of assets to the replacement cost of assets, *q*, equals the ratio of e_m to e_c. For example, if *q* equals two, earnings must fall by one-half before the firm is charging a competitive price.

MEASURES OF MARKET STRUCTURE

To examine how performance varies with structure, we also need measures of market structure. A variety of measures are used, all of which are thought to have some relation to the degree of competitiveness in an industry. We now describe some of the common measures of market structure.

Firm Size Distribution

Presumably the most important structural issue is the number and relative size of firms. We would expect firms to exercise more market power if there is only one or a few firms or if a small number of firms are very large relative to the remaining firms (such as a dominant firm-competitive fringe structure).

In most SCP studies, a measure of industry concentration is used in lieu of a full description of the size distribution of firms. Industry concentration is typically measured as a function of the market shares of some or all of the firms in a market.

Concentration Measures. By far the most common variable used to measure the market structure of an industry is the four-firm concentration ratio (C4), which is the share of industry sales accounted for by the four largest firms. It is, of course, arbitrary to focus attention on the top four firms in defining concentration ratios. Other concentration measures are used as well. For example, the U.S. government also has published eight-firm (C8), twenty-firm (C20), and fifty-firm (C50) concentration ratios.

Alternatively, one could use a function of all the individual firms' market shares to measure concentration. The most commonly used function is the Herfindahl-Hirschman Index (*HHI*), which equals the sum of the squared market shares (expressed as a percentage) of each firm in the industry. For example, if an industry has three firms with market shares of 50%, 30%, and 20%, the *HHI* equals 3,800 ($= [50\times 50] + [30\times 30] + [20\times 20]$). More attention has been paid to the *HHI* since the early 1980s, when the Department of Justice and Federal Trade Commission started using it to evaluate mergers.

Typically, empirical studies produce similar results for either the *HHI* or a C4 index. The *HHI* is the appropriate index of concentration to explain prices if firms behave according to the Cournot or other related models (see Cowling and Waterson 1976 and Chapter 1; also see Hendricks and McAfee 2005 for a generalization).

Concentration Statistics. The Bureau of the Census irregularly publishes five summary statistics for most four-digit Standard Industrial Code (SIC) manufacturing industries. For decades, the federal government has published summary statistics on industry concentration. However, the most recent publication, U.S. Department of Commerce, Economics and Statistics Administration, Bureau of Census, *Concentration Ratios in Manufacturing, 1997 Census of Manufactures* (2001), is years out of date. Traditionally, the Bureau of the Census has published four concentration measures – C4, C8, C20, and C50 – for most industries. However, for industries with very few firms, some summary statistics are suppressed for reasons of confidentiality. Since 1982, it has also reported the *HHI*.

Table 2.1. *Percent aggregate concentration in the manufacturing sector (measured by value added)*

Top firms	1947	1963	1972	1982	1992	1997
50 Largest	17	23	25	24	24	21
100 Largest	23	30	33	33	32	29
200 Largest	30	38	42	43	42	38

Sources: 1982, 1987, 1992, and 1997, U.S. Census Bureau, *Census of Manufactures: Concentration Ratios in Manufacturing*, Table 1.

Aside from concentration in individual industries, one can examine concentration in manufacturing in general. The 1997 Census of Manufactures reports concentration ratios for about 470 manufacturing industries. The C4 was below 40% in more than half of the industries, between 41% and 70% in about one-third of the industries, and over 70% in about one-tenth of the industries.

There are now more industries with low C4 ratios and fewer with high C4 ratios than in 1935. In 1935, about 47% of industries had a C4 below 40% and about 16% of industries had ratios above 70%. However, since World War II, the distribution of concentration ratios in manufacturing has not changed much. Comparisons based on value, and not on the number of firms in industries, produce similar conclusions.

There has not been a trend toward increasing aggregate concentration in the manufacturing sector based on *value added* (revenue minus the cost of fuel, power, and raw materials) accounted for by the largest firms. Table 2.1 shows that aggregate domestic concentration has increased since 1947, but has remained relatively constant since 1963. Moreover, these domestic concentration statistics overstate concentration because they ignore imports, which have grown in importance.

Most of what we know about concentration ratios concerns manufacturing industries, which comprised only about 17% of the gross domestic product (GDP) in 1996. Unfortunately, data on concentration ratios are not readily available for most individual industries outside of manufacturing. It is generally believed that ease of entry keeps most of agriculture, services, retailing and wholesale trade, and parts of manufacturing and finance, real estate, and insurance relatively unconcentrated. Moreover, some aggregate measures of concentration in the private sector show that the U.S. economy has become less concentrated over time in the sense that the share of employment and assets of the largest firms (25, 100, or 200) has declined.

White (2003) provides the first global concentration measures. As trade makes markets international, we need to pay attention to global measures. White reports that in 2001, the largest 500 global companies' employment accounted for 1.6% of the world labor force but 9.9% of OECD employment. He further notes that the large firms' profits were 0.9% of world and 1.2% of OECD GDP.

Problems with Using Concentration Measures. Unfortunately, concentration measures have two serious problems. First, seller concentration measures are affected by many factors. For example, profitability may affect the degree of concentration in an industry by affecting entry. One of the key questions we want to answer is whether a more concentrated market structure "causes" higher profits. A test of this hypothesis is only meaningful if structure affects profits but not vice versa. That is, this theory should be tested using *exogenous* measures of structure, where exogenous means that the structure is determined before profitability and that profitability does not affect structure. Using endogenous measures leads to simultaneous equation bias.

Most commonly used measures of market structure are not exogenous. They depend on the profitability of the industry. For example, suppose we use the number of firms as a measure of the structure of an industry, arguing that industries with more firms are more competitive. However, entry occurs in extraordinarily profitable industries if there are no barriers to such entry. Although, in the short run, an inherently competitive industry may have a small number of firms, in the long run, many additional firms enter if profits are high.

An exogenous barrier to entry is a better measure of structure than the number of firms. For example, if a government historically prevented entry in a few industries, those industries with the barrier should have higher profits but the higher profits do not induce additional entry.

Most SCP studies have ignored the problem of obtaining exogenous measures of market structure. In particular, the commonly used concentration measures, such as C4, are *not* exogenous measures of market structure.

The second serious problem is that many concentration measures are biased because of improper market definitions. The relevant *economic market* for a product includes all products that significantly constrain the price of that product. In order for industry concentration to be a meaningful predictor of performance, the industry must comprise a relevant economic market. Otherwise, concentration in an industry has no implication for pricing.

For example, the concentration ratio for an industry whose products compete closely with those of another industry may understate the amount of competition. If plastic bottles compete with glass bottles, the concentration ratio in the glass-bottle industry may tell one very little about market power in that industry. The relevant concentration measure should include firms in both industries. Similarly, firms classified in one industry that can modify their equipment and produce products in another industry easily are potential suppliers who influence current pricing but are not reflected in the relevant C4 ratio. If the producers of some Product *B* could profitably switch production to Product *A* (Product *B* is a *supply substitute* for Product *A*), then the producers of Product *B* should also be considered in the market for Product *A*.

Unfortunately, concentration ratios are published by the government for specific industries and products, and the definitions used do not necessarily coincide with relevant economic markets. Concentration measures are often based on aggregate national statistics. If the geographic extent of the market is local because transport costs are very high, national concentration statistics may misleadingly indicate that markets are less concentrated than is true. Some researchers use distance shipped to identify markets in which use of national data is misleading: if the distance shipped is short, the concentration in the local market may be much different from the national market concentration.

Similarly, concentration measures are often biased because they ignore imports and exports. For example, the 1997 C4 ratio for U.S. automobiles was 80%. This figure indicates a very concentrated industry; however, it ignores the imports of British, Japanese, and German cars, which accounted for more than 23% of total 1997 sales in the United States. The use of improper concentration measures, of course, may bias the estimates of the relationship between performance and concentration.

Just as seller concentration can lead to higher prices, buyer concentration can lead to lower prices. When buyers are large and powerful, their concentration can offset the power of sellers. For that reason, several researchers include buyer concentration as a market structure variable explaining industry performance. The same type of market definition problems can affect this measure. (However, many researchers argue that this measure is more likely to be exogenous than is seller concentration.)

Summary Statistic Biases. Rather than aggregating information about the relative sizes of firms into a single measure, one could examine the effects of the market shares of the first, second, third, fourth, and smaller firms on industry performance. For example, one could determine whether increases in the market share of the second firm raise prices by as much as increases in the share of the leading firm. Using this approach, Kwoka (1979) shows that three relatively equal-size firms are much more competitive than two firms.

How well do concentration measures capture information about the size distribution of firms in an industry? Golan, Judge, and Perloff (1996b) used generalized maximum entropy (GME) techniques (discussed in the Statistical Appendix) to answer the question of how well one can recover firm shares from summary statistics. To determine whether they could accurately estimate firm shares from summary statistics, they applied their method to actual data from the *Market Share Reporter* (Detroit, MI: Gale Research, 1992, 1994) in twenty industries for which there are at least eight firms and the shares reported constitute a substantial majority of the total industry.

They experimented with several approaches. For example, they used the various government concentration measures, C4, C8, C20, and C50, as well as the *HHI*. Using a Kolmogorov-Smirnov test of the hypothesis that the actual and estimated distributions are the same, they could not reject the hypothesis at the 0.05 level for any of their estimates.[5]

[5] The Kolmogorov-Smirnov test is a nonparametric test of whether two distributions are identical.

For the best estimate for each industry, the minimum correlation between the actual and estimated shares is 0.96; the correlation is at least 0.98 for seventeen industries (85%); and the correlation is at least 0.99 for eleven of our industries (55%). The best estimate of the share of the largest firm was never off by more than 2.5 percentage points, and for eleven industries, the estimate was well within one percentage point. Similarly, for sixteen of the industries, the sum of the errors for the first four firms was five percentage points or less.

They also conducted Monte Carlo (simulation) experiments in which they allowed the total number of firms to grow. They found that the accuracy of the firm share estimates for the first ten firms (the ones we care most about) does not change with the total number of firms. When there are many firms, they always estimate the shares of the small firms accurately because those shares are very small and virtually identical.

The availability of particular summary statistics greatly affects our ability to recover the size distribution of an industry. To illustrate this point, they repeatedly estimated the shares removing various summary measures from the list of explanatory variables one or two at a time. Dropping either C4 or *HHI* substantially reduced their ability to fit the distribution. However, dropping C8 and higher concentration measures had relatively little effect on their ability to fit the distribution.

If they dropped all measures save one, they found that the *HHI* contains more information than C4 or the other concentration measures. Many industrial organization researchers have recently switched from using C4 to the *HHI* as an explanatory variable in their performance equations, which is consistent with these results concerning the use of a single measure. Of course, one should use all the available summary measures so as to capture as much information about the size distribution as possible.

Barriers to Entry

Probably the most important structural factor determining industry performance is the ability of firms to enter the industry. In industries with significant long-run entry barriers, prices can remain elevated above competitive levels.[6]

Commonly used proxies for entry barriers include minimum efficient firm size (the smallest plant that can operate efficiently), advertising intensity, and capital intensity, as well as subjective estimates of the difficulty of entering specific industries. Most empirical studies do not distinguish between long-run barriers to entry and the speed with which entry can occur. The measures they use for entry barriers typically reflect both concepts.

[6] There is surprisingly little formal empirical research on entry barriers and the rate of entry. Some relevant articles are Bresnahan and Reiss (1987, 1991) and Dunn, Roberts, and Samuelson (1988).

Fraumeni and Jorgenson (1980) show that differences in rates of return across industries persist for many years. If there are no long-run barriers to entry or exit, rates of return across industries should converge. Their results indicate that there are long-run barriers, or that the rate of entry and exit is very slow so that convergence in rates of return is slow across industries, or that there are persistent differences across industries in the levels of risk that are reflected in rates of return.

Many commonly used proxies for barriers to entry, such as advertising intensity, are not exogenous. Others, such as subjective measures, have substantial measurement biases.

Unionization

If an industry is highly unionized, the union may be able to capture the industry profits by extracting them through higher wages. Moreover, the higher wages would drive prices up. Therefore, unionization may raise prices to final consumers even though profits to the firms in the industry are not excessive. It is also possible that unions could raise wages and prices and also raise profits to the industry. By making it costly to expand the labor force, unions can prevent industry competition from expanding output and driving profits down. Unionization may not be exogenous if unions are more likely to organize profitable industries.

THE RELATIONSHIP OF STRUCTURE TO PERFORMANCE

There are hundreds, if not thousands, of studies that attempt to relate market structure to each of the three major measures of market performance. This section first discusses the key empirical findings for each of the performance measures based on U.S. data. Then SCP studies based on data from other countries and on data for individual industries are examined. Finally, the section summarizes the major critiques of the results and their interpretation.

Rates of Return and Industry Structure

Joe Bain's pioneering studies were followed by a voluminous literature investigating the relationship between rates of return and industry structure. Bain (1951) investigated forty-two industries, separating them into two groups: those with a C8 ratio in excess of 70% and those with a C8 ratio below 70%. The rate of return (calculated roughly as income divided by the book value of stockholders' equity) for the more concentrated industries was 11.8%, compared with 7.5% for less concentrated industries.

Bain (1956) used his subjective judgment to classify industries by the extent of their barriers to entry. He hypothesized that profits would be higher in industries with high concentration and high barriers to entry than in other industries. Bain presented evidence that was consistent with his hypothesis.

Brozen (1971) criticized Bain's findings for two reasons. First, as Bain recognized, the industries that he studied could be in disequilibrium. Brozen showed that the industries Bain identified as highly profitable suffered a subsequent decline in their profits, whereas the industries of lower profitability enjoyed a subsequent increase in profits. In fact, for the forty-two industries of Bain's initial 1951 study, the profit difference of 4.3% that he found between the highly concentrated and less concentrated groups diminished to only 1.1% by the mid-1950s (Brozen 1971). Second, Brozen pointed out that Bain's use, in some of his work, of the profit rates of the leading firms, rather than the profit rate of the industry, could have skewed his results.

Using 1950–1960 data, Mann (1966) reproduced many of Bain's original findings. Using the same 70% concentration ratio criterion as Bain used to divide his sample into two groups, Mann found that the rate of return for the more highly concentrated group was 13.3%, compared with 8% for the less concentrated group.

Mann also investigated the relationship between profit and his own subjective estimates of barriers to entry. He found that industries with *very high* barriers to entry enjoy higher profits than those with *substantial* barriers, which in turn earn higher profits than those with *moderate to low* barriers. He confirmed Bain's predictions and earlier findings that concentrated industries with very high barriers to entry have higher average profit rates than concentrated industries that do not have very high barriers to entry.

There have been many econometric estimates of the relationships among rates of return, concentration, and a variety of other variables, such as those measuring barriers to entry (see the surveys by Weiss 1974 and Schmalensee 1989). Based on his survey of many regression studies, Weiss (1974) concluded that there was a significant relationship among profits, concentration, and barriers to entry. Studies based on more recent data tend to find only a weak relationship or no relationship between the structural variables and rates of return. For example, Salinger (1984) found, at best, weak support for the hypothesis that minimum efficient scale in concentrated industries is related to rates of return. Large capital requirements do not constitute a long-run barrier to entry unless other conditions, such as imperfect capital markets or sunk costs, are present. He found no statistical support that his other entry barrier proxy variables – such as advertising intensity – are related to rates of return.

Econometric studies linking profit to market structure often conclude that measured profitability is correlated with the advertising-to-sales ratio and with the ratio of R&D expenditures to sales. These studies also often find that high rates of return and industry growth are related.

Some researchers have studied how the speed of adjustment of capital – and hence profit – is related to concentration. Capital–output ratios rise continuously with concentration (see, for example, Collins and Preston 1969). The full explanation for the correlation between capital–output ratios and concentration is not known. One possible explanation for this result is that the plant of minimally efficient scale is so large relative to industry size that when economies of scale are important, only a few of them can fit into the industry. However, for most industries, minimum efficient scale is a small fraction of total industry demand.

It is possible that the more capital-intensive, concentrated industries use relatively more specialized capital. If so, their rates of adjustment of the capital–output ratio should be slower than those of less concentrated industries because it is usually more difficult to adjust more specialized capital stock. If highly concentrated industries adjust more slowly than unconcentrated industries, that explains why high (or low) profits take longer to fall back to (rise to) the industry average in these industries (Stigler 1963, Connolly and Schwartz 1985, Mueller 1985).

Similarly, if concentrated industries take a long time to react to demand changes, then, all else equal, good economic news should raise the value of a company in a concentrated industry more than the value of a company in an unconcentrated industry. Lustgarten and Thomadakis (1980) found that good economic news raises the stock market values of companies in concentrated industries much more than those in unconcentrated industries, and bad economic news lowers their values more.

Price–Cost Margins and Industry Structure

A gigantic literature examines the relationship between price–cost margins and industry structure. The literature varies as to which cost measures are used and which explanatory variables are included.

Price–Average Cost Margins. Following Collins and Preston (1969), many economists examined the relationship across industries between price-average variable cost margins based on Census data and various proxies for industry structure, such as the C4 ratio and the capital–output ratio. A typical regression based on data from 1958 (Domowitz, Hubbard, and Petersen 1986, 1987) is

$$\frac{p - AVC}{p} \underset{(.01)}{= .16} + \underset{(.02)}{.10C4} + \underset{(.02)}{.08}\frac{p_K K}{pq} + \text{other variables}, \tag{2.4}$$

where p is price, AVC is a measure of average variable cost, $C4$ is the four-firm concentration ratio, $(p - AVC)/p$ is the price–average variable cost margin, and $p_K K/(pq)$ is the ratio of the book value of capital to the value of output. The numbers in parentheses below each coefficient are standard errors. The $p_K K/(pq)$ term is necessary because price–average variable cost margins are used, Equation (2.3).

The sensitivity of price to increases in concentration can be derived from this equation. According to the equation, if the value of capital to annual output, $p_K K/(pQ)$, is 40% (the average value across industries), the concentration ratio of the top four firms, C4, is 50%, and if other variables are zero, the predicted price–average variable cost margin is 0.24 ($\approx$.16 + [.10 × .5] + [.08 × .4]), or $p = 1.3AVC$. That is, price is 30% above average variable cost.

If this equation holds over the entire range of possible concentration ratio values and the industry's C4 ratio doubles from 50% to 100%, the price–average variable cost margin rises to 0.29 or $p = 1.4AVC$. That is, price rises to approximately 1.4 times average variable cost, which is an increase in the price of only about 7%. Thus, even very large increases in concentration may raise price by relatively modest amounts.

For the time period 1958–1981, Domowitz, Hubbard, and Petersen (1986) found that the differential in the price–average variable cost margins between industries of high and low concentrations fell substantially over time. When they estimated a price–average variable cost equation with more recent data, the coefficient associated with the concentration ratio is much lower than its value in 1958. That is, the already small effect of concentration on price in 1958 shrinks in later years. Further, in the later period, a statistical test of the hypothesis that the concentration measure does not affect the price–average variable cost margin cannot be rejected. In general, they discovered that the relationship between price–cost margins and concentration is unstable, and, to the extent that any relationship exists, it is weak, especially in recent times.

Instead of using industry average variable cost Census data to study the relationship between the price–average variable cost margin and industry structure, other investigators, such as Kwoka and Ravenscraft (1985), use Federal Trade Commission (FTC) data to investigate price–average variable cost margins at the individual firm level.[7] The studies using individual firm data show that the link between higher concentration and higher price–cost margins is ambiguous. Some studies found that the link, if it exists at all, is very weak, whereas others discerned no link at all. They also found that the presence of a large second or third firm greatly reduces the price–cost margin that can be earned. This discovery indicates that it is a mistake to use only four-firm concentration ratios to measure market structure.

Price–Marginal Cost Margins. One of the main problems in these studies of the relationship between price–cost margins and structure is that they use average cost instead of marginal cost. If one can directly measure or accurately estimate marginal cost, then one can obtain a good measure of the Lerner index and the relationship between the price–cost margin and structure is meaningful. Unfortunately, one can rarely obtain reliable marginal cost measures.

[7] The advantage of using the firm rather than the industry as the unit of observation is that the researcher can disentangle the effect of industry concentration on a firm's price–cost margin from the effect of the efficiency of that firm alone. For example, one firm's price–cost margin may be high either because the firm is particularly efficient (low cost relative to all other firms) or because all firms in the industry enjoy a high price (lack of competition in the industry). See Benston (1985) for a critique of studies that rely on the Federal Trade Commission data.

Table 2.2. *Airline price–cost margins and market structure*

Type of market	p/MC	Share of all routes (%)
All market types	2.1	100
Dominant firm	3.1	40
Dominant pair	1.2	42
One firm (monopoly)	3.3	18
Two firms (duopoly)	2.2	19
Dominant firm	2.3	14
No dominant firm	1.5	5
Three firms	1.8	16
Dominant firm	1.9	9
No dominant firm	1.3	7
Four firms	1.8	13
Dominant firm	2.2	6
Dominant pair	1.3	7
No dominant firm or pair	2.1	~0
Five or more firms	1.3	35
Dominant firm	3.5	11
Dominant pair	1.4	23
No dominant firm or pair	1.1	0.1

Source: Weiher et al. (2002).

One example where marginal cost measures have been estimated is the airlines industry. Weiher et al. (2002) show that the markup of price over long-run marginal cost is much greater on routes in which one airline carries most of the passengers than on other routes. Unfortunately, a single firm is the only carrier or the dominant carrier on 58% of all U.S. domestic routes.

The first column of Table 2.2 identifies the market structure for U.S. air routes. The last column shows the share of routes. A single firm (monopoly) serves 18% of all routes. Duopolies control 19% of the routes, three-firm markets are 16%, four-firm markets are 13%, and five or more firms fly on 35% of the routes.

Although nearly two-thirds of all routes have three or more carriers, one or two firms dominate virtually all routes. Weiher et al. call a carrier a *dominant firm* if it has at least 60% of ticket sales by value but is not a monopoly. They call two carriers a *dominant pair* if they collectively have at least 60% of the market but neither firm is a dominant firm and three or more firms fly this route. All but 0.1% of routes have a monopoly (18%), a dominant firm (40%), or a dominant pair (42%).

The first row of the table shows that the price is slightly more than double (2.1 times) marginal cost on average across all U.S. routes and market structures. (This average price includes "free" frequent flier tickets and other below-cost tickets.)

The price is 3.3 times marginal cost for monopolies and 3.1 times marginal cost for dominant firms. In contrast, over the sample period, the average price is only 1.2 times marginal cost for dominant pairs.

The markup of price over marginal cost depends much more on whether there is a dominant firm or dominant pair than on the total number of firms in the market. If there is a dominant pair, whether there are four or five firms, the price is between 1.3 times marginal cost for a four-firm route and 1.4 times marginal cost for a route with five or more firms. If there is a dominant firm, price is 2.3 times marginal cost on duopoly routes, 1.9 times on three-firm routes, 2.2 times on four-firm routes, and 3.5 times on routes with five or more firms.

Thus, preventing a single firm from dominating a route may substantially lower prices. Even if two firms dominate the market, the markup of price over marginal cost is substantially lower than if a single firm dominates.

Other Explanatory Variables. Various studies report significant effects from other explanatory variables. Kwoka and Ravenscraft (1986) learned that industry growth has a significant and positive effect on price–average variable cost margins. Lustgarten (1975) concluded that increased buyer concentration sometimes lowers price–cost margins. Comanor and Wilson (1967) reported that a higher advertising-sales ratio may raise the price–cost margin.

Freeman (1983) showed that unions lower the price–cost margin. Salinger (1984) and Ruback and Zimmerman (1984) also found that unionism has a significant negative effect on the profits of highly concentrated industries. Voos and Mishel (1986) reported that, although unions may depress the price–cost margin, the price is not significantly above the price that would prevail in the absence of a union.

International Studies of Performance and Structure

Because international trade is more important in many other countries than in American markets, the bias from ignoring imports and exports may be more substantial in studies based on data from those countries than in those based on U.S. data. Concentration ratios based only on domestic concentration may not be economically meaningful as measures of market power. The relevant competition may well be from firms located outside a given country.

Nonetheless, despite differences across countries in sizes of domestic markets, domestic concentration ratios are correlated across countries (Pryor 1972). That is, an industry that is concentrated in the United States is also likely to be concentrated in the United Kingdom. However, the correlation is not perfect, as illustrated by Sutton (1989) for the U.S. and U.K. frozen food industries.

Regardless of which country's data are used, most studies have difficulty detecting an economically and statistically significant effect of concentration on performance (Hart and Morgan 1977, Geroski 1981). However, Encoau and Geroski (1984) found that the United States, the United Kingdom, and Japan tend to have slow rates of price adjustment in their most concentrated sectors.[8]

Performance and Structure in Individual Industries

Most studies of SCP are based on cross-sectional data rather than data for a particular industry over time (though there are exceptions, like Weiher et al. 2002). There are two serious shortcomings in cross-sectional studies of the relationship between structure and performance across different industries.

First, it is unrealistic to expect the same relationship between structure and performance to hold across all industries. Suppose that one monopolized industry has a high elasticity of demand, and another monopolized industry has a low elasticity of demand. As Equation (2.2) shows, the price–cost margin in the industry with the high elasticity of demand is lower than the price–cost margin in the industry with the low elasticity of demand. Most cross-sectional studies fail to control for differences in demand elasticities across industries, thereby implicitly assuming that the elasticities are identical across industries.

Second, it is unlikely that the C4 ratios published by the U.S. Census correspond to the concentration ratios for relevant economic markets. If concentration ratios are not defined for the proper markets, one should not expect to find any correlation between performance and concentration across different markets.

Measurement and Statistical Problems

In summary, there is, at best, weak evidence of a link between concentration and various proxies for barriers to entry and measures of market performance. Are the theories concerning the relationship between performance and structure wrong or are these studies flawed?

Although many SCP studies are well done, others are seriously flawed. These are discussed in the next section. Many of the negative findings in these studies may be due to two important problems. First, many of these studies suffer from substantial measurement or related statistical problems that are difficult to correct. Second, and more importantly, most of these studies are conceptually flawed. Many of these measurement and statistic problems were discussed earlier. Three additional problems are analyzed here.

First, concentration measures and performance measures are frequently biased due to improper aggregation across products. Because most firms sell more than one product, any estimate of profits or price–cost margins for a firm reflects averages across different products. For a firm that makes products in many different industries, aggregate statistics can be misleading. For example, the Census assigns

[8] The industrial organization of Japan is discussed in Caves and Uekasa (1976) and Miwa (1996).

firms to industry categories based on the primary products produced and includes their total value of production under that industry category. The Census also tabulates statistics at the product level, based on data from individual plants. Because a plant is less likely than a firm to produce several products, product-level data are preferable because such data are less likely to have an aggregation bias than industry-level data.

Second, as already mentioned, the performance and structural variables tend to suffer from other measurement errors. Some researchers include variables in addition to concentration to control for such measurement problems in an attempt to reduce these biases. For example, because most price–cost margins ignore capital and advertising, some economists include those two variables in their regressions of price–cost margins on concentration. The inclusion of these additional explanatory variables may not eliminate the bias if they are measured with error or determined by industry profitability (that is, endogenous). For example, researchers frequently mismeasure advertising, and advertising may be more heavily used in highly profitable industries.

Third, many studies inappropriately estimate linear relations between a measure of performance and concentration. For example, if increases in concentration have increasingly large effects on performance as the concentration rises up to a critical level and thereafter increases in concentration have relatively little additional effect, the relationship between performance and concentration will resemble an S–shaped curve: first concave and then convex to the horizontal axis. This S–shaped curve can be approximated reasonably by a straight line only if the observed levels of concentration lie in some restricted range. If concentration ratios vary from very low levels to very high levels, an estimate based on a presumed linear relationship may lead to incorrect results.

White (1976) and Bradburd and Over (1982) searched for critical levels of concentration below which price is less likely to increase as concentration increases, and threshold levels of concentration above which price is more likely to increase as concentration increases. They were only partially successful in finding such a level: there appears to be some evidence of an increase in price at C4 ratios above roughly 50% to 60%.

Bradburd and Over (1982) present evidence that the effect of concentration on an industry's performance depends on levels of past concentration. As a highly concentrated industry becomes less concentrated, price remains higher than it would if the industry had never been highly concentrated.

Conceptual Problems

The measure of performance is viewed as evidence about the existence of market power. Most SCP studies are interested in determining whether there is a relationship between performance (such as market power) and industry structure. However, the conceptual problems inherent in these studies limit their ability to identify this relationship. The two most common conceptual problems concern whether long-run performance measures are used and whether the structural variables are exogenous.

Although standard, static economic theories hold that long-run profits vary with market structure, they say nothing about the relationship of short-run profits and market structure. Thus, a SCP study based on short-run performance measures is not a proper test of the theories.

The amount of time needed to reach the long run differs by industry. At any moment, some industries are highly profitable whereas others are not. Over time, some firms exit from the low-profit industries and enter the high-profit industries, which drives rates of return toward a common level. Stigler (1963), Connolly and Schwartz (1985), and Mueller (1985) find that high profits often decline slowly in highly concentrated industries. It is only by analyzing the level of profits (or other measures of performance) and the rate at which they change that the analyst can distinguish between a long-run barrier to entry and the speed with which entry occurs. Most analyses do not make this distinction. This problem may be regarded as one of accurately measuring performance.

However, the various measurement problems with performance may not be as serious as they first appear. Schmalensee (1989) used twelve different accounting measures of profitability in a SCP study. Strikingly, although these twelve measures are not highly correlated, many of his key SCP results held over all measures.

Perhaps the more serious conceptual problem with many SCP studies is that the structural variables are not exogenous. Many researchers, after finding a link between high profits (or excessive rates or return, large price–cost margins, or high values of q) and high concentration ratios, infer improperly that high concentration rates are bad because they "cause" high profits.

However, profit and concentration influence each other. An alternative interpretation of a link between profits and concentration is that the largest firms are the most efficient or innovative (Demsetz 1973, Peltzman 1977). Only when a firm is efficient or innovative is it profitable to expand in a market and make the market concentrated. In this interpretation, a successful firm attracts consumers, either through lower prices or better products. A firm's success, as measured by both its profit and its market share, is an indicator of consumer satisfaction, not an indicator of poor industry performance. One implication of this hypothesis is that a firm's success is explained by its own market share and not just by industry concentration, as found by Kwoka and Ravenscraft (1985).

If concentration is not an exogenous measure, then an estimate of the relationship between profits and concentration, which assumes that concentration affects profits and not vice versa, leads to what is referred to as a simultaneity bias. However, Weiss (1974) estimated the relationship between performance measures and concentration using statistical techniques designed to eliminate the simultaneity bias problem and found that the different estimation procedures make little difference in the estimated relationship.

Although the regression results may not change, their interpretation does. Even a correctly estimated relationship between performance and concentration is uninformative regarding causation. High profits are not caused by concentration, but are caused by long-run barriers to entry. These barriers cause both high profits and high concentration.

Research using the SCP approach continues, though at a reduced rate. Some relatively recent works include Marvel (1978), Lamm (1981), Cotterill (1986), Schmalensee (1987), Cubbin and Geroski (1987), and Sutton (1991).

A MODERN STRUCTURE–CONDUCT–PERFORMANCE APPROACH

There is one other important modern approach to SCP by Sutton (1991, 1998). Sutton uses a game-theoretic approach to examine what happens to competition, promotional activities, and R&D as market size grows. He also addresses what happens if sunk costs are endogenous.

The original SCP literature sought to establish a systematic relationship between price and concentration. We have discussed many criticisms of this approach, but perhaps the most significant is that concentration itself is determined by the economic conditions of the industry and hence is not an industry characteristic that can be used to explain pricing or other conduct. The barrage of criticisms caused most research in this area to cease in recent years. However, Sutton has developed an approach that builds on the SCP idea of looking for systematic patterns of competitive behavior across industries, and, at the same time, addresses the endogenous determination of entry (Sutton 1991, 1998).

Sutton's research examines what happens to competition as the size of the market grows. Does the market become less concentrated? Do other dimensions of the product – such as quality, promotional activity, and R&D – change? What are the fundamental economic forces that provide the bases for systematic answers to these questions across different industries? In answering these questions, Sutton analyzes markets in which the product is either homogeneous or heterogeneous and considers the cost of entering the market or altering certain attributes of products.

Theory

Sutton examines two cases depending on whether a firm's cost of entry is an exogenous sunk cost or an endogenous sunk cost. In the former case, each firm must spend some fixed amount, F, to enter the industry. In the latter case, the amount a firm must spend to enter the industry is variable and is chosen by the firm in an effort to affect the desirability of its product by influencing certain dimensions of the product.

Exogenous Sunk Cost. To illustrate his theory, Sutton examines markets with homogeneous and heterogeneous products. Initially, we consider a market in which the firms produce a homogeneous product and the only variable on which firms can compete is price (not quality). Each firm incurs a sunk fixed cost F and has a constant marginal cost m. At low prices, the industry demand curve is $Q = s/p$, where Q is industry quantity, s is a measure of market size (total expenditure, which is assumed to be determined independent of price), and p is price. That is, for low prices and given s, the market elasticity of demand is −1. At some high price p_m, the demand curve is perfectly elastic. Thus, a monopoly would charge a price of p_m in this market.

The final equilibrium and how the equilibrium will change as the market size grows are determined by the form that competition takes. To fix ideas, Sutton considered three types of competition, each "tougher" than the next. The level of competition is lowest in a cartel in which all firms explicitly collude to set the monopoly price p_m and divide up the total cartel or monopoly profit among the n firms. Regardless of the number of firms, n, the price remains at p_m. Thus, profit per firm declines as n grows because the total monopoly profit is divided among more and more firms. The equilibrium n is the one at which that the total cartel profit is driven to zero.[9]

A more competitive market is a Cournot oligopoly. For any number of firms, n, the equilibrium Cournot price is $p(n) = m[1 + 1/(n - 1)]$.[10] Thus, the Cournot price p falls to m as n increases. The output per firm, q, equals $(s/m)[(n - 1)/n^2]$, and profit per firm is $[p - m]q - F$, which equals $s/n^2 - F$. Hence, with free entry, n equals $\sqrt{s/F}$, at which point profit per firm is zero.

Finally, consider the most competitive equilibrium, Bertrand, where price equals m for any given $n > 1$. Here, the only free-entry equilibrium has one firm with positive profit. Were a second firm to enter, it would drive price to marginal cost, so that its profit would be negative (accounting for the fixed cost).

For each model of competition, Figure 2.1 shows how price changes as n increases. As the figure illustrates, for any given $n > 1$, price is lower as competition becomes "tougher," with Bertrand being the toughest and cartel being the least tough model of competition.

[9] Let the cartel profit be $\Pi = [p - m]\,Q - nF$. The price that maximizes cartel profit is the same price that maximizes $[p - m]Q$. Define Π_m, the profit ignoring fixed costs, as the maximum of $[p - m]Q$. Then, each firm's individual profit is $\Pi_m/n - F$. In equilibrium where $\Pi = 0$, the equilibrium n equals Π_m/F.

[10] Each firm selects its output q_i to maximize its profit, which can be written as $p_i(\Sigma q_j)q_i - mq_i - F$, where $p_i(\Sigma q_j)$ is the inverse demand curve. Differentiating this expression with respect to q_i yields the first-order condition for each firm's optimal output level given its rival's output levels. Setting $q_i = q$ for all i yields the symmetric Cournot equilibrium (assuming that the resulting price is less than p_m).

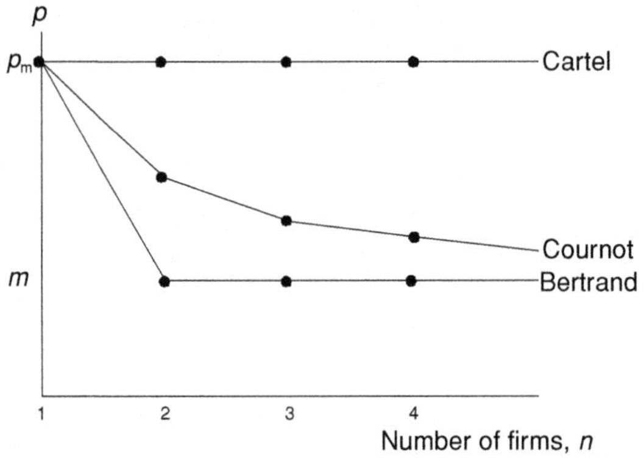

Figure 2.1. Relationship Between Prices and Number of Firms Under Three Market Structures. *Sources:* Sutton (1991, 1998).

Figure 2.2 relates a measure of equilibrium industry concentration, $1/n$, to market size s for each model of competition, where, by equilibrium market concentration, we mean that n at which total profit equals zero (or more accurately, if one additional firm enters, it will earn a negative profit.)

Figure 2.2 reveals two interesting results. First, as expected, concentration falls as market size increases for all but the most competitive game (Bertrand). The intuition for this result is that larger markets can accommodate more firms.

The second result is counterintuitive: for any given market size, when equilibrium market concentration is *higher*, the tougher the competition. Concentration is lowest for the cartel model, even though the cartel model has the highest price. The reason for this result is that tough competition leads to a low price, which discourages entry. This result illustrates that relying on concentration alone to make inferences about price and competitiveness can lead to erroneous conclusions.

The case of exogenous fixed costs with heterogeneous products has much less crisp results than the case of exogenous fixed costs with a homogeneous product. In a model with heterogeneous products, the concentration in the market depends on the nature of the game, such as how many different products one firm may produce and whether a firm has an advantage if it can choose its products before other firms choose.

Sutton's main result for heterogeneous products is that the "toughness" of competition is, in general, diminished when one moves from a homogeneous to a heterogeneous product and so (analogous to the result that occurs in the case of homogeneous product as competition weakens) the equilibrium concentration tends to fall for any given market size s. However, unlike the case of a homogeneous product, there are many possible equilibrium outcomes for any given market size, s, and the best that an economist can derive is a *lower bound* on concentration for any given s. When this lower bound is low, it means that there are very few

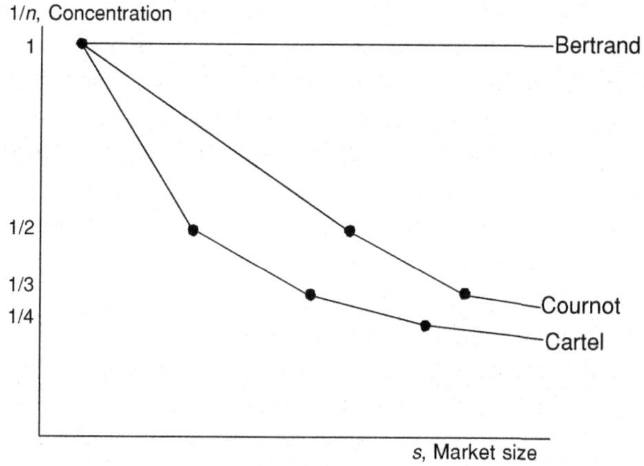

Figure 2.2. Relationship Between Concentration and Market Size Under Three Market Structures. *Sources:* Sutton (1991, 1998).

empirical predictions one can make about equilibrium concentration because any equilibrium concentration is possible as long as it exceeds the lower bound.

The property that equilibrium concentration (or its lower bound) decreases with market size s depends on the assumption that fixed costs are exogenous and that product quality is given. Given this property, all else equal, concentration should be lower in big countries than in small countries, when market size is determined by the size of country.

Although this result holds for many industries, there are some industries that are highly concentrated in both large and small countries. Sutton explains this mystery using endogenous sunk costs.

Endogenous Sunk Costs. In most markets, firms compete not just on price but also along many other product dimensions such as quality, reliability, R&D, or promotional activity. The key new assumption is that a firm may spend money to improve its product's W, an index of quality, which we will broadly interpret to include information about the product. In this model, the fixed entry cost, $F(W)$, depends on the quality index. For example, firms increase their advertising expenditures, R&D expenditures, and engineering expenditures to increase W by raising the quality of the product or by increasing consumers' perception of its quality. Firms can compete for customers by spending money to improve product quality, by lowering price, or by doing both. Here, we say that the firm has *endogenous* sunk costs because the firm decides how large an investment to make.

Paying to improve quality has two important effects. First, it raises the firm's fixed cost and perhaps its marginal cost of production if a higher quality good costs more to produce. Second, it attracts customers who were previously buying a lower quality good. These two effects can combine to reverse completely the results in the previous section in which an increase in market size is associated with a decrease in equilibrium concentration. As market size s increases, firms have an incentive to compete by improving the quality W of their product. To raise quality, a firm must incur larger sunk costs, which reduces the incentive for additional firms to enter the industry that otherwise arises from the larger s. As a result, as market size increases, concentration no longer necessarily falls. A given industry in different sized markets can remain highly concentrated, but bigger markets will have higher quality products.

For this reasoning to be valid, several assumptions need to hold. Consumers must value improvements in quality sufficiently so that they switch from lower quality products to higher quality ones. To establish the condition under which this is so, Sutton uses a model of *vertical differentiation.* In such a model, every consumer agrees on a ranking of products by quality, W, with all consumers preferring a higher quality product to a lower quality product.

Suppose that a consumer's surplus from a good of quality W equals $U = \theta W - p(W)$ where θ is a parameter reflecting the weight that the consumer places on quality and $p(W)$ is the price of a product with quality W. Because consumers differ in θ, even though all consumers prefer more W to less, some consumers place such a low value on extra W that they are willing to pay very little extra money for a high W product, whereas other consumers so enjoy extra quality that they will buy a higher quality good even if the price is relatively high. The optimal W for any consumer will depend on the price function $p(W)$, which reveals how prices rise as W rises, and on the consumer preference, θ, for quality.

Sutton proves that as long as $p(W)$ and the marginal cost of producing a high quality product do not rise "too fast" as W increases, then the equilibrium has three striking properties. First, the firms that produce the highest quality available in the market are the largest firms.

Second, an increase in market size leads to an increase in the quality of the best products in the market, higher quality products being chosen by consumers at higher prices and some lower quality products disappearing from the market. Thus, the equilibrium quality rises as the market expands.

Third, with higher quality and its attendant costs, fewer firms can afford to remain in the industry and concentration will remain high. Consequently, the property that a market remains concentrated as s increases continues to hold even where there is both horizontal and vertical differentiation as long as there is sufficient substitution between the vertical dimension (quality W) and the horizontal dimension over which consumers can have different preferences.

For both the endogenous and exogenous sunk cost cases, the key empirical predictions about concentration and market size depend on the validity of certain assumptions. The most important one is that the form of the game – Bertrand, Cournot, or cartel – remains unchanged as market size increases. In a given market, this assumption may or may not be plausible. Moreover, neither Sutton nor anyone else has made significant progress on describing the industry economic characteristics that predict the form of the game that describes the competitive process. Therefore, analogous to the criticism of the earlier literature that concentration need not be exogenous, here we have the criticism that the form of the competitive game need not be exogenous.

Empirical Research

Sutton has produced two voluminous books (1991, 1998) of studies using data from France, Germany, Italy, Japan, the United Kingdom, and the United States to test his theories, especially those concerning the endogeneity of advertising and technology. Sutton's empirical work helps explain why concentration is similar across different size countries for some industries but not others.

In Sutton (1991), he tests his theoretical predictions about the relation of concentration and market size for several industries in the food and beverage sector. He separates the industries into two types – one in which there is little advertising and the other in which there is significant advertising. The first industry type corresponds roughly to the use of exogenous sunk cost, whereas the second corresponds roughly to the case of endogenous sunk cost. For each type of industry, Sutton runs a regression on the four-firm concentration ratio, C4, similar to

$$C4 = a + b\ln(s/\sigma),$$

where s/σ is the market size divided by the size of an efficient plant. (Sutton actually uses a more complicated method because his theory predicts a lower bound to the relation between concentration and market size.) He tests and confirms that b is negative for the first type of industry, but zero for the second type, which supports his theories.

Though Sutton's work increases our theoretical and empirical understanding of the relation between concentration and competition, there are two important caveats to his results. First, as his detailed analysis of each industry in each country reveals, the assumption that the competitive game is the same across countries is not always a particularly good one. There is little research explaining why, in some countries, competition in a particular industry is more intense than in others.

Sutton identified industries and countries where competition is unusually intense and found, consistent with his theory, that the industry is more concentrated in countries such as the United States. He identifies countries with lax attitudes toward cartels and, again, consistent with his theory, finds that those industries tend to have lower concentration levels.

The second caveat is that Sutton's theory predicts a lower bound to the relation between market size and concentration. The reason for the lower bound is that there can be a multiplicity of equilibria with some having greater concentration levels than the lower bound. The theory, therefore, is unable to help us much in predicting concentration in a particular country when the lower bound is low.

Although Sutton explains that this theory of lower bounds is the most one can say under general conditions, it leaves the analyst in the uncomfortable position of having a theoretical structure that may not narrow the possible equilibria very much. Sutton's detailed history of each industry shows that many idiosyncratic factors often are critical in explaining an industry's evolution. Thus, his work provides a sobering lesson because it reveals the limits of theory to explain industrial structures.

SUMMARY

SCP studies assume that the degree of market power – our first question – can be answered using commonly available statistics as proxies for market power. These studies focus on the causes of market power – our second question. Traditionally, SCP studies use cross-sectional industry data to explain variations in market power across industries as a function of concentration and other factors.

In the following chapters, we turn to other, modern approaches to examining our key questions. These studies differ substantially from traditional SCP studies. Most recent studies concentrate on estimating market power rather than using published proxies. Because these studies usually examine only a single firm or industry over time, they cannot explain differences across industries.

PROBLEMS

Note: Answers to problems are available at the back of the book.

2.1 Suppose that the firms in a market are engaged in a Cournot game and that Firm *i*'s Lerner's index is $L_i = (p - m_i)/p = s_i/\varepsilon$, where s_i is Firm *i*'s quantity share of the market. Cowling and Waterson (1976) observed that the weighted average price–cost margin for the industry is $\sum_i (p - m_i)/p = -\sum_i s_i^2/\varepsilon = -HHI/\varepsilon$ [see Equation (1.6) in Chapter 1], where *HHI* is the Herfindahl-Hirschman Index. Suppose Equation (2.2) holds so that $m_i = AVC_i + (r + \delta)p_K K_i/q_i$. Many empirical researchers have used $(p - AVC_i)/p$ instead of $(p\ m_i)/p$ in their empirical studies. Derive an expression similar to Cowling and Waterson's equation relating $(p - AVC_i)/p$ to the *HHI* to show the effect of using this alternative measure.

2.2 Traditionally, SCP empirical studies estimated an equation relating a profit measure to a concentration measure using ordinary least squares. One of the major criticisms is that concentration is an endogenous variable. You are asked to show the relationship between a measure of profitability, p/MC, and the C4 concentration measure. Consider a monopolistically competitive industry in which firms produce a homogeneous product, demand is linear ($p = a - bQ$, where p is price and Q is total output), firms have identical cost functions (constant marginal cost m plus a fixed cost F), and they play Cournot. Firms enter until the number of firms, n, is such that the marginal firm makes a zero profit. Solve for the equilibrium number of firms, quantities, and price. (For simplicity, allow n to be a non-integer.) Show how the quantity per firm, price, number of firms, p/MC, and C4 change as F increases.

2.3 Given exogenous sunk costs, Sutton (1991, 1998) shows that, for any given market size, equilibrium market concentration is higher the more competitive is the market (the Bertrand equilibrium is more competitive than the Cournot equilibrium, which is more competitive than the cartel outcome). Why? What implications does this result have for traditional SCP empirical studies?

THREE

Industry Models of Market Power

Is a firm in an industry exercising market power? If we observe price and marginal cost, we can directly determine whether the firm sets its price above its marginal cost. Unfortunately, we usually observe only price and factors that are associated with demand and with cost; we do not have explicit information on total or marginal cost. One approach to overcoming the problem of not knowing marginal cost is to estimate the firm's behavior – or the average behavior of all firms within an industry – and marginal cost simultaneously, using a structural model. Alternatively, a researcher can use a reduced-form or nonparametric approach to determine whether firms have market power by seeing how price varies with shifts in cost (or factors that shift cost).

The structural approach has two key advantages. The model provides a direct estimate of market power. Moreover, one can use the estimated model to simulate the effects of changes in the market (as long as they do not affect the underlying market structure), which can be used for public policy debates. For example, structural models have been used to simulate the effects of mergers on price (and hence welfare): Werden and Froeb (1994), Slade (1998), Nevo (2000), and Hausman and Leonard (2005). The main disadvantage of the structural approach is that the results depend critically on a variety of assumptions concerning functional form, distributions, and other facts that are not generally known to the econometrician.

The reduced-form approach or nonparametric approach is normally based on comparative statics properties of structural models. Typically, these models have fewer data requirements and require fewer assumptions than do the structural models. They can be used to test the hypothesis that a market is competitive. However, typically, they cannot be used to answer questions about the degree of market power or to simulate the policy questions.

For simplicity in this chapter, we focus on how to estimate market power when we have only industry-level data. (In later chapters, we concentrate on models based on firm-level data.) We first go through the structural model approach for estimating market power in an oligopolistic market. Then we examine the same problem using nonparametric approaches. Next, we apply both approaches to the oligopsony problem. Finally, we present evidence as to how well these various approaches work.

STRUCTURAL APPROACH

Studies that use market-level data make a large number of assumptions in order to be able to identify and estimate a measure of market power. Most studies assume that firms' products are homogeneous, so that the average market price and total output are useful statistics. Especially in structural models, a typical assumption is that all firms are identical so that all behave in the same manner.

We illustrate a typical structural approach using a model with two basic equations: demand and marginal cost. The inverse demand function facing the market (or firm) is

$$p = p(Q, Z), \tag{3.1}$$

where p is the price, Q is the quantity of output, and Z is a vector of exogenous variables (such as income and prices of substitutes) affecting the industry demand curve but not the marginal cost, though having some overlapping variables raises no additional problems. The marginal cost curve is

$$MC = g(Q, w), \tag{3.2}$$

where w is a vector of exogenous variables (such as factor prices) that affect "industry" marginal cost but not the demand function.[1]

Just and Chern (1980), Bresnahan (1982), and Lau (1982) suggest that we use a *conduct* parameter, λ, to nest various market structures.[2] For example, we can define an *effective* or *perceived* marginal revenue function as

$$MR(\lambda) = p + \lambda p_Q(Q, Z)Q, \tag{3.3}$$

where $p_Q(Q, Z)$ is the slope of the demand curve (the partial derivative with respect to Q). If $\lambda = 0$, marginal revenue equals price and the market is competitive; if $\lambda = 1$, marginal revenue equals the marginal revenue of a monopoly; if λ lies between 0 and 1, the degree of market power lies between that of monopoly and competition, as in an oligopoly solution. With n identical firms in a Cournot (or Nash-in-quantities) equilibrium, λ equals $1/n$.

[1] This formulation suggests that the industry supply relationship depends on only industry output. Obviously if firms' cost functions differ, a more complex relationship is necessary. See Reiss and Wolak (2007) for a discussion of this issue.

[2] Some of the other analogous early work on estimating market power include Rosse (1970), Iwata (1974), Applebaum (1979, 1982), Gollop and Roberts (1979), and Bresnahan (1981a). As an alternative to using a nested family of structures, one can use non-nested hypotheses tests: see Gasmi and Vuong (1991) and Gasmi, Laffont, and Vuong (1992).

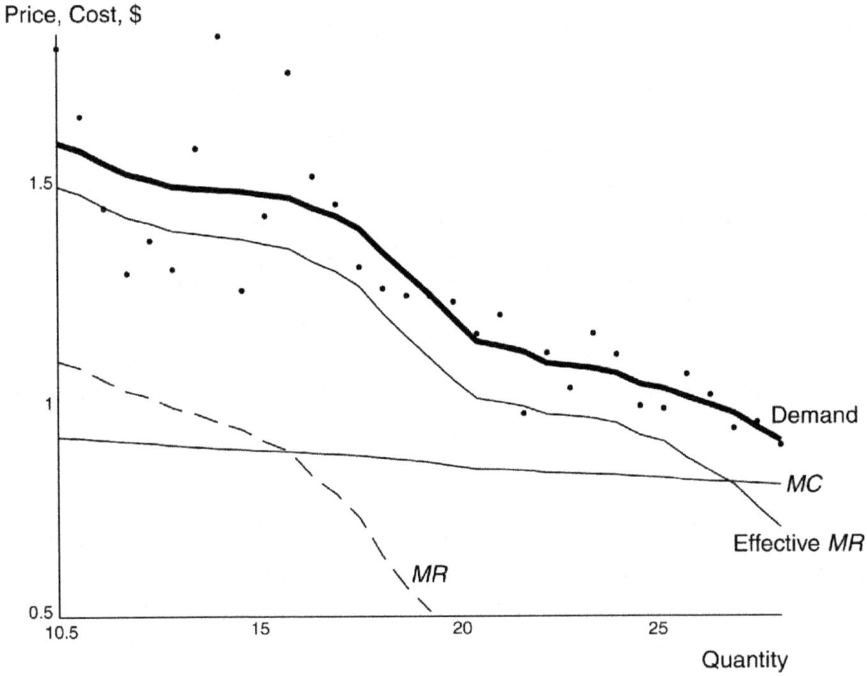

Figure 3.1. U.S. Textile Market.

The optimality or equilibrium condition is that the industry sets its effective marginal revenue, Equation (3.3), equal to its marginal cost, Equation (3.2):

$$MR(\lambda) = p + \lambda p_Q(Q, Z)Q = MC(Q, w). \tag{3.4}$$

Thus, the basic model consists of a system of two equations, the demand Equation (3.1) and the optimality Equation (3.4).

We illustrate this approach for the U.S. textile market (Perloff and Ward 1998) in Figure 3.1, in which the system of demand and optimality equations was estimated using a nonparametric method and a flexible cost function. This market is relatively unconcentrated, with market concentration ratios of 15% for 4 firms, 25% for 8 firms, 38% for 20 firms, and 52% for 50 firms, and a 113 Herfindahl-Hirschman Index for the 50 largest firms.

If this market were competitive, equilibrium would be determined by the intersection of the figure's demand curve – which is the $MR(0)$ curve – and the marginal cost curve. The figure also shows "the" marginal revenue curve, $MR = MR(1)$, which would be the relevant one if the market were completely cartelized. Finally, the figure shows the perceived or effective marginal revenue curve, $MR(\lambda)$, given the estimated $\lambda = 0.21$. We would expect to see such a λ in a Cournot equilibrium with five identical firms ($\lambda = 1/5$). The *MC* curve intersects the *MR* curve well to the left of where it intersects the effective *MR* curve, showing that the equilibrium is not very close in output space to the monopoly outcome. The equilibrium is much closer to the competitive equilibrium determined by the intersection of the demand and marginal cost curves.

Interpretations of λ

The literature provides at least two interpretations of λ (Bresnahan 1989). In the first approach, the econometrician remains agnostic about the precise game that the firms are playing and interprets λ as a measure of the gap between price and marginal cost: $p - MC = -\lambda p_Q Q$. Here, Lerner's measure is

$$L \equiv \frac{p - MC}{p} = -\frac{\lambda p_Q Q}{p} = -\frac{\lambda}{\varepsilon}, \tag{3.5}$$

where ε is the market elasticity of demand. Because λ lies in the closed set $[0, 1]$, it follows that $L \in [0, -1/\varepsilon]$. That is, λ takes on the role of $1/n$, s_i, or *HHI* in Equations (3.5) and (3.6). Thus, some econometricians argue that λ can be interpreted as an index of market power or structure. Equivalently, one can describe λ as a market demand elasticity-adjusted Lerner index: $\lambda = -L\varepsilon$.

The alternative interpretation used by many econometricians is that λ is essentially an aggregate conjectural variation. Suppose n oligopolistic firms produce identical products. Market output, Q, is the sum of the outputs of each of Firms i, q_i. Each Firm i has the same cost function $c(q_i)$, and its marginal cost is $MC = c'(q_i)$. In the usual conjectural variation story, Firm i has a constant conjecture, ν, about how its $n - 1$ rivals will respond to a change in its output: $\nu = dQ_{-i}/dq_i$, where Q_{-1} is the collective output of all the firms except for Firm i. Thus, the optimality condition Equation (3.4), for Firm i is

$$MR \equiv p + p_Q q_i[1 + \nu] = MC. \tag{3.6}$$

In equilibrium, the n firms produce identical quantities, $q = q_i$, for all i. Multiplying and dividing the second term in Equation (3.6) by n, we can rewrite this optimality condition as

$$MR = p + p_Q Q\left(\frac{1+\nu}{n}\right) = MC.$$

Because we know from the optimality Equation (3.4) that $p + \lambda p_Q Q = MC$, it follows that

$$\lambda = \left(\frac{1+\nu}{n}\right).$$

Thus, given n identical firms and $\lambda \in [0, 1]$, then $\nu \in [-1, n-1]$. Table 3.1 shows how λ, ν, and L are related for three important structures. Table 3.2 summarizes the results from a variety of early studies using the $L = (p - MC)/p$ measure.

Table 3.1. *Market structure measures*

Market structure	λ	ν	L
Competition/Bertand	0	-1	0
Cournot-Nash	$1/n$	0	$-1/n\varepsilon$
Cartel	1	$n-1$	$-1/\varepsilon$

Table 3.2. *Estimates of market power*

	Industry	$L = (p - MC)/p$	Market power
Gollop and Roberts (1979)	Coffee roasting (dominant firm)	0.06	
Just and Chern (1980)	Tomato harvesting		Yes
Sumner (1981)	Cigarette	0.50	
Appelbaum (1982)	Textile	0.07	
	Tobacco	0.65	
Lopez (1984)	Canadian food processing	0.50	
Roberts (1984)	Coffee roasting (largest firm)	0.06	
Sullivan (1985)	Cigarettes[a]		
Cotterrill (1986)	Vermont food industry		Yes
Suslow (1986)	Aluminum	0.59	
Ashenfelter and Sullivan (1987)	Cigarettes[b]		
Slade (1987)	Retail gasoline	0.10	
Lopez and Dorsainvil (1990)	Haitian coffee		Yes
Baker and Bresnahan (1988)	Breweries		
	Coors 1962–1982	0.745	
	Pabst 1962–1982	0.058	
	Anheuser-Busch 1962–1975	0.312	
	Anheuser-Busch 1975–1982	0.110	
Roberts and Samuelson (1988)	Cigarettes		Yes
Karp and Perloff (1989b)	Rice Export (largest estimate)	0.11	
Azzam and Pagoulatos (1990)	Meat	0.46	
	Livestock	1.1[c]	
	Composite meat processing	0.74[d]	
Schroeter and Azzam (1990)	Beef	0.55	
	Pork	0.47	
Buschena and Perloff (1991)	Philippines coconut oil (post 1974)	0.89	
Wann and Sexton (1992)	Grade pack pears	0.15	
	Fruit cocktail	1.41	
Durham and Sexton (1992)	Tomatoes		No
Deodhar and Sheldon (1995)	German bananas	0.26	

[a] Not very competitive, but equivalent to at least 2.5 equal-size Cournot firms
[b] Not highly noncompetitive
[c] Monopsony power
[d] Combined market power in the output and factor markets
Sources: Bresnahan (1989), Carlton and Perloff (2005).

In this second interpretation, λ is not a measure of the deviation between price and marginal cost but an aggregate conjectural variation concept associated with firms' behavior. Many game theorists have argued that the problem with this interpretation is that we can justify only a few values of λ using sound economic models, such as the Bertrand, Cournot, and collusion equilibria. Thus, they contend, we do not have a good economic theory to explain why λ could be a continuous index.[3]

Corts (1999) has attacked the alternative interpretation that λ is a measure of the gap between price and marginal cost. Corts argues that the estimated conjectural variation parameter is unbiased only if the underlying behavior is the result of a conjectural variations equilibrium and not as a measure of the gap between the price and marginal cost.

Identification

Can we identify and estimate the market-power parameter λ in the optimality equation given only data on p, Q, Z, and w, assuming we have many, varied observations? Bresnahan (1982) and Lau (1982) give conditions on the functional form such that λ is identified. As Lau (1982) notes, we can write output as a reduced-form equation of the exogenous variables, $Q = h_1(Z, w)$, and this equation is always identified. Given this functional relationship, the reduced-form expression of price is

$$p = p(Q, Z) = p(h_1(Z, w), Z) = h_2(Z, w), \tag{3.7}$$

which is always identified.[4] The optimality relationship is identified if, given an invariant demand function $p(Q, Z)$, it is not possible to find two distinct sets of the marginal cost function of the form $MC(Q, w)$ and λ that satisfy Equation (3.4).

To illustrate the identification concept, we use an example similar to that in Bresnahan (1982), in which both the demand and the marginal cost curves are linear in parameters:

$$p = \phi_0 - \phi_1 Q - \phi_2 ZQ - \phi_3 Z + u_d, \tag{3.8}$$

and

$$MC = \eta + \gamma Q + \alpha w + u_c, \tag{3.9}$$

[3] Other economists have responded that, if firms are engaged in a dynamic setting, the folk theorem (Chapter 5) shows that a range of outcomes corresponding to a range of λ are consistent with a Nash equilibrium. However, critics respond to this defense that using a static model is questionable if firms are playing a dynamic game.

[4] As Lau (1982) notes, given $Q = h_1(Z, w)$ and a nontrivial dependence of $h_2(Z, w)$ on w (which occurs if the marginal cost function depends on w nontrivially), the reduced-form equation for p in Equation (3.7), $h_2(Z, w)$, is invariant only if the demand function, $p(h_1(Z, w), Z)$, is invariant with respect to Z and w.

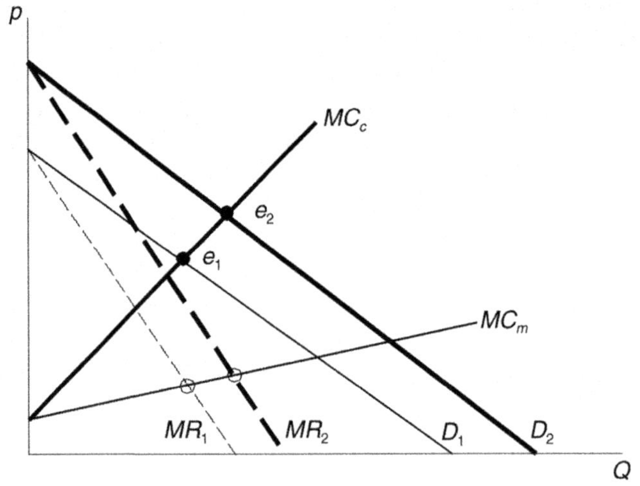

Figure 3.2. Parallel Shift of Demand Curve: Not Identified.

where u_d and u_c are error terms with zero expected means.[5] The systematic portion of the effective marginal revenue that corresponds to Equation (3.8) is

$$MR(\lambda) = p + \lambda p_Q(Q, Z) = p - \lambda[\phi_1 + \phi_2 Z]Q. \tag{3.10}$$

By equating Equations (3.10) and (3.9) and using algebra, we can derive the optimality equation as

$$\begin{aligned} p &= \eta + [\gamma + \lambda\phi_1]Q + \lambda\phi_2 ZQ + \alpha w + u \\ &= \eta + \delta_1 Q + \delta_2 ZQ + \alpha w + u, \end{aligned} \tag{3.11}$$

where $u = u_c - u_d$. If we estimate the system of Equations (3.8) and (3.11), we will obtain estimates of – among other coefficients – ϕ_2 from the demand equation and δ_2 from the optimality equation. Using these estimates, we can obtain an estimate (indicated by a hat) of the market-power parameter as $\hat{\lambda} = \hat{\delta}_2/\hat{\phi}_2$.[6] If there been no interactive term *ZQ* in the demand equation, so that ϕ_2 were identically zero, we would not have been able to identify λ in this manner. Note that we cannot obtain an estimate of λ using our estimate of the δ_1 coefficient because we lack an estimate of γ. Therefore, if $\phi_2 = 0$, there are an infinite number of pairs of λ and γ that are consistent with our estimated optimality equation.

[5] A problem with this example is that the cost function is not homogeneous of degree one if γ and η are nonzero.

[6] Zellner (1978) showed that the ordinary least squares (OLS) reduced-form estimator of a ratio possesses infinite moments of all orders and may have a bimodal distribution. Zellner (1978) and Shen and Perloff (2001) discuss several practical Bayesian and maximum entropy means of estimating such ratios.

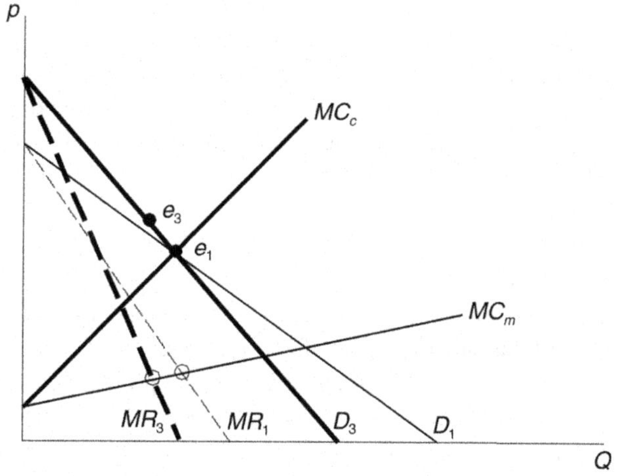

Figure 3.3. Demand Curve Rotates: Identified.

We can illustrate this example using two figures. For simplicity in the figures, we assume that the only possible solutions are that the market is competitive, $\lambda = 0$, or that the firms collude (act like a monopoly), $\lambda = 1$. In Figures 3.2 and 3.3, the initial equilibrium is shown by a solid dot labeled e_1. This equilibrium is consistent with a relatively high marginal cost curve MC_c and a competitive market – the demand curve D_1 intersects MC_c at e_1 – or a relatively low marginal cost curve MC_m and a monopoly – the marginal revenue curve MR_1 intersects the MC_m curve (hollow circle) at the same quantity as at e_1.

In Figure 3.2, we assume that a shock occurs: Z increases. Because the demand function does not have an interactive term ZQ so that $\phi_2 = 0$, this shock causes a parallel shift in the demand curve from D_1 to D_2. Consequently, the new equilibrium is e_2, which is also consistent with both a competitive and monopolistic market. Thus, in this example, the shock does not allow us to differentiate between the two possible market structures.

In contrast, in Figure 3.3, we assume that the demand function has an interactive ZQ term so that $\phi_2 \neq 0$. Consequently, when Z increases, the demand curve rotates. For simplicity, we assume that the new demand curve D_3 is rotated around the original equilibrium point e_1. Here, the resulting equilibrium is either e_1, which is consistent with competition, or it is e_3, which is consistent with monopoly. Thus, a shock allows us to discriminate between the two market structures. A rotation has no effect on a competitive equilibrium, but does affect a monopolistic one.[7]

[7] Perloff and Shen (2001) show that the linear model with the interactive term ZQ cannot be estimated because the terms on the right-hand side of the optimality equation are perfectly collinear. Later, we will examine functional forms that can be estimated.

Thus, one way to identify the market power using the Just–Bresnahan–Lau approach is to have a shock that causes a rotation in the demand curve facing the industry. For example, an ad valorem tax causes such a rotation. Similarly, if a competitive fringe with an upward-sloping supply curve enters an oligopolistic market with a homogeneous product, the residual demand curve facing the oligopolies rotates (Buschena and Perloff 1991).

More generally, Lau (1982) shows that identifying λ is impossible if and only if the inverse demand function $p(Q, Z)$ is separable in Z in the sense that we can write $p = f(Q, r(Z))$ but does not take the form $p = Q^{-1/\lambda}\, r(Z) + s(Q)$. Equivalently, the market-power parameter is identifiable if the inverse demand function is not separable in Z and the dimensionality of Z is at least two.

The only common cases in which identification is a problem are those in which the inverse demand function is linear, as in Bresnahan's example, or it has a constant-elasticity form $Q^k r(Z)$ for any $k \neq -1/\lambda$. Lau notes that, even in the latter case, identification is possible if λ is not constant: for example, if $\lambda = \lambda(Q, Z)$.[8] The key point of this discussion is that identification in this structural model is achieved by the (generally arbitrary) choice of functional form.

Estimation and Hypothesis Tests

Given that λ is in principle identified, we estimate the system of equations consisting of the demand Equation (3.1) and the optimality Equation (3.4) to obtain estimates of λ and the marginal cost. There are two major challenges facing the econometrician. The first – estimating equations with endogenous variables on the right-hand side – is well known. The second – which concerns problems that arise because the estimate of λ is the ratio of two estimated coefficients – is not as well known.

For specificity, we consider the linear example consisting of the demand Equation (3.8) and the optimality Equation (3.11). Both of these equations have endogenous variables, such as output, on the right-hand side. Thus, we need to use an instrumental variables approach (e.g., two-stage or three-stage least squares) or some other means to estimate this system of equations.

One of the major challenges facing an econometrician is to obtain good instruments. Typically, econometricians use inclusion and exclusion restrictions – an exogenous variable appears in one equation of the system but not in the other – to obtain instruments. For example, in the model consisting of Equation (3.8) and Equation (3.11), because the variable w is excluded from Equation (3.8) but is included in Equation (3.11), w is a possible instrument for the demand

[8] Gollop and Roberts (1979), Appelbaum (1982), and Spiller and Favaro (1984), among others, have modeled λ as a function of a variety of variables including output; however, there is relatively little economic theory to guide such formulations.

Equation (3.8). Similarly, restrictions on the covariance matrix and knowledge of the functional form might be used.

See Reiss and Wolak (2007) for a thoughtful discussion of these issues. As they point out, structural models can be derived from competing economic and stochastic assumptions. An advantage of a formal structural model based on economic theory is that exclusion and inclusion restrictions are explicit.

The second problem stems from the estimate of the market-power parameter being the ratio of two other estimated coefficients: $\hat{\lambda} = \hat{\delta}_2/\hat{\phi}_2$. As Zellner (1978) showed, the reduced-form estimator of a ratio possesses infinite moments of all orders (because of division by zero) and may have a bimodal distribution. Zellner (1978) and Shen and Perloff (2001) discuss several practical Bayesian and maximum entropy means of estimating such ratios.

Having estimated the system of equations, the econometrician typically wants to conduct tests concerning the market-power parameter, λ. Two approaches have been used. The first is to estimate a system of a demand Equation (3.1) and the optimality Equation (3.4), treating λ as a continuous variable. One then tests whether λ equals a value associated with a well-known model such as competition or Bertrand, Cournot, or collusive, as outlined in Table 3.1. Typically, a t-statistic is calculated for the various hypotheses or a confidence interval is reported.

However, many economists object to the idea of a continuous λ, arguing that the interpretation of λ is problematic if it does not equal the values of one of the well-known and theoretically justified models. Thus, an alternative approach is to estimate separate models corresponding to the various well-known models and then use a non-nested hypothesis test to choose among them. One of the first and a particularly elegant example is Gasmi et al. (1992). They compare their non-nested approach to the continuous λ or conjectural variations approach explicitly. They use the non-nested hypothesis tests of Vuong (1989), but several other approaches to testing are possible.

Taxes: An Application

Presumably, the main reason to estimate a structural model is to determine the degree of market power in an industry. However, an important alternative purpose may be to accurately estimate some other parameter that depends on market structure. For example, suppose we want to estimate the incidence of a tax. The tax incidence depends on the market structure as well the demand and cost curves. Consequently, if we falsely assume that a market is competitive, our estimate of the incidence will be biased.

We use a parameter λ to nest various market structure models so as to illustrate the bias.[9] Consider an industry that produces Q units of a homogeneous good and

[9] The following is based on Karp and Perloff (1989a).

faces an inverse demand curve $p(Q)$. The industry consists of n identical firms, each of which produces $q = Q/n$ in equilibrium at a variable cost of $c(q)$. If an ad valorem tax rate of t is imposed, Firm i's profit is

$$\pi_i = (1 - t)p(Q)q_i - c(q_i). \tag{3.12}$$

The firm maximizes its profit by choosing q_i such that

$$(1 - t)[p(Q) + \lambda q_i p'(Q)] - c'(q_i) = 0, \tag{3.13}$$

where $\lambda = dQ/dq_i$ is Firm i's constant conjectural variation. (Here, λ is n times larger than before, so that $\lambda = 0$ implies competition, $\lambda = 1$ is consistent with Nash-Cournot, and $\lambda = n$ implies monopoly.) In Equation (3.13), the firm sets its after-tax marginal revenue, $(1 - t)[p(q) + \lambda q_i p'(Q)]$, equal to its marginal cost, $c'(q_i)$.

If t varies during the period of observation, one could estimate the tax incidence using a reduced-form model. However, because many tax rates remain constant for many years, it may be necessary to estimate a structural model and then simulate the effect of the tax.

Suppose an economist inappropriately assumes the market is competitive and estimates a supply equation using the first-order condition in Equation (3.13) with $\lambda = 0$,

$$(1 - t)p(Q) - k'(q_i) = 0, \tag{3.14}$$

where k' is an individual firm's marginal cost. Equation (3.14) says that the after-tax price equals marginal cost. Given that t does not vary, the economist mistakes k' for c'. Given the historical t and the constant λ (and suppressing the i subscripts),

$$k'(q) \equiv c'(q) - (1 - t)\lambda q p'(nq) = h(q, t), \tag{3.15}$$

where the identity is in q. That is, given that the economist falsely assumes that the market was competitive, the economist estimates a marginal cost curve that is too high: $k'(q)$ is higher than $c'(q)$ because the demand curve slopes down ($p' < 0$). This relationship between the two marginal cost functions is shown in Figures 3.2 and 3.3 (where MC_m corresponds to c' and MC_c corresponds to k').

The economist's estimate of the effect of a change in t on q and p obviously depends on which model is estimated. In the correct model, Equation (3.13), if we totally differentiate, we find that

$$\frac{dq}{dt} = \frac{p + h_t}{h^*(q, t)}, \tag{3.16}$$

where $h^*(q, t) = (1 - t)np' - h_q < 0$ for stability; $h_q = c'' - (1 - t)[Qp'' + p'](1 + \lambda)$; and $h_t = (1 + \lambda)qp' \leq 0$, where equality in this last expression holds only if the market is competitive ($p' = 0$). Given that one falsely assumes that Equation

(3.15) holds, the estimate of dq/dt is p/h^*, which is greater in absolute value than the true value given in Equation (3.16).

Let p_λ be the predicted price at a tax rate of zero under the oligopolistic model, where λ is correctly estimated, and p_c be the comparable price where competition is assumed ($\lambda = 0$). Because demand curves slope downward, $p_\lambda > p_c$ for $\lambda > 0$. If the observed price is p, the estimated incidence falling on consumers is

$$I_m = \frac{p - p_m}{tp}, \tag{3.17}$$

for $m = \lambda$ (the correct model) or $m = c$ (the competitive model where $\lambda = 0$).

From these definitions and the inequality in prices, we conclude that

$$I_c = I_\lambda + \frac{p_\lambda - p_c}{tp} > I_\lambda, \tag{3.18}$$

for $\lambda > 0$. That is, if one falsely assumes competitive behavior, one produces an upward biased estimate of the tax incidence.

NONPARAMETRIC AND REDUCED-FORM MODELS

A main advantage of the structural model is that one obtains estimates of the market structure as well as the demand and cost curves. Unfortunately, like other estimation problems, these estimates are biased if the specification of the structural model is incorrect.

A number of economist have proposed avoiding the need to specify the structure by using a reduced-form and nonparametric approach to test for noncompetitive behavior. Sumner (1981), Sullivan (1985), Ashenfelter and Sullivan (1987), and Hall (1988) are four of the earliest and best-known approaches. A main drawback of their approach is that we do not obtain an estimate of the market structure – all we can do is test whether or not the market is competitive.

Comparative Statics

Most nonparametric approaches are based on the qualitative results from comparative statics. To illustrate the basic idea, suppose that firms face a constant marginal cost, m.[10] A shock causes the marginal cost to rise. For example, in Sumner (1981), Sullivan (1985), and Ashenfelter and Sullivan (1987), a known change in the tax rate (or difference in the tax rate across states) allows them to conduct a comparative statics experiment. If the market is competitive, then the price will increase by the same amount as the marginal cost, because the price equals the marginal cost. However, if the market is noncompetitive, price may not change by the same

[10] As noted earlier, if the marginal cost is constant, the structural model is identified even if a shock causes a parallel shift in the demand curve.

amount as the marginal cost. Thus, in principle, we can test for noncompetitive behavior by checking whether price moves disproportionately with marginal cost.

Unfortunately, we need some structure (such as the specification of the demand curve) to be able to conduct this experiment. To illustrate this point, we assume that the only alternative to a competitive structure is a pure monopoly and that the marginal cost (and hence average variable cost) is constant, m. How does the monopoly's price change as marginal cost changes?[11] The monopoly's objective is to maximize its profit through its choice of its output level

$$\max_{Q} \; [p(Q) - m]\, Q, \tag{3.19}$$

where Q is the quantity sold and $p(Q)$ is the inverse demand function. The profit-maximizing output is determined by its first-order condition:

$$Qp'(Q) + p(Q) - m = 0. \tag{3.20}$$

This expression says that the marginal revenue, $Qp'(Q) + p(Q)$, equals the marginal cost. We can rewrite this expression in terms of the market elasticity of demand, $\varepsilon = p/[Qp'(Q)]$, as the standard marginal revenue equals marginal cost condition:

$$p\left[1 + \frac{1}{\varepsilon}\right] = m. \tag{3.21}$$

Thus, the markup of price over marginal cost depends solely on the elasticity of demand:

$$\frac{p - m}{p} = -\frac{1}{\varepsilon}. \tag{3.22}$$

By totally differentiating Equation (3.20), we obtain

$$\frac{\mathrm{d}Q}{\mathrm{d}m} = \frac{1}{2p'(Q) + Qp''(Q)}. \tag{3.23}$$

Using the chain rule, we find that the change in the price in response to a change in the marginal cost is

$$\frac{\mathrm{d}p}{\mathrm{d}Q}\frac{\mathrm{d}Q}{\mathrm{d}m} = p'(Q)\frac{\mathrm{d}Q}{\mathrm{d}m} = \frac{p'(Q)}{2p'(Q) + Qp''(Q)}. \tag{3.24}$$

The numerator of the right-hand side of this equation is the slope of the inverse demand curve and the denominator is the slope of the marginal revenue curve.

According to Equation (3.24), the monopoly reduces its output so that marginal revenue increases by the same amount as its marginal cost. Consequently, price

[11] The following discussion is based on Bulow and Pfleiderer (1983).

rises by an amount equal to the ratio of the slope of the demand curve to the slope of the marginal revenue times the amount of the cost change.

If the monopoly faces a constant elasticity demand curve, $p = AQ^{1/\varepsilon}$, its marginal revenue is $p[(\varepsilon + 1)/\varepsilon]$, so $p = m\varepsilon/(\varepsilon + 1)$. Because ε is a constant that is less than -1, $\mathrm{d}p/\mathrm{d}m = \varepsilon/(\varepsilon - 1) > 1$. The monopoly uses a constant percentage markup policy: the markup is $100\varepsilon/(\varepsilon - 1)$ percent. That is, the monopoly raises the price by more than cost increases, and the amount by which it raises it depends on the elasticity of demand.

These results (that the change in price depends on the elasticity of demand and that the price increases more than in proportion to marginal cost) do not hold for all demand curves. For example, if the demand curve is of the form $p = \alpha - \beta Q^{\delta}$, where $\delta > 0$, then the monopoly's marginal revenue is $\alpha - \beta(\delta + 1)Q$ <σπ>δ </σπ>. Consequently, $p'(m) = 1/(1 + \delta) < 1$. That is, the monopoly increases its price by a constant fraction of the cost increase – not the full amount – and the markup is independent of the elasticity of demand. If $\delta = 1$ so that the demand curve is linear, then $p'(m) = 1/2$, so price always rises by one-half the increase in the marginal cost.

Finally, suppose that the demand curve is $p = \alpha - \beta \ln Q$, where $\alpha, \beta > 0$, $0 < Q < \exp(\alpha/\beta)$. Marginal revenue is $p - \beta$, so $p'(m) = 1$, hence price rises by the same amount as cost (which is what would happen in a competitive market).

Thus, without some additional knowledge, we cannot test whether the market is competitive using only information about the change in price in response to the change in marginal cost. However, this approach may require less information about specification of the demand equation than does the structural model.

Hall's Reduced-Form Approach

Hall (1988) developed one of the best-known reduced-form approaches.[12] This approach requires fewer data series than the structural model and is easier to estimate. Hall uses comparative statics results to test for market power where the null hypothesis is competition. Without supplemental information, his method does not provide an estimate of the degree of market power (see Shapiro 1987).

As Hall discusses at length, the chief weakness of his approach is that one must maintain the assumption of constant returns to scale (CRS). His market-power test is actually a joint test of both competition and CRS. Hall uses two methods. Both methods are based on the Solow residual, θ, which is an index of Hicks-neutral technical progress (that is, technical progress that is neither labor-savings nor capital-savings).

[12] Shapiro (1987), Domowitz, Hubbard, and Petersen (1986, 1988), and others use Hall's estimation methods. Shapiro (1987) discusses some of the conceptual limitations to his approach and possible solutions. Roeger (1995) provides a generalization.

For simplicity, suppose that a firm produces output Q_t in period t with a production function $\theta f(L, K)$, where θ is an index of Hicks-neutral technical progress, L is labor, and K is capital. (Hall shows that his approach generalizes to the situation in which output depends on capital, labor, and materials.) The firm buys labor at wage w. Using a well-known result by Robert Solow, under the assumption of competition and CRS, the *Solow residual* is

$$\Delta q_t - \alpha_t \Delta l_t = \theta + u_t, \tag{3.25}$$

where $\Delta q_t (= \Delta \log[Q_t/K_t])$ is the rate of growth of the output/capital ratio, α_t $(= wL/pQ)$ is the labor's factor share, $\Delta l_t (= \Delta \log[L_t/K_t])$ is the growth of the labor/capital ratio, and u_t is a random term (reflecting the random element in productivity growth).

The basic economic concept behind the Solow residual is that the observed share of labor is an exact measure of the elasticity of the production function under competition and constant returns to scale. Even without any further restrictions on the production function, we can determine the elasticity directly from data on compensation and revenue. Given this elasticity, the rate of productivity growth is the rate of growth of output minus the rate of growth of the labor/capital ratio adjusted by this elasticity. Because Solow wanted to calculate the rate of growth of production separately for each year, he added a random component, u_t, to the equation to capture nonsystematic fluctuations over time.

Suppose that there is an instrument (such as the change in the level of military spending, price of crude oil, or the political party of the President), I, that affects output, Δq_t, and employment, Δl_t, but that is uncorrelated with u and hence exogenous to Equation (3.25). Because I is uncorrelated with the right-hand side of Equation (3.25), it must also have a zero correlation with the left-hand side. Thus, Hall argues that under the assumptions of competition and constant returns to scale, the Solow residual is uncorrelated with a variable that is known neither to be the cause of a productivity shift nor to be caused by a productivity shift.

Using this result, Hall develops an *instrument test*: if the market is competitive with CRS, an appropriate instrument will have a near-zero correlation with the Solow residual. Hall argues that a "convincingly exogenous variable" that is correlated with the Solow residual refutes the joint hypothesis of competition and CRS. He then argues that a positive correlation is a sign of market power or increasing returns (which is inconsistent with competition).

To illustrate why, we assume for simplicity that there is a fixed capital stock and that technology does not change over time so that changes in output are due to changes in the labor input, ΔL_t. If $m =$ marginal cost, then a good measure of marginal cost is the change in the labor cost as output changes:

$$m = \frac{w\Delta L}{\Delta Q}. \tag{3.26}$$

We can rewrite Equation (3.26) to show that the rate of growth of output equals labor's factor share (evaluated at marginal cost), wL/mQ, times the rate of growth of labor:

$$\Delta q_t = \frac{wL}{mQ}\frac{\Delta L}{L}. \tag{3.27}$$

The ratio of price over marginal cost is $\mu = p/m$. Under competition, $\mu = 1$. In contrast, if firms have market power, $\mu > 1$. We can write the growth in output in terms of this markup, μ_t, labor's share (of revenue), α_t, and the growth of labor, Δl_t:

$$\Delta q_t = \mu_t \alpha_t \Delta l_t. \tag{3.28}$$

Hall shows that a similar equation holds when capital can change over time if we reinterpret the measure of marginal cost slightly and allow for technical change:

$$\Delta q_t = \mu_t \alpha_t \Delta l_t + \theta_t. \tag{3.29}$$

Equation (3.29) captures his basic idea (Hall, 1988, p. 926): "The relation between price and marginal cost can be found by comparing the actual growth in the output/capital ratio with the growth that would be expected given the rate of technical progress and the growth in the labor/capital ratio."

In general, θ_t is unknown: $\theta_t = \theta + u_t$.[13] Making this substitution and subtracting $\alpha_t \Delta l_t$ from both sides, we can write the Solow residual under market power as

$$\Delta q_t - \alpha_t \Delta l_t = (\mu_t - 1)\,\alpha_t \Delta l_t + \theta + u_t. \tag{3.30}$$

Hall's main result is that the covariance of the exogenous instrumental variable and the Solow residual is

$$\text{cov}(\Delta q - \alpha \Delta l, I) = \text{cov}[(\mu_t - 1)\alpha_t \Delta l_t, I]. \tag{3.31}$$

If the market is competitive, the first term on the right-hand side of Equation (3.30) is zero because $(\mu_t - 1) = 0$. If the market is not competitive, the covariance of an instrumental variable with the Solow residual differs from zero because of this term.

To perform his instrument test, we may estimate an equation of the form

$$\theta_t = \phi_0 + \phi_1 I_t + \varepsilon, \tag{3.32}$$

where I_t is the instrument, and test whether ϕ_1 is statistically significantly different from zero (in particular, positive). Although this approach allows us to test whether the market is competitive, it does not provide any information about the degree of market power if the market is not competitive.

13 If the data contain no errors and the rate of technical progress, θ_t, is known, then we can solve Equation (3.29) for the markup in each year $\mu_t = (\Delta q_t - \theta_t)/(\alpha_t \Delta l_t)$.

To look at that question, we can use the *estimation method* to obtain an estimate of the ratio of price over marginal cost, μ. If we are willing to assume that μ is constant over time, then we can estimate μ using the basic growth equation:

$$\Delta \ln\left(\frac{Q}{K}\right) = \mu\left[\tilde{\alpha}\Delta \ln\left(\frac{L}{K}\right) + \tilde{\beta}\Delta \ln\left(\frac{M}{K}\right)\right] + u, \tag{3.33}$$

where output is also a function of materials, M; $\tilde{\alpha}$ and $\tilde{\beta}$ are estimated factor shares for labor and capital (dropping the CRS assumption); and u is a random error. However, it is difficult to interpret μ unless one has additional information such as demand elasticities (Shapiro 1987).

OLIGOPSONY

So far, we have assumed that the economist is trying to determine whether there is oligopoly market power. However, in a number of industries, we are interested in whether firms have oligopsony market power.[14]

We can reformulate the structural and Hall's reduced-form models to investigate oligopsony market power (see Hyde and Perloff 1994). As before, the structural model requires more data and more explicit assumptions than does Hall's method; however, Hall's method requires that we maintain the assumption that the production function exhibits constant returns to scale (CRS).

Structural Oligopsony Model

To estimate a structural model, one must estimate all the underlying structural equations of the market. To illustrate this approach, consider a firm with monopsony power in a labor market. Suppose the labor, L, supply curve is

$$w = w(L; Z), \tag{3.34}$$

where w is the wage and Z is a vector of other relevant exogenous variables.

As in the Just–Chern–Bresnahan–Lau oligopoly power structural model, we can use a parameter λ to nest various oligopsony market structures. For example, we can define an *effective marginal cost of labor*

$$\frac{\mathrm{d}wL}{\mathrm{d}L} = w + \lambda w_L L, \tag{3.35}$$

where w_L is the slope of the supply curve. (If the supply curve has no slope, monopsony power cannot be exercised.). If $\lambda = 0$, the effective marginal cost of labor equals the wage and the market is competitive; if $\lambda = 1$, the effective marginal cost

[14] Indeed, one of the first important papers on estimating structural models, Just and Chern (1980), concerned oligopsony power. Other examples of empirical studies of oligopsony power include Love and Murniningtyas (1992), Schroeter and Azzam (1987), and Wann and Sexton (1992).

of labor equals the marginal cost of labor of a monopsony; if λ lies between 0 and 1, the degree of oligopsony power lies between the extremes of competition and monopsony.

Let the production function be $Q = f(L, K)$, where Q is output and K is capital. The optimality or equilibrium condition is that the industry sets its effective marginal cost of labor equal to the value of the marginal product of labor,

$$w + \lambda_L L = pQ_L, \tag{3.36}$$

where p is the price of output and Q_L is the marginal product of labor.

Hall's Reduced-Form Oligopsony Model

We can adapt Hall's method to estimate monopsony power. We estimate the oligopsony "markdown," $\mu = pQ_L/w$, which is the ratio of the marginal product of labor to the wage. If $\mu = 1$, the market is competitive; if $\mu > 1$, oligopsony power is being exercised.

We now derive the estimating equation given a constant level of capital, K, and ignoring technical change. The value of the marginal product is approximately $VMP = p\Delta Q/\Delta L$ (this expression holds exactly for an infinitesimal change). We can rewrite this expression for the value of the marginal product of labor as one between the growth rate of output and the rate of growth of the labor input (where θ is Hicks-neutral technical change as before):

$$\frac{\Delta Q}{Q} = \frac{(VMP)L}{pQ}\frac{\Delta L}{L}.$$

By substituting for μ and using algebra, we can rewrite this expression as

$$\frac{\Delta Q}{Q} = \mu\frac{wL}{pQ}\frac{\Delta L}{L} + \theta = \mu\eta\frac{\Delta L}{L},$$

where $\eta = wL/pQ$ is labor's share in output value. Generalizing to allow for Hicks-neutral technological progress, θ, and variable capital, we can obtain an equation that we can use to estimate μ:

$$\Delta \ln\left(\frac{Q}{K}\right) = \mu\eta\Delta \ln\left(\frac{L}{K}\right) + \theta. \tag{3.37}$$

HOW WELL THESE METHODS WORK

Do these structural and reduced-form models work well in testing for market power and in measuring it, or do these methods produce biased estimates? Two approaches have been used to judge the effectiveness of these methods. In the first, the econometrician has evidence about the true market structure and examines how well the structural model works. In the second, Monte Carlo simulations are used to examine how well these approaches work.

Tests Based on Cost Evidence

The first approach is to compare the estimated market-power parameter to what we believe to be the "truth" about the market power based on other evidence. For example, suppose that we know the true marginal cost and can thus calculate the true exercised market power. We could then ignore this information, estimate the structural model, and see whether the estimated measure of market power is consistent with the true, calculated measure.

There are two difficulties with such a comparison. First, we rarely know or can estimate the marginal cost, though there are a few exceptions. Second, the structural model estimates are conditional on assumptions about the functional form. Thus, a test comparing a structural model estimate to an observed Lerner measure is really a joint hypothesis test on the structural method and on the functional form. Consequently, recent studies that make such comparisons experiment with several functional forms.

Genesove and Mullin (1998), in a clever study, test the reliability of the structural model approach. They have data on cost for the sugar refining industry for 1880–1914 as the result of antitrust litigation. They use these data to estimate the marginal cost directly and then compare the implied market power to the value they obtained using a structural approach. Although their calculated Lerner index does not lie within the 95% confidence interval of their structural model estimate, both measures give the same qualitative answer that the market is extremely competitive. Their structural model's point estimate of the index is 0.04 compared with their calculated "true" value of 0.11 – however, both numbers are very close to zero.

Clay and Troesken (2003) use evidence from the turn-of-the-twentieth-century whiskey market to conduct a similar study. They conclude, like Genesove and Mullin (1998), that the structural approach works well for low levels of market power. In contrast, Kim and Knittle (2004) do not find that this method works well based on evidence from the (regulated) California electricity market.[15]

Oligopoly Simulations

Alternatively, we can use a Monte Carlo simulation experiment to test the effectiveness of these models.[16] We assume that the market has identical firms with Cobb-Douglas production processes and a log-linear demand function. We use this artificial market to examine how well the structural and reduced-form models perform when some of their underlying assumptions are violated.

We assume that the cost and demand functions have additive, random, uncorrelated errors representing shocks from unknown sources. The systematic portion of

[15] It is possible that some of the bias in these three studies is due to a failure to deal with the ratio problem when estimating λ.

[16] The following oligopoly simulations are from Hyde and Perloff (1995). Hyde and Perloff (1994) present similar results for oligopsony models.

the Cobb-Douglas production function can be written as $Q^* = AL^{\alpha}K^{\beta}$, where Q^* is the systematic portion of market output that does not depend on any random fluctuations in the market, L is the labor used in the industry, K is the capital, and A, α, and β are constant parameters. The corresponding cost function is also Cobb-Douglas:

$$C = A^{-1/\gamma}\gamma\left(\frac{w}{\alpha}\right)^{\alpha/\gamma}\left(\frac{r}{\beta}\right)^{\beta/\gamma} Q^{1/\gamma}e^{\varepsilon_C} \equiv C^* e^{\varepsilon_C}, \tag{3.38}$$

where $\varepsilon_c \sim N(0, \sigma^2)$, "*" indicates the systematic part of a variable (C^* is the systematic portion of costs that does not depend on ε_C), and γ, the scale parameter, equals $\alpha + \beta$. Consequently, the systematic portion of the marginal cost is

$$MC^* = A^{-1/\gamma}\left(\frac{w}{\alpha}\right)^{\alpha/\gamma}\left(\frac{r}{\beta}\right)^{\beta/\gamma} Q^{(1-\gamma)/\gamma}. \tag{3.39}$$

The demand is log-linear:

$$\ln p = \delta_0 - (\delta_1 + \delta_2 Z)\ln Q + \delta_3 Y + \varepsilon_D \equiv \ln p^* + \varepsilon_D, \tag{3.40}$$

where p is price, Z is an exogenous variable that rotates the demand curve and Y is an exogenous demand shifter (Z and Y may be the price of a substitute, a proxy for taste changes, or income), and $\varepsilon_D \sim N(0, \sigma^2)$.[17] The slope of the demand curve is $p' = -\frac{p}{Q}(\delta_1 + \delta_2 Z)$. Thus, the effective marginal revenue, Equation (3.3), is

$$MR(\lambda) = p + \lambda p' Q = p\,[1 - \lambda(\delta_1 + \delta_2 Z)]\,. \tag{3.41}$$

For the equilibrium to make sense, the effective marginal revenue must be positive, and hence $\lambda(\delta_1 + \delta_2 Z)$ must be less than one. That is, the inverse of the "effective elasticity of demand," which is λ times the inverse of the absolute value of the elasticity of demand, must be less than one.

The equilibrium condition is that effective marginal revenue equals marginal cost, or

$$\ln MR(\lambda) = \ln p + \ln\,[1 - \lambda(\delta_1 + \delta_2 Z)] = \ln MC. \tag{3.42}$$

Substituting for MC from Equation (3.39) and for $\ln p$ from Equation (3.40), we find that the log of the output demanded is

$$\begin{aligned}\ln Q &= \frac{\delta_0 + \ln[1 - \lambda(\delta_1 + \delta_2 Z)] + \delta_3 Y + \frac{1}{\gamma}\ln A - \frac{\alpha}{\gamma}\ln\left(\frac{w}{\alpha}\right) - \frac{\beta}{\gamma}\ln\left(\frac{r}{\beta}\right) + \varepsilon_D - \varepsilon_C}{\delta_1 + \delta_2 Z + \frac{1-\gamma}{\gamma}}\\ &\equiv \ln Q^* + \frac{\varepsilon_D - \varepsilon_C}{\delta_1 + \delta_2 Z + \frac{1-\gamma}{\gamma}}.\end{aligned} \tag{3.43}$$

[17] As Chapter 3 explains, λ is not identified in a log-linear model without an interaction term that rotates the demand curve, such as $Z \ln Q$.

Given the specified parameters, we can calculate Q^* using Equation (3.43).[18] By substituting Q^* into Equation (3.40), we obtain p^*.

We are interested in the degree of market power, which we measure as the Lerner index or as the price/marginal cost ratio, μ. We consider three market structures: competition ($\lambda = 0$, so that $\mu = 1$), four identical Cournot firms ($\lambda = 0.25$), and collusion ($\lambda = 1$). The parameters in the simulations are $A = 1.2, \alpha/\gamma = 1/3, \beta/\gamma = 2/3, \delta_0 = 1.8, \delta_1 = 1.2$, and $\delta_2 = -0.5$.[19] To give a patina of reality, we use actual series for w, r, and Z. The wage, w, and user cost of capital, r, are for U.S. manufacturing 1947–1981 (Berndt and Wood 1986). For Z, we use the producer price index for processed foods and farm products from the *Economic Report of the President*.[20]

Using the same series for w, r, and Z in each case, we generated 1,000 data series of thirty-five time periods by randomly drawing error terms for ε_C and ε_D. Using the equations above, we calculate the "true" Q, p, and other variables that are used in our estimation procedures.

Structural Model

As we expected, the structural model works well if it is correctly specified as a Cobb-Douglas model and does not work as well if it is incorrectly specified. When correctly specified, no particular problems are associated with the scale parameter γ, so we concentrate on the model with constant returns to scale ($\lambda = 1$). That model, consisting of Equations (3.40) and (3.43), is estimated using nonlinear three-stage least squares, where the instruments are w, r, and Z. In Table 3.3, the variance of price for the model based on ε_C and ε_D errors that are independently distributed $0.01N(0, 1)$ is virtually identical to that of the manufacturing sector (after normalizing so that the means of the two series are equal). The variance of price for the model based on error terms that are ten times larger, $0.1N(0, 1)$, is 13% larger.

We estimate the structural model in three ways. First, we estimate it correctly: we assume that the underlying technology is Cobb-Douglas.[21] Second, we estimate the system using a more general, translog specification for technology (a second-order

[18] By minimizing cost with respect to labor and capital, we obtained factor demand equations. Substituting for output into these equations, we obtain equations for L and K, which are used in Hall's method.

[19] These parameters are arbitrarily chosen. From our (nonsystematic) experimentation with other parameters, we did not find that our results are very sensitive to this particular choice. However, the results are sensitive to the choice of the number of observations and the correlation between the factor price series.

[20] In our estimation section, we examine the processed food industry. It seems plausible that demand for any one processed food depends on an index of (other) food prices.

[21] We estimated a four-equation system: the demand Equation (3.40), the optimality Equation (3.42), a share equation $s_L = \beta_1$ (where $s_L = wL/C$ and C is cost), and a cost equation $\ln(C\alpha Q) = \alpha \ln w + \beta \ln r$, where $\alpha + \beta = 1$.

Table 3.3. *Structural model (Percentage of simulations in which the hypothesis is not rejected)*

		ε_C and ε_D are distributed					
		0.1 $N(0, 1)$			0.01 $N(0, 1)$		
Market Structure, True λ	Hypothesis λ	Cobb-Douglas	Translog	Linear	Cobb-Douglas	Translog	Linear
Competition	0	94.6	93.2	10.9	94.0	92.0	0
$\lambda = 0$	0.25	0.6	0.5	1.8	0.5	0	0
	1	0	0	0	0.1	0	0
Four-Firm	0	0.6	0.2	0	0	0	0
Cournot	0.25	89.2	56.1	75.0	95.9	65.1	76.3
$\lambda = 0.25$	1	0.1	0	0.1	0	0	0
Collusion	0	0	0.2	4.7*	0	0	0
$\lambda = 1$	0.25	0	1.5	97.4*	0	0	100.0
	1	95.7	68.3	23.9*	97.5	70.8	94.6

* These numbers are averaged over the 51% of the simulations that converged.

approximation for which the Cobb-Douglas is a special case).[22] We expect the translog estimates to be less precise than those from the Cobb-Douglas model because the Cobb-Douglas restrictions to the translog are correct. Third, we estimate the model assuming the true underlying technology is linear (see Hyde and Perloff 1995).

We use t-statistics to test whether the estimated market structure parameter λ equals 0, 0.25, or 1 (competition, four-firm Cournot, and collusion). The results for the true Cobb-Douglas model, the translog model, and the misspecified linear model are shown in Table 3.3 based on 1,000 simulations of each example. The table shows the percentage of simulations in which we cannot reject each hypothesis about λ based on a standard two-tailed test at the 0.05 level.[23]

The Cobb-Douglas model does well with both size error terms. With either error term, in the correctly specified Cobb-Douglas model, we reject the false hypotheses in virtually all cases. We also fail to reject the correct hypothesis in virtually every case. For example, with the smaller error term, we fail to reject collusion in 97.5% of the 1,000 simulations when the true model is $\lambda = 1$.

The translog model performs nearly as well as the Cobb-Douglas model when the market is competitive, but does not perform as well when the market is four-firm Cournot ($\lambda = 0.25$) or collusive ($\lambda = 1$). For example, with the smaller error term, when the market is competitive, we fail to reject the competitive hypothesis in 94.0% of the simulations when we use the Cobb-Douglas specification, and in 92.0% of the simulations when we use the translog specification. When the true λ is 0.25, we fail to reject the four-firm Cournot hypothesis in 95.9% of the replications for the Cobb-Douglas model but only 65.1% for the translog.

If we use the incorrectly specified linear model, we cannot distinguish clearly between the hypotheses, even with a small error term.[24] When the true model is competitive, the linear model rejects both correct and incorrect hypotheses in almost all simulations. When the true λ is 0.25, the linear model performs "better" than the translog model in rejecting false hypotheses and failing to reject the true one. When the true λ is 1, the linear model fails to reject the false hypothesis that $\lambda = 0.25$ more times than the true hypothesis that $\lambda = 1$. We also found that, with the large error term, we could not estimate the linear model in half the simulations when the true λ is one.

[22] We estimate a four-equation system: The demand Equation (3.40), the share equation, $s_L = \beta_1 + \beta_3[\ln r - \ln w]$, a cost equation, $\ln(C/Q) = \alpha \ln w + \beta \ln r + 0.5\gamma_{11}(\ln w)^2 + \gamma_{12}(\ln w)(\ln r) + 0.5\gamma_{22}(\ln r)^2$, and a new optimality equation, $p = [1 - \lambda(\delta_1 + \delta_2 Z)]^{-1} \times \exp(\beta_0 + \beta_1 \ln w + (1 - \beta_1)\ln r + \beta_3(\ln w)(\ln r) - 0.5\beta_3(\ln w)^2 - 0.5\beta_3(\ln r)^2)$.

[23] One might argue for using one-tailed tests, especially when testing the competitive ($\lambda = 0$) and collusive ($\lambda = 1$) hypotheses, which are bounds on the range of λ. However, we observed the same pattern of results when we used one-tailed tests.

[24] With the misspecified linear model, the results are very sensitive to the scale parameter γ. With $\gamma = 0.9$ or 1.1, we reject all the hypotheses in almost all cases. The exception is when $\lambda = 0.25$ and $\gamma = 0.9$, where we fail to reject the hypothesis $\lambda = 0$ in 81.9% of the simulations and $\lambda = 0.25$ in 43.4% of the simulations. However, the reason for this failure is that the linear model is collinear (Perloff and Shen 2001).

Table 3.4. *Hall's estimation method*

Market structure, true λ	Average $\hat{\mu}$	Average p/MC	Fail to reject the null hypothesis (%): Competition, 0.1 $N(0,1)$	Competition, 0.01 $N(0,1)$	True model, 0.01 $N(0,1)$
Competition ($\lambda = 0$)	.996	1.00	98.5	98.4	98.4
Four-firm Cournot ($\lambda = 0.25$)	1.084	1.16	98.9	12.1	90.3
Collusion ($\lambda = 1$)	1.569	2.29	85.9	6.2	40.7

Hall's Reduced-Form Model

We can test whether the market is competitive (given our maintained assumption of constant returns to scale) using either of Hall's methods. The estimation method uses Equation (3.39). After estimating the price–marginal cost ratio, μ, one uses t-statistics to test the hypothesis that $\mu = 1$. In the instrument test, one uses instrumental variables to test the competitive hypothesis. In the estimation method, if the market is not competitive, μ is greater than one, but the relationship between μ and particular market structures is not known unless one has additional information such as the demand elasticity (Shapiro 1987).

In Table 3.4, the second column shows the average estimate of μ, $\hat{\mu}$, across the simulations for each of the three market structures. The third column shows the average price–marginal cost ratio based on the true simulation model. When the market is competitive, the average estimate of μ is 1. When the market is not competitive, $\lambda = 0.25$ or 1; however, the mean value of $\hat{\mu}$ is less than the true price–marginal cost ratio.

The last two columns show the percentage of simulations in which we fail to reject various null hypotheses using the smaller error terms: $0.1N(0, 1)$ at the 0.05 level using a two-tailed test. The test for competition is the test that $\mu = 1$. Hall's test correctly fails to reject the hypothesis 98.4% of the time when the market is competitive; however, it incorrectly fails to reject in 12.1% of the simulations when $\lambda = 0.25$ and 6.2% when $\lambda = 1$. The last column tests whether the estimated μ equals the average p/MC (which, of course, one could not know in a real-world problem). Because the estimated μ in the collusive case is very low, we reject equality in nearly 60% of the cases.

Unlike the structural model, Hall's model is very sensitive to the size of the errors. When the larger errors are used, $0.1N(0, 1)$, we fail to reject competition in virtually all cases.

As we explained earlier (and Hall discusses at length), Hall's test is actually a test of the joint hypotheses of competition and constant returns to scale. To see how sensitive this approach is to deviations from constant returns to scale, we allow γ to range between 0.8 and 1.2 using 0.1 increments. For each γ, the model is simulated 200 times.

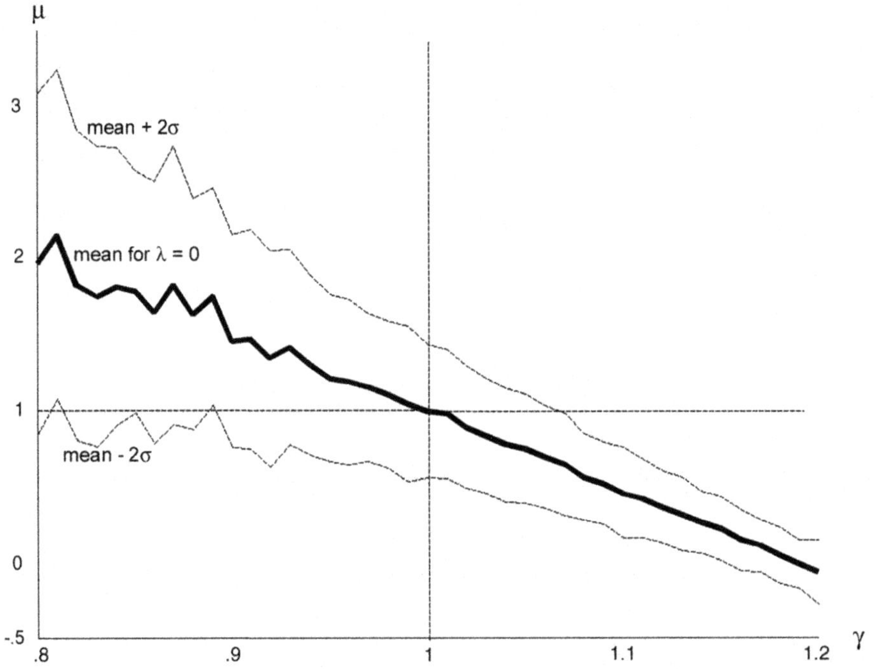

Figure 3.4. Hall's Estimation Test of Competition when Firms Are Price Takers.

The thick, solid line in Figure 3.4 shows how the mean of the estimates of μ varies with γ when the true model is $\lambda = 0$.[25] When there are decreasing returns to scale ($\gamma < 1$), the estimate of μ is well above 1; with increasing returns to scale ($\gamma > 1$), μ is well below 1. Also in the figure are two dotted lines that show, for a given γ, the mean μ plus or minus two standard deviations. Based on this example, relatively small deviations from constant returns can affect hypothesis tests of competition substantially. Hall's test works well, however, with constant returns to scale.

Figure 3.5 shows the same thick, solid line for the mean μ for the $\lambda = 0$ model as in Figure 3.4. It also shows the corresponding lines for the average μ when $\lambda = 0.25$ or $\lambda = 1$. The average μ line in Figure 3.5 for the collusive model is slightly lower than the dotted line in Figure 3.4 for the average μ for the $\lambda = 0$ model plus two standard deviations. As Figure 3.5 shows, with increasing returns to scale, a less competitive market could be mistaken for a competitive one: the $\lambda = 0.25$ and $\lambda = 1$ curves equal 1 for any γ greater than 1. Similarly, with decreasing returns to scale, falsely rejecting competition becomes more likely.

We also examine Hall's instrumental variable test of the competitive hypothesis (Equation 3.44). It is not obvious how we should construct the instrument.

[25] However, the "competitive model" of $\lambda = 0$ does not make sense in the presence of increasing returns to scale.

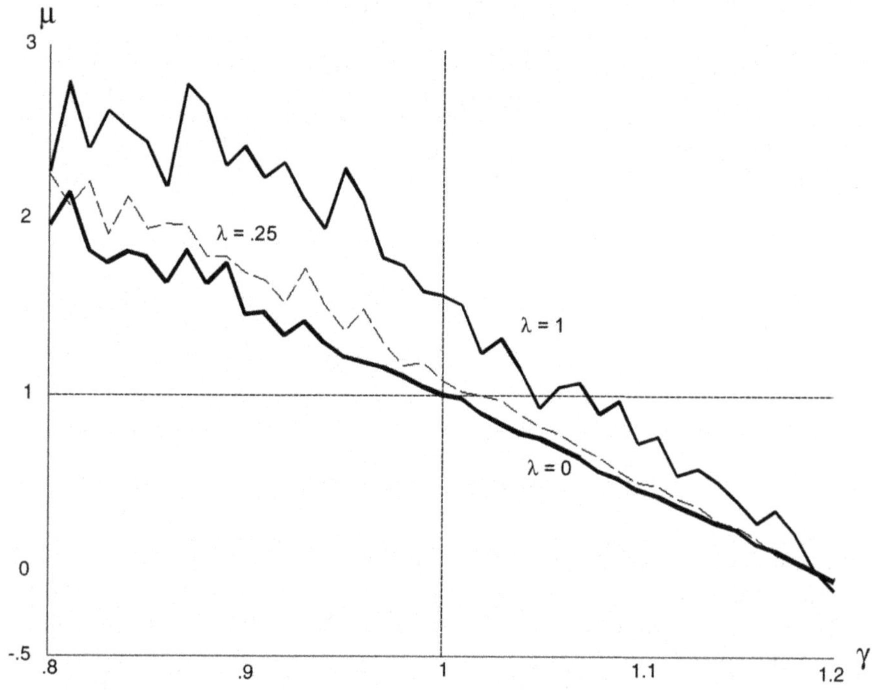

Figure 3.5. Hall's Estimation Test of Competition under Three Market Structures.

Following Hall's suggestion on how to choose instruments, we want to construct an instrument that is correlated with the change in the inputs or output but uncorrelated with the error term u_t in Equation (3.42). Consequently, we construct an instrument, I, that is the weighted average, $\omega\Delta\ln(L/K) + (1-\omega)\zeta$, of a random error term, $\zeta \sim N(0, 0.1)$, and the change in the logarithm of the labor–capital ratio, where ω is the weight.[26] The larger ω, the less noisy is the instrument – the more highly correlated it is with the growth of the labor–capital ratio.

The outcomes of these experiments using $\omega = 0.1$, 0.5, and 0.9 are shown in Table 3.5. The table shows how the instrument is correlated with $\Delta\ln(L/K)$ and with the Solow residual, θ. Based on this test for all ω, we almost never reject the competitive hypothesis when the true model is competition. We are correctly likely to reject competition if the instrument is highly correlated with $\Delta\ln(L/K)$ and θ, and we are incorrectly likely to fail to reject the competitive hypothesis when the instrument is not highly correlated with $\Delta\ln(L/K)$ and θ.

How well does the model work when the constant returns to scale assumption is violated? Figure 3.6, where $\omega = 0.2$ and $\lambda = 0$ (competition), presents various tests of competition as γ, the scale parameter, varies. The thick, solid line shows the

26 We also experimented with instruments created by using random error terms that were correlated with the errors in the labor equation. However, this approach did not work well.

Table 3.5. *Hall's instrument method*

True market structure, λ	Instrument weight, ω	Corr $(I, \Delta\ln [L/K])$	Corr (I, θ)	% Not rejected*
Competition	.1	.17	.01	95.5
$\lambda = 0$	.5	.84	.01	96.5
	.9	1.0	.01	98.0
Four-Firm Cournot	.1	.17	.11	90.5
$\lambda = 0.25$	.5	.84	.48	12.5
	.9	1.0	.56	3.0
Collusion	.1	.17	.09	89.5
$\lambda = 1$	.5	.84	.53	7.5
	.9	1.0	.63	.1

* Percentage of simulations for which the hypothesis of competition is not rejected.
Note: Instrument is $\tilde{I} = \omega\Delta\ln(L/K) + (1-\omega)\zeta$, where $\zeta \sim N(0, 0.1)$. Corr$(I, \Delta\ln [L/K])$ is the correlation coefficient between I and $\Delta\ln [L/K]$.

percent of cases in which competition is rejected based on a standard two-tailed t-test. As Hall notes, however, there is no plausible interpretation of a negative correlation (a world with price below marginal cost), so one might one want to use a one-tailed test, which is shown as a dashed line in the figure. The dotted line

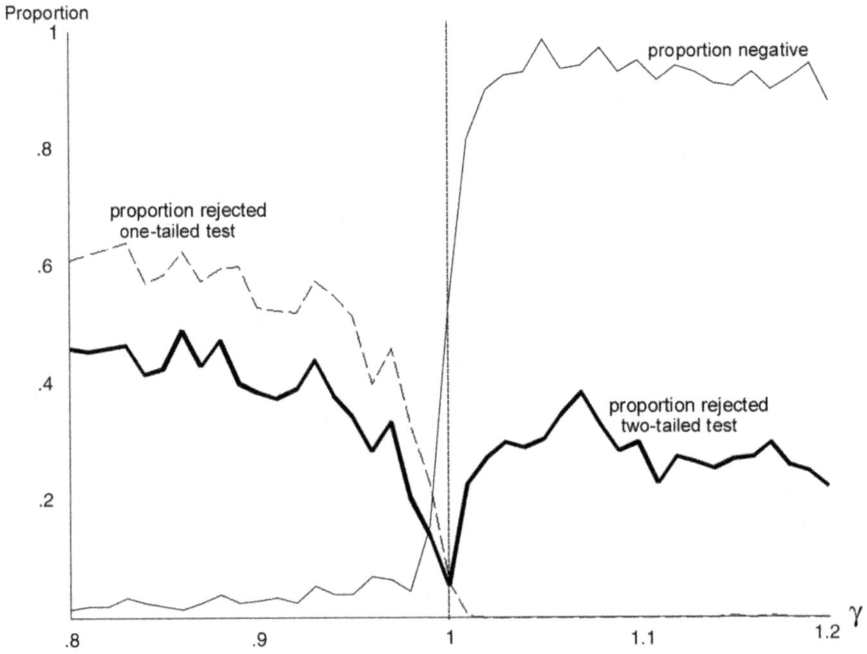

Figure 3.6. Hall's Instrument Test of Competition where $\lambda = 0$.

shows the actual percentage of negative correlations. Again, with constant returns to scale, Hall's test works well. With decreasing returns to scale, competition is incorrectly rejected in a higher percentage of cases.

For larger ω, the two-tailed test rejects competition in virtually all cases for any γ much different than 1. For example, if $\omega = 0.5$, the competitive hypothesis is accepted virtually all of the time when $\lambda \,\varepsilon\, (0.98, 1.02)$ and rejected in virtually all simulations for other γ.

With increasing returns to scale, finding an implausible negative correlation between the Solow residual and the instrument is very likely. Based on a one-tailed test, one would not reject competition; however, based on a two-tailed test, one might incorrectly reject competition because the correlation is too negative. Figure 3.6 shows that the probability of getting a negative correlation is virtually zero for γ much below 1, and the probability is virtually 1 for γ more than slightly greater than 1.

Empirical Comparisons

These simulation results indicate a number of potential problems for both approaches. However, we wondered whether these approaches produce similar or dissimilar results in the real world. If the results are similar, one might be more willing to dismiss worries about these potential problems.

We tried to compare the two approaches using four-digit Standard Industrial Code (SIC) data for food, beverages, and tobacco industries.[27] Both approaches may have problems with industry data if the firms in these industries differ substantially in their behavior. Although we can assume this problem away in our simulations, we cannot assume it away in our empirical work.

Possibly for this reason, we were unsuccessful in obtaining plausible estimates based on an industry-level structural model: the estimated price–cost margins were negative for many industries.[28] In Table 3.6, we show three Hall estimates in which the production function depends on labor, capital, materials, and energy.

We used five instruments (one at a time) in Hall's instrument test for competition.[29] For three instruments – the party of the President, the percentage change in military expenditures, and the percentage change in the U.S. population – the

[27] See Hyde and Perloff (1995) for a description of the data and sources. All prices are deflated by the gross national product (GNP) deflator.

[28] We estimated Almost Ideal Demand System (AIDS) equations and used the same functional form for the marginal cost for each equation. By experimenting with the specification for each industry, we probably could estimate separate specifications with plausible results for most of the industries. However, we did not want to use different specifications for each industry, nor did we want to extensively experiment with the specification, thereby creating a pretest estimator bias.

[29] Hall (1988) gives a lengthy justification for why military spending, the world oil price, and the political party of the president are appropriate instruments. He questions the appropriateness of M1 (a measure of money supply).

Table 3.6. *Industry results*

Industry SIC	Hall instrument test (t-statistic) Oil	M1	Hall estimated markup μ (a. s. e.)
Red meat 2011	−0.92	0.31	−0.79[b] (0.40)
Poultry 2013	−0.09	0.45	0.77 (0.62)
Butter 2021	0.47	0.63	0.58 (.31)
Cheese 2022	−0.38	1.44	0.64 (.26)
Condensed milk 2023	−2.00	1.00	0.13 (.23)
Fluid milk 2026	1.31	−3.10[a]	2.00 (1.32)
Flour 2041	−3.25[a]	2.13[a]	−0.05[b] (.18)
Malt Beverage 2082	−3.75[a]	3.00[a]	0.19 (.34)
Wine 2084	0.21	−0.48	0.09 (.53)
Distilled liquor 2085	−0.40	−0.05	2.70 (1.07)
Cigarettes 2111	−1.75	0.48	2.47 (.77)
Cigars 2121	0.38	−0.09	1.39 (.47)

[a] Statistically significantly different from zero at the 5% level based on a two-tailed test.
[b] Statistically significantly different from one at the 5% level based on a two-tailed test.

hypothesis of competition could not be rejected for any industry (these t-statistics are not reported in Table 3.6). For the other two instruments – the percentage change in the price of oil and the percentage change in the M1 money supply – the t-statistics on this test are shown in Table 3.6.

In three cases (flour and malt beverages for oil and fluid milk for M1), the estimated coefficient on the instrument is statistically significantly negative. This result is difficult to explain, although our simulation results indicate that this outcome may be consistent with competition. Using oil as the instrument, we never reject competition: no coefficient is statistically significantly positive. Using M1 as the instrument, we reject competition for flour and malt beverages.

SUMMARY

In principle, modern static studies have at least five advantages over the structure–conduct–performance (SCP) approach. First, these studies estimate market power rather than relying on a crude accounting proxy. Second, the estimating equation is based on formal economic maximizing models, so that theory-related hypotheses can be tested directly. Third, the studies use exogenous variables (comparative statics results) to explain variations in market structure rather than endogenous variables such as concentration ratios and advertising. Fourth, it is straightforward to build industry-specific institution factors into the analysis. Fifth, there is no need to use the heroic assumption in most SCP analyses that there is symmetry across industries (e.g., that market demand elasticities are equal). Nonetheless, such modern studies depend crucially on properly specifying the model and may be very sensitive to misspecifications.

Both the structural and reduced-form approaches to estimating or testing market power have strengths and weaknesses. The advantage of the structural model is that it provides an estimate of the degree of market power, unlike the reduced-form approach, which only asks whether firms have market power. The reduced-form approach is relatively easy to use and requires relatively fewer data and explicit assumptions.

In simulation experiments, the structural model works well if it is properly specified even with random error terms that are substantially larger than generally observed in manufacturing markets. However, it performed badly when misspecified.

The big danger of using structural models is choosing the wrong structure. However, the use of a more flexible functional form, such as the translog, substantially reduces our ability to determine noncompetitive market structures due to loss of efficiency in estimation. For example, in our simulations, when the true structure is four-firm Cournot, the translog estimates were between 4 and 8.5 times more likely to incorrectly reject this market structure than would an estimate based on a correctly specified Cobb-Douglas model. Because the structural model is sensitive to specification – especially to false specifications – it may be prudent to check the results from a structural model against those obtained using Hall's technique or other methods.

Our most disturbing result concerning the structural model is that we could not estimate plausible market structure parameters for most of the four-digit SIC manufacturing markets we examined using a fairly general structural model specification. This result suggests that many existing estimates of such models required extensive experimentation with specification, which brings the statistical tests based on those estimates into question.

Although the reduced-form or nonparametric method is relatively easy to use and requires relatively fewer data, it is not clear that it is less subject to specification bias than the structural model. Our simulation results confirm that Hall's methods work well when an industry has constant returns to scale, which is a critical assumption. Unfortunately, we find that the results from these methods are very sensitive to deviations from constant returns to scale in either direction. Decreasing returns to scale lead to consistent overestimates of the price markup, and increasing returns to scale lead to underestimates. Moreover, the size of the random error in the simulations had a large impact on the ability of the Hall test to reject false hypotheses. The degree of market power based on Hall's estimate of the price–marginal cost markup cannot be determined without additional information.

Based on our empirical analysis of four-digit SIC data, Hall's two tests of competition produce results that differ nonsystematically across industries. Further, we find that the markup estimate is sensitive to the choice of input factors included in the model specification.

In conclusion, as one might have expected, the structural and Hall's reduced-form approaches can be used effectively under ideal conditions. If one is reasonably sure that firms have constant returns to scale and one only wants to test for competition, Hall's method is attractive because it is easier to use and less sensitive to specification bias than is the structural model. If one is not sure about constant returns or one needs an estimate of the degree of market power, a structural model may be used. However, one must be confident in one's specification to trust the estimated market power.

PROBLEMS

Note: Answers to problems are available at the back of the book.

3.1 There are n firms in an oligopolistic industry. Because each firm produces a homogeneous good, we can write the market inverse demand function as $p(Q)$, where Q is the sum of the outputs of the individual firms, q_i, $i = 1, \ldots, n$. Each Firm i has a conjectural variation of ν_i with respect to the output of all other firms. Firm i's cost function is $c_i(q_i)$, and the cost functions vary across firms. Write the first-order, profit-maximizing condition for each firm. Sum across the n conditions, divide by n, and solve for the average conjecture. Discuss under what conditions interpreting the average conjecture as a constant over time makes sense.

3.2 It would be very useful if we have clear-cut comparative statics results that would let us distinguish between competitive and noncompetitive markets. Suppose each firm has a constant marginal cost m. As we discussed in the chapter, a change in a constant marginal cost causes an equal change in price for a competitive industry. However, the change in price may be more, equal to, or less than the change in marginal cost for a monopoly depending on the shape of the demand curve. In particular, if we know that the inverse market demand curve is linear, $p = a - bQ$, the monopoly will change price less than in proportion to marginal cost, so we can use the comparative statics result to distinguish between monopoly and competition. Now, suppose that the n identical firms in the market are price setters. Can we use the same type of comparative statics result to distinguish between competition and oligopoly (using a conjectural variation model) or between competition and monopolistic competition? Given your results, what can you conclude about your ability to distinguish market structures if you do not know about entry conditions in the market?

3.3 Let the demand and marginal cost curves be linear as given by Equations (3.8) and (3.9), so that the optimality condition is Equation (3.11). Assume that the equation holds exactly (the error term, ε, is identically equal to zero) and that the marginal cost does not vary with output ($\gamma = 0$). Show that, even if the linear model is correctly specified and identified, this model has a fundamental problem of multicollinearity because the regressors in Equation (3.11), the constant, ZQ, and Q, are perfectly collinear. *Hint*: Solve for the equilibrium value of Q by substituting p from Equation (3.8) into Equation (3.11). Then show that the right-hand-side variables in the optimality equation, Q and ZQ, are perfectly collinear by demonstrating that the weighted sum of these two variables is a constant.

FOUR

Differentiated-Product Structural Models

In the previous chapter, we discussed how to estimate a market-level model in which all firms sell a homogeneous product. In this chapter, we generalize this one-sector structural model to include many firms (or markets) that may sell differentiated products. The emphasis in most of these generalized models is on the role of factors that affect demand in determining market power.

There are at least three reasons for generalizing the model of market power to allow for multiple firms and products. First, we can better examine the role of product differentiation in determining market power. A firm differentiates its product to affect its demand curve – presumably causing it to shift out and to become relatively less elastic – which increases the firm's market power.

Second, we can use such models to examine how factors other than differentiation that vary across markets affect market power. Typically, structure–conduct–performance studies compare market power or its causes across industries, whereas most early structural models focused on a single industry. By extending the structural approach to allow estimation of the market power that exists for many industries, we can model the markups as a function of entry costs or other factors that affect these markups.[1]

Third, we can test more complicated hypotheses than with the one-sector model. In the one-sector model, we usually assume that all firms produce homogeneous output, have identical cost functions, and behave identically. If firms differ, we have to tell some story as to how the estimated market-power parameter reflects an average of behavior. In contrast, if we allow firms to differ and estimate separate equations for each firm, we can test these previously maintained hypotheses.

Most studies use one of two approaches to estimating market power with multiple firms with differentiated products. Both approaches are based on a structural model that generalizes the one-sector model.

[1] A number of papers, such as the structural model of Bhuyan and Lopez (1997) or the Hall-method studies of Domowitz, Hubbard, and Petersen (1986, 1988), have examined market power for a variety of markets, but they did not constrain the demand curves to be derived from a single utility function or part of a demand system, which is the focus of this chapter.

Several of the earliest studies derive residual demand curves for individual firms from the full structural model. These studies take into account both demand and cost factors, and estimate a market-power or conjectural variation parameter directly.

More recently, econometricians have estimated full systems of demand and optimality functions. In most of these studies, econometricians have focused primarily on how to estimate the demand side of the model and have paid less attention to the supply side. For example, some researchers have carefully estimated the demand system and thereby obtained an estimate of the demand elasticities, which they used along with the assumption that marginal costs are constant to infer the degree of market power or Lerner's measure for each product.

Most of the recent studies use one of two approaches to specify and estimate the demand system. In one, a demand model is estimated based on market-level data using a flexible functional form and imposing restrictions from economic theory such as adding up, symmetry, and homogeneity properties. We refer to this approach as neoclassical demand system estimation.

In the other approach, researchers use consumer or other micro data to estimate the consumer demand system, typically without imposing restrictions from economic theory. The best-known studies using this approach employ a random utility model. We discuss the three models – residual demand, neoclassical demand systems, and random utility model – in turn.

RESIDUAL DEMAND

We showed in Chapter 1 – especially the discussion concerning Equations (1.3) and (1.4) – that, if a firm maximizes its profit, then the degree of market power it faces depends on its residual demand elasticity. If there are many firms producing close substitutes, it is not always straightforward to use this approach because one needs to estimate all the relevant own- and cross-price elasticities. Some researchers have estimated residual demand curves for some or all of the firms in a market. Important early examples of residual demand or other differentiated product studies include Bresnahan (1981a, 1987), Baker and Bresnahan (1988), Spiller and Favaro (1984), Suslow (1986), Gelfand and Spiller (1987), and Slade (1987).

The inverse demand curve facing Firm i is[2]

$$p_i = D(q_i, Q_{-i}, Z), \tag{4.1}$$

where Z is a vector of exogenous demand variables and Q_{-i} is a vector of outputs of all possible substitutes for q_i, including the output of all other firms in the industry and possibly outputs from some other industries. The demand for the output of any other firm can be written similarly.

[2] The following discussion is based on Baker and Bresnahan (1988). We have slightly modified their notation and presentation.

The marginal cost facing Firm *i* is $MC_i(q_i, W, w_i,)$, where *W* is a vector of industrywide factor prices and w_i is a vector of firm-specific factor prices not contained in *W*, such as the shadow-rental prices of nontraded assets. More generally, the firm might also face some firm-specific factor prices, which we ignore for simplicity.

The optimizing behavior of each of the other individual firms is determined by setting marginal cost equal to the effective marginal revenue, *EMR*, as in Chapter 3:

$$EMR_j(q_j, Q_{-j}, Z, \lambda_j) = MC_j(q_j, W, w_i) \quad \text{for} \quad j \neq i, \tag{4.2}$$

where λ_j is a conduct parameter that indexes the oligopoly solution and hence determines the firm's conjecture $\partial q_k/\partial q_j$ (as in Chapter 3) and $EMR_j = p_j + q_j \sum_k (\partial p_j/\partial q_k)(\partial q_k/\partial q_j)$.

One could now estimate a structural model by estimating demand Equation (4.1) and optimality Equation (4.2). If this approach is feasible, one obtains estimates of the behavioral parameters λ_i for each firm. Until recently, researchers believed that estimating a large system of equations of this form was infeasible.

Instead, several studies used a residual demand approach. One drawback of this approach is that these studies obtained only the joint impact on market power through the slope of the residual demand curve.

The first step in deriving a single-firm residual demand curve is to solve the demand equations and optimality equations for the other firms simultaneously so that we can express the vectors of prices and quantities of the other firms in terms of the exogenous variables and relevant parameters including the behavioral ones. By so doing, we can write

$$Q_{-i} = E_{-i}(q_i, Z, W, w_{-i}, \lambda_{-i}), \tag{4.3}$$

where the "$-i$" subscript indicates a vector of all relevant outputs or behavioral parameters except for Firm *i* and w_{-i} is the union of the firm-specific factor prices for the other firms. Each element of this function is a partial reduced form. The only remaining endogenous variable is q_i.

The next step is to substitute Equation (4.3) into Firm *i*'s inverse demand, Equation (4.1), to obtain an expression for the inverse residual demand facing Firm *i*:

$$p_i = \tilde{R}(q_i, E_{-i}(q_i, Z, W, w_{-i}, \lambda_{-i}), Z).$$

By eliminating redundant variables, we can rewrite this equation more simply as

$$p_i = R(q_i, Z, W, w_{-i}, \lambda_{-i}). \tag{4.4}$$

This inverse residual demand function is conditional on the firm's own quantity, structural demand variables, industry factor prices, other firms' cost variables, and other firms' behavioral parameters. The excluded exogenous variable we need to estimate Equation (4.4) is w_i, which appears in Firm *i*'s marginal cost and hence its optimality equation but does not appear in Equation (4.4).

Baker and Bresnahan (1985, 1988) illustrate how this approach can be used to estimate the market power of beer manufacturers. Baker and Bresnahan (1985) show how this approach can be used to determine whether the firms were colluding and what would be the effect of mergers.

NEOCLASSICAL DEMAND SYSTEM

Over the last couple of decades, a number of studies used market-level data to estimate differentiated product demand systems for automobiles, beer, breakfast foods, and a number of other goods. A few of the best-known studies include Bresnahan (1981a, 1987) and Hausman (1997).

In this approach, a system of demand equations is estimated using restrictions from economic theory. Based on these estimates and some information about cost curves, the econometrician then uses the estimated elasticities of demand to determine the degree of market power.

One way to do so is to simultaneously estimate a demand system for several goods and a market-power parameter and a marginal cost function for each good. If properly specified, using a system approach is more efficient than estimating a demand curve for each good in isolation because the system estimator makes use of information obtained from demand theory, such as price homogeneity restrictions, as well as correlations in error terms (e.g., by using Zellner's seemingly unrelated equations method).

The basic idea is that the econometrician specifies an incomplete system of demand equations for the n goods and another n optimality (first-order, profit-maximizing) equations. These $2n$ equations are the generalization of the two-equation system described in Chapter 3, which consisted of a single demand equation and a single optimality equation.

Given that there are often hundreds of differentiation products, the econometrician would have to estimate hundreds or thousands of parameters. Doing so may be impossible because the number of parameters exceed the number of observations available. Thus, econometricians have simplified the traditional neoclassical demand model (e.g., by arbitrary aggregation assumptions or by constraining all cross-price elasticities to be equal for some subset of products).

Multilevel Demand Specifications

Researchers who have relatively few observations often use a multilevel demand specification, which is flexible despite using relatively few parameters. Well-known examples include the Hausman et al. (1994), and Hausman (1997) studies of cereal and the Hausman and Leonard (2004) study of toilet paper.

Each consumer is assumed to make a series of decisions, which can be specified as separate stages or levels of the decision-making process. For example, at the first (highest) level, consumers choose how much of their budgets to allocate to a particular type of product such as automobiles or cereal. At the second stage, consumers allocate their budget across the different categories of the differentiated product, such as children or adult cereals. In the third and final stage, consumers pick a particular product within a category, such as Cheerios or cornflakes within the adult category.

By using a multistage approach, the econometrician is implicitly restricting some of the cross-price elasticities: changes of prices of cereals in the adult category do not affect demand for children's cereals. However, such models can still allow for flexible estimates of cross-price elasticities within a particular category: the change in the price of Cheerios affects the demand for cornflakes.

An Almost Ideal Demand System Example

Perhaps the simplest approach is to estimate an incomplete demand system for n goods, where the econometrician assumes that consumers' utility functions are additively separable in all goods except for these n.[3] We illustrate this approach using the linear approximate version of the almost ideal demand system (LA/AIDS) model of Deaton and Muellbauer (1980).[4]

The AIDS demand system consists of budget-share equations for each good, where the budget share for good i is $s_i = p_i q_i / X$, p_i and q_i are the price and quantity of the ith good, and X is the total expenditure on all relevant goods. The budget-share equations are

$$s_i = \alpha_i + \sum_j \gamma_{ij} \ln p_j + \beta_i \ln(X/P), \tag{4.5}$$

where α_i, γ_{ij}, and β_i are structural parameters and P is the relevant price index:

$$\ln P = \alpha_0 + \sum_i \alpha_1 \ln p_i + \frac{1}{2} \sum_i \sum_j \gamma_{ij} \ln p_i \ln p_j.$$

The LA/AIDS model replaces this price index with Stone's (1953) geometric approximation:

$$\ln P = \sum_i s_i \ln p_i.$$

3 Most studies simply treat the n equation demand system as though it were a complete system and do not discuss what happened to the other goods. However, it is possible to estimate a properly specified, incomplete demand system that is consistent with utility maximization: see LaFrance (1990, 2004).

4 The following discussion is based on Hyde and Perloff (1998). We use the linear approximation for simplicity. Given current powerful computers, a researcher would be better advised to use the Almost Ideal Demand System (AIDS) model rather than the linear approximation in an actual study.

The corresponding uncompensated own-price, ε_{ii}, and expenditure elasticities, η_i, of demand (Green and Alston, 1990) are

$$\varepsilon_{ii} = -1 + \frac{\gamma_{ii}}{s_i} - \beta_i,$$

$$\eta_i = 1 + \frac{\beta_i}{s_i}.$$

The adding up, homogeneity, and symmetry conditions imply that

$$\begin{aligned} \sum_j \gamma_{ij} = \sum_i \gamma_{ij} = \sum_i \beta_i = 0, \\ \sum_i \alpha_i = 1, \\ \gamma_{ij} = \gamma_{ji}. \end{aligned} \tag{4.6}$$

Again, one way to capture an entire family of possible equilibria is to equate marginal cost with a measure of effective marginal revenue, $p_i + \lambda_i p_i'(q_i)q_i$, where $\lambda_i \in [0, 1]$ is a parameter that reflects market power in industry *i*. As in Chapter 3, $\lambda_i = 0$ implies price taking, $\lambda_i = 1$ corresponds to collusion, and intermediate cases are represented by λ_i that lie strictly between 0 and 1 corresponds to other oligopoly equilibria. In general, the optimality equation for good *i* is

$$p_i + \lambda_i \frac{\partial p_i}{\partial q_i} q_i = c_i'(q_i), \tag{4.7}$$

where $c_i'(q_i)$ is the marginal cost function for firms in industry *i*.

For example, in an application of this method to Australian retail sales of various meats, Hyde and Perloff (1998) assume that the marginal cost for each good reflects constant returns to scale and is linear in wholesale price and wages so that

$$c_i'(q_i) = a_i + b_i v_i + d_i w, \tag{4.8}$$

where v_i is the wholesale price of meat *i*, *w* is an index of retail wage costs common for all meats, and a_i, b_i, and d_i are parameters.

In the LA/AIDS model, the slope of each demand curve, holding total expenditure on all goods, *X*, and other prices p_j, $j \neq i$, constant, is

$$\frac{\partial p_i}{\partial q_i} = -\frac{p_i}{q_j}\left[\delta_{ij} - \frac{\gamma_{ij}}{s_i} + \beta_i \frac{s_j}{s_i}\right]^{-1}, \tag{4.9}$$

where δ_{ij} is an element of the Kronecker δ, where $\delta_{ij} = 0$ if $i \neq j$ and $= 1$ if $i = j$. In the case in which each firm sells all goods, Equation (4.7) generalizes to

$$p_i + \lambda_i \sum_j q_j \frac{\partial p_j}{\partial q_i} = c_i'(q_i). \tag{4.10}$$

By substituting Equations (4.8) and (4.9) into the optimality condition, Equation (4.10), and rearranging terms, we obtain an optimality equation we can estimate:

$$p_i = \left[a_i + b_i v_i + d_i w - \frac{\lambda_i s_i}{q_i} \sum_{j \neq i} \frac{p_j q_j}{\gamma_{ij} - \beta_i s_j}\right] \left[1 - \frac{\lambda_i}{1 - \frac{\gamma_{ii}}{s_i} + \beta_i}\right]^{-1}. \tag{4.11}$$

The full structural model is obtained by estimating the LA/AIDS demand system, Equation (4.5), subject to the price-homogeneity and symmetry restrictions, Equation (4.6), together with the optimal pricing conditions for each good, Equation (4.11). All the parameters in this system, including λ_i, are identified. Because of the homogeneity restrictions on the demand system, one demand equation may be omitted.

Estimation

If the market power or conjectural variation parameters are identified, a common approach to estimating such a system of equations is to use some form of three-stage least squares. Given today's powerful computers and statistical programs, many researchers use nonlinear three-stage least squares because that provides a simple way to impose the nonlinear coefficient restrictions. For example, as Chapter 3 discusses, the market-power parameter is a ratio of other parameters.

As always, researchers face several problems in estimating a system of equations. First, we can only estimate market power or conjectural variation parameters if they are identified. Second, estimation is feasible only if we have an adequate number of instruments.

Identification. The identification problem of market power, λ_i, or conjectural variation, ν_i, parameters is analogous to that discussed in Chapter 3, where we had only one sector and one parameter. We can illustrate the basic idea using an example from Nevo (1998).

In a duopoly, the firms set prices rather than quantities. Both demand and marginal cost are linear functions.

The demand functions, which are not necessarily consistent with utility maximization, are

$$q_i = \alpha_0 + \alpha_{i1} p_1 + \alpha_{i2} p_2 + Y' \alpha_{i3} + \varepsilon_i, \quad i = 1, 2. \tag{4.12}$$

The marginal cost functions are

$$MC_i = \beta_{i0} + W' \beta_{i1}, \quad i = 1, 2. \tag{4.13}$$

Both Y and W may be vectors. We assume that Y and W differ and that the dimension of W is such that the parameters of the demand functions are identified.

As in Equation (3.3), we write the firm's first-order conditions using parameters that nest the family of possible equilibria:

$$p + \Omega Q(p) = MC, \tag{4.14}$$

where p, $Q(p)$, and MC are 2 $\times 1$ vectors and Ω is a matrix consisting of the market-power parameters. By substituting Equations (4.12) and (4.13) into Equation (4.14), we can write the optimality relationships as

$$\begin{aligned} p_i &= \beta_{i0} + W_i'\beta_{i1} - A\left[\lambda_{jj}\frac{\partial q_j}{\partial p_j}q_i - \lambda_{ji}\frac{\partial q_i}{\partial p_j}q_j\right] + \eta \\ &= \beta_{i0} + W_i'\beta_{i1} - A(\lambda_{jj}\alpha_{jj}q_j - \lambda_{ji}\alpha_{ij}q_j) + \eta, \qquad (4.15) \\ & \qquad i = 1,\ 2; \quad j = 3 - i = 2,\ 1, \end{aligned}$$

where

$$A = \left[\lambda_{11}\lambda_{22}\frac{\partial q_2}{\partial p_2}\frac{\partial q_1}{\partial p_1} - \lambda_{11}\lambda_{22}\frac{\partial q_2}{\partial p_1}\frac{\partial q_1}{\partial p_2}\right]^{-1} = (\lambda_{11}\lambda_{22}\alpha_{22}\alpha_{11} - \lambda_{12}\lambda_{21}\alpha_{21}\alpha_{12})^{-1}.$$

Given that the demand parameters are identified, a necessary condition for the market-power parameters ($\lambda_{11}, \lambda_{12}, \lambda_{21}, \lambda_{22}$) to be identified is that the dimension of the exogenous variables in the demand equation, Y, is at least two. This example can be generalized for more than two firms, of course.

Instruments. However, as Nevo notes, it may be difficult to find a large enough number of exogenous variables that influence demand but are uncorrelated with the shock in the pricing equation. For example, although marketing variables might be included in the demand equation, they are probably correlated with the pricing decision. Although seasonal parameters that influence demand are appropriate, the researcher may not have enough of them. Thus, Nevo concludes that identifying a large number of market power or conjectural variation parameters may be difficult in practice.

Finding appropriate instruments becomes even more difficult when each firm produces several brands. Then, unobserved quality variation may introduce spurious correlation between average price and average sales across brands. A low-quality brand would tend to have fewer sales than other brands for some fixed price. However, the low-quality item is likely to be paired with a relatively low price because price is chosen optimally by the firm. To account for this source of endogeneity, one might use a fixed-effects model with a dummy for each brand to capture unobserved quality variation at the brand level.[5] However, one might still be concerned about endogeneity and wish to use instruments. Following Hausman (1997), some researchers who have a cross-section of city data over time have argued that city-specific valuations of products are independent across cities but

[5] For this approach to work, one needs a large number of time periods so as to avoid the identification issue in Chamberlain (1982).

are correlated within a city over time. They then argue that prices of a brand in another city are a valid instrument because prices are correlated across cities due to a common marginal cost. However, the cross-city independence assumption is difficult to believe, especially for firms that engage in national advertising (see also the discussion in Reiss and Wolak, 2007). A superior approach, when feasible, is to use factor cost data that vary across products.

Hypothesis Tests

By estimating separate equations for each firm rather than a single model for the industry, we can test more complex hypotheses that allow various firms to behave differently. For example, using firm-specific data and separate equations for each firm, we can estimate conjectural variation, ν_i, or market-power, λ_i, coefficients for each firm, where the optimality equation for each firm is of the form of Equation (3.6). One of the first examples of this approach with continuous parameters is Gollop and Roberts (1979), who estimated separate parameters for various groups of coffee processors. Gasmi et al. (1992) estimated separate models using non-nested hypothesis tests for both Coke and Pepsi within the cola market.

To illustrate how to formulate the market power hypotheses to be tested, we use a duopoly example in which both firms produce a homogeneous product and have constant and equal marginal costs. If we want to test the hypothesis that both firms are engaged in a Cournot game, we can test whether the conjectural variation parameter ν for each firm equals zero or that each firm's market-power parameter λ equals one-half.

Now suppose that we want to test the hypothesis that one firm is a Stackelberg leader and the other is a follower – a test that would be difficult, if not impossible, to conduct with a single-market model. To test whether the potential follower is using a Cournot conjecture, we need to test whether its conjecture is zero. Because a Stackelberg leader maximizes profit subject to the constraint of the other firm's reaction or best-response function, its conjecture, ν, is the slope of the follower's best-response function.

Let $p(q_1 + q_2)$ be the inverse demand function for the homogeneous good. Suppose each firm's cost function is $mq_i + F$, so that it has a constant marginal cost m. Then, the profit of the follower Firm 1 is $p(q_1 + q_2)q_1 - (mq_1 + F)$, so its best-response function is determined by its first-order condition:

$$p(q_1 + q_2) + q_1 p'(q_1 + q_2) - m = 0. \tag{4.16}$$

By totally differentiating, we can show that the slope of the follower's best-response function is:

$$\frac{dq_1}{dq_2} = -\frac{p' + q_1 p''}{2p' + q_1 p''}. \tag{4.17}$$

This best-response function is downward sloping if $p' + q_1 p'' < 0$ because the denominator is negative by the second-order condition. For example, if the inverse demand curve is linear, then $p'' = 0$ and the slope of the best-response curve is $-1/2$.

The Stackelberg leader, Firm 2, maximizes its profit $p(q_1 + q_2)q_2 - (mq_2 + F)$ subject to the best-response function of the follower, Equation (4.16). Its first-order condition is:

$$p + q_2\, p' \left[\frac{\mathrm{d}q_1}{\mathrm{d}q_2} + 1\right] - m = 0. \tag{4.18}$$

We can substitute the expression for $\mathrm{d}q_1/\mathrm{d}q_2$ from Equation (4.17) into Equation (4.18).

We would get the same outcome if, instead, the Stackelberg leader uses a conjecture, $\nu = \mathrm{d}q_1/\mathrm{d}q_2$, such that its first-order condition is:

$$p + q_2\; p'\,[1 + \nu] - m = 0. \tag{4.19}$$

For example, we would get the Stackelberg equilibrium if the inverse demand curve were linear and $\nu = \mathrm{d}q_1/\mathrm{d}q_2 = -1/2$. For nonlinear inverse demand curves, ν depends on the shape of the curve and is not a constant. Given our estimated demand curve, we can test whether ν is consistent with our Stackelberg-leader hypothesis.

RANDOM PARAMETER MODEL

The other major approach to specifying a demand system – the predominant one at the moment – is to use a random parameter utility model. Such studies typically use consumer rather than market data.

Linear Random Utility Model

A widely used approach to estimating the demand elasticity is to use a linear random utility model from Perloff and Salop (1985; henceforth PS) and Anderson, de Palma, and Thisse (1992; henceforth AdPT).[6] In the PS model, Consumer j's conditional indirect utility is[7]

$$\tilde{V}_{ij} = a - p_i + \theta\zeta_{ij},$$

where a is the attribute or quality of a good (initially the same for all goods), p_i is the real price of firm i's product (initially each firm produces a single product), ζ_{ij} is a random variable with mean zero, and θ is the preference intensity: the higher

[6] The following discussion is based on Perloff and Ward (2000).

[7] The extension of these models to include an outside good is straightforward: see Salop (1979), Perloff and Salop (1985), or Anderson, de Palma, and Thisse (1992).

the value of θ, the less important price is in determining which variant a consumer buys. Each of the n firms produces a differentiated product. For simplicity, each of the N consumers buys one unit, so the sum of their demands, Q_i, is N. If ζ_{ij} is distributed independently and identically distributed with CDF $F(\bullet)$ and density $f(\bullet)$, m is the constant marginal cost, and n is the number of firms, the (symmetric) short-run equilibrium price is

$$p = m + \frac{\theta}{n(n-1)\hat{\Gamma}(n)}, \tag{4.20}$$

where $\hat{\Gamma}(n) = \int_{-\infty}^{\infty} f^2(\zeta)\,[F(\zeta)]^{n-2} d\zeta$. Thus, price is proportional to marginal cost and the additive markup over marginal cost in Equation (4.20) is proportional to θ. Increasing the number of firms decreases the short-run equilibrium price if and only if $(n+1)\hat{\Gamma}(n+1) - (n-1)\hat{\Gamma}(n) > 0$ for an integer number of firms n. Even though $\hat{\Gamma}(n+1) < \hat{\Gamma}(n)$ by inspection, the condition for a price decrease need not hold. Indeed, for some distributions $F(\bullet)$, price may increase with n. One distribution where the price decreases is the logit.

PS show that, when the number of firms become arbitrarily large ($n \to \infty$), the price approaches the marginal cost if (a) the support of $f(\bullet)$ is bounded from above or if (b) the $\lim_{\zeta\to\infty} f'(\zeta)/f(\zeta) = -\infty$ when the support from above is unbounded. For example, given the upper bound condition in (a), as the number of firms grows very large, consumers find more varieties that they value near the upper bound of the support of the density function, so that competition drives price to marginal cost. A similar intuition applies for condition (b). If we use a probit distribution, condition (b) holds so that the limit is perfect competition. However, if neither condition (a) nor (b) holds, the limiting case is monopolistic competition with price strictly above marginal cost, given positive entry costs. With the logit distribution, the equilibrium price falls monotonically with n to a limit of $m + \mu$.[8] The limiting case is relevant if either the number of firms in the market becomes arbitrarily large or if the fixed cost becomes arbitrarily small.[9]

Now we consider a generalization of the linear random utility models in PS and AdPT. Each firm sells one or more products, where i is the product index and n is the total number of products across all firms. In each period, the indirect utility for consumer j is

$$\tilde{V}_{ij} = a_i - p_i + \varepsilon_{ij} + \zeta_{ij},$$

where ε_{ij} is distributed multivariate normal and ζ_{ij} is distributed IID extreme value. By using two error terms with different distributions, we avoid forcing the

[8] The limit occurs where $\mu = \sigma\sqrt{6}/\pi$ (AdPT, p. 188). Even more striking as PS show, the limit for the standardized exponential is $m + \mu$ and the price is independent of n for $n \geqq 2$.

[9] With free entry, then the long-run equilibrium number of firms is uniquely determined as the implicit solution to (AdPT, p. 189) $n^2\,(n-1)\,\hat{\Gamma}\,(n) = N\theta/K$, where K is the fixed production cost per firm.

equilibrium to have the particular properties of either the logit or the probit. We could weight these two error terms to allow the model to range between the two extremes.

By integrating to concentrate out ζ_{ij}, we derive a multinomial logit share equation for item i purchased by individual j:

$$\tilde{S}_{ij} = \frac{e^{(a_i - p_i + \varepsilon_{ij})/\mu}}{\sum_{k=1}^{n} e^{(a_k - p_k + \varepsilon_{kj})/\mu}}, \tag{4.21}$$

where μ is the scale parameter on the type 1 extreme value. By integrating over individuals j, we can concentrate out the ε_{ij} terms and obtain the item's share:

$$S_i = \int \tilde{S}_{ij} f(\varepsilon) d\varepsilon. \tag{4.22}$$

Consequently, if each consumer buys one unit (or any constant number) so that the total number of units purchased is N, then the demand equations are

$$Q_i = NS_i. \tag{4.23}$$

Although one interpretation of μ in these equations is the scale parameter, AdPT (p. 78) provide another way of viewing it. They show that a representative consumer's utility function (where we suppress the individual's index) consistent with these multinomial logit share equations is given by

$$U = \begin{cases} \sum_{i=1}^{n} a_i Q_i - \mu \sum_{i=1}^{n} Q_i \ln \frac{Q_i}{N} + Q_0 & \text{if} \sum_{i=1}^{n} Q_i = N, \\ -\infty & \text{otherwise} \end{cases} \tag{4.24}$$

where Q_0 is an outside good. The second term on the right-hand side of Equation (4.24) is μ times N times a version of the entropy measure. It captures the variety-seeking behavior of the representative consumer. All else the same, the larger μ (which plays a role similar to the preference intensity parameter θ in the PS model), the greater is the preference for diversity. When $\mu \to 0$, diversity is not valued explicitly and the consumer buys solely the variant with the largest net surplus, $a_i - p_i$; and when $\mu \to \infty$, consumption is divided equally among all available variants.

We can now use these demand equations to derive a firm's multiproduct optimal pricing strategy. We start by examining how an item's share varies with item price, which we obtain by differentiating Equation (4.22):

$$\frac{\partial S_i}{\partial p_i} = \frac{1}{\mu} \int \tilde{S}_{ij} \left(\tilde{S}_{ij} - 1 \right) f(\varepsilon) d\varepsilon. \tag{4.25}$$

In setting its prices, the firm must take into account how changing the price of one item in its product line can cannibalize the demand of another item. In each period, suppose that a given firm sells h products, so that it maximizes its profit of

$$\pi = \sum_{k=1} (p_k - m_k)\, Q_k - hF - \tilde{F}, \tag{4.26}$$

where k indexes only those items sold by that particular firm, marginal cost per item is constant at m_k, the fixed cost associated with item k for that firm is F, the overall fixed cost for the firm is $\tilde{F}$, and the time parameter is suppressed. The firms' equilibrium is Nash-Bertrand. Using Equation (4.25), we can write the first-order condition for profit maximization of Equation (4.26) as

$$\frac{\partial \pi}{\partial p_k} = \sum_l (p_l - m_l) \frac{N}{\mu} \int S_{kj}(S_{kj} - 1) f(\varepsilon) d\varepsilon + N S_k = 0.$$

By rearranging terms, we find that

$$\sum_l (p_l - m_l) = \frac{\mu S_k}{S_k - \int \tilde{S}_{kj}^2 f(\varepsilon) d\varepsilon}, \tag{4.27}$$

for each firm.

Whether there is too little or too much diversity depends, in part, on whether competition is localized – as in a spatial or Hotelling model (Salop, 1979) – or all firms compete with each other – as in a representative consumer or Chamberlin model (Spence 1975, Dixit and Stiglitz 1977, and PS). Deneckere and Rothschild (1992) construct a model of demand that nests the Salop (1979) and PS models. Deneckere and Rothschild show that adding an extra brand benefits fewer consumers in a spatial model (where competition is localized) than in a representative consumer model. Consequently, there are too many brands in a spatial model but there may be too many or too few in a representative consumer model.

Estimating the Random-Parameter Model

Researchers estimate a random-parameter discrete-choice model of individual consumer behavior that corresponds to this theoretical model (see Berry et al. 1995; Train 1998; and Nevo 2000a, 2000b, 2001). Sometimes researchers know consumers' choices vary, but they do not have information about individuals' choices or their personal characteristics. Sometimes they have data on only consumers' aggregate consumption. Thus, they model demand as depending on observed and unobserved (by the econometrician) product characteristics and price. They capture these unobserved effects using random parameters.

Consumer j chooses an item i produced each period t. Consumer j's indirect utility is

$$\tilde{V}_{ijt} = X_{it}\beta_j + \zeta_{ijt},$$

where X_{it} is a vector of observed product characteristics, β_j is a vector of coefficients that are unobserved for each consumer j and that vary randomly over consumers due to differences in tastes, and ζ_{ij} is an unobserved random term.

The econometrician can (arbitrarily) choose which distribution to use in the random-parameter model. Many researchers use a generalization of the logit called the random-parameter logit (RPL) or mixed logit.[10] They assume that ζ_{ijt} is independently and identically distributed extreme value independent of β_j and X_{it}. However, there are many other possibilities, such as random-parameter probit.

RPL allows coefficients β_j to vary across the population rather than being common for all. We can decompose the coefficient vector for each consumer, β_j, into the sum of the population mean, β, and an individual deviation, η_j, that represents the consumer's taste relative to the average tastes of all consumers. For example, we may assume that η_j is distributed IID normal. We can rewrite utility as

$$\tilde{V}_{ijt} = X_{it}\left(\beta + \eta_j\right) + \zeta_{ijt} \equiv X_{it}\beta + \varepsilon_{ijt} + \zeta_{ijt}.$$

As we show below, we can estimate β, but we do not observe η_j for each consumer. Thus, the unobserved portion of utility is $X_{ij}\eta_j + \zeta_{ijt} \equiv \varepsilon_{ijt} + \zeta_{ijt}$. This term is correlated over products and time because of the common term η_j. That is, we assume that a given consumer has the same tastes among products and over time (however, we allow some product characteristics to vary over time by adding interactions between those characteristics and a time trend).

RPL generalizes logit by allowing the coefficients of characteristics to vary randomly over characteristics rather than be fixed. RPL avoids three unattractive restrictions of the usual logit or nested logit models that have traditionally been employed in demand studies (Train, 1998).[11] First, in logit or nested logit models, the coefficients of variables that enter the model are assumed to be the same for all products, which implies that different products with the same observed characteristics have the same value for each explanatory variable. Consequently, the logit predicts that a change in the attributes of one alternative changes the probabilities of the other alternatives proportionately (and the nested logit makes the same assumption within a nest). Second, the logit model has the "independence from irrelevant alternatives" (IIA) property, and nested logit has IIA within each nest.[12] Third, where repeated choices are made over time, logit and nested logit assume that unobserved factors are independent over time (in the absence of time trend terms).

[10] For an excellent user guide to practically estimating a random-parameter logit model, see Nevo (2000b).

[11] In a nested logit model, the decision maker makes decisions at two or more stages (as in the multistage demand systems previously discussed). For example, a consumer might decide between having a carbonated or noncarbonated drink in the first stage, and then choose between an orange or lemon flavored drink in the second stage.

[12] IIA means that the odds ratio of choosing between any two options in the multinomial logit is independent of the other alternatives.

In contrast, the RPL allows the unobserved portion of utility to be correlated across products and time. Consequently, RPL coefficients are not the same across all products, RPL lacks the IIA property of the traditional logit or nested logit models, and choices may vary over time. For example, we allow consumers' tastes for certain types of products (e.g., sparkling juice drink) to change over time. Indeed, the RPL model can exhibit very general patterns of correlation over products and time. McFadden and Train (2000) argue that any pattern of substitution can be represented arbitrarily closely by an RPL.[13]

The RPL model can also capture much of the flavor of nested logit by using a zero-one dummy variable for each nest (for example, a flavor, a type of product, or a brand). By allowing the coefficient of each nest-specific variable to vary randomly, we obtain correlation in unobserved utility among alternatives within each nest, while not inducing correlation across nests.

Suppressing the time, t, index, noting that $a_i \equiv X_i\beta$ and $\varepsilon_{ij} \equiv X_i\eta_j$, and integrating out the ζ_{ij} term that is distributed IID extreme value, we can rewrite share Equation (4.21) as

$$\tilde{S}_{ij} = \frac{e^{(X_i\beta - p_i + \varepsilon_{ij})/\mu}}{\sum_{l=1}^{n} e^{(X_l\beta - p_l + \varepsilon_{lj})/\mu}}. \tag{4.28}$$

We now integrate out the population distribution of the taste parameter ε_{ij}, which is distributed IID normal to obtain Equation (4.22):

$$S_i = \int \tilde{S}_{ij}\, f(\varepsilon)\mathrm{d}\varepsilon.$$

We cannot evaluate the product shares directly because the high-dimensional integral is difficult to calculate analytically. Instead, we approximate the product share using simulations. In particular, S_i is approximated by a sum over randomly chosen values of ε_{ij}. A value of ε_{ij} is drawn from its distribution and used to calculate the share in Equation (4.22). This process is repeated for, say, fifty draws, and the average of the share $\tilde{S}_{ij}$ is taken as the approximate choice probability. By construction, we have an unbiased estimator, the variance of which decreases as the number of draws increases. The simulated estimator is smooth (e.g., twice differentiable), which helps in the numerical search for the maximum of the simulated log-likelihood function. It is strictly positive for any realization of the finite draws, so that the log of the simulated probability is always defined. See Lee (1992) and Hajivassiliou and Ruud (1994) for the asymptotic distribution of the maximum simulated likelihood estimator based on smooth probability simulators with the number of repetitions increasing with sample size. Under regularity conditions,

[13] Actual substitution patterns may be more complex than is allowed in typical models. For example, Allenby and Rossi (1991) find that consumers are more likely to switch up to high-quality brands than down in response to price promotions.

the estimator is consistent and asymptotically normal (McFadden, 1989). When the number of repetitions rises faster than the square root of the number of observations, the estimator is asymptotically equivalent to the maximum likelihood estimator.

Similarly, we can calculate the associated expenditure function (cf., AdPT, p. 79),

$$Z = \overline{U} - N\mu \ln\left[\int \sum_{i=1}^{n} e^{(a_i - p_i + \varepsilon_{ij})/\mu} f(\varepsilon) d\varepsilon\right], \tag{4.29}$$

for any utility level $\bar{U}$. This expression provides the dollar value of the exact consumer benefit from increased product variety.

Finally, we calculate the own- and cross-price elasticities of demand, which we use later to predict price changes. The own-price elasticity for item i is

$$E_{ii} = \frac{p_i}{\mu\ S_i} \int \tilde{S}_{ij} \left(\tilde{S}_{ij} - 1\right) f(\varepsilon)\, \mathrm{d}\varepsilon, \tag{4.30}$$

which must be negative. If we used a straight logit, this expression simplifies to $E_{ii} = p_i(S_i - 1)/\mu$. Thus, a product's own-price elasticity is roughly proportional to its own price. The cross-price elasticity (effect of a change in the price of good k on the quantity of good i) is

$$E_{ik} = \frac{p_k}{\mu\ S_i} \int \tilde{S}_{ij}\ \tilde{S}_{kj}\ f(\varepsilon)\, \mathrm{d}\varepsilon, \tag{4.31}$$

which must be positive. That is, all goods are substitutes. With a standard logit, the cross-price elasticity simplifies to $E_{ik} = p_k S_k/\mu$.

An increase in one good's price, holding all other goods' prices fixed, causes the shares of other goods to rise for *any* discrete-choice model (Perloff and Ward 2000 – see Problem 4.2). For the logit, eliminating a good causes other goods' shares to rise, increasing their own-price elasticities. Consequently, the price of all other goods will rise in a logit model where each firm produces a single good. However, in RPL or other more general models, the elasticity, and hence price, may rise or fall. Thus, by generalizing the logit model, we permit greater flexibility in elasticities and pricing.

Market Power

If we lack reliable measures of marginal cost, we have the same problem in identifying market power and marginal cost as in the previous structural models. We can use the estimated demand system to infer the degree of market power and the marginal costs if we are willing to make strong assumptions. For example, if we assume that the manufacturing marginal cost is constant, then the demand elasticities are sufficient to identify market power: the Lerner measure of market power depends solely on the elasticities of demand.

If a firm makes a single product and maximizes its profit, the relevant Lerner index is $L = (p - c)/p = -1/e$, where e is its own-price elasticity. On the other hand, if the firm produces many products and engages in a Bertrand-Nash game with other firms, then its first-order conditions for profit maximization are given by Equation (4.27).

Alternatively, the vector of Lerner markups can be written in terms of cross-price elasticities (see, e.g., Hausman 1997):

$$\hat{L} = -(E')^{-1}S, \tag{4.32}$$

where S is the vector of the shares of the items and $\hat{L}$ is a vector whose kth element is L_k, the Lerner price–cost markup for item k, times S_k, item k's share (of the firm's total sales). Thus, the Lerner index for item k, L_k, is the kth row of the (inverted transposed) matrix times the column vector S divided by S_k. Essentially, what this equation tells us is that the relevant elasticity of demand for the item is a weighted average of its own-price elasticity and the cross-price elasticities of the other items the firm makes. We call this weighted elasticity the *multiproduct elasticity*.

The matrix E has negative own-price elasticities on the diagonal and positive cross-price elasticities – all items are substitutes – off the diagonal: see Equations (4.30) and (4.31). As the firm lowers the price of one item, it gains sales from that item (because its own-price elasticity is negative) but it cannibalizes sales from its other items (due to the positive cross elasticities). Consequently, the multiproduct elasticity for an item is less elastic than is the own-price elasticity.

Some of the best-known applications of this approach to estimating market power in a differentiated goods market are Berry et al. (1995), Goldberg (1995), Nevo (2001), and Pinske et al. (2002). Berry et al. and Goldberg study the U.S. automobile industry, Nevo examines the ready-to-eat cereal industry, and Pinske et al. analyze the retail gasoline market.

Berry et al. (1995) estimate their automobile demand system using product-level price and quantity data. Their demand estimates reflect the sum of individual purchase probabilities, which they require to equal actual new car market shares. Goldberg (1995) uses household-level, new car purchasing data to estimate the probabilities that a household purchases a given model. She then uses these household probabilities to determine the demand curve that firms face.

Nevo (2001) decomposes his estimated price–cost margins into margins caused by product differentiation, multiproduct firm pricing, and potential price collusion. He concludes that the first two effects explain most of the observed price–cost differentials.

Pinske et al. (2002) provide an alternative approach in which the differentiation is due to spatial competition. They use a semiparametric approach to estimate cross-price response coefficients.

SUMMARY

In recent years, researchers have extended the industry-level model (Chapter 3) to examine the behavior of firms that may produce differentiated products. By doing so, they can examine richer questions. For example, it would be very difficult, if not impossible, to examine whether a market is Stackelberg using a market-level approach; however, it is straightforward to construct and test a model of Stackelberg behavior if we can separately model the behavior of the individual firms in the market.

Two major approaches have been used to look at markets with (possibly) differentiated products. Both are based on a generalization of the single-market structural model in Chapter 3 to a multifirm structural market.

The first approach is to estimate the residual demand facing each firm. Starting from the multifirm structural model, one derives an inverse residual demand function that is conditional on the firm's own quantity, structural demand variables, industry factor prices, other firms' cost variables, and other firms' behavioral parameters.

The second approach is to estimate the full system of demand and optimality equations. Researchers typically specify the demand system in one of two ways. Some estimate a neoclassical demand model based on market-level data. They use a flexible functional form and impose restrictions from economic theory such as adding up, symmetry, and homogeneity properties.

In the other approach, consumer or other micro data are used to estimate consumer demands, typically without imposing restrictions from economic theory. The best-known studies using this approach employ a random utility model.

A key advantage of all of these models over the previous aggregate structural model is better estimates of the demand and optimality equations. The older structural model aggregates across firms and brands. If the firms' products are differentiated or they behave differently, such aggregation may be inappropriate. In contrast, these more general models allow own- and cross-elasticities to vary across brands, which presumably results in more reliable demand estimates.

That said, the fundamental problem of estimating market power remains. As in the one-sector structural model, reliability depends critically on identifying both market power and costs. Many researchers have identified these parameters within their models by making heroic assumptions about costs, such as constant returns to scale, because they lacked detailed data on costs.

PROBLEMS

Note: Answers to problems are available at the back of the book.

4.1 Suppose that we are confident that the market has a two-firm, Stackelberg equilibrium. Using the first-order conditions Equations (4.16) and (4.19), show that we can estimate the Stackelberg leader's conjecture ν using only information about the observed output levels.

4.2 Show that an increase in the price of one good implies that the share of each of the other goods must rise for any discrete-choice model. Let the conditional indirect utility for good i be $\tilde{V}_i = X_i\beta - p_i + \varepsilon_i$. Now calculate the probability that a consumer chooses good i over any of the other n goods and show that the probability that a consumer purchases this good rises as the price of another good increases.

4.3 Suppose you have estimated a system of demand and optimality equations for a market with several firms, each of which produces several differentiated items or brands. How can you use that model to predict (simulate) the price or Lerner markup effect of a merger between two of the firms? Can you say anything about the change in the elasticity for any one item?

FIVE

Strategic Reasons for a Dynamic Estimation Model

Until now, we have discussed estimating market power under the assumption that firms engage in a sequence of static games: In each period, a firm maximizes its current profit given its belief about how its rivals behave and assuming that actions in other periods do not affect behavior in this period. We now examine how to model games in which firms interact over many periods: where they play a dynamic game. Each firm maximizes its expected present discounted value of the stream of its future profits. When each firm solves a dynamic optimization problem in which its payoff depends on the behavior of other firms, the industry equilibrium is the solution to a dynamic game. We want to use observations on firms' behavior to measure the extent of competition in a dynamic game.

The manner in which we estimate market power depends on the reason for the dynamics: the type of game that firms play. We distinguish between two types of reasons – *strategic* and *fundamental* – why firms might play a dynamic game rather than a sequence of static games. If dynamic interactions arise because firms think that their rivals will respond in the future to their current action, we say that the reason for the dynamics is strategic. If a firm solves a dynamic rather than a static problem because its current decision affects a stock variable that affects its future profits, we say that the reason for the dynamics is fundamental.

Of course, firms may play a dynamic rather than a static game for both strategic and fundamental reasons, but these reasons are distinct. For example, unlike oligopolistic firms, a monopoly or competitive firms cannot have strategic reasons to engage in a dynamic game. When the reason for dynamics is fundamental, firms have to solve a dynamic problem even *in the absence of strategic considerations.* When dynamics arise because of fundamentals, the nature of the optimization problem is different in an oligopoly and in a competitive industry or monopoly, but in both cases (strategic or fundamental) the problem is dynamic. Regardless of whether the reason for the dynamics is fundamental or strategic, the firms' environment changes endogenously.

Although dynamics may be important for both strategic and fundamental reasons, it is clearer to discuss them separately. This chapter examines environments in which the only reason for dynamics is strategic. We start by reviewing basic concepts from game theory involving many period games, including subgame perfection and the Folk theorem (briefly discussed subsequently) of supergames. Next, we explain their role in the estimation problem. We close the chapter by reviewing empirical applications of games in which dynamics arise because of strategic rather than fundamental reasons.

In Chapter 3, we explained how to estimate a measure of competition in the case in which firms ignore the past and the future in deciding their current action – that is, where firms play a sequence of one-shot games. We used a structural estimation method, such as conjectural variations or a market-conduct parameter to nest a range of "reasonable" (or at least familiar) equilibrium outcomes. This family of outcomes includes the important cases of competitive, Bertrand, Cournot-Nash, and monopolistic equilibria. The equilibrium conditions for these special cases typically involve demand and cost shifters, so these exogenous variables enter the regression equations. The market-power index is a parameter in this system of equations. Its estimated value measures the closeness of the actual market structure to one of the special cases, say a competitive market.

Here, we consider the case in which firms care about the future, and they understand that actions in the future will depend upon decisions made today. This setting provides a rationale for equilibrium outcomes that are "between" the familiar equilibria, such as those identified by the static conjectural variations or market-conduct approach described in earlier chapters. More importantly, dynamic strategic considerations lead to new types of estimation models.

SUPERGAMES

We consider a repeated game, or supergame, in which firms know that, with positive probability, they will interact with their rivals infinitely many times. Each firm's objective is to maximize the expected present discounted value of its stream of current and future profits. We need additional terminology to discuss such games.

The *history* of the game consists of the past values of those variables that the firm knows. For example, a firm may be able to observe its rivals' past prices or sales, so those variables are part of the history. In other settings, a firm may know only its own past sales and the price it received; it does not know – and therefore cannot condition its decisions upon – its rivals' past prices or sales. Thus, its rivals' variables are not part of the game's history for the firm. A *decision rule* for a firm is a function that maps the history into an action, such as a price, quantity, or advertising. A *Nash equilibrium set of decision rules* – a rule for each firm – has the property that each firm's decision rule is a best response to other firms' decision rules. Given a particular history and given that other firms use their equilibrium decision rule, each firm maximizes its objective by using its equilibrium decision rule. An *outcome* is the trajectory of actions that result when firms use their decision rules, starting from a particular history.

We need to distinguish between a firm's action and its decision rule that (together with the history) generates this action. The econometrician may be able to observe the action, but at best can infer the decision rule. In the one-shot game, the equilibrium conditions depend on demand and cost shifters. In the repeated game, the equilibrium actions may also depend on the history of the game. Consequently, the econometrician has to decide whether to include the history as conditioning variables in the estimation equations for a dynamic game. This issue does not arise in a static game.

A *subgame* is a game that begins with a particular history. An equilibrium is *subgame perfect* if the set of decision rules constitute an equilibrium for any possible history – that is, for any possible subgame – not merely for the subgames that arise in equilibrium. Thus, the set of subgame perfect equilibria is a subset of the set of equilibria. We can use an example to illustrate the distinction between *equilibrium* and *subgame perfect equilibrium.* Suppose there are two firms, each with a discount factor of δ. Each firm can use one of two prices, H and L (high and low). The big firm's dominant strategy is H; that is, H maximizes this firm's current period profits, regardless of the other firm's action. The small firm's dominant strategy is L. This firm's single-period profit is higher when both firms use H rather than when both firms use L. Its profit is still higher when it uses L and the big firm uses H because the small firm captures a larger market share. The following payoff matrix is an example that is consistent with this description.

Small Firm \ *Big Firm*	*H*	*L*
H	10 3	8 1
L	7 4	5 2

The large firm's actions are given in the columns, and the small firm's actions are on the rows. The top right element in each cell is the single-period payoff of the large firm, and the bottom left element is the single-period payoff of the small firm.

One candidate for an equilibrium decision rule instructs both firms to begin by using H and then to use H if both firms have used H in every period in the past, and otherwise to use L. The small firm can "cheat" by using L when it is "supposed to" use H. Cheating – or in a more general setting, the use of any action not prescribed by the equilibrium strategy – can cause the breakdown of cooperation. A decision rule with this characteristic is known as a trigger strategy. If both firms use this strategy, the trajectory consists entirely of both firms choosing H each period. H is a dominant strategy for the large firm in the one-period game: a best response to any action of the small firm. The large firm is obviously willing to use this candidate decision rule, provided that the small firm does so, because the large firm is never "instructed" to use L on the equilibrium trajectory.[1] If the small firm follows the candidate strategy, its payoff is $3/(1-\delta)$; if it deviates while the large firm adheres to the candidate strategy, the small firm's payoff is $4 + 2\delta/(1-\delta)$. The small firm prefers to follow the candidate strategy if the first expression is greater than the second; that is, if $\delta > 0.5$. If this inequality is satisfied, the candidate is an equilibrium strategy, given that the decision rule for each firm is a best response to the other firm's decision rule.

Although the candidate is an equilibrium strategy, it is not a subgame perfect equilibrium. To establish subgame perfection, it is not enough to confirm that the candidate decision rule remains an equilibrium rule for subgames along the equilibrium path – in this example, a sequence in which both firms choose H. If either firm were to deviate and use L, the ensuing history is "off the equilibrium path" – it would contain an L. Subgame perfection requires that the decision rule is a best response given histories both on and off the equilibrium path. For a subgame off the equilibrium path, the big firm would not want to use the candidate decision rule. In this example, the candidate is a best response for the big firm on the equilibrium path but not off the equilibrium path; hence, it is not subgame perfect.

Subgame perfection requires that firms cannot commit to behaving in a manner that would be suboptimal *ex-post*. A firm cannot promise to behave in a certain way if a certain contingency (history) arises, as a means of affecting the probability that the contingency arises. In the previous example, the requirement of subgame perfection prohibits the big firm from threatening to use L in the event that the small firm cheats. More generally, the requirement of subgame perfection rules out the use of threats or promises that are not credible (because they are *ex post* suboptimal). Subgame perfection is usually considered a reasonable restriction for the econometrician to impose. In Chapter 8, we compare estimates of market power with and without the restriction of subgame perfection.

The *Folk theorem* of supergames states that if players are sufficiently patient – δ is sufficiently close to one – then any feasible, individually rational payoff can be supported in a subgame perfect equilibrium (Fudenberg and Tirole 1993, Chapter 5.1). A payoff is *individually rational* if it is greater than or equal to the minimum payoff that a player can guarantee. This theorem implies that in general there exists a continuum of subgame perfect (noncooperative) equilibria to infinitely repeated games. Although the simple punishment strategy described earlier is not subgame perfect, more complicated strategies can be devised to support cooperative behavior when the discount rate is small. Those strategies involve not only punishment for deviation from cooperative behavior, but also punishment for failing to punish a deviation, punishment for failing to punish a deviation from the obligation of punishing a deviation, and so on.

[1] An equilibrium does not literally "instruct" agents. This figure of speech is a shorthand way of saying that an agent behaves in a manner that is consistent with the equilibrium.

We can use a variation of our last example – a prisoners' dilemma – to illustrate the weaker claim that there may be multiple subgame perfect equilibria. We now assume that the firms are symmetric; the noncooperative Nash equilibrium to the one-shot game is for each firm to use *L*; and the cooperative equilibrium (the cartel solution) is for both firms to use *H*:

		Firm 1	
		H	*L*
Firm 2	*H*	10 10	15 2
	L	2 15	5 5

The decision rule that instructs firms to use *L* for every possible history is obviously a subgame perfect equilibrium. If firms expect their rivals to always use *L*, they will do likewise, regardless of what has occurred in the past (regardless of the history). As with the previous example, a candidate strategy instructs firms to use *H* in the first period and then to use *H* in each subsequent period if both firms have used *H* in all previous periods, and to use *L* otherwise. If δ is sufficiently large, this candidate is also subgame perfect. In a subgame in which both firms have always used *H* in the past, a firm expects its rival to use *H* in the current period. This firm gains five in the current period by cheating (using L rather that H) but it expects the deviation to cost it five in every subsequent period, for a present discounted loss of $5\delta/(1-\delta)$. For $\delta > 0.5$, the loss from cheating exceeds the benefit. At any subgame that includes *L* in the history, each firm expects its rival to always use *L*, so its optimal action is to use *L*. Here, unlike in the previous example, it is *ex post* optimal for a firm to *punish* a rival that cheated, and this credible threat of punishment prevents cheating. We conclude that for $\delta > 0.5$, the candidate strategy is subgame perfect.

Both firms are harmed in the punishment phase, relative to cooperation. If, for some reason, a firm deviates, leading to a low price, it might seem reasonable that firms would be able to "renegotiate" to reduce or eliminate the punishment phase. If this kind of renegotiation were possible, the threat of the punishment described earlier (use *L* forever, following a deviation) would not be credible and therefore would not be able to sustain cooperation. However, more complicated strategies can sustain cooperation. (See Chapter 5.4 of Fudenberg and Tirole 1993.)

In this deterministic setting, firms would always cooperate, providing that they begin by cooperating. The econometrician would observe a sequence of high prices, possibly with a very low variance. Given estimates of demand and cost functions, the econometrician would be able to recognize that these prices are "high" by comparing them to the cartel price. However, the lack of variability of prices would make it difficult to estimate the demand function, so as a practical matter it might be difficult to determine whether prices are actually high or low. In a stochastic setting, with a more complicated trigger strategy consisting of finite punishment phases, random shocks may lead to intervals of cooperation interspersed with intervals during which firms punish their rivals. In that case, the econometrician observes a more volatile sequence of prices. The greater variability of output may make it easier to estimate a demand function (and therefore to compare the actual to the cartel price). However, the presence of the punishment phases may make it harder to identify the type of strategy that firms are using. For the game whose payoffs are given in our second example, the outcome in one subgame perfect equilibrium is identical to the noncooperative equilibrium to the one-shot game; the outcome in another subgame perfect equilibrium is identical to the outcome under collusion. More generally, there may be uncountably many subgame perfect equilibria to repeated games. The outcomes of some of these equilibria may be indistinguishable from collusion, and others may be indistinguishable from static noncooperative behavior (depending on, for example, the discount factor).

EMPIRICAL IMPLICATIONS

From an economic (as opposed to a legal) standpoint, it does not matter whether firms choose the cartel price because they have formed an explicit cartel or because they are playing a noncooperative game and using trigger strategies. It is reasonable to try to measure how closely the industry behavior resembles that of a cartel, or a perfectly competitive industry, even if we cannot expect data on prices and quantities to tell us whether firms collude. In a static setting, there are a small number of familiar outcomes, including perfect competition, collusion, and noncooperative Nash (in which firms choose price, quantity, or some other decision variable). One criticism of the structural models in Chapter 3 is that the econometrician assumes that firms play a static game, but the outcome may lie "between" recognizable equilibria. Given that such intermediate outcomes are not well-known equilibria to the one-shot game, the point of using a game-theoretic model as the basis for empirical analysis has been challenged.

However, if firms recognize that they might interact infinitely many times, there are many subgame perfect equilibrium outcomes that are not equilibria to the one-shot game. Thus, the adoption of a dynamic rather than a static framework provides a justification for measures of market power that might otherwise appear ad hoc. The estimates of market power in the static games described in Chapter 3 can be re-interpreted in light of the theory of repeated games. In that case, the theory is used to explain only why the outcome (such as the price or quantity) in a non-cooperative equilibrium lies between the outcomes under perfect competition or a cartel at a level not equal to the Nash equilibrium of the one-shot game. The econometrician attempts to estimate a parameter that measures the extent to which the observed outcome deviates from the competitive or collusive outcome.

More importantly, the theory of repeated games can be used as a basis for developing empirical models that are qualitatively different from the static conjectural variations models described in previous chapters. Because theory does select a particular equilibrium for a given game, the econometrician needs to make additional assumptions to obtain an estimation model. The remainder of this chapter reviews two different approaches to formulating empirical models based on repeated games. The first approach assumes that firms use trigger strategies, and the second assumes that firms use strategies that are continuous in the history.

MODELS OF REPEATED GAMES WITH TRIGGER STRATEGIES

The deterministic repeated games we have just reviewed do not provide a basis for estimation models. In the trigger strategy equilibria to these games, the credible threat of punishments supports (some degree of) implicit cooperation. In equilibrium, these punishments do not occur. The equilibrium outcome, as distinct from the equilibrium strategy, consists of a string of constants – not the kind of data set that permits estimation of behavior. To obtain an estimation model based on trigger strategies, we need to introduce some reason why cooperation breaks down in equilibrium, and we need to specify the information that firms use to condition their actions.

The models proposed by Rotemberg and Saloner (1986) and Green and Porter (1984) are examples of repeated game models that provide a basis for estimation. Empirical applications attempt to test whether observed behavior is consistent with the implications of these models. Both these models assume that tacit cooperation is supported by the threat of reversion to noncooperative actions: firms use trigger strategies. The extent of the cooperation changes randomly, due to the presence of random shocks.

We first consider a simplified version of Rotemberg and Saloner's model. (Problem 5.2 provides a more formal statement of the model, using a numerical example.) In this version, there are two price-setting firms and two states of nature, associated with high and low demand. Firms' payoffs are higher when both cooperate than when both cheat (cut prices), but cheating is a dominant strategy for the one-shot game – as in the second example. Firms are able to observe their rival's price and they know the current state of demand. An independently and identically distributed shock determines whether the demand for the industry product is strong or weak. Firms' profits in a period depend on the demand shock and on the prices that firms use in that period.

Firms use a simple punishment strategy: they behave "cooperatively" as long as their rival has behaved cooperatively in the past. Cheating by any firm causes all firms to use the noncooperative Nash equilibrium price (of the one-shot game) at every period in the future. The cooperative price is the price closest to the collusive price that can be sustained by the threat of future noncooperative pricing following cheating. The cooperative price leads to the highest level of industry profits within a period, subject to the constraint that arises from firms' self-interested behavior, together with the use of a relatively unsophisticated punishment strategy. Typically, the cooperative price is strictly lower than the collusive price.

Firms always cooperate in equilibrium, so the econometrician never observes a punishment phase. Here, however, the state of demand changes randomly, leading to a possible change in the firms' actions even though firms remain in the cooperative phase. That is, the degree of cooperation can vary with demand. The degree of cooperation is measured by a decreasing function of the difference between the collusive price and the actual (equilibrium) price; this difference is zero when there is "complete cooperation." If the equilibrium price during a cooperative phase is much lower than the collusive price, it is natural to think of the degree of cooperation as being small. Thus, the measurement of the degree of cooperation within any period requires two prices: the equilibrium price, which is observed, and the collusive price, which is not observed (except under complete cooperation).

The testable hypothesis from this model is that higher demand is negatively correlated with the degree of cooperation. This hypothesis is a statement about the relation between demand and the *difference* between two prices – the collusive price and the equilibrium price. The hypothesis states that an increase in demand raises the equilibrium price by less than the collusive price, so that the difference in the two increases. The hypothesis does not state that the equilibrium price falls when demand is higher, although this possibility can arise for some parameterizations. One way to interpret the hypothesis is that booms (outward shifts in the demand curve) are associated with price wars. This price war is peculiar because it it might be associated with higher prices.

To obtain intuition for the testable hypothesis, we consider the special case in which the equilibrium price (in a cooperative phase) is equal to the cartel price when demand is low. We want to explain why the equilibrium price must be lower than the cartel price when demand is high. The equilibrium price during a cooperative phase balances the benefit of cheating in the current period and the subsequent loss due to lower prices in the punishment phase.

The cost of cheating equals the expected present discounted difference between the future cooperative profits and future noncooperative profits. When the demand shock is independently distributed, the current value of the demand shock provides no information about its future values, so the *cost of cheating is the same under low and high demand.* The benefit of cheating – unlike the cost of cheating – depends on the current demand shock. Moreover, the benefit of cheating tends to be greater when demand is relatively strong. Stronger demand is associated with a higher marginal revenue curve. At the cartel price, the firm's current increase in profit resulting from undercutting its rival is greater when demand is stronger. To offset the increased temptation to cheat, it is necessary to reduce the benefit of cheating. This reduction can be achieved by cooperating imperfectly (using a price lower than the cartel price) when demand is strong.

More formally, denote the equilibrium cost of cheating as C, the expected discounted value of the difference in the stream of future profits under cooperative and noncooperative behavior. This value is the same in both states of the world (high and low demand) because the current state provides no information about the future. The equilibrium value of C depends on the prices that firms use when they behave cooperatively. Let Δ^k, $k = strong, weak$, be the difference in single-period profit under cooperation and noncooperation when the state of demand is k. This difference depends on the levels of the cooperative prices. Letting μ be the probability that demand is strong, we have

$$C = \delta\left(\mu\Delta^{strong} + [1-\mu]\Delta^{weak}\right)(1-\delta)^{-1}.$$

Denote as C^{cartel} the cost of cheating if firms were to use the cartel prices under both weak and strong demand (in a cooperative phase). If the threat of reversion to noncooperative prices is not powerful enough to support cartel prices, all equilibrium values of C are lower than C^{cartel}. Denote the single-period net benefit of cheating when the rival firms use the cartel price and demand is $k = weak, strong$ as B^k. (The net benefit is the difference in payoff under cheating and under cooperation.) For reasons explained earlier, the benefit of undercutting the cartel price is likely to be higher under strong demand, implying that $B^{strong} > B^{weak}$. If this equality holds, it is possible that

$$B^{strong} > C^{cartel} > B^{weak}.$$

This inequality states that the threat of reverting to noncooperative behavior could support cartel prices when demand is weak, but not when demand is strong.

If this inequality holds, the threat of reverting to noncooperative behavior cannot sustain cartel pricing. In order to support some degree of cooperation under strong demand, using the threat of reverting to noncooperative behavior, it is necessary to lower the benefit of cheating when demand is strong. That is, the cooperative price under strong demand must be below the cartel price. This change reduces the benefit of cheating, B^{strong}, more than it reduces the cost of cheating, C. The latter depends on future expected profit differentials, which are weighted averages of profit differentials in both high and low demand states. Consequently, by using a price lower than the cartel level during periods of high demand, it is possible to discourage cheating during these periods. The cost of cheating may still be large enough to sustain the cartel price during periods of weak demand.

The assumption that the demand shocks are serially uncorrelated is important because it implies that the cost of cheating is the same in each state of nature. If demand shocks were positively serially correlated, as is likely to be the case when the intervals of time are short (as with monthly or quarterly data), the cost of cheating is greater when demand is high. This higher cost of cheating tends to balance the higher benefit of cheating, making it more likely that cooperation can be sustained when demand is high. That is, positively correlated demand shocks tend to undermine the main result of this model. Kandori (1991) and Haltiwanger and Harrington (1991) study the model with correlated demand shocks.

In the equilibrium to this game, as with the deterministic supergames previously discussed, firms never enter a punishment phase in equilibrium. The econometrician always observes cooperation, but the extent of the cooperation varies inversely with the strength of market demand. By observing prices and demand shifters, the econometrician may be able to determine whether this prediction is consistent with the data.

Rotemberg and Saloner (1986) do not directly test the predictions of the model, but they summarize evidence that indirectly supports these predictions. First, they point out that price adjustment during the business cycle is sluggish. If a fall in demand triggered price wars, one might (arguably) expect to see larger price decreases during downturns in the cycle. They also find that price–marginal cost ratios are countercyclical in more concentrated industries. If decreases in demand triggered price wars in oligopolistic industries, the movements in this ratio would be procyclical. They also claim that the price wars in the automobile and railroad industries occurred during booms, not busts.

Green and Porter (1984) develop a model in which cooperation breaks down following a sufficiently bad shock. In their model, each firm chooses its production level. Firms observe the market price but not their rivals' output levels or the realization of the demand shock. A firm is tempted to cheat by selling more than the cooperative level, thereby increasing its profits and its market share. Cooperative behavior is enforced by the threat of reversion to noncooperative behavior (such as selling at the Cournot level). This punishment phase lasts for a known number of periods. After this punishment phase in which firms have carried out the punishments decreed by the equilibrium strategies, firms revert to a cooperative phase. (Problem 5.3 provides a formal description of the model, using a numerical example.)

The firms' calculations are complicated by the difficulty of detecting a rival's cheating. A firm cannot determine whether the price in a period is low because of a bad demand shock, or because a rival sold more than the cooperative level. A firm needs to be willing to retaliate in order to deter cheating. However, profits during a punishment phase are lower, so firms do not want to enter such a phase unnecessarily.

Components of the equilibrium include the duration of the punishment phase, the quantities that firms sell during the cooperative and the punishment phases, and a price level that triggers entry into the punishment phase. In equilibrium, during a cooperative phase firms sell the cooperative level. If the price falls below the critical level (because of a bad demand shock), the firms enter a punishment phase.

In this equilibrium – as in all the other trigger strategy equilibria that we have considered – firms never cheat. When the price falls below the critical level, they do not "think that it is likely" that a rival has cheated. Rather, they begin the punishment phase because – by construction – it is optimal for them to do so, given their beliefs about what their rivals will do. That is, firms collectively punish themselves to prevent cheating later. This model implies that a sufficiently bad demand shock triggers the breakdown of cooperation – the opposite conclusion from Rotemberg and Saloner's model.

Porter (1983) and Lee and Porter (1984) test variations of the Green and Porter model using U.S. railroad pricing data from the 1880s. During this period, a cartel, the Joint Executive Committee (JEC), controlled the railroad grain shipments from Chicago to the East Coast. The cartel agreement specified the members' market shares. Firms were allowed to choose the price of shipments, and required not to exceed their allocated market share. The JEC kept weekly accounts, so firms were able to determine aggregate shipments and their market shares.

The starting point for developing the empirical model is the same as in the static models considered in previous chapters. The equilibrium condition for Firm i in period t is

$$p_t\left(1+\frac{\theta_{it}}{\alpha}\right)=MC_{it},$$

where α is the demand elasticity, MC is marginal cost, and the parameter θ determines the extent of cooperation. The cartel, Nash-Cournot, and Bertrand equilibria to the one-shot games are obtained when θ_{it} takes the values 1, s_{it} (Firm i's market share), or 0, respectively. Multiplying the firm's equilibrium condition by s_{it} and summing over i (using the fact that market shares sum to 1) leads to the market equilibrium condition

$$p_t\sum_i s_{it}\left(1+\frac{\theta_{it}}{\alpha}\right)=p_t\left(1+\frac{\theta_t}{\alpha}\right)=\sum_i s_{it}\,MC_{it},$$

where $\theta_t\equiv\sum_i s_{it}\theta_{it}$. The value of the parameter θ_t varies, depending on whether the industry is in a cooperative or a noncooperative phase. If the econometrician knows whether each observation is associated with a punishment or a cooperative phase, it is possible to estimate the parameters of the model, including the values of θ in each phase, using two-stage least squares. These estimated values of θ provide estimates of the extent of cooperation and punishment in the two phases, as in static conjectural variation models.

When the econometrician does not know the regime, it is necessary to use the data to determine whether a particular observation is associated with a punishment or a cooperative phase. One approach is to use a switching regression technique. In the simplest case, the econometrician assumes that there is a fixed probability, μ, that an observation is associated with a cooperative phase. The empirical problem requires estimating μ, and also allocating observations between the two regimes. For a given allocation across regimes, the remaining parameters can be estimated as if the regime were known. The estimate of μ and the allocation across regimes are chosen to maximize a pre-specified likelihood function.

Porter (1983) applies this estimation method to the railroad data. During noncooperative periods, output was at approximately the Nash-Cournot level, and was consistent with the level often assumed to be used during a punishment phase. Price was approximately 66% higher, quantity 33% lower, and profit 11% higher in cooperative versus noncooperative periods. These results are therefore consistent with the Green and Porter (1984) model of trigger strategies. Hajivassilious (1989) reaches similar conclusions. However, Town (1991) finds that price wars were not related to demand fluctuations. This finding is contrary to the predictions of both the Green and Porter (1984) and the Rotemberg and Saloner (1986) models. Domowitz et al. (1987) find little evidence of price wars either in booms or recessions.

Suslow (1998) presents evidence that conflicts with the predictions of the Rotemberg and Saloner (1986) model. In an examination of pre–World War II cartels, she finds that a cartel is more likely to break down during recessions and depressions. Recent theoretical developments have built on the Rotemberg and Saloner and the Green and Porter models. For example, Athey et al. (2004) study an infinitely repeated Bertrand game in which firms receive independent and identically distributed cost shocks. In important cases, the equilibrium involves no price wars. Using a two-player game in which firms imperfectly monitor their rival's actions, Matsushima (2004) shows that the collusive outcome can be sustained when the discount factor is close to one.

MODELS OF REPEATED GAMES WITH CONTINUOUS STRATEGIES

In the trigger strategy models, certain observations – such as low sales or a low market price – trigger a temporary or permanent breakdown in cooperation. During a punishment phase, firms behave noncooperatively, perhaps by using the noncooperative Nash price or quantity associated with the one-shot game. These strategies are discontinuous in the history; a small difference in the history can lead to a large difference in behavior. An alternative is for firms to use strategies that are continuous in the history. With these strategies, a small deviation from cooperation causes a small change in the history, and leads to a small punishment. Slade (1989) models a price-setting game with continuous reaction functions. In the deterministic version of this model, symmetric duopolies face known linear demand. Goods are imperfect substitutes, so the Bertrand-Nash equilibrium to the one-shot game involves a price greater than marginal cost. We subtract marginal costs (assumed constant) from the demand intercept. Treating this difference as the demand intercept of a "new" demand function, we can write the model as if marginal costs are equal to zero.

In general, a firm's choice of the current price might be a function of the entire history; but, in this model, firms condition their current price on only their rival's price in the last period. In the first period, a firm sets the endogenous, cooperative price $p_0^i = \hat{p}$. (The superscript identifies the firm and the subscript identifies the time period; $\hat{p}$ is the cooperative price.) In subsequent periods, it matches its rival's last period deviation from this price by R^i times that deviation, so Firm i follows the strategy:

$$p_t^i = \hat{p} + R^i\left(p_{t-1}^j - \hat{p}\right), \ \ j \neq i, \tag{5.1}$$

where $0 \leq R^i \leq 1$ is exogenous. Hereafter we assume that the equilibrium is symmetric, so we drop the superscript on this parameter and write the slope of the reaction function as R. The empirical implementation of the model does not assume either duopoly or symmetry.

Suppose that Firm i uses the strategy given by Equation (5.1). In a symmetric equilibrium, firm j's best response to this strategy must be to use the price $\hat{p}$. This requirement determines the unique value of $\hat{p}$. That is, associated with the strategy given by Equation (5.1), there is a unique Nash equilibrium price, $\hat{p}$. This price is a function of the discount factor, the (exogenous) parameter R, and the demand parameters. (Problem 8.1 uses a numerical example to show how the equilibrium price can be determined.)

The parameter R plays a role analogous to the conjectural variations parameter in static models, but there is one important difference. Here firms think that rivals will respond in the subsequent period – not in the same period – to a deviation in the current period. Therefore, in this model, the literal interpretation of R as a conjecture of other firms' response makes sense. In the static models, in which firms move simultaneously, we interpret the conjectural variations parameter as either an *ad hoc* representation of dynamics or, less controversially, as an index of market power.

A large value of R means that firms punish deviations more strongly; therefore, larger values of R imply that the equilibrium outcome is closer to the cooperative outcome. For $R = 0$, the equilibrium value of $\hat{p}$ equals the Bertrand-Nash level; and, for $R = 1$, the equilibrium value of $\hat{p}$ converges to the cartel level as the discount factor approaches one. On the equilibrium trajectory, each firm always charges $\hat{p}$.

The Nash equilibrium strategy given by Equation (5.1) is not subgame perfect: if one agent deviates, it is not a best response for the other agent to use this strategy. A strategy is said to be ε-subgame perfect if an agent loses no more than ε by following that strategy rather than using its best response. The strategy given by Equation (5.1) is ε-subgame perfect provided that the discount factor is sufficiently close to one.

We want to understand the relation between the discount factor and ε-subgame perfection. Let the annual discount rate be r. If a period lasts for $1/n$th of a year, the discount factor for a period is $\delta = (1/[1+r])^{1/n}$. A large discount factor for a period is equivalent to a short period (large n); that is, a large discount factor is equivalent to the ability to respond rapidly to a deviation. If agents use the strategy given by Equation (5.1) following a deviation and if δ is close to one, the price converges quickly to $\hat{p}$. Here, the price returns quickly to a neighborhood of the equilibrium value $\hat{p}$. Once the price is close to this equilibrium value, using the strategy given by Equation (5.1) is approximately a best response. Therefore, provided that n is large, agents lose a small amount (less than ε) by always following the strategy given by Equation (5.1). This model, and the extension that includes stochastic demand, is therefore appropriate in industries in which the reaction time is short.

Events that look like price wars arise in equilibrium if the demand parameters change randomly. In any period, there is a small chance that these parameters change their value. The parameters δ and R are assumed fixed. The endogenous price $\hat{p}$ is a function of the parameters of the model, including the demand parameters. Therefore, when a change in demand occurs, the previous value $\hat{p}$ is no longer part of a Nash equilibrium strategy. Firms do not know the new demand parameters, so they are not able to calculate the new equilibrium value of $\hat{p}$. If firms are Bayesians, they are able to update and improve their estimate of the demand parameters by making use of the observed prices and quantities. In the linear model with normal random variables, the particular Bayesian updating rule is known as the Kalman filter. If the change in demand parameters causes the demand curve to shift to the left, firms respond by lowering prices.

The equilibrium price $\hat{p}$ depends on the demand parameters. There is another price, $\hat{p}^e$, that depends on firms' expectations of the demand parameters. During the learning phase, firms have an incentive to use a price that is lower than $\hat{p}^e$. Thus, the learning phase looks like a price war. As firms get better information about the demand parameters, the price $\hat{p}^e$ converges to the value of $\hat{p}$ that corresponds to full information about demand. Prices are not only lower but also more variable while firms are learning about the demand parameters, relative to periods when these parameters are known.

Slade (1987) uses daily price data for Vancouver gas stations to attempt to determine whether firms use continuous reaction functions or trigger strategies, and to estimate the extent of tacit collusion. The parameter R is an index of the extent of collusion, given that a larger value of R leads to a higher equilibrium price $\hat{p}$. During a cooperative phase, it is not possible to distinguish between the use of a trigger strategy or a continuous reaction function. Both types of punishment are capable of supporting cooperation. However, during a punishment phase, the two types of strategies lead to different kinds of behavior. The econometrician needs data from a punishment phase in order to assess what type of strategy firms use.

A common assumption is that, when firms use trigger strategies, they revert to the noncooperative Nash equilibrium actions during a punishment phase. (For example, Rotenberg and Saloner's model of price wars under random demand uses this assumption. As we mentioned in our discussion of the Folk theorem, many other types of punishments can be part of an equilibrium strategy.) In a price-setting game, this assumption means that firms revert to Bertrand-Nash prices. With continuous reaction functions, on the other hand, equilibrium prices during the punishment phase depend on previous prices, as in Equation (5.1).

The price war is precipitated by a demand shock. The punishment phase is really a learning phase, during which time firms attempt to learn the values of the new demand parameters. The econometrician uses observations on firm behavior during a punishment/learning phase to determine what kind of strategy firm use. If firms use trigger strategies, they set prices equal to the Bertrand-Nash price of the one-shot game that corresponds to their beliefs about the new demand parameters. If they use continuous strategies, they condition their price on the rival's lagged price as in Equation (5.1).

To obtain an estimation equation under the assumption that firms use continuous reaction functions, take the first difference of Equation (5.1) and add a random error u_t (with mean zero). The result is

$$\Delta p_t^i = R\Delta p_{t-1}^j + u_t; \quad j \neq i, \tag{5.2}$$

where Δ denotes the first difference. If firms use trigger strategies, they would like to use the Bertrand-Nash price corresponding to the unknown demand parameters. In this case, the price they use in the current period is a function of the prices they expect their rivals to use in the same period. By taking the first difference of this relation, we obtain an equation of the same form as Equation (5.2), except that the variable on the right side is Δp_t^j rather than Δp_{t-1}^j. The two models can be nested in the following estimation equation

$$\Delta p_t^i = \alpha R\Delta p_t^j + (1-\alpha)R\Delta p_{t-1}^j + u_t, \quad j \neq i, \tag{5.3}$$

where $0 \leq \alpha \leq 1$. The actual estimation equation is more complicated than Equation (5.3) because there are more than two firms (so R is a matrix rather than a scalar) and the industry is not symmetric. However, to describe the empirical model in a simple manner, we retain the assumption of a symmetric duopoly.

The hypothesis that firms use trigger strategies is consistent with $\alpha = 1$ and the hypothesis that they use continuous reaction functions is consistent with $\alpha = 0$. For the Vancouver gasoline price data, statistical tests fail to reject the hypothesis that $\alpha = 0$ and they reject the hypothesis that $\alpha = 1$, thus favoring the hypothesis that firms use continuous reaction functions rather than trigger strategies.

As noted earlier, under the assumption of continuous reaction functions, the steady-state equilibrium prices depend on the slopes of the reaction function: on the value of R. A larger value of R implies more cooperative behavior in the steady state. The estimated values of R imply pricing behavior that is more cooperative than the Bertrand-Nash outcome, but less cooperative than the cartel outcome. Thus, these estimated slopes imply that implicit collusion exists, but is imperfect.

In Slade's study, the steady-state prices implied by the reaction functions (estimated using data during the period of a price war) are close to the observed prices during the subsequent period of price stability (the period during which the uncertainty about demand has been resolved, and firms return to cooperative behavior). The average price for the sample period is indistinguishable from the Bertrand-Nash price. In this case, aggregation of the data over time during the period of a price war destroys the evidence of implicit collusion. The time-series data make it possible to distinguish between a punishment phase supported by reversion to the one-shot Nash equilibrium (the use of a trigger strategy) and a punishment phase supported by continuous reaction functions. Time-averaged data cannot distinguish between these two possibilities for this data set.

In another empirical application using the same data, Slade (1992) relaxes the assumption that the slope of the reaction function, R, is a constant. The more general formulation of the model with continuous reaction functions is that R changes according to

$$R_t = \alpha + \beta R_{t-1} + \varsigma p_{t-1} + \gamma DP_{t-1} + u_t, \tag{5.4}$$

where DP_{t-1} is an indicator function that takes the value one if the previous change in price was positive, and takes the value zero otherwise; as above, u_t is a random error with mean zero. (Again, the actual formulation is more complicated because there are more than two firms, and the firms are not symmetric. The parameters that we treat as scalars are actually matrices in the empirical study.) This formulation allows the slope of the reaction function to depend on the price level (if $\varsigma \neq 0$) and it allows the reaction to differ depending on whether the rival increased or decreased its previous price (if $\gamma \neq 0$).

The estimation model consists of a linear demand function, Equation (5.2) with R replaced by R_t, and Equation (5.4). Equation (5.2) is referred to as the *measurement equation* and Equation (5.4) as the *state equation*. The state variable is not observed; the state equation provides the law of motion for this latent variable. The state variable appears as a nonstationary parameter in the measurement equation, which also contains variables that are observed. The measurement equation is used to estimate the unobserved state variable, in much the same way as constant parameters are estimated in standard regressions. The state equation imposes structure on the change in the error that appears in the regression. This model is estimated using the Kalman filter. The estimates of ς are statistically insignificant, indicating that the slope of the response function does not vary with price (or possibly that the model is misspecified). The estimates of γ are significantly different from zero and they vary in sign (for different types of rivals). Firms respond asymmetrically to price increases and decreases. The parameters β are significantly different from zero, indicating a systematic change in the slope of the reaction functions over time. The estimated long-run equilibrium value of R (the steady state of Equation (5.4)) implies long-run equilibrium prices that are higher than the Bertrand-Nash level. Again, there is evidence that the firms' strategies support some degree of tacit collusion.

SUMMARY

The theory of repeated games explains why there are typically many subgame perfect noncooperative equilibria when firms interact over many periods. Depending on the discount factor, some of these noncooperative equilibria are indistinguishable from collusion and others are identical to the equilibria of the one-shot game. The theory of repeated games therefore rationalizes the existence of equilibria that are "between" the familiar equilibria (competition, Bertrand, Cournot, and cartel) of static models. In this sense, the theory of repeated games provides a game-theoretic basis for estimating static market conduct (or conjectural variation) models.

More importantly, the theory also provides a basis for constructing qualitatively different empirical models. There have been two prominent lines of research here, using either trigger strategies or continuous reaction functions.

With trigger strategies, the qualitative features of the equilibrium depend on the information firms use to determine their actions. We discussed two models in which positive demand shocks might be associated with increased or decreased (tacit) collusion depending on firms' information set. In the equilibria to both games, firms never actually cheat. In one game, cooperation appears to break down or to be reduced in circumstances in which the temptation to cheat is greater. In the other game, cooperation actually does break down for a time due to an exogenous shock, but not due to cheating.

The equilibrium with continuous reaction functions is "approximately" subgame perfect when the discount factor is large. In this equilibrium, firms never cheat and they never need to punish each other. However, random demand shocks mean that there are periods during which firms are groping toward a new equilibrium as they learn the new demand parameters. These periods look like price wars, because price tends to be more variable and (given a bad demand shock) the price is below its long-run level.

PROBLEMS

Note: Answers to problems are available at the back of the book.

The computations required to answer these questions are straightforward, but some are tedious. Before attempting them, you may want to learn how to use a symbolic math solver. A couple of hours invested in learning to use one of these programs will have a handsome payoff. The authors' favorite is Maple or MuPad, which are built-in features of Scientific Workplace.

5.1 [This problem illustrates how the threat of noncooperation can support cooperative behavior as part of a noncooperative equilibrium.] Suppose that duopolists sell differentiated products. The inverse demand for Firm $i = 1, 2$ is $p_i = a - q_i - bq_j$, where $0 < b < 1$. Firms have zero cost of production. The firms' common discount factor is δ.

a. Calculate the single-period payoff when firms use the cooperative level of sales. Calculate the single-period payoff in the symmetric Nash-Cournot equilibrium and the single-period payoff if a firm cheats when its rival sells at the cooperative level. Use these quantities to find the smallest discount factor needed to support the collusive outcome when cheating is punished by Cournot competition in each period following cheating.

b. Calculate the single-period payoff when firms use the cooperative price level. Calculate the single-period payoff in the symmetric Bertrand equilibrium and the single-period payoff if a firm cheats when its rival sets its price at the cooperative level. Use these quantities to find the smallest discount factor needed to support the collusive outcome when cheating is punished by Bertrand competition in each period following cheating.
c. Compare the critical discount factors in the two cases. What conclusion can you draw from this comparison? In particular, in this model is it "harder to sustain cooperation" (in the sense that a larger discount factor is needed) under price or quantity competition?
d. Discuss the effect of b on the critical discount factors.

5.2 [This question illustrates the essence of the Rotemberg and Saloner model.] Let $p = a_k - (q_1 + q_2)$ be industry demand in state $k = H, L$, where $aH > aL$ (so that demand is greater in the "high" state, $k = H$.) Firms have zero cost of production, and they observe the state of nature. Suppose that if any firm has "cheated" in the past, both players use Nash-Cournot actions in every subsequent period. The states of nature are serially uncorrelated, with $\mu = Prob(a = a_H)$. The discount factor is δ.

a. Calculate the collusive levels of output in the two states of nature, q_H^c, q_L^c, and use these levels to calculate the expected value of the present discounted value of firms' payoff under collusion. (Take the expectation before the current state is known.)
b. Calculate the Nash-Cournot levels of output in the two states, and use these values to calculate the expected value of the present discounted value of firms' payoff in a symmetric Nash-Cournot equilibrium. (Take the expectation before the current state is known.)
c. Calculate C^{cartel}, defined in the text as the present discounted value of the expectation of the cost of cheating, given that firms use the collusive quantity in the cooperative phase.
d. Calculate the single-period net benefit of cheating in state $k = H, L$ (the difference in payoff under cheating and under cooperation). Using this result, find the critical discount factor below which a firm wants to cheat in state i.
e. Using the result just determined, what is the smallest discount factor that sustains the collusive outcome?
f. Now specialize by setting $a_L = 5$, $a_H - 10$, and $\mu = 0.5$. Confirm that for these parameter values, the minimum discount factor needed to sustain cooperation in both states is $\delta = 0.643$. Suppose that the discount factor is $\delta = 0.5$, so that it is not possible to sustain cooperation in both states of nature. What is the highest price and the highest level of profits that can be sustained in the high state? How does this level of profit compare to the

level under full cooperation? [*Hint*: to solve this problem, denote as χ (a value to be determined) the highest level of profits that can be sustained in the high state. Find the level of (symmetric) output that supports this level of profit (in the high state). Denote this value of output as y (a function of χ). When the rival uses output y, find the benefit to a firm of cheating in the current period. (This benefit is also a function of χ.) Given this level of profit, find the present discounted value of the expectation of the cost of cheating, when the discount factor is $\delta = 0.5$. Setting the benefit of cheating equal to the cost of cheating, solve for χ. Using this solution, find y and the equilibrium price in the high state.]

g. Suppose that instead of being serially uncorrelated, the demand shocks are correlated. Let μ_H be the probability that there is a high state in the next period, given that the current state is high. Let μ_L be the probability that there is a high state in the next period, given that the current state is low. How does this complication affect the results to the previous questions? (You need not do any calculations. Just explain how you would solve the model.)

5.3 [This problem illustrates the basic idea in the Green and Porter model.] The inverse demand facing duopoly firms is

$$p = 5 + \varepsilon - (q_1 + q_2), \quad \text{where } \varepsilon \sim \textit{Uniform}\,(0, 0.5).$$

Firms never observe the demand shock, ε, or their rival's output. They choose their own output, and they observe the market price. The discount factor is 0.8. In the cooperative phase, firms produce the collusive level. If the price falls below a critical level, denoted p^c, firms revert to a punishment phase that lasts for five periods. During the punishment phase, firms produce at the Nash-Cournot level. After the punishment phase, firms revert to the cooperative phase.

Find the critical price level p^c that supports the decision rules just described as a noncooperative equilibrium. Using this value, what is the probability that the industry enters a punishment phase, and what is the expected value of being in a cooperative phase?

Hint: first, find the output level, q^m, that maximizes industry-expected profits. Our final objective is to find a threshold price, p^c (the price that triggers punishment) such that when a firm believes that its rival is using q^m in a cooperative phase, it is optimal for the firm to also use q^m.

Second, find the single-period noncooperative level of expected profits and use this value to calculate the expected present value of receiving these profits for five periods (the duration of the punishment phase); denote this value as V. *Note that* q^m and V *are numbers*. This fact makes it relatively easy to perform the following calculations. Denote as q the (endogenous) level that a firm sells in a cooperative phase, given that it believes that its rival is selling q^m. Remember that our problem is to find the critical price p^c such that it is optimal for a firm to set $q = q^m$, given that the firm believes its rival is selling this quantity.

Third, using the uniform distribution, find the probability that $p \leq p^c$ when the firm uses q and its rival uses q^m. Denote this probability (a function) as $\rho(q, p^c)$. Given the uniform distribution, this function is piecewise linear. Assume that at the equilibrium, $0 < \rho < 1$; that is, the equilibrium is interior. This assumption will be confirmed upon completion of the exercise.

Fourth, the payoff for a firm in the cooperative phase, given that it expects its rival to use the cooperative output level, is *J*, which satisfies the relation

$$J = \max_q \{[5.25 - (q^m + q)]q + 0.8[(1 - \rho)J + \rho(V + (0.8)^5 J)]\}.$$

This equation is an example of a dynamic programming equation (DPE). The first term on the right side in curly brackets is the expected payoff in the current period if the firm sells q when it believes that its rival is selling q^m. The second term is the present value of continuation profits. With probability $1 - \rho$, a firm finds itself in a cooperative phase in the next period, in which case the present discounted value of its future profits is *J*. With probability ρ, a firm finds itself in a punishment phase, in which case its present discounted value of expected profits is $(V + [0.8]^5 J)$.

Fifth, write the first-order condition for q in the maximization problem just described. Notice that the problem is concave, so the solution to this first-order condition gives the optimal action. This first-order condition gives q as a function of *J*. Our assumption that a firm's optimal (equilibrium) action is q^m enables us to solve for (i.e., to obtain a numerical value for) *J*. Substitute this value of *J*, together with $q = q^m$ into the DPE, and solve for the trigger price p^c and the value of ρ. [The complete solution to this problem is relatively straightforward because we assumed a linear demand, a uniform distribution, and the specific numerical parameter values.]

SIX

Dynamic Games Involving Economic Fundamentals

We now focus on games in which dynamics arise because of changes in economic fundamentals. This type of game is often referred to as a *dynamic game* or a *stochastic game*. When agents move in continuous time, rather than at discrete stages, it is often called a *differential game*. Hereafter we use the term dynamic game, where it is understood that the dynamics involve (a change in) an economic fundamental and not only the kind of strategic dynamics considered in the previous chapter. In this chapter, we concentrate mainly on the economic theory of these models. In the following chapter, we concentrate on the estimation of these models.

Fundamental sources of dynamics complicate the estimation of market power. The presence of dynamics means that we have to be cautious about interpreting evidence of market power. In particular, the previously used Lerner index (the price–marginal cost difference divided by price) is not an appropriate measure of market power when a firm solves a dynamic problem. When the industry is dynamic, a competitive equilibrium does not, in general, require that price equals static marginal production cost; hence, the Lerner index may either understate or overstate the extent of market power. For example, in a dynamic competitive market for a nonrenewable resource, price equals marginal extraction costs plus the resource rent; in this case, a positive Lerner index does not imply imperfect competition.

In a dynamic setting, the competitive condition requires that the price equals *full marginal cost*, which is the sum of static marginal production costs and a function involving the shadow value of a stock. This shadow value measures the change in the present discounted value of the flow of future profits resulting from a marginal change in the stock. The definition of the stock depends on the context; for example, it may be the amount of a natural resource, the amount of goodwill or knowledge, or the level of a quasi-fixed input (defined as an input whose level is costly to adjust).

Pindyck (1985) discusses a measure of market power that takes into account the dynamics. This measure involves an aggregation over time of the ratios of price minus full marginal cost over price. Though this measure is appealing for its theoretical grounding, it is difficult to calculate even when the exact market structure is known because it requires the solution to a control problem. The next two chapters examine approaches to estimating market structure that use only the necessary conditions (not the solution) to optimal control problems.

We begin by describing several fundamental reasons for dynamics. We emphasize the difference between these reasons and the strategic reasons for dynamics considered in the previous chapter. We then discuss a detailed example that is used to explain the difference between Markov Perfect and open-loop equilibria. We also use this example to discuss the reason for multiplicity of Markov Perfect equilibria when strategies can be discontinuous. We use a second example to explain why Markov Perfect equilibria are typically not unique even when we restrict strategies to be differentiable. We then discuss the relationship between equilibria in dynamic games and conjectural variations equilibria in static games. We close this chapter with a discussion of the empirical implications of the theory.

FUNDAMENTAL REASONS FOR DYNAMICS

To clarify the distinction between fundamental and strategic reasons for dynamics, we provide examples of a fundamental source of dynamics that arise in production or demand. In both cases, we explain why the removal of the fundamental source of dynamics causes a monopoly's or a competitive firm's problem to become static. However, this is not the case for oligopolistic firms. Even if the fundamental source of dynamics is removed, oligopolistic firms might need to solve dynamic problems because of the kinds of strategic considerations discussed in the previous chapter.

Production Fundamentals

Initially, we assume that firms are price takers with respect to inputs. The firms' factors of production are variable, fixed, or quasi-fixed, depending on the cost of changing their level. The average cost of changing the level of a variable input does not depend on the speed of the change. The cost of changing the level of a fixed input is prohibitive. Inputs are quasi-fixed when the cost of changing the level of the input is a convex function of the speed of the change. That is, the average cost of changing the level of quasi-fixed inputs increases with the size of the change within a period; these inputs have nonlinear adjustment costs. The category to which an input belongs may depend on the time horizon considered by the firm. Over a very short period, most inputs are fixed, but over a long period of time, most are variable or quasi-fixed.

In many dynamic problems, in which a period lasts from several months to a few years, it is reasonable to think of capital as a quasi-fixed input. For example, the total cost of constructing a new factory in one year may be greater than the cost of constructing the same factory over a period of two years because it is more expensive to make changes quickly. The cost of building two factories may be more than twice the cost of building one new factory in the same period of time.

Labor may also be a quasi-fixed input. A rapid reduction in the labor force may require large severance payments, whereas a gradual reduction can be achieved more cheaply by means of attrition.

A growing empirical literature attempts to estimate adjustment costs and to distinguish between variable and quasi-fixed inputs in competitive markets. Pindyck and Rotemberg (1983), Epstein and Denny (1983), Hayashi and Inoue (1991), Luh and Stefanou (1991), Fernandez-Cornejo et al. (1992), Anderson (1993), Burh and Kim (1997), Hall (2002), and other papers attempt to quantify adjustment costs in different sectors and for different factors.

Suppose that capital is a quasi-fixed input and all other inputs are variable. A firm's equilibrium profit in a period – its restricted profit function – is a function of its own and of rivals' levels of capital. Its own level of capital affects its profit directly by affecting its cost of production. Its rivals' levels of capital affect their production decisions, affecting the output price, thereby affecting the profits of all firms.

When production involves quasi-fixed inputs, a firm needs to solve a dynamic optimization problem, regardless of the market structure. Because the quasi-fixed input affects the equilibrium level of profit within a period, and because investment changes the future levels of the quasi-fixed input, current investment affects future profit flows. The firm's optimal current investment decision depends on the current level of the quasi-fixed input and on its beliefs about future variables such as prices. The actual level of investment in the current period also affects the equilibrium level of investment (for all firms) in subsequent periods. A single firm's deviation from the equilibrium investment path in the current period alters the future stock of the quasi-fixed input, thereby changing all firms' incentives to invest in subsequent periods.

This consideration is important for oligopolistic firms in which investment plays a strategic role. When choosing investment, a monopoly or a competitive firm needs to take into account only how future profits depend (directly) on the trajectory of the quasi-fixed input. An oligopolistic firm must also take into account how rivals might respond in the future to the change in its capital stock. These responses create an indirect link between future profits and future stocks of the quasi-fixed input.

The change from monopoly or a competitive industry to oligopoly alters the type of dynamic problem that the firm solves. However, the firm's problem is dynamic in all market settings. The firm's problem is dynamic due to an economic fundamental – the quasi-fixed stock – rather than industry structure.

If quasi-fixed inputs are not important to production, it is reasonable to model a monopoly or a competitive firm as solving a sequence of static problems. In each period, the firm chooses input levels to maximize current profits. The current level of inputs has no direct effect on future profits or future decisions. There is no fundamental reason why a firm should condition its current decisions on previous input levels.

If the market structure is oligopolistic rather than competitive or monopolistic, there may be strategic reasons for a firm to solve a dynamic problem even when there are no quasi-fixed inputs. Each firm may think that its rivals' current decisions depend on what has happened in the past, as with the punishment strategies discussed in the previous chapter. It is then rational for each firm to take into account how its current decision will affect the rivals' future decisions. The source of dynamics in this case is strategic rather than fundamental. The oligopolistic firm solves a dynamic problem, whereas the same firm in a competitive or monopolistic setting would solve a sequence of static problems.

Demand Fundamentals

There are a number of reasons why current demand may depend on past actions, so that firms operate in a dynamic environment. We discuss advertising and consumer switching examples.

Advertising can create a stock effect (see Chapter 7). Current advertising may have long-lasting effects by increasing the number of the firm's (or firms') customers today and in the future. The value of current advertising depends on the current stock of potential customers. If the firm already has most of the potential buyers in its customer base, the value of additional advertising may be small. Because current advertising also affects the future stock of potential customers, it affects optimal future advertising levels. This link between the optimal decisions in different periods makes the firm's problem dynamic, even in the absence of strategic considerations. For example, a monopoly must solve a dynamic optimization problem when deciding on its current level of advertising.

Strategic considerations complicate an oligopolistic firm's dynamic problem. A firm's pool of potential customers may depend on its rivals' past advertising levels as well as its own. Consequently, it is rational for the firm to form beliefs about how its rivals will respond to a change in the stock of their customers caused by the change in its advertising. This stock effect may alter the benefit of current advertising. Again, the marginal benefit of advertising may be small if a firm has already attracted most of the potential buyers.

Customer switching costs may result in dynamics. Some consumers might be willing to incur a cost when they experiment with, or switch to, a new brand if the current price differential is sufficiently large. Similarly, customer switching cost may be associated with costs of acquiring information about an unfamiliar good. Even a monopoly needs to solve a dynamic optimization problem because the current price affects the future stock of loyal consumers (those who incur a switching or experimentation cost to try the monopoly's good).

Once again, strategic considerations complicate an oligopolistic firm's dynamic problem, but strategic issues are not the source of the dynamics. An oligopolistic firm's optimal current price depends on its current stock of loyal consumers. That stock depends on the price history of all firms. Consequently, it is rational for a firm to realize that its current price can influence its rival's future decisions, via the effect on future stocks of loyal customers.

In a variation of this model, oligopolistic firms sell a homogeneous good, but there are consumer costs of switching between this and some other good, the price of which is treated as exogenous. Here, the price at a point in time depends on current aggregate sales and also on lagged price or quantity. (Chapter 7 discusses this sticky price model in greater detail.)

If the effect of advertising on future demand is negligible in the first example, or if consumers' switching costs are negligible in the second example, the fundamental source of dynamics is unimportant. A monopoly may choose current advertising or current sales to solve a static problem. However, an oligopolistic firm might still need to solve a dynamic problem. If firms think that their rivals' decisions depend on the history of advertising or sales, then it is rational for them to consider how their current decisions will affect their rivals' future decisions. Each firm then solves a dynamic problem because of strategic considerations.

A DYNAMIC GAME WITH A QUASI-FIXED INPUT

This example formalizes the model in which the dynamic fundamental is related to production. Reynolds (1987) and Driskill and McCafferty (1989) analyze this type of game. Suppose that production for Firm i in period t involves only two inputs – a quasi-fixed input named capital, K_{it}, and a variable input named labor, L_{it}. (We treat capital and labor as scalars, but in a more general setting they may be vectors.) For simplicity, suppose that there are only two firms. A bold variable with a single time subscript denotes a vector of variables in that time period; for example, $\mathbf{L}_t = (L_{1t}, L_{2t})$. The vector $\mathbf{x}_t$ contains exogenous variables that affect firms' profits in period t, such as demand and cost shifters. The profit *excluding investment costs* of Firm i in period t is given by the function $\Pi_i(\mathbf{L_t}, \mathbf{K_t}, \mathbf{x_t})$. Because the vector $\mathbf{x}_t$ can contain the time index, there is no loss in generality in assuming that the function Π_i is stationary.

We adopt the convention that investment in the current period increases capital in the subsequent period. Firm i's investment in period t is I_{it} and its level of capital in the subsequent period is

$$K_{i,t+1} = \rho K_{it} + I_{it}, \tag{6.1}$$

where ρ is the fraction of capital that survives into the next period, so that the depreciation rate is $1 - \rho$. The current level of capital is a predetermined variable because it depends on the previous value of capital and the investment decision in the last period. The cost of investment is $c(I_{it}, K_{it})$, a convex function of I_{it}.

As we discussed earlier, the convexity of the investment cost means that capital is a quasi-fixed input and is therefore a source of *fundamental* dynamics. This convexity means that the necessary conditions to the firm's optimization problem depend on the (predetermined) value of capital. Thus, investment decisions in the current period affect the optimal investment decision in subsequent periods, regardless of the strategic interaction (or lack of it) among firms. If the investment costs were linear, this intertemporal link between decisions would vanish.

In this example, we assume that firms buy capital. Nothing of importance changes if they rent rather than buy capital, provided that the cost of changing the level of capital is convex. We assume that investment costs depend only on investment and capital, but in a more general case we can include $\mathbf{x}_t$ as an argument of the investment cost function.

Each firm chooses labor and investment in each period. Because capital is predetermined at the beginning of the period, the choice of labor determines the firm's current output; the two firms' labor choices determine aggregate output and the market price in the current period. The investment decisions determine the levels of capital in the subsequent period. We refer to the choice of L_{it} as a *static decision* because it has a direct effect on only current period profits – it does not have a direct effect on future outcomes. However, the choice of labor in the current period might affect future profits because of the kinds of strategic reasons described in the previous chapter. That is, the labor choice may have *indirect* effects. For example, firms might be using a trigger strategy that involves labor; hiring more than a threshold level of labor – and thereby increasing production above a threshold level – may cause implicit cooperation to break down. However, the choice of labor in the current period has no *fundamental* (that is, nonstrategic) effect on the subgame in which firms find themselves in the next period. In contrast, the current choice of investment does have this kind of fundamental effect on next period's subgame because it affects the next period production costs, via the level of capital. We refer to the choice of investment as a *dynamic decision.*[1]

The presence of a stock variable (quasi-fixed capital, in this case) does not exclude the possibilities of the kinds of dynamic strategic interactions that arise in repeated games. These dynamic strategic interactions can be the source of multiple subgame perfect equilibria in games with stock variables, for essentially the same reasons as in repeated games without economic fundamentals. Because we want to focus on the quasi-fixed input (or some other industry fundamental) as the source of dynamics, we exclude the kinds of strategic considerations described in the previous chapter.

We achieve this simplification by assuming that the static decision in each period is a function of the *directly payoff-relevant state variable* $\mathbf{z}_t = (\mathbf{K}_t, \mathbf{x}_t)$. The vector $\mathbf{z}_t$ contains agents' *information state*; it is described as *directly payoff-relevant* to distinguish it from other state variables that might be only *indirectly payoff-relevant.*

[1] The assumption that the static and dynamic decisions occur at the same frequency is not necessary. For example, if there is a fixed cost of investing, the dynamic decision may be made infrequently, whereas the static decision is made often. This change requires additional notation, but does not affect the point of this example.

For example, the history of actions would affect a firm's payoff if decisions are conditioned on that history. However, this effect would be *indirect*: the history affects the payoff only because it affects actions. In contrast, $\mathbf{z}_t$ affects payoffs regardless of whether it affects actions. Decision rules that depend only on the directly payoff-relevant state variable (hereafter, referred to simply as the *state variable*) are called Markov strategies.[2] The qualifier *Markov* means that the action depends only on the current state, not on the manner in which the state was reached – that is, not on the history. The "state variable" (which is a vector here) contains two types of states: $\mathbf{K}_t$ changes endogenously, and $\mathbf{x}_t$ changes exogenously.

Suppose that the equilibrium Markov decision rule for the static choice, for Firm i, is given by the function $L_{it} = l_i(\mathbf{z}_t)$. The Markov assumption excludes history-dependent choices. The function $l_i(\mathbf{z}_t)$ depends on the manner in which firms interact in each period. For example, in each period, each firm might choose current labor to maximize its own current profits, treating capital as a parameter and taking as given their rival's choice of labor. In this case, the outcome is the Nash-Cournot equilibrium to the one-period game with payoffs $\Pi_i(L_t, K_t, \mathbf{x}_t)$. Alternatively, firms may be able to explicitly cooperate on the choice of labor. For example, they might choose labor to maximize joint profits, or they might use an *ad hoc* sharing rule for total output (and thus for labor inputs) that depends on the relative capital shares.

Cooperation with respect to a static decision variable and competition with respect to the dynamic decision variable can co-exist, as in Fershtman and Muller (1987). This kind of limited cooperation might occur if the static decision occurs at frequent and known intervals, but the dynamic decision occurs randomly and infrequently. For example, the arrival time of a new technology may be random. When such a technology becomes available, firms choose how much of their existing plant to replace (the dynamic decision). It might be easier to cooperate with respect to a static decision, such as monthly purchases of an input. Another example arises when the arrival time of the new technology is endogenous. Firms invest in research and development (R&D), and the first firm to develop the technology obtains a patent. Firms may be able to cooperate (perhaps imperfectly) in sharing the market, without being able to cooperate on R&D expenditures. Of course, exactly the opposite possibility might also arise. In some industries, we see joint R&D ventures between firms that do not explicitly collude in setting price or output. In either case, there may be a different degree of cooperation with respect to different types of decisions.

[2] *Marginal payoff-relevant* is a more accurate modifier than *payoff-relevant*, but we use the latter because it is the standard term. The important characteristic of these state variables is that they affect an equilibrium condition (optimality condition), so that they affect a decision rule. If a state variable appears in the payoff in an additively separable function, independent of decision variables, then it would be payoff-relevant but would not be an argument of the decision rules. We ignore these kinds of variables, and assume that payoff-relevant state variables do affect an equilibrium condition.

Cooperation with respect to the static decision might lower the present discounted value of firms' profits and increase consumer welfare. This possibility arises because firms' incentive to invest may be much greater when aggregate output (or the labor input) is chosen cooperatively, and each firm's share of output depends on its capital stock. For example, if firms behave as a cartel with respect to the output decision, the share of output within a period might be allocated efficiently across firms. In that case, a firm's output share depends on the relation between its and its rivals' marginal costs. Because marginal costs depend on capital, a firm's share of output in this scenario depends on the capital stock of all firms. Firms might overinvest (from the standpoint of industry profits) in order to be able to capture a large share of the subsequent cartel profits, leading to a lower cost curve. The actual price depends on the cost curve – and thus on the level of investment – and on whether firms choose the price cooperatively. The cartel price for the low cost curve (high investment) may be below the noncooperative price that corresponds to the higher cost curve (low investment). In addition, the present discounted value of profits (profits from sales minus investment costs) may be lower when firms collude with respect to the static decision output but not the dynamic decision (investment), as in Gatsios and Karp (1992).

Disadvantageous cooperation may seem implausible, but it nevertheless can emerge as a subgame perfect equilibrium. Consider the simplest case, in which the investment decision is made only once, at the beginning of the game, and the static decision is made infinitely often thereafter.[3] Given the investment decision, subsequent cooperation is a subgame perfect equilibrium if the discount rate is sufficiently low (as explained in Chapter 5). Cooperation as an outcome may be more plausible than noncooperation.

If firms believe that cooperation will occur with respect to the static decision in the future, and if their share of cartel profits depends on their share of industry capital, firms have an incentive to overinvest (from the standpoint of aggregate industry profits) in the first stage. They also have an incentive to overinvest when the subsequent static decisions are made noncooperatively, but the difference in the magnitude of this incentive can be substantial, depending on the manner in which the splitting rule for cartel profits varies with capital.

This possibility illustrates the difficulty of drawing welfare conclusions based on indices of competition. Even if we are able to overcome the practical problems of measuring these indices, they might be misleading if they estimate the degree of competition with respect to only a subset of the firms' decision variables. We might, for example, correctly measure a high degree of cooperation with respect to

[3] Problem 6.1 provides a two-stage example of the possibility that limited cooperation can lower industry profits. In the first stage, firms decide noncooperatively whether to make an investment that reduces production costs. The second stage of the game represents all future periods: the second period payoff equals the present discounted value of the equilibrium payoffs in all future periods, as a function of the investment decision in the first period.

static decisions. If the dynamic decisions were fixed, it would be correct to conclude that this industry structure benefits firms and harms consumers. However, because the dynamic decisions may depend on the extent of cooperation at a later stage of the production process, those welfare conclusions might be wrong. In principle, it is possible to estimate separate indices for the degree of cooperation with respect to static and dynamic decision variables, although we do not know of any such attempts.

OPEN-LOOP RULES

We now assume that the modeler knows the equilibrium Markov decision rule for the *static* decision variable, $L_t(\mathbf{K}_t, \mathbf{x}_t)$. In this subsection, we do *not* assume that the decision rule for the dynamic variable (investment) is Markovian. Substituting the static decision rule into Firm *i*'s profit function, we obtain the reduced-form profit function

$$\pi_i(\mathbf{K}_t, \mathbf{x}_t) \equiv \Pi_i\,(\mathbf{K}_t, \mathbf{L}(\mathbf{K}_t, \mathbf{x}_t))$$

The rest of this chapter uses this reduced-form profit function.

At time *t*, the firm knows the state variable $\mathbf{z}_t = (\mathbf{K}_t, \mathbf{x}_t)$ and wants to maximize its expectation of the present discounted value of profits net of adjustment costs:

$$PDV_{it} \equiv E_{it} \sum_{\tau=1}^{\infty} (\pi_i\,\{\mathbf{K}_\tau, \mathbf{x}_\tau\} - c\,(I_{it},\, K_{it}))\delta^{\tau-t}. \tag{6.2}$$

The operator E_{it} represents the firm's expectations conditional on its information at period *t*. The firm bases its current decision on its expectations about the future sequences of both the endogenous and the exogenous state variables, $\mathbf{K}_t$ and $\mathbf{x}_t$.[4]

To simplify the discussion, we assume for the time being that $\mathbf{x}_t$ is a constant parameter, so we can ignore it. With this simplification, the game consists of the payoff in Equation (6.2), the equations of motion for capital in Equation (6.1), and the initial (predetermined) level of capital at the beginning of the game. In the absence of exogenous uncertainty (because we are treating $\mathbf{x}_t$ as a constant), the expectations operator in Equation (6.2) refers to Firm *i*'s beliefs about its rival's

[4] A note on estimation: failure to include exogenous state variables in the estimation equations will almost certainly result in bias, for the usual reason of misspecification due to an omitted variable. In a stochastic setting, the nature of the estimation problem depends on (1) whether firms understand that they will obtain new information in the future and (2) whether they have rational expectations about the evolution of $\mathbf{x}_t$. At the end of this chapter we return to the first of these two questions, since it has an important bearing on the meaning of "*open-loop*." Although we do not discuss the second issue, it is worth noting that the failure to impose the correct restrictions implied by rational expectations results in less efficient estimators (as does the failure to impose any other true restriction). These econometric issues are distinct from the game-theoretic issues that we want to emphasize here.

future levels of capital. We are now in a position to consider the various types of equilibria.

In the simplest equilibrium, firms choose the entire sequence of investment – and thus, the entire sequence of capital stocks – at the initial time, s, where the capital stock is $\mathbf{K}_s$. If t is an arbitrary future time, then $\tau = t - s$ equals the number of periods until that time. In most cases, we set $s = 0$, but it is useful to retain s as a parameter in order to describe the situation in which the strategy is revised so that the initial time changes. Decision rules that depend on the current calendar time and the information (the state variable) known at the initial time are called *open-loop*.

In the noncooperative Nash open-loop equilibrium, Firm *i's* equilibrium open-loop (OL superscript) investment rule is $I_{i,s+\tau} = I_i^{OL}(\tau, \mathbf{K}_s)$ for $\tau \geq 0$; the level of investment given by this rule is the best response to the rival's decision rule.[5] The decision rule is a function of capital stock at the initial time, $\mathbf{K}_s$, not of the capital stock at the time investment actually occurs, $\mathbf{K}_{s+\tau}$. In this equilibrium, the firm conditions its action at time $t \geq s$ on the information that it has at time s.

For symmetric firms, the degree of difficulty of characterizing the open-loop equilibrium is similar to the degree of difficulty of characterizing the equilibrium in the corresponding one-firm dynamic problem. In many cases of interest, there is a unique symmetric open-loop Nash equilibrium in which firms are symmetric. In the following discussion of open-loop policies, we focus on the symmetric Nash equilibrium and we assume existence and uniqueness. (If firms are heterogeneous, the open-loop Nash equilibrium in an oligopoly has higher dimension than the one-firm problem; the higher dimension naturally adds some complications.)

Time Consistency of Open-Loop Rules

The open-loop equilibrium is *time-consistent*, meaning that the open-loop equilibrium decision rule remains an equilibrium rule for subgames on the equilibrium path. If firms solve the game at time s and play according to their open-loop Nash equilibrium rules for an arbitrary number of periods, and then re-solve the game, the resulting equilibrium path is the same as the path that would have resulted under the initial solution.

More formally, we can substitute the equilibrium investment rule $I_{i,s+\tau} = I_i^{OL}(\tau, \mathbf{K}_s)$ into Equation (6.1) and solve the difference equation to obtain the function $\mathbf{K}_{s+\tau} = K^{OL}(\tau, \mathbf{K}_s)$. The arguments of this function are the number of

[5] We assume that the environment is stationary and we write the action at time $s + \tau$ as a function of τ rather than $s + \tau$. If, for example, there were exogenous technical change, it would be important to retain as an explicit argument calendar time rather than merely the number of periods in the future. If $s = 0$, there is no distinction between calendar time and the number of periods in the future.

periods in the future, τ, and the value of capital at the initial time, when the open-loop equilibrium was computed. For $t = s + \tau$, values of capital given by $\mathbf{K}_t = \mathbf{K}_{s+\tau} = K^{OL}(\tau, \mathbf{K}_s)$ are said to be "on the equilibrium path." If we choose an arbitrary time $\tau \geq s(\tau \geq 0)$ with capital on the equilibrium path (so that $\mathbf{K}_{s+\tau} = K^{OL}(\tau, \mathbf{K}_s))$ and re-compute the open-loop equilibrium at that time, this "new" open-loop equilibrium equals the continuation from time t onward of the original open-loop equilibrium computed at time s.[6] That is, for $\tau \geq 0$ and $\tau' \geq 0$,

$$\mathbf{K}_{\tau+s} = K^{OL}(\tau, \mathbf{K}_s) \Rightarrow I_i^{OL}\left(\tau', \mathbf{K}_{\tau+s}\right) = I_i^{OL}(\tau' + \tau, \mathbf{K}_s). \tag{6.3}$$

The first equality states that, at time $\tau + s$, the state is on the equilibrium path determined at time s. The second equality states that the open-loop paths calculated at times $\tau + s$ and s are the same for every time after $\tau + s$. (Later in this chapter we explain how the inclusion of exogenous stochastic state variables changes the meaning of "open-loop".)

Different Approaches to Obtaining Necessary Conditions

Dynamics are "relevant" even when firms use open-loop strategies because the dynamic constraint – the equation of motion for capital – must hold. Investment in one period affects the level of capital and therefore profits in subsequent periods. However, there is no strategic role for dynamics with open-loop policies. Both firms make all their decisions at the initial time, so neither firm can use current investment to influence its rival's future decisions. The open-loop assumption renders the game "strategically static."

This property diminishes the appeal of the open-loop equilibrium concept, but it provides a useful simplification. It means that the noncooperative open-loop Nash equilibrium can be obtained by solving an optimization problem rather than an equilibrium problem. For example, the equilibrium to a perfectly collusive industry can be obtained by solving the cartel's optimization problem. Similarly, the equilibrium to a competitive industry can be obtained by solving a social planner's problem (under the appropriate convexity assumptions). The Nash-Cournot equilibrium can also be obtained by solving a (different) optimization problem, as we show subsequently. Slade (1994, 1995) discusses this approach to calculating the equilibrium to a game; Hansen et al. (1985) illustrates the idea using a game with a nonrenewable resource.

[6] The time consistency of the open-loop equilibrium arises because the Nash assumption makes firms strategically symmetric in the sense that each firm takes the other firm's sequence of actions as given. If one firm were able to announce its investment trajectory, with the view to influencing its rival's decisions – for example, if the equilibrium were Stackelberg – the open-loop equilibrium would not, in general, be time consistent. However, even in the Stackelberg case, the open-loop equilibrium is time consistent in special circumstances, as discussed by Xie (1997) and Karp and Lee (2003).

All of these maximands – cartel profits, social welfare, and the "artificial" maximand associated with the Nash-Cournot equilibrium – can be nested in a single, more general maximand. This method of obtaining a particular equilibrium by solving an optimization problem rather than using the necessary conditions for that equilibrium (such as the firms' first-order conditions) works for both a static game and for the open-loop equilibrium to a dynamic game.

This method does not work when noncooperative firms use Markov Perfect strategies. That is, it is not possible in general to obtain a Markov Perfect noncooperative equilibrium simply by solving a single-agent optimization problem. (The final section of Chapter 7 discusses a method for estimating industry structure when firms use Markov Perfect strategies.)

There is sometimes a computational advantage to obtaining an equilibrium by solving an optimization problem rather than by finding a fixed point in the best-response mapping. Beginning with an optimization problem also provides an approach to estimating market power. We can compare the estimated parameter (or vector of parameters for an asymmetric equilibrium) of the general maximand with those values associated with familiar equilibria (competitive, collusive, and Nash-Cournot). This comparison provides a measure of the distance between the actual outcome and one of these known equilibria.

It does not matter whether the economist thinks of the index of market power as an argument in the maximand of a single-agent decision problem (as in the preceding paragraphs) or as an argument in the equilibrium conditions to an oligopoly (as in the conjectural variations model that we studied earlier). In the former case, the economist uses the first-order conditions of an "artificial" single-agent maximization problem, and in the latter she/he uses the set of first-order conditions of the oligopolies. These are merely two different ways of nesting different degrees of cooperation within a single set of estimation equations.

A third equivalent approach, in the case of a symmetric equilibrium, is to replace the "true" derivative of price with respect to quantity with the industry's belief (or conjecture) concerning the change in that derivative, and then solve the industry's problem using this conjecture. As the relation between the true and the conjectured derivative varies, we again obtain different outcomes. For particular values of the conjecture, we obtain the familiar equilibria.

To illustrate these three equivalent approaches for obtaining the necessary conditions, consider the problem in which market demand is $p = a - bQ$ and Q is aggregate. If q is the output of one of the n symmetric firms, and each firm's cost is zero, the profit of a typical firm is $\pi = (a - bQ)q$. In a symmetric equilibrium, where the conjecture that firm i makes about the behavior of its rivals is $\frac{dQ_{-i}}{dq_i} = v$, the equilibrium condition is

$$a - b\left(1 + \frac{v+1}{n}\right)Q = 0.$$

The method of solving an "artificial" optimization problem that has been used to obtain the Nash-Cournot equilibrium involves the "industry" maximizing

$$\Pi = \left(a - b\left(1 + \frac{\nu + 1}{n}\right)\frac{Q}{2}\right)Q$$

with respect to Q, leading to the same necessary condition.

In the third approach, the industry maximizes sales, PQ, using the conjecture that $\frac{dp}{dQ} = -\frac{b(\nu+1)}{n}$, leading to the necessary condition $p - b\frac{\nu+1}{n} = 0$. By evaluating this condition at $p = a - bQ$, we obtain the same equilibrium condition. These three approaches are merely different ways to obtain a family of equations that nest, within a single equation, the necessary conditions for certain well-known equilibria.

The relations between different equilibria on the one hand and different objective functions or conjectures on the other are obvious in the simple static example given. The more interesting point is that they also hold for an open-loop equilibrium in a dynamic game – an observation that we use in Chapters 7 and 8.

SUBGAME PERFECTION AND MARKOV STRATEGIES

The lack of strategic dynamics means that the open-loop Nash equilibrium is (typically) not subgame perfect. (Fershtman, 1987, shows that there are exceptions to this statement. He identifies a class of games for which the open-loop equilibria are subgame perfect.) If a firm were to deviate from the open-loop equilibrium – that is, not use its open-loop equilibrium investment rule – the state would be *off the equilibrium trajectory*: $K_{s+\tau} \neq K^{OL}(\tau, K_s)$ for some $\tau > 0$. The continuation of the original equilibrium is not an equilibrium for the subgame that begins at such a point. In other words, instead of Equation (6.3), we have

$$K_{\tau+s} \neq K^{OL}(\tau, K_s) \Rightarrow I_i^{OL}(\tau', K_{\tau+s}) \neq I_i^{OL}(\tau + \tau', K_s). \tag{6.4}$$

The lack of subgame perfection explains why theorists and empiricists are skeptical of open-loop equilibria.[7]

Our previous comments regarding the multiplicity of history-dependent subgame perfect equilibria apply here. If firms are able to condition their current level of investment on the history of the game, many different outcomes are possible. Chapter 5 discussed the empirical difficulties of estimating market structure in repeated games when firms use history-dependent strategies. These problems are magnified in a game with a dynamic constraint such as Equation (6.1), simply because such games are more complex. Therefore, for many theoretical and most empirical applications, we need to consider a smaller class of strategies.

[7] Problem 6.2 provides a two-period example of an open-loop equilibrium that is time consistent but not subgame perfect.

The obvious candidate is Markov strategies: decision rules that depend only on the directly payoff-relevant state variable. A subgame perfect Markov equilibrium is referred to as a *Markov Perfect equilibrium* (MPE). This refinement eliminates many outcomes, but there is no reason to expect it to yield a unique outcome. It is often possible to use a "bad" MPE as a credible threat to support a Pareto superior MPE. The presence of the endogenous stock and the restriction to Markov strategies cause some complications, but the basic idea of these trigger strategies is similar to the trigger strategies that support cooperation (or something approaching cooperation) in a supergame. (In a supergame, the noncooperative equilibrium to the one-shot game – or some other "bad" outcome – is a credible threat if firms deviate from cooperative actions.)

In our example, suppose that firms are symmetric and that $\partial^2 \pi_i / \partial K_i \partial K_j < 0$. This inequality implies that Firm i's incentive to invest (thereby increasing its level of capital) is lower at higher levels of its rival's stock. In the noncooperative setting, a firm therefore has an incentive to increase its stock of capital to discourage its rivals' subsequent investment levels. Because all firms have this incentive, there exists a noncooperative equilibrium in which the steady-state level of capital is higher than the cooperative steady state. The cooperative steady-state level of capital, denoted K^c, is the steady state to the problem of maximizing the present discounted value of industry profits. Thus, there exists a MPE, the "bad MPE," for which the steady-state level of capital is higher, and the steady-state flow of profits lower than under cooperation. If a firm believes that its rival will use the bad MPE strategy whenever $K_{it} > K_i^c$ and that, for $K_{it} \leq K_i^c$, its rival will choose investment in order to keep its capital at or below the cooperative level, the firm has an incentive to make sure that its own stock never exceeds the cooperative level. If investment is constrained to be non-negative, this incentive is strong if δ, the discount factor, and ρ, the fraction of capital that survives into the next period, are large. If δ is large, profits near the steady state receive greater weight than profits along the transition path in the firm's calculation of the present discounted value of the payoff. Given that investment is non-negative, if ρ is large, it takes a long time or it might be impossible for a firm to drive the stock to the region where its rival behaves cooperatively.

The basic idea in this example is that the type of strategy that firms use depends on the region in which they find the state. The desire to avoid driving the state to a region where competition is strong and profits are low may be enough to induce cooperative investment decisions when the state is in a "good" region (e.g., a region where capacity is less than or equal to the industry profit-maximizing level). Fudenberg and Tirole (1993, Chapter 13) give examples of the multiplicity of MPE in an investment game in which investment is irreversible, the investment rate is bounded above, and the cost of investment is linear.

Dutta and Sundaram (1993) provide examples of the multiplicity of MPE in a game in which firms extract a renewable resource, such as fish; here, the state variable is the stock of the resource. A possible equilibrium outcome in this game is that the stock of the resource is driven to a low level (leading to a low flow of resource rents), or exhausted (leading to zero resource rents). Agents do not have sufficient incentive to conserve the resource, because they believe that their rivals will take whatever they leave. This outcome is known as the "tragedy of the commons." The (credible) threat that all firms will behave in this way if the stock falls below a certain level, may be enough to keep the stock at a high level.

Given that the strategy depends on the current level of the stock, and not directly on the history of actions, the strategy is Markov (rather than history-dependent). However, these strategies are similar to the trigger strategies discussed in Chapter 5, insofar as in both cases a "good" outcome is supported by means of a credible threat to punish "bad" behavior. There are many MPE of this type.

DIFFERENTIABLE MARKOV PERFECT STRATEGIES

The examples of multiple MPE described previously involve strategies that change discontinuously if the state moves from one region to another. In the first example, firms behave cooperatively if production capacity (or capital stock) is low, and they behave competitively when capacity is high. In the second example, firms conserve the resource when the stock is high, but a low stock triggers the tragedy of the commons. From an estimation point of view, it would be possible, in principle, to use switching regressions (as in Porter's 1983 supergame model) to estimate strategies that change abruptly as the state passes from one region to another. However, we are not aware of applications of switching regressions in games with dynamic fundamentals. For the purpose of estimating market structure, these kinds of discontinuous Markov Perfect strategies seem to be of limited use.

The aforementioned examples of multiple MPE involve discontinuous strategies (a sudden change in behavior when the state crosses a threshold). This discontinuity is needed because the credible threat of triggering the "bad" MPE is used to induce firms to remain in the region of state space where they behave (somewhat) cooperatively. Restrictions on the strategy space can eliminate this kind of equilibrium. A possible restriction, beyond Markov Perfection, is that the equilibrium actions change "smoothly" as the value of the state variable changes. For example, we can require the strategy to be differentiable in the state variable. This restriction eliminates discontinuous strategies and, therefore, it removes the possibility of using a bad MPE to support other (better) MPE. This restriction therefore eliminates the reason for multiplicity illustrated in the previous examples.

The restriction to smooth strategies can therefore be viewed as a refinement because it eliminates certain types of equilibria. In addition, the researcher might consider smooth strategies as more plausible than the kinds of discontinuous strategies used in the examples just given. An objection to those kinds of (discontinuous) strategies is that the equilibrium threshold (the value of the state variable that triggers the discrete change in behavior) is largely arbitrary. Because the assumption of rationality does not determine the level of the threshold, it is hard to understand how firms could compute the threshold; they need this information in order to solve their optimization problem. The basis for this objection is essentially that there are "too many" equilibria, and no explanation for how firms' interaction leads to a particular equilibrium. This same objection applies to many areas of game theory. A counterargument is that the multiplicity of equilibria is a feature of the real world, and not a failure of the theory.

Even though the restriction to differentiable (and therefore continuous) strategies reduces the set of equilibria, it typically does not result in a unique equilibrium. The explanation for the multiplicity with differentiable strategies is easier to understand in the context of a continuous time model with a single state variable, where the theory was developed, rather than in the discrete stage model with two state variables (the capital levels for the different firms).[8] The following discussion of a continuous time model is based on Tsutsui and Mino (1990). We use this example both to explain the reason for multiplicity and to emphasize the difference between open-loop and Markov Perfect equilibria.

A STICKY PRICE MODEL

Suppose that there are two symmetric oligopolists selling in a market with sticky prices. The price is fixed at a point in time t. The long-run equilibrium relation between price, p_t, and aggregate quantity, $Q_t = q_{1t} + q_{2t}$, is given by $p_t = P(Q_t)$. If the current price exceeds this equilibrium price, price falls, and if it is below this price, the price rises. The change in price is given by

$$\dot{p} \equiv \frac{\mathrm{d}p}{\mathrm{d}t} = \alpha\left[P\left(Q_t\right) - p_t\right], \tag{6.5}$$

where α is a speed-of-adjustment parameter. If α is large, price adjusts rapidly. The firm faces convex production costs, so the firm never wants to produce at an infinite rate. If Firm i produces at rate q_{it}, its instantaneous flow of profits is $\pi(p_t, q_{it})$. The present discounted value of profits for Firm i is

$$\int_{s=t}^{\infty} e^{-r(s-t)}\pi\left(p_s, q_{is}\right)\mathrm{d}s. \tag{6.6}$$

Equation (6.6) gives the payoff to the game and Equation (6.5) is the dynamic constraint. In this game, the payoff-relevant state consists of a single variable, the price p_t. In order to solve its maximization problem, Firm i forms beliefs about its rival's decision rule. In a MPE, the rival uses a state-dependent decision rule. Firm i's belief about the rival's decision rule is $q_{jt} = q^e(p_t)$, which we assume is

[8] Most econometric applications use discrete-time models because they are easier estimate. A recent paper by Doraszelski and Judd (2005) provides a setting in which continuous-time games are easier to estimate. Kamien and Schwartz (1991) provide an excellent introduction to continuous-time optimal-control methods.

differentiable. Given these beliefs, we can eliminate q_{jt} from Firm i's problem by writing $Q_t = q_{it} + q^e(p_t)$. Firm i solves a "standard" optimal control problem, except that this problem involves the unknown function $q^e(p_t)$. We need to find this function, together with the solution to Firm i's problem. Suppressing the time index, the Hamiltonian to this problem is

$$H_i = \pi(p, q_i) + \mu_i \alpha \left[P\left(q_i + q^e(p)\right) - p \right]. \tag{6.7}$$

The co-state variable $\mu_i(t)$ is the shadow value for Firm i of the price. It gives the marginal change in the value of the firm's program resulting from a marginal change in the state variable, the current price.

Assuming an interior equilibrium, $q(t) > 0$, the necessary conditions to this problem consist of Equation (6.5), the transversality condition, $\lim_{t\to\infty} e^{-rt}\mu_i(t) = 0$, and

$$\frac{\partial H_i}{\partial q_i} = \frac{\partial \pi}{\partial q_i} + \alpha \mu_i \left(\frac{\partial P}{\partial Q} \right) = 0, \tag{6.8}$$

$$\dot{\mu}_i = r\mu_i - \pi_p(p, q_i) - \mu_i \alpha \left(\frac{dP}{dQ}\frac{dq^e}{dp} - 1 \right). \tag{6.9}$$

Equation (6.9) contains the derivative of the firm's belief about its rival's decision rule; in equilibrium, this belief is correct. The appearance of this derivative in the firm's necessary condition shows the importance of the assumption that strategies are differentiable.

The rival firm has an analogous control problem. In a symmetric equilibrium, each firm has the same expectations about its rival's decisions and the same necessary conditions. In equilibrium, the firm's expectations are confirmed, so the function $q^e(p)$ is the solution to (both) firms' problems. More formally, denote the equilibrium decision rule for Firm i – the solution to the firm's decision problem – as $q(p)$. This solution depends on the firm's beliefs about its rival's decision rule $q^e(p)$. In a symmetric equilibrium, the solution to the rival's control problem is the same as Firm i's, so we denote it as $q(p)$ as well. In equilibrium, where the actual and the expected behavior must be the same,

$$q(p) \equiv q^e(p). \tag{6.10}$$

The Markov assumption implies that firms' decision rules depend on the state variable, p. In an open-loop equilibrium, in which decisions depend only on the initial state and calendar time, each firm thinks that its rival would not respond to a change in the state. Therefore, the term dq^e/dp in Equation (6.9) is identically zero in an open-loop equilibrium. This simplification makes the open-loop equilibrium much easier to characterize. The other necessary conditions are the same in the open-loop and Markov equilibria.

Multiplicity of Equilibria

In order to understand the reason for the multiplicity of symmetric differentiable MPE, it is useful to think about how one would go about computing an equilibrium, using the necessary conditions for optimality and the equilibrium condition implied by symmetry, Equation (6.10). (The same logic applies if firms are not symmetric, but the description is more complicated.) We show that the equilibrium conditions involve one fewer equation than the number of unknowns. Therefore, the necessary conditions for a MPE are not, in general, sufficient to determine a unique equilibrium.

Using Equation (6.10), we replace q_i and q^e with $q(p)$ in Equations (6.5), (6.8), and (6.9) and define $m(p) \equiv dq/dp$. Given the identity in Equation (6.10), this definition implies that $m(p) \equiv dq^e/dp$. In contrast, in an open-loop equilibrium, the agent treats the rival's future actions as fixed (not a function of the state). Therefore, $m(p) = 0$ in the open-loop equilibrium. In a standard one-agent control problem (rather than a game), in which there is no rival, $dq^e/dp = 0$, the function $m(p)$ also vanishes.

At least in principle, we can use Equation (6.8) to solve for aggregate output at a point in time as a function of the price and the co-state variable at that time. We write this relation as $2q_t = Q_t = Q(p_t, \mu_t)$.[9] It is simple to obtain q as a (possibly implicit) function of (p, μ) by using Equation (6.8), because this is an algebraic rather than a differential equation. Of course, we do not know the values of the arguments of this function, p_t, and μ_t.

When we substitute the function $Q(p_t, \mu_t)$ into Equations (6.5) and (6.9), we obtain a system of two ordinary differential equations for p and μ involving the unknown function $m(p)$. In order to solve these two differential equations, we need two boundary conditions. The initial price provides one boundary condition. In many standard infinite horizon control problems, the second boundary condition is given by the requirement that the system converge to a steady state. Setting the time derivative of p and μ given in Equations (6.5) and (6.9) equal to zero (to solve for the steady state), we find that the following two algebraic equations hold at the steady state:

$$\alpha\,[P\,(Q(p,\mu) - p] = 0, \tag{6.11}$$

$$r\mu - \pi_p(p, Q(p,\mu)) - \mu\alpha\left(\frac{dP\,(Q\,(p,\mu))}{dQ} m(p) - 1\right) = 0 \tag{6.12}$$

where $P(Q(p, \mu))$ is the function $P(Q)$, used in Equation (6.5), evaluated at $Q = Q(p, \mu)$.

[9] In practice, we may be able to obtain the function $Q(p_t, \mu_t)$ only implicitly, but this complication would not affect the basic idea of the solution algorithm described subsequently; it would only complicate the implementation of that algorithm.

In a standard (one-agent) control problem or in an open-loop equilibrium, where $m(p) = 0$, we can solve Equations (6.11) and (6.12) to obtain steady values of p and μ. With these values, we can find the initial value of μ such that the system of differential equations for (p_t, μ_t) converges to the steady state. With this boundary condition, we can solve the pair of ordinary differential equations to find the equilibrium trajectories for (p_t, μ_t) and then use the function $q_t = Q_t/2 = Q(p_t, \mu_t)/2$ to find the equilibrium trajectory for the output of a single firm. For values of p between the initial and steady-state values, we then know the relation between output and price. That is, for this interval of prices, we can find the equilibrium control rule, the function $q(p)$. This method is sometimes referred to as *synthesizing* the feedback rule from the open-loop solution. For certain special functional forms, it is possible to obtain a closed-form solution. In general, however, numerical methods are needed to implement this algorithm (or a variation of it).

Matters are different in an MPE to a differential game because of the presence of the unknown function $m(p)$ in Equation (6.12). Equations (6.11) and (6.12) do not enable us to find the three unknowns, the steady-state values p_∞, $m_\infty \equiv m(p_\infty)$, and μ_∞. Tsutsui and Mino (1990) refer to this indeterminacy as an *incomplete transversality condition.*

If we knew the value of m_∞, we could solve for the steady-state values p_∞, μ_∞ in Equations (6.11) and (6.12) and then find the solutions to the differential equations for the price and the co-state variable. In the process, we would construct the equilibrium decision rule $q(p)$ and its derivative $m(p) = dq/dp$. The details of the procedure are more involved than those of the previously described algorithm for the one-agent control problem or the open-loop equilibrium, but the basic idea is similar. Because the necessary conditions for a MPE do not pin down a unique value of m_∞, these conditions do not select a unique steady state or a unique decision rule. The incomplete transversality condition is equivalent to a missing boundary condition for the state.

Thus, there typically exists a family of differentiable MPE, indexed by the parameter m_∞, or equivalently, indexed by the steady state.[10] A steady state is *asymptotically stable* if, for all initial conditions in the neighborhood of the steady state, the equilibrium trajectory converges to the steady state. (We discuss the idea of asymptotic stability more fully subsequently, and in Problem 6.3.) The requirement of stability places bounds on the set of equilibrium steady states. This requirement reduces the family of differentiable MPE but does not lead to uniqueness.[11]

[10] The non-uniqueness is associated with the lack of a boundary condition for the state variable when $t = \infty$. In some problems, there is a *natural boundary condition* that produces uniqueness. For example, if the state variable is a *nonrenewable* natural resource, as in Karp (1992), it must eventually decline to an exogenous level (such as zero). This level is the natural boundary condition for the state. Here, the unique differentiable symmetric MPE can be obtained by solving an ordinary differential equation.

[11] Problem 6.3 shows the reader how to obtain the unique steady state in a symmetric open-loop equilibrium, and the set of asymptotically steady states in a differentiable MPE.

Each member of this family of MPE is defined over a subset of state space. That is, the MPE decision rule that causes price to converge to a particular steady state is defined for a particular interval of prices including, of course, the steady state. Changing the steady state changes the domain of the decision rule. In some settings, there may be a reason to require that the decision rule is defined at least over a particular region. The requirement that the MPE decision rule be defined over a particular interval eliminates some stable MPE, but again, need not lead to uniqueness.

Selecting a Particular Equilibrium

For applied theory or empirical work, we usually want to study a specific equilibrium, rather than a family of equilibria. There are two practical means of selecting a particular equilibrium. One method replaces the upper limit of infinity by a finite value T in the definition of the payoff Equation (6.6). This finite horizon problem can be solved backwards (from the final time). Doing so typically results in a unique equilibrium. We can index this equilibrium by T and then study its limit as $T \to \infty$.[12] Driskill (2002) provides examples of this approach.

Another approach selects a particular equilibrium decision rule on the grounds of its simplicity. In the sticky price example, if the function π is linear-quadratic in its arguments and the function P is linear, the resulting problem is a linear-quadratic differential game. For this game, there exists a linear equilibrium decision rule. This linear decision rule is the same as the rule that we obtain when we begin with a finite horizon problem and take limits as $t \to \infty$.

COMPARING OPEN-LOOP AND MARKOV EQUILIBRIA

In both Markov and open-loop equilibria, firms understand that a change in their actions (e.g., a deviation from the equilibrium action) causes a change in the state variable. In a Markov equilibrium, firms realize that rivals will respond to a change in the state variable. In an open-loop equilibrium, firms believe that rivals will not respond to such changes. Because it is (typically) optimal for firms to respond to a change in the state variable, the Markov assumption attributes greater rationality to firms, and is more in keeping with economists' inclination to assume that agents are rational. Whether the Markov assumption is more consistent with how firms actually behave is an empirical question.

Comparing the outcomes in the two types of equilibria is not straightforward because the symmetric open-loop equilibrium is typically unique, whereas the symmetric MPE is not. However, if we are willing to select a MPE, the comparison can be made. For example, games in which the payoffs are quadratic in the state and

[12] This situation provides an example of *discontinuity at infinity*. There is a unique equilibrium for $t < \infty$, but a family of equilibria that includes the limit of the unique equilibrium at $t = \infty$.

control variables, and the equation of motion is linear in these variables ("linear-quadratic games"), always have a MPE equilibrium decision rule that is linear in the state variable (the "linear equilibrium"). We can compare the linear MPE to the unique open-loop equilibrium in this game. It is natural to ask whether the Markov assumption weakens or strengthens competition between firms, relative to the open-loop assumption. The answer depends on the specifics of the game. Lapham and Ware (1994) compare the open-loop and Markov Perfect steady-state equilibria for the discrete time linear-quadratic game. Jun and Vives (2004) study the continuous time linear-quadratic model. Both papers examine the linear equilibrium to the respective games.

In order to understand the comparison of open-loop and Markov Perfect steady states, we can use insights from the distinction between strategic complements and substitutes in static games. In a static game, this distinction depends on the slope of a firm's best-response function. Actions are *strategic substitutes* if a firm wants to decrease its action as a consequence of its rivals' increased action. Actions are *strategic complements* if a firm wants to increase its action as a consequence of rivals' increased action. For example, if duopoly firms choose quantities and the goods are substitutes in consumption, the best-response functions are (typically) negatively sloped: a higher output by a firm lowers its rival's marginal revenue curve, making it optimal for its rival to produce less.[13] In this quantity-setting game, actions are strategic substitutes. If firms choose prices, the best-response functions are typically positively sloped: if a firm raises its price, its rival's marginal revenue curve shifts up, making it optimal for the rival to charge a higher price. In this price-setting game, actions are strategic complements.

The best-response function in static games determines how a firm would want to respond to an arbitrary action by its rival if it were able to make such a response. However, the assumption of simultaneous moves precludes the ability to actually respond. In contrast, when firms use Markov strategies in a dynamic game, they are able to respond to their rivals' actions, although they respond in later periods. This difference between static and dynamic games causes the meaning of strategic substitutability and complementarity to differ across the two types of games. In a static setting, the distinction turns on the direction of the desired contemporaneous response to a rival's action, whereas in a dynamic game the distinction turns on the actual future response to a rival's action. The actual future response depends on how a firm's current action changes the state variable in the next period, and how this change alters the rival's decision in the subsequent period.

Consider the continuous time sticky price model. At the steady state, where $Q = Q_\infty$ and $p = p_\infty = P(Q_\infty)$, a small deviation from equilibrium by one firm

[13] Let $\pi(q_1, q_2) = p(q_1, q_2)q_1 - c(q_1)$ be Firm 1's profit function in the static duopoly, where $p(q_1, q_2)$ is Firm 1's inverse demand function. Assuming that π is concave in q_1, Firm 1's best-response function is downward sloping if and only if $\pi_{q_1 q_2} \equiv p_{q_1 q_2}(q_1, q_2)q_1 + p_{q_2}(q_1, q_2) < 0$.

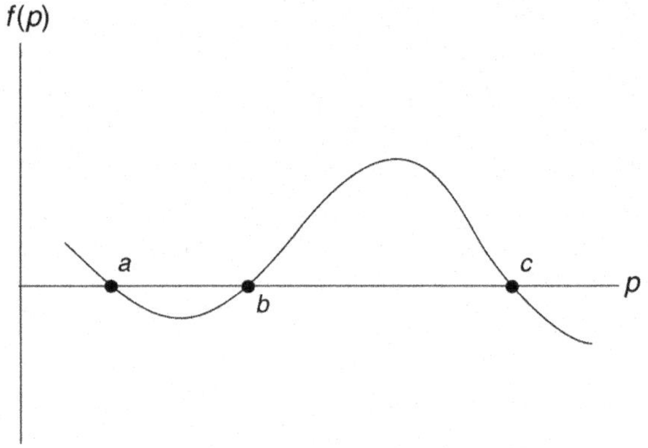

Figure 6.1. Graph of $f(p)$.

causes the price to change by $\alpha[dP(Q)/dQ]$, evaluated at $Q = Q_\infty$. This change in price induces the other firm to change its level of sales in "the next instant" by $\alpha[dP(Q_\infty)/dQ]m_\infty$. If this expression is negative (respectively, positive), the actions are strategic substitutes (respectively, complements). Because $\alpha P'(Q) < 0$, for actions to be strategic substitutes, it is necessary that $m(p_\infty) > 0$.

When we substitute the equilibrium control rule into the equation of motion, we obtain an equation for $\dot{p}$ that depends on the current price: $\dot{p} = \alpha f(p)$, with $f(p) \equiv P(Q(p)) - p$. Asymptotic stability of the steady state requires that the graph of $\alpha f(p)$ has a negative slope at the steady state. Given that $\alpha > 0$, this condition requires that $f'(p) < 0$ evaluated at the steady state. This inequality is equivalent to

$$\frac{d[(Q(p)) - p]}{dp} = P'(Q)\frac{dQ}{dp} - 1 = 2P'(Q)\,m(p) - 1 < 0. \tag{6.13}$$

Figure 6.1 graphs the function $f(p)$ for a case in which $f(p) = 0$ has three roots, denoted a, b, and c. Each of these prices is a steady state, but only points a and c are asymptotically stable. Consider a region slightly below point a or point c. In such a region, price is increasing, so the price moves toward the steady state (a or c). Similarly, in a region slightly above either point, price decreases toward the steady state. Thus, both the points a and c are asymptotically stable in this example. In contrast, at any point close to but not exactly equal to point b, the price moves away from point b so this steady state is unstable. The second equality in Equation (6.13) uses the assumption that there is a symmetric equilibrium with two firms, so $dQ(p)/dp = d[2q(p)]/dp = 2m(p)$. Thus, in a duopoly market, stability implies only that $P'(Q)\,m(p) < 0.5$, evaluated at the steady state. Stability is not sufficient to establish that actions are strategic substitutes in this game.

A sufficient condition for actions to be strategic substitutes is that $m(p_\infty) > 0$. If this equality holds, a higher output in the current period lowers future price, lowering the rival's future equilibrium output. Here, the Markov behavior gives a firm an incentive to produce that is absent under the open-loop assumption: lower future sales by the rival. This benefit to the firm is absent under the open-loop equilibrium, in which firms assume that rivals do not respond to changes in the state. Consequently, equilibrium sales tend to be higher in a (Nash) MPE, and the equilibrium price lower, relative to an open-loop equilibrium.

In the example with quasi-fixed inputs, investment is less attractive for a firm that faces a rival with large capital stocks (assuming $\partial^2\pi_i/\partial K_i\partial K_j < 0$). At least in the linear equilibrium to the linear-quadratic game, the equilibrium investment rule is decreasing in the rival's capital stock. Here, a firm has an incentive to invest more for a given level of capital, in order to make it less attractive for its rival to invest in the future. Again, actions are strategic substitutes. Steady-state equilibrium investment is higher (and profits are lower) in the linear MPE than in the open-loop equilibrium. The Markov Nash equilibrium is more competitive (less collusive) than the open-loop equilibrium. In a game in which actions are strategic complements, this comparison is reversed.

For the linear equilibrium to the linear-quadratic game, it is possible to determine whether actions are strategic substitutes or complements by explicitly solving for the equilibrium. However, as our calculations with the sticky price model illustrate, the necessary conditions for a steady-state, stable equilibrium typically do not enable us to determine whether actions are strategic substitutes or complements in a more general setting.

For purposes of theory, the qualitative differences among outcomes under different equilibria is important. For empirical purposes, the quantitative difference may matter more. We return to this topic in Chapter 8.

MARKOV PERFECT EQUILIBRIA AND CONJECTURAL VARIATIONS

As we noted earlier, we can index members of the family of differentiable MPE by the parameter m_∞. The value of this parameter pins down the steady-state price using Equations (6.11) and (6.12), and thus determines the steady-state sales of each firm in the symmetric equilibrium. This steady state, together with the other necessary conditions, determines the equilibrium control rule and the equilibrium trajectory. The parameter m_∞ is the equilibrium response of either firm to a movement of the state variable away from its steady-state value. This equilibrium response is identical to the response that rivals anticipate. That is, because firms know each other's equilibrium decision rule, m_∞ is equal to a firm's belief about its rival's response to a change in the steady-state value of the state.

In the late 1970s, economists attempted to append dynamics to a static game by adding a conjectural variation parameter. If viewed literally, this parameter describes how a firm thinks that its rival would respond if the firm were to change its own decision. As we described in Chapter 3, many econometric studies use the relation between the conjectural variations parameter and the index of market power.

Changes in the value of the conjectural variations parameter cause the equilibrium outcome to vary from the cartel to the competitive outcome. The conjectural variation is said to be *consistent* if the value of the conjectural variations parameter equals the optimal response of the rival (Bresnahan 1981b and Kamien and Schwartz 1983): a firm's beliefs are correct in equilibrium. However, the requirement of consistency does not, in general, select a unique conjectural variations parameter without additional assumptions. One such assumption is that Firm i believes that its rival's decision is linear in its (Firm i's) output: the rival's response is of the form $q_j = \alpha + \beta q_i$. Here, Firm i's conjectural variation parameter, β, is a constant. The assumption of linear conjectures, together with the requirement of consistency, typically result in a unique value of α and β and a unique equilibrium output. The main rationale for the assumption of linearity is its simplicity.

Conjectural variation models were introduced because they added an element of dynamics that seemed to make the model more descriptive of how firms behave. The requirement that conjectures be consistent is compatible with economists' conception of firms' rationality. However, the consistency requirement, without further *ad hoc* restrictions, did not produce a unique equilibrium. One response to this was that the conjectural variations model was doomed because it added dynamics in an *ad hoc* manner; it was necessary to introduce dynamics into the primitives of the game – the economic environment.

The kinds of dynamic games studied in this chapter attempt to do exactly that. The value of m_∞ in a MPE is analogous to a consistent conjectural variations parameter in a static model. However, we have seen that even if we require subgame perfections and also assume that firms use strategies that are differentiable in the directly payoff-relevant state variable – that is, we assume differentiable Markov Perfect rules – non-uniqueness survives, albeit in a more subtle form.

The reasons for the non-uniqueness in the static conjectural variations equilibrium and in the dynamic MPE are similar. In the sticky price model, the value of $\alpha\ [\mathrm{d}P(Q_\infty)/\mathrm{d}Q]\ m_\infty$ can be interpreted as a consistent conjectural variation in that it represents Firm i's belief of the first-order effect on its rival's decision, of Firm i's departure from equilibrium. The Markov Perfect equilibrium conditions do not pin down the value of this consistent conjectural variation unless we make additional assumptions.

EMPIRICAL IMPLICATIONS

The most important empirical implication of this last section is that assumptions about the type of equilibrium may not be enough to identify a specific outcome and the exact game/strategy played. Even if we knew the decision variable that firms use (such as investment or output) and we knew that they play noncooperatively and we were also willing to assume a particular type of equilibrium (such as differentiable MPE), we should not expect to be able to predict the exact equilibrium decision rule or the exact outcome. Consequently, when we observe only a particular realization (a time-series) of the equilibrium outcome – corresponding to a particular realization of the exogenous random variables – we confront a formidable problem in trying to determine the game that firms are playing.

For example, suppose that we assume the equilibrium is symmetric and we are able to observe, with some noise, aggregate output in the neighborhood of the steady state. There is (in many cases of interest) a unique competitive and a unique collusive steady state, but as we have emphasized, there is typically a continuum of locally stable differentiable MPE steady states. (If we drop the assumption of differentiability, we obtain still more equilibria.) Some of these may be close to the competitive or the collusive steady state, making it difficult to use noisy observations to distinguish between noncooperative play and competition or collusion. Further, given the range of possible noncooperative equilibria, it might not be informative to conclude that the equilibrium is noncooperative. It may be more useful to measure how close the particular noncooperative equilibrium is to collusion or to perfect competition.

This multiplicity of equilibria, coupled with technical problems associated with estimating dynamic models, provides a rationale for using summary measures in empirical work or using simple equilibrium concepts such as open-loop. Just as with static games, it may be impossible to determine whether firms are explicitly cooperating, or whether they are using noncooperative strategies, the outcome of which is similar to the cooperative outcome. The distinction between these two possibilities may be essential for antitrust analysis, but irrelevant for policy analysis. Instead, we may attempt to measure the extent to which the observed outcome is consistent with a particular type of cooperation, or a particular type of noncooperation. Economic models typically make a sharp distinction between cooperative and noncooperative behavior. Social interactions, including those mediated by markets, often lie on a continuum strictly between the two extremes of cooperation and noncooperation.

This observation motivates the material in the next chapter that emphasizes estimation of open-loop models. The simplicity of the open-loop equilibrium together with the posibility of nesting a family of necessary conditions (corresponding to different open-loop equilibria) are arguments for using it. The complexity that arises in estimating Markov strategies, due to multiple MPE, strengthens the appeal of trying to estimate an open-loop equilibrium. We made a similar point in Chapter 5, in which we suggested that the multiplicity of subgame perfect equilibria in supergames provides a rationale for using a static model with an index of market structure for empirical purposes.

By imbedding a market structure parameter in an empirical model that assumes that strategies are open-loop, we can estimate an index of market power. For particular values of this index, corresponding to perfectly competitive or collusive markets, this open-loop equilibrium and the MPE are identical. For other values of the index, we have a simple measure of the departure from competition or collusion.

The major disadvantage of the open-loop model is that it credits firms with "too little" rationality. The major disadvantage of the Markov Perfect assumption is the difficulty of estimating the model. The lack of uniqueness of Markov equilibria may not be a major drawback if one is interested primarily in estimating the parameters of the primitive functions or the parameters that describe the industry's structure (collusive, noncooperative, or competitive). The estimation identifies the parameters of the equilibrium that actually occurs. However, the lack of uniqueness may be a more important problem if the objective is to use the estimated parameters to estimate the effect of a change in regulatory policy. The difficulty is that the change in policy may cause a different type of equilibrium to arise.

The second empirical implication concerns the possibility that firms' degree of cooperation varies over different decision variables. Even if the econometrician were able to estimate accurately the degree of cooperation with respect to a particular variable, the welfare conclusions might be ambiguous. For example, correctly identifying that firms cooperate with respect to a decision that is made at frequent intervals (such as advertising, or the choice of a variable input) does not necessarily mean that this cooperation benefits firms or harms consumers if the firms do not cooperate with respect to a different decision variable. More generally, when firms choose two or more decision variables, cooperative behavior with respect to only one variable has ambiguous effects on both industry profits and social welfare.

This possibility is simply an illustration of the theory of the second best. From the standpoint of the firms, the first best requires collusion with regard to both the static and dynamic decision variables. When firms compete over both types of variables, there are two "distortions" – two sources of departure from the optimality conditions for maximizing industry profits. The removal of one of these "distortions" might either raise or lower industry profits, as the theory of the second best describes. From the standpoint of social welfare, the first best requires that firms exercise no market power. If firms behave noncooperatively with respect to both types of decision variables, there are two sources of departure from the optimality conditions that maximize social welfare: the two "distortions." Increased collusion with respect to one decision variable magnifies one distortion, but for reasons familiar from the theory of the second best, this change might either increase or decrease social welfare.

When firms' degree of cooperation differs over various variables, the econometrician who tries to estimate the degree of cooperation with respect to a particular variable may obtain biased estimates of the extent of that cooperation. Consider again the example of quasi-fixed inputs. If the econometrician assumes noncooperative behavior with respect to the static decision (the choice of a variable input within a period) but firms actually cooperate with respect to that variable, the econometrician obtains biased estimates of the parameters of the restricted profit function. The equilibrium decision rule for investment depends both on the extent of cooperation with respect to that variable, and on the actual restricted profit function. Biased estimates of the restricted profit function may lead to a biased estimate of the degree of cooperation with respect to investment.

In principle, it would be possible to estimate an index of cooperation with respect to a static decision, using the methods described in previous chapters. This index could be used to construct the restricted profit function. Using this function and assumptions about the investment cost function, it would be possible to estimate an index of cooperation with respect to the dynamic decision, using methods discussed in later chapters. This estimation problem would be formidable. It would require time-series data on the static and dynamic decisions, input costs, and demand-side variables, and (ideally) information that could be used to estimate the nonconvex investment costs. The resulting estimates of cooperation would still be vulnerable to the criticism that the indices are *ad hoc* – the same criticism made against these indices in simpler settings.

A third empirical issue arises if we try to determine whether firms use open-loop or a Markov Perfect (or some other feedback) strategy. In order to distinguish between these two, it might seem reasonable to estimate which variables are significant in firms' decision rules. The open-loop decision rule is a function of the *initial* state variable and calendar time, whereas the MPE rule is a function of the *current* state variable. One estimation strategy is to see which of these two possibilities is more nearly consistent with the data. To conduct such a test, we could run separate regressions of the firms' decision rules, using different regressors, and compare the results using a non-nested hypothesis test.

An apparent problem with this procedure is that the econometrician has no way of knowing the initial state. There is, for example, no reason to suppose that the first period of a time series coincides with the first period of the game. Luckily, this problem is not important because the initial state (whatever its value) is a constant for the game. The initial state can therefore be subsumed in the constant term in a regression.

A more subtle but more serious problem makes this estimation procedure of doubtful value. The problem with it is that it may not test what it is intended to test because the open-loop model conflates two hypotheses. The first of these is the hypothesis that firms take their rivals' future decisions as exogenous. That is, each firm acts as if rivals will not respond in the future to the firm's actions that affect the endogenous state variable. In the first example, this hypothesis implies that each firm thinks that its rivals will not respond to a change in the firm's capital stock (a change caused by current investment). In the second example, the hypothesis implies that each firm thinks that its rivals will not respond to a change in the price (a change caused by the firm's current output). This hypothesis is the one that we want to test. The second hypothesis contained in the open-loop model is that firms do not respond (and do not expect to respond) to new information about *any* state variable.

These two hypotheses might seem to be essentially the same, but this appearance arises because in discussing the dynamic model we suppressed the exogenous state variables (demand and cost shifters) in order to emphasize the strategic difference between open-loop and Markov equilibria. Any empirical model has to include exogenous state variables that are likely to evolve randomly. If firms have even a modest degree of rationality, they take into account their current information on all state variables (including both exogenous demand and cost shifters and endogenous variables such as levels of quasi-fixed capital) when choosing their current decision. Attributing this degree of rationality to firms does not, however, imply that they take into account the effect of their current actions on their rivals' future decisions (as in a MPE). To emphasize the difference between these two different degrees of rationality, we need to consider the meaning of "open-loop" in a stochastic setting.

DIFFERENT WAYS TO INTERPRET OPEN-LOOP EQUILIBRIUM

There is an obvious difference between the following two claims: (1) Firms do not think their current actions influence their rivals' future actions; and (2) Firms do not expect to change their own decisions when they receive new information in the future. In a *deterministic* setting, in the open-loop equilibrium firms do not receive any new information. In a deterministic setting, we make only the first claim in assuming that firms use open-loop strategies; there is no ambiguity. In contrast, in a stochastic setting – most empirically interesting settings – we have to be clear about which of these claims we have in mind when we adopt the open-loop assumption.

There is room for confusion here because game theorists imported the term *open-loop* from optimal control theory. The meaning of the term is not exactly the same in the two settings. Game theorists have in mind Claim (1) when adopting the open-loop assumption. Further, the term was imported principally to be used in a deterministic setting. In contrast, in the optimal control setting, Claim (1) is uninteresting (because there are no rival controllers in a one-agent problem); the open-loop assumption is interesting only if the environment is stochastic.

For the purpose of studying *empirical* dynamic oligopolies, we have to decide whether the open-loop assumption means one or both of these two claims. It certainly means the first claim because that is what game-theorists have in mind when they use the term. In most contexts – including this book – it *does not* mean the second claim; that claim is tangential to the strategic feature of equilibrium. Thus, in a stochastic setting, when we say that firms use open-loop policies, we mean that they think that rivals will not respond in the future to their actions in the current period. In general, firms may or may not understand that their own future actions will be conditioned on future information, but (we assume) they do condition their current action on current information.[14]

[14] In a one-agent stochastic control problem, a decision rule is said to be "open-loop" if all decisions are conditioned only on information available at the initial time. The decision-rule is "open-loop with revision" if the decision maker at time *t* conditions the time *t* decision on

This assumption (our interpretation of the meaning of "open-loop" in a stochastic setting) means that the firms' decision rules have the same arguments in both the open-loop and the MPE. Therefore, even with a perfect set of observed data, the economist (econometrician) has no possibility of distinguishing between the two equilibria simply by determining which variables belong in a regression in which the dependent variable is the firm's decision.

Our interpretation of the meaning of *open-loop* makes it possible to estimate an index of market power in an open-loop setting using a variety of methods, as described in the next chapter. There, we assume that firms *do* understand that their future policies will be conditioned on their future information – the opposite of Claim (2). Consequently, we can estimate the market structure by estimating an Euler equation or by solving a stochastic dynamic programming problem, as the next chapter illustrates.

SUMMARY

This chapter reviewed elements of the theory of dynamic games that are important in understanding how to estimate dynamic game models. We pointed out that, with history-dependent strategies, there is typically a multiplicity of equilibria, for essentially the same reason as in repeated games. Most applications of dynamic games assume that agents use either open-loop or Markov decision rules.

Open-loop Nash equilibrium rules are time consistent, but typically not subgame perfect. (In contrast, open-loop Stackelberg equilibrium rules are typically not even time-consistent.) With open-loop strategies, we can nest a family of equilibria – including competitive, noncooperative Nash, and collusive equilibria – by means of a market performance parameter or one of the other devices used in static models.

Under the Markov model, it is possible to construct equilibria that are supported by credible threats, as in repeated games. The restriction to strategies that are continuous in the state eliminates these kinds of equilibria. However, there (typically) exists a continuum of MPE, even with the added restriction that the strategies are differentiable. This multiplicity is due to the *incomplete transversality condition* or the lack of a natural boundary condition. It is analogous to the multiplicity of *consistent conjectural equilibria* in static games. Markov steady-state equilibria may be more or less competitive than the corresponding open-loop equilibrium depending on whether actions are strategic substitutes or complements.

The possibility that a continuum of MPE exists makes it more difficult for the observer to distinguish between noncooperative outcomes and either competitive

information available at time t, but acts as if all future decisions are also conditioned only on information available at time t. With a "feedback" decision rule, the decision maker at time t conditions information at time t on current information, and understands that all future decisions will be conditioned on information that become available in the future.

or collusive outcomes. Therefore, there is a higher level of uncertainty associated with one's claim that a particular equilibrium is noncooperative. Econometricians, in that case, may want to use an index that measures how close the observed outcome is to the competitive or collusive outcome.

PROBLEMS

Note: Answers to problems are available at the back of the book.

6.1 This question illustrates that limited cooperation may reduce the industry's profits. The example uses two games, both of which contain two stages. The two games differ only in the *assumed* behavior in the second stage. This difference leads to different *equilibrium* first-stage behavior. In the first game, firms are assumed to behave cooperatively in the second stage, and noncooperatively in the first stage, representing "partial cooperation." In the second game, firms behave noncooperatively in both stages; that is, there is no cooperation. In the first stage of each of the two games, the two firms simultaneously decide whether to make an investment, costing x, that reduces their production costs. (Firms are identical prior to their investment decision.) In the second stage, firms choose output levels. Firms sell a homogeneous product. If the firm takes action I, it invests; and if it takes action N, it does not invest.

In the first game (partial cooperation), firms choose output levels in the second stage to maximize industry profits. The payoff matrix depends on the first-period investment decisions, given that firms cooperate in the second stage to maximize joint profits.

Payoffs in the First Game (Partially Cooperative)

		Firm 1	
		I	N
Firm 2	I	$20-x$ (top right) $20-x$ (bottom left)	0 (top right) $40-x$ (bottom left)
	N	$40-x$ (top right) 0 (bottom left)	15 (top right) 15 (bottom left)

In each cell, the bottom left payoff shows what Firm 2 earns and the top right payoff is Firm 1's earnings. For example, if both firms invest and there is cooperation in the second stage, each firm obtains a second-stage payoff of 20 and incurs a first-stage cost of x, for a payoff of $20 - x$. As noted in the text, the second-stage payoff can be interpreted as the present discounted value of all future payoffs, which depend on first-period investment decisions.

In the second game, firms choose output levels noncooperatively in the second stage. Again, their payoffs depend on their first-stage investment decisions.

Payoffs in the Second Game (Noncooperative in Both Stages)

		Firm 1	
		I	*N*
Firm 2	*I*	15− x $15-x$	4 $30-x$
	N	30− x 4	12 12

a) What assumption about production costs leads to the payoff structure in the partially cooperative game? (Hint: notice that the *second-stage* industry profits are the same regardless of whether one firm or both firms invest in the first period.)

b) For each game, obtain the (expected) payoff in a symmetric equilibrium as a function of x. Note that for some range of x there is a unique pure strategy equilibrium, and for some range there is a unique mixed strategy equilibrium (see Chapter 9 for a brief review of mixed strategies). For the case of the mixed strategy equilibrium, you need to find the mixed strategy as a function of x, and then use this mixed strategy to calculate a firm's expected equilibrium payoff.

c) For what values of x does second-stage cooperation lead to a lower (expected) payoff, compared with second-stage noncooperation? Provide the economic explanation for this result.

d) Describe a "reasonable" outcome if firms are able to cooperate on both the investment and the output decision.

6.2 This question uses a two-period model to show that a time-consistent open-loop equilibrium is not necessarily subgame perfect. Firm 1 can choose U or D in each of the two periods. Firm 2 chooses U or D in the first period, and does not move in the second period. Consider two versions of this game, which differ depending on when the decisions are made. These two games have different equilibria.

The following game tree shows the extensive form of the game under the assumption that firms simultaneously choose their first-period actions, and Firm 1 chooses its second-period action knowing which first-period actions both firms chose.

A firm's "information set" is the information that the firm has when making its decision. In the initial period, each firm's information set consists of the possible moves and the resulting payoffs. Because firms move simultaneously in the first period, a firm does not know its rival's first-period action when it chooses its own first-period action: neither firm's first-period information set contains the rival's move in that period. Firm 2 does not move in the second period. When Firm 1 moves in the second period, it knows its own and its rival's first-period actions, so these actions are in Firm 1's information set in the second period.

The first number beneath each node in the game tree identifies the firm (1 or 2). The second number is identifies the information set. Because both firms have the same information at the beginning of the game, the second number in the first three nodes is the same (a "1"). The second firm's information is the same regardless of whether the first firm moves *U* or *D*. To emphasize this point, the game tree shows dotted lines between the two nodes labeled 2:1. In the second period, Firm 1 has different information, depending on the first-stage actions. The first and second numbers after the final nodes in the tree represent the payoffs to Firms 1 and 2, respectively. For example, if both firms play *U* in the first period and Firm 1 plays *D* in the second period, Firm 1 obtains a payoff of zero and Firm 2 obtains a payoff of six.

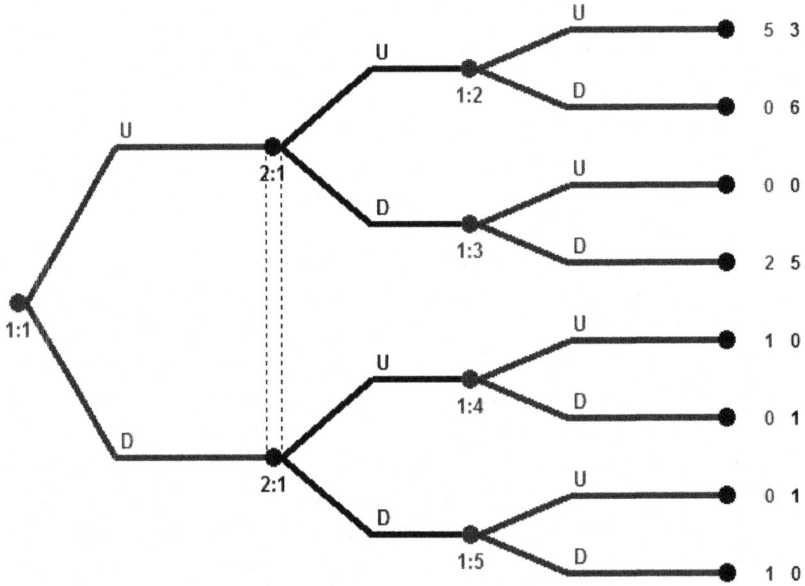

Working backward, find the subgame perfect equilibrium to this game by finding the optimal second-period action for Firm 1, conditional on each possible subgame (i.e., each second-period node of the game tree). There are four subgames, each corresponding to a different combination of first-period actions. Use this information to find the equilibrium payoff corresponding to each possible subgame. Use those payoffs to find the equilibrium first-period actions for the two firms, and the resulting equilibrium payoffs. Note that this subgame-perfect equilibrium is unique.

Next, consider the open-loop equilibrium corresponding to the payoffs in the game tree. In the open-loop equilibrium, firms choose their trajectories of actions simultaneously in the first period. Firm 1 has a period 1 and 2 action, so this firm has four possible trajectories: *UU*, *UD*, *DU*, and *DD*. (For example, *UD* means that Firm 1 chooses *U* in the first stage and *D* in the second stage.) Firm 2 moves only in period 1, so it has only two possible "trajectories": *U* or *D*. Find the equilibrium to this game. Confirm that it is time-consistent. In other words, if both firms play their equilibrium first-period action, Firm 1 has no incentive to deviate from the second-period (open-loop) equilibrium action.

Comment: the open-loop equilibrium is different from the subgame perfect equilibrium. Because the subgame perfect equilibrium is unique, the open-loop equilibrium is not subgame perfect (even though, in this example, it is time-consistent).

6.3 This problem shows how to obtain the unique steady state in a symmetric open-loop equilibrium, and the set of states that are candidates for a symmetric differentiable MPE. These are "candidate" steady states because they satisfy the *necessary* equilibrium conditions, including asymptotic stability.[15]

Suppose that steady state inverse demand is linear in quantity: $P(Q) = 1 - Q$. If a firm produces at rate q, its instantaneous cost of production is $\frac{q^2}{2}$, so the firm's flow of profits is

$$\pi = pq - \frac{q^2}{2}.$$

The rest of this problem uses the notation for the sticky price model in the text.

a) Write (each) firm's equilibrium sales as $q(p)$. Find a differential equation, of the form $dq/dp = q'(p) = m(p) = g(q, p)$, that the equilibrium control rule must satisfy. That is, obtain an explicit expression for the function $g(p)$. To obtain this equation, proceed as follows: Use the linear inverse demand in the first-order condition, Equation (6.8). Solve this equation for the costate variable μ and differentiate the result with respect to time, to obtain an equation for $\dot{\mu}$. Use this equation, Equation (6.9), and your expression for μ to obtain the function $g(q, p)$. Then use the notation $\nu = \alpha/r$ to write g as a function of ν.

[15] A more challenging problem – not considered here – is to confirm that a candidate satisfies sufficient conditions. A partial solution to this problem involves finding a particular candidate that can be shown to satisfy sufficient conditions, and then using continuity to show that neighboring candidates also satisfy sufficiency, at least for some region of the state space.

b) Find the set of candidate steady states (an interval of p) in a differentiable MPE. To find this set, proceed as follows: in a MPE, Equation (6.5) implies

$$\dot{p} = \alpha \left(1 - 2q(p) - p\right),$$

so $(1 - p)/2 = q$ at a steady state. Because $\alpha > 0$, asymptotic stability requires that

$$-2q'(p) - 1 = -2m - 1 < 0,$$

so $m > -1/2$ at an asymptotically stable steady state, defined in the text. Using the notation from part (a), and the steady-state condition, this stability condition can be written:

$$m = g(p, q) = g\left(p, \frac{1-p}{2}\right) > -0.5.$$

To complete the answer, find the interval of p for which the last inequality is satisfied.

c) What happens to the interval of candidate steady states as v approaches the limiting values of zero and infinity? What is the economic explanation of this result?

d) Find the unique open-loop steady state. You can start from "first principles" by using the open-loop necessary conditions, Equations (6.8) and (6.9), with $dq/dp = 0$. Alternatively, you can use the steady-state condition obtained in part (b) of this question, and set $m = 0$. (Because $m = 0$ for all p in the open-loop equilibrium, this equality must also hold at the steady state.) Write the open-loop steady state as a function of v and compare that to the set of candidate steady states in the MPE. What is the economic explanation for this comparison?

SEVEN

Estimation of Dynamic Games Involving Economic Fundamentals

The previous chapter explained the difference between open-loop and Markov Perfect equilibria. The Markov Perfect equilibrium assumes that firms are rational, insofar as they expect their rivals to respond to changes in the state variable; the equilibrium is subgame perfect. In contrast, the open-loop equilibrium is (in most cases) not subgame perfect. For this reason, the Markov Perfect equilibrium is more consistent with the standard assumption of firms' rationality. However, the open-loop equilibrium is easier to estimate. We start by showing how to estimate open-loop equilibria using two examples of discrete-time, dynamic games with different types of data and objectives. We then briefly discuss an estimation approach when firms use Markov Perfect strategies.

OVERVIEW OF TWO EXAMPLES

The first of our two discrete-time examples, the *sticky price model*, shows how to estimate an index of market power in a dynamic setting when the econometrician has only industry-level (rather than firm) data. The market power ("conjectural variation") parameter nests a family of equilibria, including the leading cases of competition, cartel, and symmetric Cournot.

The second example, which is based on Roberts and Samuelson (1988) – the *RS model*, includes the open-loop equilibrium as a special case. In this example, the econometrician has firm-level data. Because the econometrician assumes that firms behave noncooperatively, rather than estimate an index of market structure, the econometrician is interested in estimating a particular feature of the noncooperative behavior and the implication of that behavior.

We use the first example to explain how to estimate a simple dynamic oligopoly model. We simplify the problem by using a market structure parameter and the open-loop assumption, which eliminates dynamic strategic considerations. Thus, the remaining complications are associated with the dynamics of the model rather than the oligopoly setting.

As with the static market structure or conjectural variations models, we make no pretense of identifying the "true game" that firms play. The goal is to estimate an index that measures the extent to which the observed outcome is closer to one or another of the leading equilibria. A literal interpretation of this parameter is that it represents a firm's belief concerning rivals' response in the same period. This literal interpretation is not consistent with the assumption that firms move simultaneously within a period. In a static game, the conjectural variations model might be defended as an *ad hoc* means of incorporating dynamics. That interpretation is clearly not appropriate here, where dynamics are an explicit part of the model. The parameter is only an index of the degree of collusion or market structure.

In Chapter 6, we used a static model to show that it is possible to obtain the leading symmetric equilibria in three ways: by using an optimization problem based on firms' profits and having a conjectural variation with respect to aggregate output; by using a single-agent optimization problem that involves a single-period objective equal to industry profits and a conjectural variation with respect to the price; or by solving a fictitious optimization problem (with no conjectural variations parameter). In a (simultaneous move) static model, a firm makes all of its decisions at a single point in time: at a single information set. In an open-loop equilibrium to a dynamic game, it is as if firms choose their entire trajectory of future actions at the initial time – that is, at a single information set. Therefore, the open-loop assumption renders the dynamic game "strategically static": firms have no incentive to use current decisions to influence future state variables as means of influencing their rivals' future actions. This feature makes it possible to find symmetric equilibria using the same three methods, listed above, as in the static game.

The second example is an oligopoly model in which the dynamics arise because firms' advertising affects the stock of goodwill, which affects total market demand and firms' market share. If firms take their rivals' sequence of future advertising levels as given, the equilibrium is open-loop; if firms recognize that rivals' future advertising will respond to changes in the state variable (the stock of goodwill), the equilibrium is Markovian.

We first derive the estimation equation under the open-loop assumption, and then under the Markov Perfect assumption. By comparing these equations, we illustrate why the Markov model is more difficult to estimate. We then describe Roberts and Samuelson's approach, which allows firms to recognize that rivals might respond to changes in the stock in only the next period.[1] In addition, the

[1] In general, a change in the state variable in the next period causes changes in the values of the state variable in subsequent periods. In a Markov equilibrium, the latter changes cause changes in the equilibrium control rules in subsequent periods. In the RS model, firms ignore those future changes in the control rules (beyond the next period).

firm's conjecture about its rivals' response is not constrained to equal the rivals' equilibrium response. This equilibrium is a hybrid because it includes the open-loop equilibrium as a special case, and it has a flavor of the Markov equilibrium.

Roberts and Samuelson (RS) use firm-level data. They are interested in two empirical questions: (1) Do firms recognize that their current actions affect rivals' decisions in the next period? (2) Is the primary effect of a firm's advertising to enlarge the total market or to increase that firm's market share? RS assume that the equilibrium is Nash in advertising. In contrast, our sticky price model assumes that the econometrician has only industry-level data, and the empirical question is whether the industry behaves competitively or collusively. We do not assume that the observed outcome is a particular price-setting or quantity-setting Nash equilibrium. The differences in the data, the empirical questions, and the assumptions distinguish the different modeling approaches. The difference in the source of dynamics – sticky prices in one case and durable stocks of goodwill in the other – is incidental.

A market power or conjectural variations parameter appears in both models, but because of the differences in the data, assumptions, and empirical questions, this parameter takes a different form and serves a different function in the two models. In the RS model, the parameter measures a firm's belief about its rivals' response in the next period. This literal interpretation is consistent with the assumption that firms move simultaneously within a period. The magnitude and statistical significance of the parameter shed light on whether firms are rational, in the sense that they understand that rivals will respond to changes in the stock of goodwill.

THE STICKY PRICE MODEL

The demand function in period t is

$$p_t = \alpha_{0t} + \alpha_{1t} Q_t + \alpha_{2t} p_{t-1} + \alpha_{3t} Q_{t-1} + \varepsilon_t, \tag{7.1}$$

where ε_t is a demand shock at period t with mean zero and a constant variance. (If $\alpha_{2t} \equiv \alpha_{3t} \equiv 0$, the model is static.) The coefficients in Equation (7.1) are functions of $\mathbf{z}_t$, a vector of exogenous, possibly stochastic, demand shifters: $\alpha_{it} \equiv \alpha_i(\mathbf{z}_t)$, where $i = 0, 1, 2, 3$. This demand function is a discrete-time version of the sticky price model in Chapter 6. The current price depends on lagged price, current and lagged quantity, the exogenous shifters, and the demand shock. The long-run equilibrium price function, which we obtain by equating current and lagged price and equating current and lagged quantity, is

$$p = \frac{1}{1 - \alpha_{2t}} \left[\alpha_{0t} + (\alpha_{1t} + \alpha_{3t}) Q + \varepsilon_t \right].$$

Although the demand function is linear in prices and quantity, its intercept and slope coefficients are general functions of exogenous variables. We consider three specializations of this model:

(1) $\alpha_3(\mathbf{z}) \equiv 0$;
(2) $\alpha_i(\mathbf{z}), i = 1, 2, 3$, are functions of known (non-random) variables, such as time;
(3) $\alpha_i, i = 1, 2, 3$ are constants.

These three assumptions lead to different estimation equations.

In a symmetric, n-firm equilibrium, the output of a representative firm is $q = Q/n$. This firm's cost function in period t is $C_t \equiv C(q_t, \mathbf{y}_t)$, and its marginal cost is $c_t \equiv c(q_t, \mathbf{y}_t)$, where $\mathbf{y}_t$ is a vector of exogenous cost shifters. The firm's profit in the period is $\pi_t = p_t q_t - C_t$. At time t, the firm knows the value of the current exogenous variables $\mathbf{x}_t \equiv (\mathbf{y}_t, \mathbf{z}_t)$, but we assume that it does not know the current demand shock ε_t, so that Q_t and ε_t are uncorrelated.[2] The firm knows (or has beliefs about) the process that generates the random variables.

There are several types of demand uncertainty in this model beyond the additive demand uncertainty conditional on realizations of the current exogenous variables. Firm (or industry) actions in the current period do not affect the variance of the current price. However, at time t, the firm is uncertain about future partial derivatives of the demand function because (in general) it does not know future values of $\mathbf{z}$. Current actions can affect the mean and the variance of future prices. For example, large sales in the current period lower the current price and thereby affect the lagged price and quantity in the next period. The exact effect on next period's demand function depends on the realization of the demand shifter. The equilibrium quantity in the next period $(t+1)$ depends on next period's demand function, and thus on the price and quantity in the current period (t). This dependence may be affected by the realization of the demand shifters in the next period. The firm does not know the exact future price and quantity or the marginal effects of current actions on these variables or on the variance of the price.

The firm's objective is to maximize the present discounted value of its expected profits, using the discount factor δ:

$$\mathrm{E}_t \sum_{\tau=0}^{\infty} \delta^{\tau} \pi_{t+\tau}.$$

The equilibrium value of the firm's payoff – its value function – is $J(p_{t-1}, Q_{t-1}, \mathbf{x}_t)$. This equilibrium payoff depends on the predetermined endogenous variables

[2] This assumption is incorrect if the firm – but not the econometrician – knows one of the demand shifters. Here, the variable that is omitted from the econometric model is part of the error term, causing it to be correlated with industry output. To estimate Equation (7.1), the econometrician must use an instrumental variables estimator.

(p_{t-1}, Q_{t-1}) and the exogenous vector $\mathbf{x}_t$ of demand and cost shifters. We assume that this vector contains all variables that the firm uses to predict future values of these exogenous variables.

The Dynamic Programming Equation

We want to obtain the estimation equations corresponding to the open-loop equilibria characteristics to a variety of industrial structures, including competitive, cartel, and Cournot, indexed by Λ. As in the static model, we nest different equilibria by assuming that the firm acts as if $dQ/dq_t = \Lambda$, a constant. We obtain the competitive equilibrium if $\Lambda = 0$, the Cournot equilibrium if $\Lambda = 1$, and the cartel equilibrium if $\Lambda = n$. (Because we assume a symmetric equilibrium, we can use the same index for the conjecture with respect to all the firm's rivals' output levels.)

The firm's dynamic programming equation is

$$J(p_{t-1}, Q_{t-1}, \mathbf{x}_t) = \max_{q_t} \mathrm{E}_t \{\pi_t + \delta J(p_t, Q_t, \mathbf{x}_{t+1})\}. \tag{7.2}$$

This equation states that the equilibrium value of the firm's payoff in period t (the value function on the left of the equation) equals the maximized value of the expectation of the sum of current profits, π_t, and the discounted *continuation profits* (the last term in brackets on the right). We use the abbreviations $J_p(t+1) = J_p(p_t, Q_t, \mathbf{x}_{t+1})$ and $J_Q(t+1) = J_Q(p_t, Q_t, \mathbf{x}_t + 1)$ to denote the *shadow values.* The shadow value of a state variable is the partial derivatives of the value function with respect to that state variable. For example, $J_p(t)$ (the shadow value of the state p at time t) equals the expected change in the present discounted value of the firm's payoff due to a small change in the lagged price at time t.

Using the "conjectural variation" $\mathrm{d}Qt/dqt = \Lambda$ and assuming an interior equilibrium, the first-order condition is

$$\mathrm{E}_t\{[p_t - c_t + \alpha_{1t}\Lambda q_t] + \delta\Lambda[J_p(t+1)\alpha_{1t} + J_Q(t+1)]\} = 0. \tag{7.3}$$

This equation states that the expected change in the present discounted value of profit due to a change in current sales is zero at the optimum. This expectation is the sum of the expectation of marginal profit in the current period (the three terms in the first square brackets) plus the discounted expected change in future profits (the terms in the second square bracket, which are multiplied by $\delta\ \Lambda$).

Our objective is to obtain a necessary condition for equilibrium that involves only the *primitive* demand and cost functions and the parameter Λ. That is, we want to eliminate the endogenous (and unknown) shadow values. The resulting equation can be used to estimate the conjectural variations parameter and, if necessary, unknown parameters in the demand and cost function.

Define the equilibrium control rule (the solution to Equation (7.3)) as the function $q^*(p_t, Q_t, \mathbf{x}_{t+1})$. Substitute this function in Equation (7.2) to obtain the maximized dynamic programming equation:

$$J(p_{t-1}, Q_{t-1}, \mathbf{x}_t) = \mathrm{E}_t\{\pi(q^*) + \delta J(p_t, Q_t(q^*), \mathbf{x}_{t+1})\}. \tag{7.4}$$

We take the derivative of both sides of Equation (7.4) with respect to p_{t-1}, Q_{t-1} using the envelope theorem and the open-loop assumption (which states that rivals' controls do not respond to changes in the state variable). We also use the previously stated assumption that α_{2t} and α_{3t} are known at time t; this assumption allows us to pass the expectations operator through these variables. The result is

$$J_p(t) = \alpha_{2t}[q_t + \delta \mathrm{E}_t J_p(t+1)], \tag{7.5}$$

$$J_Q(t) = \alpha_{3t}[q_t + \delta \mathrm{E}_t J_Q(t+1)]. \tag{7.6}$$

Equations (7.5) and (7.6) link the shadow values of an endogenous state over time. For example, Equation (7.5) states that the shadow value of price at time t equals the marginal effect of lagged price on current profit, $\alpha_{2t}q_t$, plus the discounted effect of lagged price on the expectation of the next period shadow value of price, $\delta\alpha_{2t}E_t J_p(t+1)$.

The Euler Equation for a Special Case

We first derive the Euler equation for the simpler case, in which lagged quantity does not affect the current price, $\alpha_{3t} \equiv 0$. This assumption eliminates one channel by which current actions affect the future. The current aggregate sales have no direct effect on the future demand function, although they can still have an indirect effect via the lagged price in the future. For this special case, Equation (7.6) implies that $J_Q(t) \equiv 0$. Given this identity, the lagged value of aggregate quantity has no effect on the firm's expectation of its present discounted flow of profits. This result follows because the lagged quantity has no direct effect on current or future revenues, and the open-loop assumption rules out history-dependent strategies. Thus, given that $\alpha_{3t} \equiv 0$, there is a single endogenous state variable (lagged price) in this model, which greatly simplifies the necessary condition for optimality.

We will need the expression for the shadow value of price at time $t+1$ because this function appears in the necessary condition, Equation (7.3). By advancing Equation (7.5) by one period (replace t with $t+1$) and taking expectations conditional on information at time t, we obtain

$$\mathrm{E}_t J_p(t+1) = \mathrm{E}_t\{\alpha_{2t+1}[q_{t+1} + \delta E_{t+1} J_p(t+2)]\}. \tag{7.7}$$

Using the identity $J_Q(t) \equiv 0$, we can rewrite the first-order condition, Equation (7.3), as

$$-\frac{\mathrm{E}_t p_t - c_t + \alpha_{1t}\Lambda q_t}{\delta\Lambda\alpha_{1t}} = \mathrm{E}_t J_p(t+1). \tag{7.8}$$

Once again, we used the assumption that at time t, the firm knows the exogenous vector $\mathbf{x}_t$, to justify moving the expectations operator. Therefore, we take the expectations in Equation (7.3) only with respect to the current price, p_t, and the shadow value of price in the next period $J_p(t+1)$. The arguments of this value function depend on the value of variables that are unknown at time t. Even if the firm knew the current demand shock – and therefore knew the current price – the function $J_p(t+1)$ would be random because it depends on $\mathbf{x}_{t+1}$, which is unknown at time t.

Combining Equations (7.7) and (7.8), we obtain the Euler equation given that $\alpha_{3t} \equiv 0$:

$$\begin{aligned} &\mathrm{E}_t p_t - c_t + \alpha_{1t}\Lambda q_t - \delta\alpha_{1t}\mathrm{E}_t\left\{\alpha_{2t+1}\left(\frac{p_{t+1} - c_{t+1}}{\alpha_{1t+1}}\right)\right\} \\ &\quad = \mathrm{E}_t p_t - c_t + \alpha_{1t}\Lambda q_t - \delta\alpha_{1t}\mathrm{E}_t\left\{\alpha_{2t+1}\left(\frac{\mathrm{E}_{t+1}\left(p_{t+1} - c_{t+1}\right)}{\alpha_{1t+1}}\right)\right\} = 0. \quad (7.9) \end{aligned}$$

The first equality uses the law of iterated expectations and our assumption that $\mathbf{x}_{t+1}$ is known at time $t+1$. As Λ takes different values, Equation (7.9) produces the necessary conditions for various market structures. For $\Lambda = 0$, it is obvious that

$$\mathrm{E}_s(p_t - c_t) = 0 \quad \text{for all } s \tag{7.10}$$

satisfies Equation (7.9). Equation (7.10) is the necessary condition for the competitive equilibrium: expected price equals marginal cost in each period. For $\Lambda = 1$, Equation (7.9) produces the necessary condition for the Cournot open-loop equilibrium (by construction). Given the assumption that firms are symmetric, a straightforward calculation shows that for $\Lambda = n$, Equation (7.9) produces the necessary condition for the cartel equilibrium.

Other Approaches to Deriving the Euler Equation. Instead of beginning with the representative firm's optimization problem and using the firm's conjectural variations with respect to industry output, we could have used either of the two alternate methods described in Chapter 6. The first alternate method replaces the representative firm's single-period profits, π_t, with a single-period objective function that nests the (1) single-period social welfare (used to obtain the necessary condition for the competitive equilibrium), the (2) aggregate industry profit (used to obtain the necessary condition for cartel equilibrium), and (3) a function that produces the necessary condition for the open-loop Cournot equilibrium.

The second alternate method uses a single-period payoff function equal to the industry's profit, $\pi^I \equiv p_Q - nC(Q/n, y)$, where

$$nC(Q/n, y) \equiv C^I(Q, y; n) \tag{7.11}$$

is the industry's cost function. This method uses a "conjectural variation" parameter, μ, with respect to price rather than output. In this setting, the industry's dynamic optimization problem is solved under the assumption that $\mathrm{d}p_t/\mathrm{d}Q_t = \mu\alpha_{1t}$. For appropriate value of the market structure parameter, we obtain the Euler equation for the competitive ($\mu = 0$), Cournot ($\mu = 1/n$), and cartel ($\mu = 1$) equilibria. For example, if $\mu = 0$, then each firm in the industry acts as a price taker in every period. These actions produce the competitive equilibrium. If $\mu = 1$, the optimization problem requires the maximization of the present discounted value of the industry's profits, using the correct conjecture $\mathrm{d}p_t/\mathrm{d}Q_t = \alpha_{1t}$. The solution to this problem maximizes the industry's profits, and therefore gives the cartel solution. If $\mu = 1/n$, the conjectured marginal single-period industry profits (suppressing the time subscript) is

$$\begin{aligned}\frac{d\pi^I}{dQ} &= \frac{\alpha_1}{n}Q + p - C_Q^I(Q, y; n) = \frac{\alpha_1}{n}Q + p - C_q(q, y)\\ &= \alpha_1 q + p - C_q(q, y).\end{aligned} \tag{7.12}$$

(The second equality in Equation (7.12) uses Equation (7.11) and the third equality uses the assumption of symmetry.) Thus, the conjectured marginal industry profit equals the actual single-firm marginal profits. Consequently, the Euler equation to the industry optimization problem when $\mu = 1/n$ is identical to the Euler equation to the single-firm optimization problem when $\Lambda = 1$; the solution to this Euler equation gives the open-loop symmetric Cournot equilibrium.

More formally, we can begin with the dynamic programming equation for the case in which the single-period payoff is the industry's profit: the industry analog to Equation (7.2). Taking the first-order condition to this problem, using the conjectural parameter μ, and repeating the manipulations that led to Equation (7.9), we obtain an Euler equation that involves the parameter μ rather than Λ and the industry cost function, rather than the firm's cost function. Given our maintained hypothesis that firms are symmetric, the single-firm cost function and the industry cost function contain the same information when n is known.

Thus, the three methods (the procedure that led to Equation (7.9) and the two alternates that we just sketched) all lead to a family of equilibrium conditions that nests the leading (extreme) cases. The econometrician who has input prices and industry input levels can estimate the industry cost function, Equation (7.11), using input demand equations.

The Estimation Model. Our estimation model consists of Equations (7.1) (the demand equation) and (7.9) (the Euler equation). If cost data are available, the input demand system (not shown) and Equation (7.11) comprise a third set of estimation equations.

By assuming that the equilibrium is symmetric and that firms use open-loop strategies and by using an index to nest market structures, we eliminate many of the complexities caused by strategic interactions. The Euler equations that determine the equilibrium in the game have the same structure as the Euler equations for a cartel or a social planner; they differ only in the value of the conjectural variations parameter. Therefore, we can use the methods developed for the nonstrategic models to estimate the Euler equations for the game.

An extensive literature discusses how to estimate Euler equations in nonstrategic settings. Hansen and Singleton (1982) provide one of the early discussions of the application of the method of moments to estimate dynamic models. Many subsequent papers have used this method or variations based on it to estimate Euler equations.

The General Model

The estimation problem is more complicated when the identity $\alpha_{3t} \equiv 0$ does not hold so that the current price depends on lagged aggregate quantity. Here, the lagged quantity affects the present discounted value of future profits, so the identity $J_Q(t+1) \equiv 0$ does not hold. As a consequence, Equation (7.8) is invalid. This more general case illustrates how an apparently small change in a primitive function (in this case, the demand function) complicates the estimation of a dynamic model. As we have eliminated most strategic complications by employing a conjectural variations model together with the open-loop assumption, these additional complications arise because of the dynamics.

We assume that we know the functional forms for the primitive functions, demand and cost. However, we do not know the functional form of the value function, unless we actually solve the optimization problem. Therefore, our objective is to obtain an equilibrium condition that involves the primitive functions and the conjectural variation parameter, but that does not contain the partial derivatives of the value function. By so doing, we can estimate the model without solving the control problem.

To obtain an estimation equation in this more general setting, we begin by advancing Equation (7.6) by one period and taking expectations conditioned on information at time *t*. The result is

$$\mathrm{E}_t J_Q(t+1) = E_t\{\alpha_{3t+1}[q_{t+1} + \delta \mathrm{E}_{t+1} J_p(t+2)]\}. \tag{7.13}$$

We use Equation (7.13) to eliminate $J_Q(t+1)$ from Equation (7.3), thereby obtaining

$$\begin{aligned} \mathrm{E}_t \{ & p_t - c_t + \alpha_{1t}\Lambda q_t + \delta\Lambda[J_p(t+1)\alpha_{1t} \\ & + (\alpha_{3t+1}[q_{t+1} + \delta \mathrm{E}_{t+1} J_p(t+2)])]\} = 0. \end{aligned} \tag{7.14}$$

Our next step is to eliminate $J_p(t+2)$ from Equation (7.14). Rearranging Equation (7.5) and advancing the result one period gives

$$\left(\frac{J_p(t+1)}{\alpha_{2t+1}} - q_{t+1} \right) = \delta \mathrm{E}_{t+1} J_p(t+2). \tag{7.15}$$

Using Equation (7.15) to eliminate $J_p(t+2)$ from Equation (7.14), we obtain

$$\begin{aligned} & \mathrm{E}_t\left[p_t - c_t + \alpha_{1t}\Lambda q_t + \delta\Lambda\left\{J_p(t+1)\left(\alpha_{1t} + \frac{\alpha_{3t+1}}{\alpha_{2t+1}}\right)\right\}\right] \\ & \quad = p_t - c_t + \alpha_{1t}\Lambda q_t + \delta\Lambda \mathrm{E}_t\left\{J_p(t+1)\left(\alpha_{1t} + \frac{\alpha_{3t+1}}{\alpha_{2t+1}}\right)\right\} = 0. \end{aligned} \tag{7.16}$$

The first equality follows from the assumption that current values of α_{it} are known at time t, so we can pass the expectations operator through these variables. However, when the future values of these variables are unknown at time t, the first-order condition involves the expectations of a product of $J_p(t+1)$ and the random variable $\alpha_{3r+1}/\alpha_{2t+1}$, which complicates estimating the Euler equation.

We would like to eliminate the endogenous (unknown) function $J_p(t+1)$ from Equation (7.16) to obtain an estimation equation involving only the primitive functions, as in Equation (7.9). We have two ways of achieving this goal. The first requires an additional assumption concerning the demand function, and the second, and more complicated approach, introduces a numerical computational step into the estimation problem.

An Additional Assumption about Demand. We can use an additional equation in order to eliminate $J_p(t+1)$ from Equation (7.16). Rather than using Equation (7.15) to eliminate $J_p(t+2)$ from Equation (7.14) as we did to obtain Equation (7.16), we can eliminate $J_p(t+1)$ instead. If we eliminate $J_p(t+1)$ from Equation (7.14), we obtain

$$\begin{aligned} & \mathrm{E}_t\left\{p_t - c_t + \alpha_{1t}\Lambda q_t + \delta\Lambda\left(\alpha_{1t}\alpha_{2t+1} + \alpha_{3t+1}\right)q_{t+1}\right\} \\ & \quad + \delta\Lambda \mathrm{E}_t\{\delta\left(\alpha_{1t}\alpha_{2t+1} + \alpha_{3t+1}\right)J_p(t+2)\} = 0. \end{aligned} \tag{7.17}$$

Equations (7.16) and (7.17) involve the shadow values in different periods. If we advance Equation (7.16) by one period and take expectations conditional on information at time t, we obtain an equation involving $J_p\,(t+2)$:

$$\mathrm{E}_t\left\{p_{t+1} - c_{t+1} + \alpha_{1t+1}\Lambda q_{t+1}\right\} + \delta\Lambda \mathrm{E}_t\left\{\left(\alpha_{1t+1} + \frac{\alpha_{3t+2}}{\alpha_{2t+2}}\right)J_p(t+2)\right\} = 0. \tag{7.18}$$

Equations (7.17) and (7.18) both contain $J_p(t+2)$; but, in each equation, this function is multiplied by a different term involving α_{is}, where $s = t+1$ or $s = t+2$. We cannot pass the expectations operator through these terms because they are random at time t. Unless we make additional assumptions, we cannot use these two equations to eliminate the endogenous function $J_p\,(t+2)$ from the estimation equation.

The simplest assumption is that the functions $\alpha_i(\mathbf{z}_t)$, $i = 1, 2, 3$, are not random: The firm knows the evolution of $\alpha_i(\mathbf{z}_t)$, $i = 1, 2, 3$.[3] With this assumption, the only random elements are future values of $\alpha_0(\mathbf{z}_t)$, the current and future additive demand shock, and the cost shifters. Thus, this assumption allows us to pass the expectations operator through the terms involving the demand shifters in Equations (7.17) and (7.18) and to solve for $E_t J_p(t+2)$.

We now turn to the case n which $\alpha_i(\mathbf{z}_t)$, $i = 1, 2, 3$, are nonrandom. Here, we can use Equation (7.18) to obtain

$$-\frac{\mathrm{E}_t\{p_{t+1} - c_{t+1} + \alpha_{1t+1}\Lambda q_{t+1}\}}{\delta\Lambda\left(\alpha_{1t+1} + \dfrac{\alpha_{3t+2}}{\alpha_{2t+2}}\right)} = \mathrm{E}_t\{J_p(t+2)\}.$$

Substituting this expression into Equation (7.17), we find that

$$\begin{aligned}&\mathrm{E}_t\{p_t - c_t + \alpha_{1t}\Lambda q_t + \delta\Lambda(\alpha_{1t}\alpha_{2t+1} + \alpha_{3t+1})q_{t+1}\}\\ &\quad - \delta(\alpha_{1t}\alpha_{2t+1} + \alpha_{3t+1})\alpha_{2t+2}\frac{\mathrm{E}_t\{p_{t+1} - c_{t+1} + \alpha_{1t+1}\Lambda q_{t+1}\}}{(\alpha_{1t+1}\alpha_{2t+2} + \alpha_{3t+2})} = 0. \qquad (7.19)\end{aligned}$$

As a check for the consistency of calculations, we note that, if $\alpha_{3t} \equiv 0$, Equation (7.19) is the same as Equation (7.9).

In summary, if firms regard the demand shifters other than the intercept as nonstochastic, Equation (7.19) is the appropriate Euler equation for estimation. We can estimate this equation using the Method of Moments, together with the demand function (and, if data are available, the cost function).

We have a much simpler Euler equation if the demand slopes are constant over time. This assumption allows only the demand intercept and the cost function to depend on exogenous (and changing) variables. In this case, Equation (7.19) becomes

$$\begin{aligned}&\mathrm{E}_t\{p_t - c_t + \alpha_1\Lambda q_t + \delta\Lambda(\alpha_1\alpha_2 + \alpha_3)q_{t+1}\}\\ &\quad - \delta\alpha_2\mathrm{E}_t\{p_{t+1} - c_{t+1} + \alpha_1\Lambda q_{t+1}\} = 0. \qquad (7.20)\end{aligned}$$

Random Demand Shifters. We now discuss the estimation model when we treat the demand shifters as random, so that $\alpha_i(\mathbf{z}_t)$ is random. In this case, we replace the unknown function in Equation (7.16) with an infinite series. We first solve Equation (7.5) to obtain

$$J_p(t) = \mathrm{E}_t\left\{\sum_{\tau=0}^{\infty}\left(\prod_{s=0}^{\tau}\alpha_{2t+s}\right)\delta^\tau q_{t+\tau}\right\}. \qquad (7.21)$$

[3] An alternate assumption is that the functions $\alpha_i(\mathbf{z}_t)$ are random but orthogonal to $J_p(t+2)$. That assumption would be difficult to defend (except possibly as an approximation): it requires that the cross partial derivative $J_{pz}(\,) \equiv 0$. Because the function J is endogenous, we cannot impose this restriction in a simple manner.

Next, we advance this equation by one period and substitute the result into Equation (7.16) to obtain

$$\mathrm{E}_t\{p_t - c_t + \alpha_{1t}\Lambda q_t\} + \delta\Lambda f(x_t) = 0 \tag{7.22}$$

$$f(\mathbf{x}_t) \equiv \mathrm{E}_t\left\{\left(\sum_{\tau=0}^{\infty}\left(\left(\prod_{s=0}^{\tau}\alpha_{2t+1+s}\right)\delta^{\tau}q_{t+1+\tau}\right)\right)\left(\alpha_{1t}+\frac{\alpha_{3t+1}}{\alpha_{2t+1}}\right)\right\}. \tag{7.23}$$

Equation (7.22) is the Euler equation for this model and Equation (7.23) is a definition. In contrast to the previous Euler Equations (7.9) and (7.19), Equation (7.22) involves the expectation of an infinite number of future exogenous ($\mathbf{x}_t$) and endogenous (q_t) variables. To be able to use this equation to estimate the model, we need to be able to evaluate the function $f(\boldsymbol{x})$ conditional on the parameter estimates. This computation is an example of the kinds of technical complications that arise in estimating dynamic models. The future (random) values of $\alpha_i(\mathbf{z}_t)$ and q_t are correlated, so it would be incorrect to simply replace these functions by their expected values in evaluating the function $f(\boldsymbol{x})$, defined in Equation (7.23).

One method of using Equation (7.21) to estimate industry structure uses the following algorithm:

Step 1: (a) Obtain an estimate of the parameters of $\alpha_i(\mathbf{z}_t)$ by estimating the demand function Equation (7.1). (b) Estimate a time-series model of the process that generates $\mathbf{x}_{t+\tau}$ as a function of $\mathbf{x}_t$. (Recall our assumption that the vector $\mathbf{x}_t$ contains all the variables that the firm uses to predict future values of $\mathbf{x}$.) (c) Estimate the equilibrium control rule $q_t^e = q^e(\mathbf{x}_t)$. (Here we choose the functional form of q^e and estimate the parameters of that function using observations of q_t and $\mathbf{x}_t$.)

Step 2 (The Monte Carlo step): Using the three sets of parameters from parts (a), (b), and (c) of Step 1, generate samples of $\alpha_{i,t+\tau}, q_{t+\tau}$ for $1 \leq \tau \leq T < \infty$ conditional on $\mathbf{x}_t$. For each sample, approximate the value of the term in curly brackets in Equation (7.23) by replacing the infinite upper limit of the sum with T. Average over the sample to obtain an estimate of the expectation of this sum and an approximation of $f(\mathbf{x}_t)$, called $\hat{f}(\mathbf{x}_t)$. Repeat this step for all of the values of $\mathbf{x}_t$ in the actual sample to generate the pseudo-observations $\hat{f}(\mathbf{x}_t)$.

Step 3: Replace the unknown value $\hat{f}(\mathbf{x}_t)$ by its approximation $\hat{f}(\mathbf{x}_t)$ and use the resulting equation to estimate the remaining unknown parameter, Λ.

Estimation Using the Dynamic Programming Equation. An alternative to estimating the Euler equation is to work directly with the dynamic programming equation. The increase in computing power and the improvement in numerical algorithms make this an increasingly attractive option. This approach was pioneered by John Rust (1987 and 1994), who modeled an agent who solves a discrete choice problem so that the agent has a finite number of choices. A number of recent papers explore efficient algorithms for solving these types of estimation problems; see, for example, Aguirregabiria and Mira (2002).

Even if the decision variable is price or quantity, the model can sometimes be well approximated using a discrete choice model. This approximation selects a finite number of intervals for the decision variable, and treats all observations from within the same interval as identical. For example, we might think of firms as choosing prices as whole dollars. (Chapters 9 and 10 provide an example of approximating a continuous choice set using a finite choice set in a static model.)

Although the mechanics of estimating a dynamic model depend on the specific features of the model (including whether the control space is discrete or continuous), the basic elements of the process are general. Here we provide an overview of the process.

In principle, we can estimate all of the parameters of the sticky price model, except the market power parameter, without using the dynamic optimization model. The dynamic equation for the price, Equation (7.1), can be estimated using time-series methods, and the cost function can be estimated directly or using factor demand equations.[4] If there were no data on factor prices and inputs, the parameters of the cost equation could be estimated using the necessary conditions to the dynamic optimization problem. In order to keep the discussion simple, we will assume all parameters except for the market power parameter can be estimated without using the necessary conditions for dynamic optimization. Thus, we describe a situation in which the dynamic optimization model is used only to estimate the market power parameter.

However, it is worth noting that in some models, parameters of the profit function can be recovered only by using the necessary conditions to dynamic optimization. The convex adjustment cost model in the next chapter, and models that describe a firm's entry into and exit from the industry, are two examples of such models. We seldom, if ever, have data that include explicit measures of adjustment costs (in the first example) or entry/exit costs (in the second example), ruling out a "standard" regression. In these cases, we can (typically) estimate the unknown cost parameters by using observations of dynamic optimization.

The economically relevant range for Λ, encompassing competitive and collusive behavior, is $[0, n]$. We want to know which value in that range best describes the observed outcome, conditional on our estimates of the remaining parameter values. We treat those estimates as given henceforth. We select a finite number of values of Λ in the relevant range, and for each of these values we solve the Dynamic

[4] Even where it is possible to estimate some parameters, such as those in Equation (7.1), without using the conditions for dynamic optimization, we may gain statistical efficiency by simultaneously estimating all parameters. The complexity of the estimation involving dynamic optimization makes this simultaneous estimation approach unattractive. We want to use the dynamic optimization conditions to estimate as few parameters as possible.

Programming Equation (7.2). Solving this equation means finding a value function $J(p_{t-1}, Q_{t-1}, \mathbf{x}_t)$ and a control rule given by

$$q^*(p_{t-1}, Q_{t-1}, \mathbf{x}_t) = \arg\max \mathrm{E}_t \{\pi_t + \delta J(p_t, Q_t, \mathbf{x}_{t+1})\}.$$

In general, there is no analytic solution to this problem (however, we present one exception in the next chapter). Therefore, we need numerical methods to obtain an approximate solution: functions that approximate the value function and the control rule. There are a number of excellent books that describe these methods – see, for example, Judd (1999) and Miranda and Fackler (2002). The difficulty that these methods encounter is that the numerical problem quickly becomes very large as the number of possible values of the state variable(s) increases; this difficulty is known as "the curse of dimensionality." Suppose, for example, that we want to evaluate the value function and control rule at each of ten possible values for each of m state variables. In that case, we need to evaluate the functions at 10^m points. In the sticky price example, there are two endogenous state variables, lagged price and current quantity. However, the vector $\mathbf{x}$ may contain a number of exogenous state variables, and these also contribute to the curse of dimensionality. Much of the art of solving dynamic problems lies in choosing a parsimonious specification, which might be achieved by limiting the number of state variables or by reducing the number of values that we allow these variables to take (ten, in the example above), or choosing a tractable functional form (as in Rust, 1987).

Given an approximation to the optimal control rule, conditional on the choice of Λ, we can obtain the approximately optimal value of the decision variable for each value of the state variable in our sample. We call these the *estimated* values of the control variable because they are our estimates of the optimal values. We can evaluate a loss function using these estimated values of the decision variable and their actual, observed values. This loss function contains Λ as an (implicit) argument because a change in the value of this parameter will change the approximation of the control rule, thus changing our estimated values of the decision variable. By minimizing the loss function over Λ, we obtain a point estimate of this parameter.

The simplest loss function is the sum of squared differences between the actual and the estimated values of the control variable. If our model explains why the observed and the optimal control rules differ, we might have a basis for choosing a different loss function. Earlier, we proceeded as if we had the "correct model" and, in addition, knew all of the parameters of the model except for Λ. If both of those assumptions were true, then at the correct value of Λ, the actual and the estimated values of the control variable would be identical. Unfortunately, neither of those assumptions is true. We need to decide how to relax the assumptions in order to explain the discrepancy between the actual and the estimated values of the control variable.

There is no shortage of ways to explain the discrepancy. One explanation is that agents commit "optimization errors." That is, if they truly behaved optimally, they would use the value that we estimate (once we have selected the correct value of Λ), but something causes them to make an error and choose a different value for their control variable. If we make assumptions about the optimization error, this type of explanation enables us to interpret the loss function as a likelihood function, and we can then impute statistical properties to the estimate of Λ.

A slightly different explanation for the discrepancy between observed and estimated values of the control variable is that the econometrician's representation of the firm's behavior is only a model, not an accurate description of what the firm does. Consequently, we have no reason to think that the model's predictions would exactly predict actual behavior.

It is difficult to imagine a situation in which either of these explanations would be false. Firms do not literally solve these dynamic optimization problems, so even if the econometrician's description of firms' objectives and constraints were exactly correct, the firm would not behave exactly optimally. In addition, the econometrician does not have exactly the right description of the firms' environment. Nevertheless, these explanations can both be criticized as being *ad hoc*. In addition, they do not provide guidance for choosing the loss function. For example, should different observations receive the same weight in this loss function?

For the purpose of providing a theoretical basis for the loss function, we need to impose more structure on the estimation problem. One possibility is that firms and the econometrician have different information, so the econometrician is not solving exactly the same control problem as the industry does. There are many plausible ways that information might differ. For example, the underlying model could be correct, but firms know the true values of the model parameters in the price and cost equations, and the econometrician has only estimates.

To be concrete, we suppose that there is a single parameter in the cost function about which the firm is fully informed and for which the econometrician has a subjective distribution (based perhaps on estimation of the cost function). Using draws from this distribution, we can solve the control problem conditional on Λ for each value of the draw to obtain the optimal control rule and obtain estimates of the optimal controls. The random sample of values of the cost parameter represents a distribution of the estimated optimal control for each value of the state variable. We could calculate the mean and variance of each of these distributions and use them to evaluate a loss function. Mechanically, we would imbed an optimal control subroutine in a Monte Carlo outer loop.

In short, one can invent a wide range of ways in which to specify the loss function that is used to estimate Λ. The basis for all of these is the approximate solution to a dynamic programming problem. In contrast, the estimation of Λ by means of the Euler equation uses only a necessary condition for optimization. In particular, the Euler equation estimation does not impose a transversality condition, which is another necessary condition for (most) optimization problems. Both of these estimation approaches can be used because – as we have emphasized – the market-power parameter formulation eliminates the difficult strategic issues. Instead of having to find an equilibrium to a game, we have the simpler problem of finding a solution to an optimization problem.

A Related Dynamic Oligopoly Model

Before discussing a second example of the estimation of a dynamic model, we briefly consider Steen and Salvanes' (1999) empirical study of the Norwegian salmon market. This study is interesting in the present context because it provides a very different development of the sticky price model that we previously discussed. In contrast to our treatment, they assume that the firm solves a sequence of static problems rather than a dynamic problem. This assumption eliminates many of the interesting issues arising from dynamics, but it enables the authors to focus on some econometric issues inherent in the use of time-series data.

We emphasized that price rigidities cause the industry's problem to be dynamic unless the firms in the industry are price takers. The solution to an oligopolistic industry's problem leads to an Euler equation, which can be used to identify the industry's structure. Steen and Salvanes ignore the dynamic optimizing behavior of the firm/industry by assuming that firms solve a succession of one-period problems. Consequently, the equilibrium supply relation involves only current and lagged variables *and not the expectation of future variables* (which appears in the Euler equation).

They estimate an error correction model involving conjectural variations. As in the static models considered in previous chapters, the estimation model consists of a demand function and a supply relation; the latter equates *perceived marginal revenue* (modeled using conjectural variations) and marginal cost. In contrast to the static framework used in earlier chapters, both the demand function and the supply relation here are dynamic even though the firm solves a sequence of static problems. The model allows for short-run departures from long-run equilibrium. These short-run deviations may be caused by a variety of factors, including random shocks, sluggish adjustment, and seasonal shifts in supply or demand.

The estimated parameters provide information on the long-run equilibrium demand and supply relations as well as on the dynamic adjustment toward a long-run equilibrium. This formulation also includes two types of conjectural variations parameters. One conjectural variation parameter measures the long-run equilibrium market power. Another set of conjectural variation parameters measure the extent of market power during the adjustment toward a long-run equilibrium.

The obvious drawback of Steen and Salvanes' modeling approach is that it assumes that firms are myopic and, in that respect, are not rational agents. The benefit of this approach is that by ignoring forward-looking behavior, they obtain a much simpler model, which enables them to distinguish between market power in a long-run equilibrium and market power in transit to such an equilibrium.

A DYNAMIC MODEL WITH ADVERTISING

We now consider a model based on RS in which the stock of consumer goodwill is the source of the dynamics. This stock decays over time and can be increased by advertising. Thus, the stock of goodwill is similar to a stock of capital that depreciates and that can be renewed by investment. The industry stock of goodwill – the sum of firms' stocks – determines the aggregate size of the market. For given prices, a firm's stock of goodwill relative to the aggregate stock determines the firm's market share.

The advertising and the sticky price models are dynamic for different fundamental reasons. More importantly, the two models illustrate different empirical objectives. Our discussion of the sticky price model emphasized the use of a market-power parameter to measure the extent of collusion. In contrast, we assume that there is a Nash-in-advertising equilibrium in the RS model; we do not consider the possibility that firms behave collusively with respect to advertising or that they believe that they cannot affect the stock of goodwill. Our primary estimation objective is to determine whether firms use open-loop strategies or whether they recognize that their actions in the current period may affect their rivals' actions in the future. Our secondary objective is to determine whether the main effect of a firm's advertising is to increase its own market share or to increase the aggregate size of the market.

We simplify the RS model by assuming that there is a single type of cigarette instead of two types (high and low tar), as in their data set. After describing the model, we obtain the Euler equation under the assumption that firms use open-loop strategies, and then under the assumption that firms use Markov strategies. We then describe the hybrid model that RS actually estimate.

Firm i's stock of goodwill in period t is G_{it} and its advertising level is A_{it}. The fraction $1-\alpha$ of lagged goodwill decays within a period, and advertising in the current period increases the current stock of goodwill. Thus, the equation of motion for the stock of goodwill is

$$G_{it} = \alpha G_{it-1} + A_{it}. \tag{7.24}$$

The vector of industry stocks is $\mathbf{G}_t \equiv (G_{it}, \mathbf{G}_{-it})$, where $\mathbf{G}_{-it}$ is the vector of stocks for all firms other than Firm i. Current advertising affects the stock of goodwill in the current period, so the endogenous state variable at time t is $\mathbf{G}_{t-1}$. Firms' decisions at time t determine the value of $\mathbf{G}_t$. The vector of industry advertising is $\mathbf{A}_t = (A_{it}, \mathbf{A}_{-it})$, where $\mathbf{A}_{-it}$ is the advertising of its rivals. The sum of firms' stocks of goodwill (the aggregate industry stock of goodwill) is $GT_t \equiv \sum_i G_{it}$. Firm i's demand is $q_{it} = q_i(\mathbf{G}_t, \mathbf{z}_t)$, where $\mathbf{z}_t$ is a vector of demand shifters, including prices, p_t. The firm's cost of advertising is $\psi_{it} = \psi_i(A_{it}, \mathbf{y}_t)$ and its cost of production is $c_{it} = c_i(q_{it}, \mathbf{y}_t)$, where $\mathbf{y}_t$ is a vector of cost shifters. The vector $\mathbf{x}_t \equiv (\mathbf{y}_t', \mathbf{z}_t')'$ contains the exogenous demand and cost shifters. The firm's single-period profit is

$$\pi_{it}(\mathbf{G}_{t-1}, \mathbf{A}_t, \mathbf{x}_t) = p_{it}q_{it} - c_{it} - \psi_{it}. \tag{7.25}$$

The firm wants to maximize the present discounted value of profits, with discount factor equal to δ. Its value function is $J_i(\mathbf{G}_{t-1}, \mathbf{x}_t)$ and its dynamic programming equation (DPE) is

$$J_i(\mathbf{G}_{t-1}, \mathbf{x}_t) = \max_{A_{it}} \{\pi_{it} + \mathrm{E}_t \delta J_i(\mathbf{G}_t, \mathbf{x}_{t+1})\}, \tag{7.26}$$

subject to the constraint given by Equation (7.24). In writing this equation, we assume that the firm can observe or predict the equilibrium values of the arguments of current profits, $(\mathbf{G}_{t-1}, \mathbf{A}_t, \mathbf{x}_t)$. Therefore, the expectations operator does not operate on π_{it}. (This assumption would not be correct if firms have private information. In that case, they would not be able to predict their rivals' current decisions, so current profits would be under the expectations operator.)

In reality, firms probably make a number of strategic choices, including pricing and advertising decisions. However, this model investigates only the strategic choice of advertising. The endogeneity of prices is recognized at the estimation stage, where the authors use instrumental variables. However, at the optimization stage, prices are taken as fixed. When considering a variation in advertising levels, firms do not consider how the resulting change in goodwill, and the associated change in the demand function, will change the equilibrium price. Although unrealistic, this assumption makes a difficult estimation problem tractable.

In the next two subsections, we obtain the necessary conditions (Euler equations) first under the assumption that firms use open-loop strategies and then under the assumption that they use Markov Perfect strategies. These derivations help clarify the distinction between the two types of equilibria. They also make it easier to understand the hybrid model that RS estimate.

The Open-Loop Equilibrium to the Advertising Model

The Nash-in-advertising assumption is that firms take their rivals' current advertising levels as given. If firms also take their rivals' future advertising levels as given, we have an open-loop Nash equilibrium. In this case, we derive the Euler equation in the same manner as we used in the previous example with sticky prices. The Euler equation is a necessary condition for optimality that is stated in terms of the primitive functions, rather than the endogenous function $J_i(\mathbf{G}_{t-1}, \mathbf{x}_t)$ and its derivatives.

The first-order condition to the firm's maximization problem, Equation (7.26), is

$$-\frac{\partial \pi_{it}}{\partial A_{it}} = \delta \mathrm{E}_t \frac{\partial J_i(\mathbf{G}_t, \mathbf{x}_{t+1})}{\partial G_{it}}. \tag{7.27}$$

An additional unit of advertising in the current period affects profits in the current period and changes the stock of goodwill available at the beginning of the next period by one unit. The value of a marginal change in the stock of goodwill – its shadow value – equals the partial derivative of the value function. The first-order condition requires that the sum of the marginal effect of advertising on current profits and the expected discounted shadow value of goodwill must equal 0 for all t.

We eliminate the *max* operator in Equation (7.26) by replacing the decision variable A_{it} with its optimal value, and then take the derivative (of both sides of the resulting equation) with respect to the state variable G_{it-1}. Using the envelope theorem and Equation (7.24), we obtain

$$\frac{\partial J_i(\mathbf{G}_{t-1}, \mathbf{x}_t)}{\partial G_{it-1}} = \frac{\partial \pi_{it}}{\partial G_{it-1}} + \delta\alpha \mathrm{E}_t \left\{ \frac{\partial J_i(\mathbf{G}_t, \mathbf{x}_{t+1})}{\partial G_{it}} \right\}. \quad (7.28)$$

It is important to understand the role of the envelope theorem in deriving this equation in order to understand why the equilibrium condition changes once we drop the open-loop assumption and consider Markov strategies. To simplify the descriptions, suppose that there are only two firms, Firm i and Firm j. A change in G_{it-1} changes the optimal value of A_{it}. However, because A_{it} maximizes the right side of Equation (7.26), a small change in the value of this variable has only a second-order (negligible) effect on the value of the payoff. The envelope theorem says that in considering the effect of a change in G_{it-1} on the value function, we can ignore the induced change in A_{it}. By virtue of the open-loop assumption, the change in G_{it-1} has no effect on Firm j's advertising. In contrast, under the assumption of Markov Perfection, the change in G_{it-1} does affect Firm j's advertising. Because Firm j's advertising is chosen to maximize Firm j's payoff (not Firm i's payoff), the change G_{it-1} and the resulting change in Firm j's actions has a first-order effect on Firm i's payoff. We return to this point when we discuss the Markov Perfect equilibrium.

Advancing Equation (7.28) by one period, taking expectations conditional on the information at time t and then multiplying by δ, we obtain

$$\delta E_t \frac{\partial J_i(G_t, x_{t+1})}{\partial G_{it}} = \mathrm{E}_t \delta_t \left\{ \frac{\partial \pi_{it+1}}{\partial G_{it}} + \delta\alpha \mathrm{E}_{t+1} \left\{ \frac{\partial J_i(G_{t+1}, x_{t+2})}{\partial G_{it+1}} \right\}\right\}. \quad (7.29)$$

Substituting Equation (7.27) into (7.29) gives the Euler equation for the open-loop equilibrium:

$$\frac{\partial \pi_{it}}{\partial A_{it}} + \delta \mathrm{E}_t \left\{ \frac{\partial \pi_{it+1}}{\partial G_{it}} - \alpha \frac{\partial \pi_{it+1}}{\partial A_{it+1}} \right\} = 0. \quad (7.30)$$

The Euler equation has the following interpretation. A necessary condition for optimality of the firm's plan is that *any* perturbation of that plan must lead to a zero first-order change in the firm's payoff.[5] Because this condition must hold for

[5] This requirement is the same as in a static maximization problem, where, at an interior optimum, the derivative of the maximand with respect to the control is zero. Here, the first-order Taylor approximation of the payoff evaluated at the optimal decision equals the value of the payoff evaluated at that point. In other words, a small movement away from the optimal decision leads to no first-order change in the payoff.

any perturbation of the candidate trajectory, it must hold for the following specific perturbation: In period t, let Firm i increase its advertising by a small amount, ε, and decrease its advertising in the next period, $t+1$, by the amount $\varepsilon\alpha$. This perturbation leaves unchanged the advertising and stock levels in all periods $t+k$, $k>1$, so we only need consider the effects of the perturbation on profits in periods t and $t+1$. The first term in Equation (7.30) is the effect on current profits of this perturbation. The second term is the discounted expectation of the effect of this perturbation on profits in the next period. That effect consists of the change in profits due to the increased value of the state, minus the change in advertising costs due to the decreased level of advertising. The Euler equation requires that the sum of these effects must be zero.

The Markov Perfect Equilibrium to the Advertising Model

We now explain how the equilibrium condition changes when firms use Markov strategies. The first-order condition, Equation (7.27), is unchanged, but Equation (7.30) no longer holds under Markov strategies. In deriving Equation (7.30), we used the envelope theorem and the assumption that other firms' *future* advertising levels do not change when G_{it} (or A_{it-1}) changes. A change in the current state variable, $G_{it\text{-}1}$, causes the equilibrium values of A_{it} to change. Because A_{it} maximizes the right side of Equation (21), the change in this variable has only a second-order effect on the payoff, by the envelope theorem. In a Markov equilibrium, a change in the current state variable, G_{it-1}, also causes the equilibrium values of A_{-it} to change. However, A_{-it} does not maximize the right side of Equation (7.26) so, in general, a change in this variable has a first-order effect on the payoff. In taking the derivative of the value function with respect to G_{it-1}, we need to consider this effect when we drop the open-loop assumption.

With Markov strategies, when we differentiate the DPE with respect to G_{it-1}, instead of Equation (7.28) we obtain

$$\frac{\partial J_i(\mathbf{G}_{t-1}, \mathbf{x}_t)}{\partial G_{it-1}} = \frac{\partial \pi_{it}}{\partial G_{it-1}} + \delta\alpha \mathrm{E}_t\left\{\frac{\partial J_i(\mathbf{G}_t, \mathbf{x}_{t+1})}{\partial G_{it}}\right\} + K_{it}, \tag{7.31}$$

where K_{it} is defined as

$$K_{it} \equiv \mathrm{E}_t\left\{\frac{\partial \pi_{it}}{\partial \mathbf{A}_{-it}} + \delta\frac{\partial J_i(\mathbf{G}_t, \mathbf{x}_{t+1})}{\partial \mathbf{G}_{-it}}\right\}\frac{\partial \mathbf{A}_{-it}}{\partial G_{it-1}}. \tag{7.32}$$

The K_{it} function in Equation (7.31) is not included in Equation (7.28). The K_{it} function is the change in Firm i's profits due to an increase in its rivals' advertising – the curly brackets in Equation (7.32) – times the change in advertising induced by the change in G_{it-1}.[6]

[6] Because G_{-it} is a vector when Firm i has more than one rival, the partial derivatives in Equation (7.27) are also vectors. Thus, K_{it} is the product of a row vector and a column vector. In order not to encumber the notation, we do not include transpose signs in the equations. We can always define the vectors of partial derivatives in such a way that the transpose signs are unnecessary.

To evaluate the K_{it} function, we need the vector of partial derivatives,

$$\frac{\partial J_i(G_t, x_{t+1})}{\partial G_{-it}} \equiv \frac{\partial J_i(t+1)}{\partial G_{-it}},$$

which we obtain by differentiating Equation (7.26) with respect to G_{-it}. The result is[7]

$$\frac{\partial J_i(t)}{\partial \mathbf{G}_{-i,t-1}} = \frac{\partial \pi_{it}}{\partial \mathbf{G}_{-i,t-1}} + \delta\alpha \frac{\partial E_t J_i(t+1)}{\partial \mathbf{G}_{-i,t}} + \frac{\partial \mathbf{A}_{-i,t}}{\partial \mathbf{G}_{-i,t-1}} \left\{ \frac{\partial \pi_{it}}{\partial \mathbf{A}_{-i,t}} + \delta \frac{\partial E_t J_i(t+1)}{\partial \mathbf{G}_{-i,t}} \right\}. \tag{7.33}$$

We simplify this equation by using the following definitions,

$$\eta_{it} \equiv \frac{\partial J_i(t)}{\partial \mathbf{G}_{-i,t-1}}; \quad \mu_{it} \equiv \frac{\partial \pi_{it}}{\partial \mathbf{G}_{-i,t-1}} + \left\{ \frac{\partial \pi_{it}}{\partial \mathbf{A}_{-i,t}} \right\} \frac{\partial \mathbf{A}_{-i,t}}{\partial \mathbf{G}_{-i,t-1}};$$

$$\varpi_{it} \equiv \delta \left(\alpha \mathbf{I} + \frac{\partial \mathbf{A}_{-i,t}}{\partial \mathbf{G}_{-i,t-1}} \right),$$

where $\mathbf{I}$ is an identity matrix whose dimension equals the number of Firm i's rivals. With these definitions, we rewrite Equation (7.33) as

$$\eta_{it} = \mu_{it} + \varpi_{it} \mathrm{E}_t \eta_{it+1}. \tag{7.34}$$

The solution to Equation (7.34) is

$$\eta_{it} = \mathrm{E}_t \sum_{\tau=0}^{\infty} \left(\prod_{s=1}^{\tau} (\varpi_{it+s}) \right) \mu_{it+\tau}; \quad \prod_{s=1}^{0} (\varpi_{it+s}) \equiv 1. \tag{7.35}$$

We are now able to proceed as in the case with open-loop strategies. We use Equations (7.31), (7.32), and (7.35) to write

$$\frac{\partial J_i(t)}{\partial G_{it-1}} = \frac{\partial \pi_{it}}{\partial G_{it-1}} + \delta\alpha E_t \left\{ \frac{\partial J_i(t+1)}{\partial G_{it}} \right\} + \left\{ \frac{\partial \pi_{it}}{\partial \mathbf{A}_{-it}} + \delta \eta_{it} \right\} \frac{\partial \mathbf{A}_{-it}}{\partial G_{it-1}}.$$

By advancing this equation by one period and taking expectations with respect to the information available at time t, we obtain

$$\mathrm{E}_t \frac{\partial J_i(t+1)}{\partial G_{it}} = \mathrm{E}_t \left\{ \frac{\partial \pi_{it+1}}{\partial G_{it}} + \delta\alpha \left(\frac{\partial J_i(t+2)}{\partial G_{it+1}} \right) + \left(\frac{\partial \pi_{it+1}}{\partial \mathbf{A}_{-it+1}} + \delta \eta_{it+1} \right) \frac{\partial \mathbf{A}_{-it+1}}{\partial G_{it}} \right\}. \tag{7.36}$$

The reader can assume that Firm i has only one rival and interpret all the partial derivatives as scalars without losing the thread of the argument.

[7] When Firm i has more than one rival, $\partial \mathbf{A}_{-i,t}/\partial \mathbf{G}_{-i,t-1}$ is a matrix because both $\mathbf{A}_{-i,t}$ and $\mathrm{G}_{-i,t-1}$ are vectors.

Substituting Equation (7.27) into (7.36), we get the Euler equation under Markov strategies:

$$\frac{\partial \pi_{it}}{\partial A_{it}} + \delta \mathrm{E}_t \left\{ \frac{\partial \pi_{it+1}}{\partial G_{it}} - \alpha \left(\frac{\partial \pi_{it+1}}{\partial A_{it+1}} \right) \right\} + \delta \mathrm{E}_t \left\{ \left(\frac{\partial \pi_{it+1}}{\partial \mathbf{A}_{-it+1}} + \delta \eta_{it+1} \right) \frac{\partial \mathbf{A}_{-it+1}}{\partial G_{it}} \right\} = 0. \tag{7.37}$$

The Euler equations under open-loop and Markov strategies, Equations (7.30) and (7.37), differ due to the presence of the third term in Equation (7.37). This term represents the change in Firm i's expected payoff due to the rival firms' response to Firm i's increased stock of goodwill in period $t+1$. The change in this payoff consists of the change in profits in period $t+1$ and the discounted stream of the change in profits in all subsequent periods. The function η_{it+1} captures this second change.

Equation (7.22), the Euler equation associated with the open-loop equilibrium to the "general" sticky price model, and Equation (7.37), the Euler equation associated with the Markov Perfect equilibrium (MPE) to the advertising model, resemble each other superficially. They both involve an infinite sequence of expectations of future endogenous variables, the function f in the first case and the function η in the second. However, the estimation problems in the two cases are significantly different. We previously described a strategy for estimating the parameters in Equation (7.22). The application of a similar strategy for the open-loop problem here involves solving the optimal control problem to find the equilibrium control rule, conditional on estimates of the parameters of the primitive functions.

In principle, the same kind of algorithm can be used to estimate Markov strategies, but the search algorithm is more complicated. To evaluate Firm i's Euler equation, we need to know how the other firms respond to a change in the state variable. That is, we need estimates of the vector $\partial \mathbf{A}_{-it}/\partial \mathbf{G}_{it-1}$ and the matrix $\partial \mathbf{A}_{-it}/\partial \mathbf{G}_{-it-1}$. To obtain those estimates, we need to estimate the Euler equations for the other firms. In other words, we have to solve a dynamic game rather than a control problem.

The Hybrid Model

RS estimate a model similar to Equation (7.37) except that they set η_{it} equal to zero and $\partial A_{-it+1}/\partial G_{it} = \zeta_i$, a constant vector of conjectural variations. This partial derivative is a conjecture about how rivals will respond in the *next* period to a change in Firm i's advertising in this period – unlike the conjectural variation that we used in the sticky price model. The *hybrid* Euler equation is

$$\frac{\partial \pi_{it}}{\partial A_{it}} + \delta \mathrm{E}_t \left\{ \frac{\partial \pi_{it+1}}{\partial G_{it}} - \alpha \left(\frac{\partial \pi_{it+1}}{\partial A_{it+1}} \right) \right\} + \delta \mathrm{E}_t \left\{ \left(\frac{\partial \pi_{it+1}}{\partial \mathbf{A}_{-it+1}} \right) \zeta_i \right\} = 0. \tag{7.38}$$

RS's simplification means that Firm i considers only the next-period effect on its profits due to the rivals' response to the change in the stock of goodwill, caused by Firm i's advertising. In addition, these responses are described by an arbitrary linear conjecture. This conjecture need not satisfy the equilibrium conditions associated with the rivals' optimization problems. These two assumptions make estimation of the model tractable. The resulting model is more general than the open-loop model because firms consider the possibility of some response by rivals. A statistical test of whether the conjectural variation parameters are zero provides a test for the open-loop assumption.

The endogenous state variable, the firms' stocks of goodwill, is not observable. In order to use Equation (7.38) for estimation, we need the derivatives of profits or sales with respect to goodwill. By assuming that quantity demanded and market shares are linear functions of goodwill stocks, RS avoid the need to estimate demand functions. For example, the change in Firm i's output due to a change in its stock of goodwill is simply

$$\frac{\partial q_{it}}{\partial G_{it}} \equiv S_{it}\frac{\partial Q_t}{\partial GT_t} + Q_t\frac{\partial S_{it}}{\partial G_{it}} = \omega_{i1} S_{it} + \omega_{i2} Q_t, \tag{7.39}$$

where S_{it} is Firm i's market share, Q_t is aggregate demand, GT_t (previously defined) is the aggregate stock of goodwill, and ω_{i1}, ω_{i2} are parameters. The first part of Equation (7.39) is an identity, and the second part follows from the assumption that aggregate demand and market shares are linear in the stock of goodwill. RS also estimate a system of factor demands in order to obtain estimates of marginal costs of production. They use a Tornqvist index over the prices of advertising in different media as a proxy for the marginal cost of advertising.

Treating prices as predetermined, we can use Equations (7.24), (7.25), and (7.39) to write the Euler equation (7.38) as a function of observable or constructed (estimated) variables and of the parameters to be estimated. To complete the model, the authors estimate a separate equation in order to determine whether the primary effect of advertising is to increase market share or total market size. They assume that a firm's market share is a linear function of its own stock of goodwill and the aggregate stocks of rivals. They apply the Koyck transformation to this equation, using the assumption that the decay rate for goodwill is the same for all firms. The result is an estimation equation that gives a firm's current market share as a linear function of its previous market shares and of its and its rivals' advertising in the current period.

The authors find that advertising affects the size of the market for low-tar but not for high-tar cigarettes, but it does not affect the market share for either type. (However, the market share is affected by the number of brands that a manufacturer sells.) In the low-tar market, firms benefit from rivals' advertising, but in the high-tar market, this advertising has a negligible effect. The point estimates of the dynamic conjectural variation parameters are negative and statistically significantly different from zero.

The finding that the market-size effect dominates the market-share effect (at least for low-tar cigarettes) means that one firm's advertising creates positive externalities for its rivals. In this case, a firm with a negative conjectural variation advertises less than a naïve firm that believes that rivals will not respond to changes in goodwill stocks. In other words, the equilibrium in this hybrid model is more collusive than in the open-loop model: actions here are strategic complements. Statistical tests do not reject the hypothesis that the level of advertising maximizes joint profits.

ESTIMATION OF MARKOV PERFECT EQUILIBRIA

The past ten years has seen an explosion of papers that estimate MPE. This section provides a brief overview of the objectives and the methods of this literature. Recent papers, including Pakes et al. (2004) and Bajari et al. (2004), provide new estimation methods and reviews of earlier work.

The papers in this literature seek to estimate parameters of dynamic games, such as the parameters of entry and exit costs and adjustment costs. These papers begin with the assumptions that firms behave noncooperatively, the decision variable (such as investment) is known, and firms use Markov Perfect strategies. The papers in this literature do not estimate an index of market power. A key focus of this book is to estimate such an index.

The parameters of firms' profit functions – the entry and exit costs or the investment cost – may be of intrinsic interest if, for example, we want to assess the importance of adjustment costs. These parameters might also be useful to conduct policy experiments. For example, given estimates of the parameters of a game, we could determine how the equilibrium changes following a change in a regulatory policy. However, the (likely) multiplicity of MPE creates problems in interpreting the results of such an experiment. Firms may be using a particular MPE under an existing regulatory environment. A change in this environment could cause them to shift to a different equilibrium. In addition, there are some subtle identification issues in these games.

Although it is often interesting to obtain parameter estimates for the profit function, conditional on the maintained assumption that firms play a particular noncooperative game, arguably it is equally or more important to determine the kind of game that they are playing. We may want to estimate whether firms are actually behaving as Nash oligopolists, or whether they are competitive or collusive. Although the recent literature on estimating dynamic games has (to the best of our knowledge) ignored this question, the methods developed by this literature can be adapted to address the question. Salgado (2007) applies the methods described here to estimate oligopoly power in the computer chip market. A variety of types of equilibria can be obtained by solving a dynamic game in which an agent seeks to maximize the expectation of the present value of the stream of its future single-period payoffs. The single-period payoff is the firm's profit (inclusive of entry or exit costs or adjustment costs) in the noncooperative equilibrium, social surplus in the competitive equilibrium (under the assumption of convex technology), and industry profits in the collusive equilibrium.

It is not possible, in general, to find the solution to a MPE by finding the solution to a single optimization problem. Therefore, we cannot estimate the parameters of a MPE by estimating the parameters of a single optimization problem. (It would be convenient if it were possible to do so because it is easier to estimate the parameters of a control problem than to estimate the parameters of a dynamic game.) For example, if firms use Markov strategies and play noncooperatively, each wanting to maximize its own profits, we cannot "usefully"[8] find an optimization problem, the solution to which is identical to the MPE of the game. However, it is straightforward to represent a single optimization problem as a game: when the optimization problem has more than one decision variable, invent fictitious players, each of whom chooses one or more of the decisions, and all of whom have the same objective, which is identical to the objective of the original optimization problem. The Nash equilibrium to this fictitious game is obviously identical to the solution to the original optimization problem. For example, suppose that the two firms collude in choosing output to maximize duopoly profits. In this case, it clearly makes no difference if we think of each of the two firms choosing their own output to maximize duopoly profits, taking as given the other firm's decision rule, or if we think of a cartel as choosing output for both firms to maximize duopoly profits. The first scenario describes a (peculiar sort of) noncooperative game, and the second scenario describes a single-agent optimization problem. In much the same way, the noncooperative equilibrium with price-taking firms (a game) reproduces the equilibrium of a social planner (a single-agent optimization problem). The estimation procedure described in this subsection nests different equilibrium structures by solving a single game, using different parameters in the objective function.

For example, suppose that there are two firms and that the inverse demand function, $p(q)$, is linear with slope b; Firm i's costs depend on its capital, $c(k_i, q_i)$; and there are convex costs of adjusting capital, $\Delta(I_i)$, as in the model discussed in Chapter 6. Let γ and ν be two non-negative parameters, the sum of which is no greater than one. Firm i's single-period objective can be written as

$$\pi_i = pq_i + (1-\gamma)\, pq_{-i} - (1-\gamma-\nu)\frac{b}{2}(q_i + q_{-i})^2 - c(k_i, q_i) - \Delta(I_i), \tag{7.40}$$

[8] We include the modifier "usefully" for the following reason. In some cases we *can* find an optimization problem, the solution to which is identical to the MPE of the noncooperative dynamic game. However (at least for the cases with which we are familiar), this procedure requires knowing the MPE to the dynamic game. Thus, the procedure seems to be of little practical use, since it requires knowing the thing that we are using the procedure to discover. In contrast, if firms use *open-loop* strategies, we can construct the optimization problem (which, when solved, produces the open-loop equilibrium to the game) simply by knowing the primitives (not the solution) to the original game.

where we suppress the time index. Consider the MPE to the dynamic game in which each firm's single-period payoff has the form of Equation (7.40) and each firm chooses an investment policy. The parameters of the demand function and the restricted cost function $c(k_i, q_i)$ can be estimated using standard static methods; γ and ν and the parameters of the adjustment cost function, $\Delta(I_i)$, need to be estimated using the equilibrium conditions of the dynamic game.

For $\gamma = 1$ and $\nu = 0$, the payoff in Equation (7.40) is the single-period profit of Firm i, so the equilibrium to the game is the noncooperative equilibrium. For $\gamma = 0$ and $\nu = 1$, the payoff in Equation (7.40) is the single-period industry profits so the equilibrium to the game is the collusive equilibrium. Finally, for $\gamma = 0$ and $\nu = 0$, the payoff is social surplus so the equilibrium to the game is the competitive equilibrium. In order to nest all three equilibria, we need to use two parameters.

As the weights in the convex combination (γ, ν) vary, the estimated equilibrium becomes "closer" to one of the three types of industry structure. By testing hypotheses regarding the value of these parameters, it is possible to test the nature of the industry equilibrium (under the maintained assumption of Markov Perfection) instead of assuming that the equilibrium is noncooperative Nash.

The measure of market structure in this setting is a vector (γ, ν) rather than a single index. Although the three values of (γ, ν) –, the ordered pairs $(0, 0)$, $(1, 0)$, and $(0, 1)$ – correspond to perfect competition, Nash-Cournot, and collusive equilibria, a point in the unit square (i.e., the point (α_1, α_2) with $0 \leq \alpha_i \leq 1$) does not have an obvious economic interpretation. Such a point does not represent an outcome that is either "between competition and Nash-Cournot" or "between Nash-Cournot and collusive."

For example, suppose we have two estimates of the market structure parameters (γ, ν) – A $= (0.001, 0.2)$ and B $= (0.8, 0.001)$. Estimate A implies a market that is closer (using the Euclidean norm) to collusion than to Nash-Cournot, and estimate B reverses this ranking. This observation, and the fact that collusion is certainly "less competitive" than the Nash-Cournot outcome, implies that estimate B is associated with a more competitive market structure than estimate A. However, estimate A is closer to $(0, 0)$ than is estimate B, which suggests that (if we adopt the Euclidean distance as a metric for market power) estimate A is associated with a more competitive market. Of course, the Euclidean distance has no particular appeal in this setting, but the same kind of contradiction arises if we use a different metric.

The problem is that there is a natural ranking of market structures, going from perfect competition to Nash-Cournot to collusion, but a two-dimensional measure of market structure does not preserve this ranking. There is a simple remedy to this problem. The estimation procedure uses a search over parameter space, and the econometrician chooses the relevant space. We can obtain a one-dimensional measure of market power by restricting the parameter space for (γ, ν) to a curve in the unit square. If we choose the curve to consist of the "bottom edge" and the "Northwest-Southeast" diagonal of the unit square (rather than the entire unit square), then, as we move along this curve (beginning at $(0, 0)$), the index represents an increasingly collusive market structure. If we wanted to impose additional prior information, we could restrict parameter space further. For example, if we were convinced that the equilibrium was "between" noncooperative and collusive, we would limit parameter space to the Northwest–Southeast diagonal of the unit square; equivalently, we would set $\gamma = 1 - \nu$. Similarly, if we were willing to maintain the assumption that the equilibrium was "between" competitive and noncooperative, we would set $\nu = 0$.

The paper by Pakes and McGuire (1994) is one of the earliest explorations of the estimation of MPE using general function forms (not the linear-quadratic form discussed in the next chapter). They provide an algorithm to estimate a dynamic game of product quality with firm entry and exit, and they illustrate it using simulations. The basis for this algorithm is the approximate solution to firms' dynamic programming equations. This approach is costly in terms of computer time, limiting the size of the model that can be estimated.

Recent proposals, such as those described by Pakes et al. (2004) and Bajari et al. (2004), (building on earlier work by Hotz and Miller 1993 and others), offer less computationally demanding approaches. We use the model in Equation (7.40) to explain the basic idea of this estimation strategy, adapted for the purpose of estimating market structure. The starting point is the observation that there exists a *dynamic duality* between the single-period profit function and the value function, which means that information about one of these functions can be used to recover information about the other.[9]

The dynamic programming equation associated with the single-period profit function in Equation (7.40) is

$$J_i(\mathbf{s}_t) = \max_{y_{it}} \mathrm{E}\left\{\pi_{it} + \delta J_i(\mathbf{s}_t)\right\}, \tag{7.41}$$

where $\mathbf{s}_t = (\mathbf{x}_t, \mathbf{k}_{t-1})$ is the vector of exogenous states $\mathbf{x}$ and endogenous but predetermined levels of capital $\mathbf{k}$, and $y_{it} = (q_{it}, I_{it})$ is Firm i's vector of controls at time t. (We assume that the vector $\mathbf{s}$ contains a random variable whose current value is known.) Denote $y_{it}^* = y_i(\mathbf{x}_t, \mathbf{k}_{t-1})$ as the optimal control rule for Firm i, given that all other firms use their equilibrium control rules $\mathbf{y}_{-it}^* = \mathbf{y}_{-i}(\mathbf{x}_t, \mathbf{k}_{t-1})$. Using Equation (7.41), we have

$$J_i(\mathbf{s}) = \mathrm{E}_{\mathbf{s}, y_i^*, y_{-i}^*}\left\{\sum_{\tau=0}^{\infty} \delta^{\tau} \pi(\mathbf{y}_{t+\tau}^*, \mathbf{s}_{t+\tau})\right\}. \tag{7.42}$$

Optimality implies that for any policy $y_{it}' \neq y_{it}^*$ the following inequality holds:

$$\mathrm{E}_{\mathbf{s}, y_i^*, y_{-i}^*}\left\{\sum_{\tau=0}^{\infty} \delta^{\tau} \pi(\mathbf{y}_{t+\tau}^*, \mathbf{s}_{t+\tau})\right\} \geq \mathrm{E}_{\mathbf{s}, y_i', y_{-i}^*}\left\{\sum_{\tau=0}^{\infty} \delta^{\tau} \pi(\mathbf{y}_{-i,t+\tau}^*, y_{t+\tau}', \mathbf{s}_{t+\tau})\right\}. \tag{7.43}$$

[9] This observation provides the basis for an earlier literature on estimating dynamic models, pioneered by Epstein (1981).

The expectations in this expression are conditioned on the current value of the state variable ($\mathbf{s}$), and the firm's beliefs about the policy function that all firms will use. If Firm i thinks that all other firms are using their equilibrium policy functions, then Firm i's best response is to use its equilibrium policy function.

A tremendous saving in computation is achieved when the single-period profit function is linear in unknown parameters. We assume that the demand parameters and the parameters of the production cost have already been estimated, and we treat them as known for the purpose of estimating the remaining parameters, denoted by the vector θ. For our example, θ contains the weights γ, ν and the parameters of the investment function, Δ. We assume that Δ is linear in unknown parameters. Note that we do not assume that Δ is linear in investment, a requirement that is inconsistent with the assumption of convex adjustment costs. For example, Δ can be a polynomial in investment; the unknown parameters in this case are the coefficients of the polynomial. With this example, Δ is linear in the unknown parameters, as we require. Consequently, π is linear in the unknown parameters.[10] Given this assumption, we can write

$$\pi_{it} = \pi_i(y_{it}, \mathbf{y}_{-it}, \mathbf{s}_t) = W_i(y_{it}, \mathbf{y}_{-it}, \mathbf{s}_t)\theta, \tag{7.44}$$

where $W_i(y_{it}, \mathbf{y}_{-it}, \mathbf{s}_t)$ is a vector of *known* functions with the same dimension as θ. Only the parameters θ need to be estimated.

Given this linearity assumption, the expectations in inequality – Equation (7.43) – are linear in parameters. That is, for any decision rule $\mathbf{y}$ (not just the equilibrium rule), we can write

$$\mathrm{E}_{\mathbf{s},\mathbf{y}}\left\{\sum_{\tau=0}^{\infty}\delta^{\tau}\pi_i(\mathbf{y}_{t+\tau}, \mathbf{s}_{t+\tau})\right\} = \mathrm{E}_{\mathbf{s},\mathbf{y}}\left\{\sum_{\tau=0}^{\infty}\delta^{\tau}W_i(\mathbf{y}_{t+\tau}, \mathbf{s}_{t+\tau})\right\}\theta. \tag{7.45}$$

Thus, we can rewrite Inequality (7.43) as

$$E_{\mathbf{s},\mathbf{y}^*}\left\{\sum_{\tau=0}^{\infty}\delta^{\tau}W_i(\mathbf{y}^*_{t+\tau}, \mathbf{s}_{t+\tau})\right\}\theta \geq E_{\mathbf{s},y'_i,\mathbf{y}^*_{-i}}\left\{\sum_{\tau=0}^{\infty}\delta^{\tau}W_i(\mathbf{y}^*_{-i,t+\tau}, y'_{t+\tau}, \mathbf{s}_{t+\tau})\right\}\theta. \tag{7.46}$$

[10] The current choice of output, q, is a static decision variable, as defined in this chapter. It would be more efficient to eliminate this variable from the maximization in Equation (7.40) by replacing the profit function defined in Equation (7.40) with the restricted profit function: the function that gives the firm's equilibrium single-period revenue minus production costs as a function of the exogenous state variables and the endogenous levels of capital (for all firms). This restricted function would not be linear in the weights γ and ν. Therefore, in order to eliminate the static decision variable and still maintain linearity in parameters, we would begin with the restricted single-period payoff functions corresponding to those of the firm, the industry, and the social planner, and take a convex combination of those three functions. This modification would be straightforward, but we do not pursue it because our objective is merely to explain the principles of the estimation strategy.

The action y' is an arbitrary deviation from the equilibrium action, y^*. Ideally, we would like to require that Inequality (7.46) holds for every possible initial condition $\mathbf{s}$ and for every possible deviation y', but in general it is not possible to impose this condition. Even in the case in which the control and state space are both finite, there would typically be too many possibilities to require that Inequality (7.46) hold for every possible combination.

We describe the algorithm for estimating the unknown parameters θ in three steps. We assume that the demand and production (but not adjustment) costs have been previously estimated. Thus, the algorithm is conditional on those estimates.

Step 1 obtains an estimate of the vector

$$V_i(\mathbf{s}_t; \mathbf{y}^*) \equiv E_{\mathbf{s},\mathbf{y}^*} \left\{ \sum_{\tau=0}^{\infty} \delta^{\tau} W_i(\mathbf{y}^*_{t+\tau}, \mathbf{s}_{t+\tau}) \right\}, \tag{7.47}$$

which appears on the left side of Equation (7.46). The first argument of $V_i(\mathbf{s}_t; \mathbf{y}^*)$ is the value of the exogenous state variable at a point in time; the second argument, $y^*(\mathbf{s})$, is the equilibrium control rule, a function. The variable $\mathbf{y}^*_{t+\tau}$ appearing on the right side of Equality (7.47) equals $\mathbf{y}^*(\mathbf{s}_{t+\tau})$; it is the value of the control at a point in time $t+\tau$ (as distinct from the control rule) when the value of the state variable is $s_{t+\tau}$.

Part a. First we estimate the parameters of the equation of motion (not shown) for the exogenous state variables $\mathbf{x}$. Recall that this vector includes variables such as factor costs and demand shifters. This estimation uses standard time-series methods.

Part b. We also estimate the vector of equilibrium control rules $y^*(\mathbf{s})$. To achieve this, we regress agents' observed actions against the state $\mathbf{s}$, using a flexible functional form. This estimation does not involve the equilibrium conditions for dynamic optimization.

Part c. The estimation in Parts a and b also produce estimates of the variance of the random terms in both the equation of motion of the exogenous states and in the control rule. We draw random sequences consisting of T elements, taken from distributions with these variances. We choose T sufficiently large that δ^T is very small; we will use a discounted sum consisting of T elements to approximate a discounted sum consisting of infinitely many terms. For each random sequence, we simulate future values of the state $\mathbf{s}$ and the control $\mathbf{y}$ (using our parameter estimates from Parts a and b). For each random sequence we approximate the vector of infinite sums

$$\sum_{\tau=0}^{\infty} \delta^{\tau} W_i(\mathbf{y}^*_{t+\tau}, \mathbf{s}_{t+\tau})$$

by replacing the upper limit ∞ by T. We then average over many such sequences to obtain an estimate of the vector in Equation (7.47), which we denote as $\hat{V}_i(\mathbf{s};\mathbf{y}^*)$. We obtain analogous estimates for the other firms.

Step 2 obtains an estimate that is used to evaluate the right side of Equation (7.46). The right side of this equation involves the function

$$V_i(\mathbf{s}_t;\mathbf{y}^*_{-i},\ y'_i) \equiv E_{\mathbf{s},y'_i,\mathbf{y}^*_{-i}}\left\{\sum_{\tau=0}^{\infty}\delta^{\tau}\,W_i(\mathbf{y}^*_{-i,t+\tau},\ y'_{t+\tau},\ \mathbf{s}_{t+\tau})\right\}. \tag{7.48}$$

Again, the arguments $\mathbf{y}^*_{-i}$, y'_i in the left side of (7.48) are functions: the equilibrium control rule for firms other than i and the (deviation) control rule for Firm i. We have an estimate of the function $\mathbf{y}^*_{-i}$ from Step 1.b. The estimation problem would be extremely difficult if we had to evaluate Inequality (7.46) for all possible functions y'_i. Fortunately, instead of considering all possible deviations, it is sufficient to consider "one-step deviations"; that is, deviations in which Firm i deviates from the equilibrium decision in the current period, and then uses the equilibrium decision rule in all subsequent periods. (See Bajari et al. 2004.)

Part a. Let y'_i be a one-step deviation; y'_i is a sequence consisting of the current action (the first element of the sequence) and future actions (all subsequent elements of the sequence). The fact that it is a "one-step" deviation means that the first element of this sequence (the action in the current period, time t) is not equal to the equilibrium action $y^*(s_t)$, but all subsequent elements do equal the corresponding equilibrium action. For this deviation, we have

$$\begin{aligned}
&V_i(\mathbf{s}_t;\mathbf{y}^*_{-i},\ y'_i)\\
&= \mathrm{E}_{\mathbf{s},y'_i,\mathbf{y}^*_{-i}}\left\{\sum_{\tau=0}^{\infty}\delta^{\tau}\,W_i(\mathbf{y}^*_{-it+\tau},\ y'_{t+\tau},\ \mathbf{s}_{t+\tau})\right\}\\
&= \mathrm{E}_{\mathbf{s}_t,y'_i,\mathbf{y}^*_{-i}}\left\{W_i(y_{it},\ \mathbf{y}^*_{-it},\ \mathbf{s}_t) + \delta \mathrm{E}_{\mathbf{s}_{t+1},\mathbf{y}^*}\left\{\sum_{\tau=0}^{\infty}\delta^{\tau}\,W_i(\mathbf{y}^*_{t+\tau+1},\ \mathbf{s}_{t+\tau+1})\right\}\right\}\\
&= \mathrm{E}_{\mathbf{s}_t,y'_i,\mathbf{y}^*_{-i}}\left\{W_i(y_{it},\ \mathbf{y}^*_{-it},\ \mathbf{s}_t) + \delta \mathrm{E}_{\mathbf{s}_{t+1},\mathbf{y}^*}\,V_i(\mathbf{s}_{t+1};\mathbf{y}^*)\right\}.
\end{aligned} \tag{7.49}$$

The first equality in Equation (7.49) repeats the definition in Equation (7.48). The second equality uses the assumption that Firm i is using a one-step deviation. Firm i uses $y'_{it} \neq y^*_i(\mathbf{s}_t)$ in the current period and then switches to the equilibrium control rule $y^*_i(\mathbf{s}_t)$ for subsequent periods. The third equality uses Equation (7.47).

Part b. We use the estimate of the equilibrium control rule $\mathbf{y}^*$ from Step 1b and the estimator $\hat{V}_i(\mathbf{s}_t;\mathbf{y}^*)$ from Step 1c, together with Equation (7.49) to obtain an estimate of $V_i(\mathbf{s}_t;\mathbf{y}^*_{-i},\ y'_i)$ for many one-step deviations for Firm i. We denote this estimate as $\hat{V}_i(\mathbf{s}_t;\mathbf{y}^*_{-i},\ y'_i)$. We obtain analogous estimates for each firm.

Step 3 of the algorithm produces an estimate of the parameter θ, using the estimates of $\hat{V}_i(\mathbf{s}_t; \mathbf{y}^*)$ and $\hat{V}_i(\mathbf{s}_t; \mathbf{y}^*_{-i}, y'_i)$ that we obtained from Steps 1 and 2. We have these estimates for many values of the state $\mathbf{s}$ and for many one-step deviations y'_i. We want to find the value of θ that approximately satisfies

$$(\hat{V}_i(\mathbf{s}_t; \mathbf{y}^*) - \hat{V}_i(\mathbf{s}_t; \mathbf{y}^*_{-i}, y'_i))\theta \geq 0. \tag{7.50}$$

Equation (7.50) is the estimation analog of Equation (7.46). We choose θ by minimizing a loss function, based on Inequality (7.50).

There are many potential loss functions. In order to describe the simplest of these, define a particular combination of a one-step deviation and initial condition, $(y'_i, \mathbf{s})$, as ω_k; the index k runs over all the combinations of initial states and one-step deviations that we chose in Steps 1 and 2. Define

$$g(\omega_k, \theta) = (V_i(\mathbf{s}) - V'_i(y'_i, \mathbf{s}))\theta, \tag{7.51}$$

and define $K(\theta)$ as the set of indices k for which $g(\omega_k, \theta) \geq 0$ is violated. The loss function in this case is[11]

$$\sum_{k \in K(\theta)} g(\omega_k, \theta)^2.$$

Bajari et al. (2004) provide more details for this estimation strategy, including the large sample properties of the estimator.

The assumption that the single-period profit function is linear in the unknown parameters is central to the algorithm. This assumption leads to tremendous computational savings because it means that the expectation of the present discounted stream of profits is multiplicatively separable in the unknown parameters and the control rule, as shown in Equation (7.45). This fact means that we can estimate the value function in two steps. From Equations (7.42) and (7.45), the value function is

$$J_i(\mathbf{s}) = \mathrm{E}_{\mathbf{s}, y^*_i, y^*_{-i}} \left\{ \sum_{\tau=0}^{\infty} \delta^\tau \pi(\mathbf{y}^*_{t+\tau}, \mathbf{s}_{t+\tau}) \right\} = \mathrm{E}_{\mathbf{s}, \mathbf{y}^*} \left\{ \sum_{\tau=0}^{\infty} \delta^\tau W_i(\mathbf{y}^*_{t+\tau}, \mathbf{s}_{t+\tau}) \right\} \theta. \tag{7.52}$$

We have explained how to use Monte Carlo methods to estimate the vector

$$\mathrm{E}_{\mathbf{s}, \mathbf{y}^*} \left\{ \sum_{\tau=0}^{\infty} \delta^\tau W_i(\mathbf{y}^*_{t+\tau}, \mathbf{s}_{t+\tau}) \right\}.$$

The important feature of this model is that the estimation of this vector is independent of θ. Therefore, we only need to compute the approximation to

11 A more complicated variation uses a weighted sum of squares, where the weights reflect the relative importance of the pseudo-observation ω_k. This variation may increase the efficiency of the estimator, just as weighted least squares improves the efficiency of ordinary least squares.

the infinite sum once (for each initial condition $\mathbf{s}$). With this estimate (and the information obtained from Step 2 of the algorithm), we can use the optimality condition to estimate θ. Without the assumption that the single-period payoff is linear in unknown parameters, we would need to compute an approximation to the infinite sum for each estimate of θ (and for each initial condition $\mathbf{s}$).

Given the importance of the linear-in-parameters assumption, it is worth asking whether it is empirically limiting. In our view, this assumption is less limiting than it might appear. Many highly nonlinear functions can be well approximated by low-order polynomials, for example, by using Chebyshev polynomials (see Judd 1999 or Miranda and Fackler 2002). These polynomials are linear in parameters. When beginning with a primitive payoff function that is not linear in parameters, the researcher has to make a choice between two approximations. The first alternative is to approximate the primitive function using a function that is linear in parameters (e.g., by using Chebyshev polynomials). The second alternative is to carry on with the original primitive function (nonlinear in parameters) and then approximate the resulting value function, as described in the previous paragraph. The first alternative is much simpler because the approximation needs to be carried out only once.

The estimator described in this section is a "first-stage" estimator, which we now denote as $\theta(1)$. At $\theta = \theta(1)$ the estimated decision rules approximately satisfy the necessary conditions for optimality, Inequality (7.46). The estimated decision rules used in this stage were obtained by regressing observed actions against state variables, without using any optimality condition. A "second stage" estimator, $\theta(2)$, proceeds as aforementioned, except that the original estimates of the decision rules are replaced by updated estimates that use the optimality conditions and $\theta(1)$. The algorithm given in Aguirregabiria and Mira (2002) can (we conjecture) be modified to obtain second and higher stage estimates.

SUMMARY

We discussed the estimation approaches of two models that differ in the fundamental reasons for dynamics. These models were used to address different empirical questions. The sticky price model provides a straightforward dynamic generalization of the static conjectural variation models used in the first part of this book. The conjectural variations parameter provides an index that measures the extent to which the observed outcome is closer to a competitive or collusive equilibrium. The necessary condition for optimality, the Euler equation, is the basic estimation equation, just as the first-order conditions to static optimization problems are the basis for estimating static models.

We illustrated how an apparently small change in the underlying demand function can lead to a substantial complication in the Euler equation. In a simple case, the Euler equation involves expectations of the decision variable in the next period. In a more complicated case, the Euler equation involves the expectation of an infinite sequence of future decision variables.

The advertising model assumed that the equilibrium was Nash-in-advertising. There, the objective was to determine whether firms use naïve (open-loop) or a more sophisticated strategy in which they recognize that rivals may respond to changes in the endogenous state variable. We derived the Euler equation under the assumption that firms use open-loop strategies and also under the assumption that they use Markov decision rules to illustrate why the estimation problem is more difficult in the second case. We then described a hybrid model that reduces to the open-loop equilibrium when a particular parameter is set equal to zero. This model can test the hypothesis that firms use open-loop strategies.

The final section of this chapter described a recently developed technique for the estimation of the parameters of the objective function in a game in which firms use Markov Perfect strategies. Using an example, we showed how this estimation strategy can be modified so that it permits the identification of the industry structure. That is, it enables the researcher to test whether firms are playing a noncooperative game, acting collusively, or behaving as price takers.

PROBLEMS

Note: Answers to problems are available at the back of the book.

7.1 You are asked to use the methods described in Chapter 7 to obtain the estimation equation for a duopoly under the open-loop assumption. Suppose that a regulator wants to achieve a target level of emissions, e^*, and does so by using a unit emissions tax τ. The tax in the next period is adjusted depending on whether current aggregate emissions exceed or fall short of the target: $\tau_{t+1} = \alpha\,(e_t - e^*)$, where $0 < \alpha < 1$ is a speed of adjustment parameter. In the first period (time 0), the "previous" tax is taken as given. Higher emissions reduce a firm's abatement costs, increasing its profits. Exclusive of the tax, Firm i's profits are increasing and concave in its own emissions, $\pi_{it} = \pi_i\,(E_{it})$. Its tax payments in period t are $\tau_t E_{it}$ and aggregate emissions are $E_t = E_{1t} + E_{2t}$. The firm's discount rate is δ. Assume that the equilibrium is symmetric.

a) Write down the optimization problem for each firm. What is the firm's control variable, and what is the state variable?

b) In this setting, what are the three market structures that correspond to the three leading cases (competitive, Nash-Cournot, collusive) discussed in the text?

c) Use a conjectural variation (or market index) model, with parameter λ, to nest the leading cases in part (b).

d) Obtain the Euler equation for the model in part (c). Discuss how you would estimate this model.

e) For the simple case in which $\pi_{it} = \pi_i(e_{it}) = (1 - e_{it}/2)\, e_{it}$, find the steady state as a function of λ and α. Interpret this result.

7.2 This question illustrates the difference between an open-loop and (differentiable) MPE. Use the same structure of the game as in question 7.1.

a) Obtain the Euler equation for the conjectural variation model when firms use MPE.

b) How would you estimate this model?

c) Specialize the conjectural variation parameter to obtain the Euler equation for the noncooperative Nash equilibrium. Using the quadratic model $\pi_{it} = (1 - e_{it}/2)\, e_{it}$, what can you say about the steady state?

EIGHT

Estimation of Market Power Using a Linear-Quadratic Model

Using what we developed in the preceding chapters, we now show how to estimate market power using a dynamic model in which firms incur costs that are quadratic in the change of output and face linear demand functions. Because demand is linear in output, revenue is quadratic in output. The equation of motion – a definition stating that output in this period equals output in the previous period plus the change in output – is linear. Thus, the single-period payoff is a linear-quadratic function of the endogenous state variable (lagged output) and the control variable (the change in output). In addition, the constraint is linear in these variables.

This model is a special case of the model of quasi-fixed inputs discussed in Chapter 6. We know that there is a linear equilibrium to this model, defined for all values of the state variable (lagged outputs). If we restrict attention to this linear equilibrium, we can obtain a measure of market power under either the open-loop or Markov Perfect assumption. This model illustrates the methods discussed in Chapters 6 and 7. The ability to write the equilibrium conditions in closed form, as a function of the index of market power, makes this model easy to estimate.

The linear-quadratic specification makes it possible to compare, in a simple manner, equilibria under the open-loop and Markov Perfect assumptions. In Chapter 6, we noted that these equilibria typically produce different outcomes, and that it is frequently possible to learn something about the qualitative difference between these outcomes, at least in the neighborhood of the steady state. The linear-quadratic specification enables us to examine the quantitative difference between the two equilibria: open loop and Markov Perfect. For a given measure of market power, we can determine the magnitude of the difference in the price trajectory and steady state. We can also see how the estimate of market power depends on whether we assume that firms use open-loop or Markov policies. That is, we can get a sense of whether the Markov assumption really matters for empirical work. This is important because the researcher rarely knows the exact game played by the firm(s).

For general functional forms, open-loop models are easier to estimate, as our discussion of the advertising model in Chapter 7 illustrated. That chapter also noted that Markov equilibria for general functional forms can be estimated, either by using numerical methods to solve the Dynamic Programming Equation or by using simulated values of the value function. Either of those approaches requires a combination of other compromises, such as reducing the dimension of the state vector, approximating a continuous control and state space using a discrete grid, or requiring that an optimality condition holds only for a subset of possible state-and-control combinations. Roberts and Samuelson's hybrid model represents another compromise, because it has features of both the open-loop and the Markov model. This chapter explores a different compromise, based on a functional form that permits closed-form solutions to the equilibrium conditions of both open-loop and Markov equilibria.

We would like to know whether the differences implied by open-loop and Markov equilibria are large. We assess this difference by comparing the indices of market structure and the corresponding steady-state prices under the two equilibria assumptions. Our comparison is based on a linear-quadratic model, and unfortunately we do not know how the difference between open-loop and Markov equilibria depends on the primitive functions. Therefore, the evidence we present concerning the different equilibria assumptions may not be applicable for other functional forms or for other values of the parameters we use in the linear-quadratic models investigated.

We begin by defining the model. We then discuss the relation between this model, a static model, and the model of quasi-fixed inputs studied in Chapter 6. We describe some of the implications of the linear-quadratic structure, and explain why these simplify the estimation problem. We use the model to estimate market power in the international rice and coffee markets. In these empirical applications, the agent is taken to be a country rather than a firm. The material in this chapter is based on Karp and Perloff (1989b, 1993a, 1993b, 1993c, 1996). Deodhar and Sheldon (1995) used this model to estimate international trade in bananas.

ASSUMPTIONS AND DEFINITIONS

There are $n \geq 2$ firms in an industry. Firm i ($i = 1, 2, \ldots, n$) sets output at the price-taker level, at the collusive level, or at an intermediate, oligopolistic level that lies between the two extremes.

Demand is linear and adjustment costs are quadratic. In period t, firms i face the inverse linear demand curve

$$p_{it} = a_i(t) - \sum_{j=1}^{n} b_{ij} q_{jt}. \tag{8.1}$$

For much of our discussion, we use the less general case, where $b_{ij} = b$, in which case Equation (8.1) simplifies to

$$p_{it} = a_i(t) - b \sum_{i=1}^{n} q_{it} = a_i(t) - bQ_t. \tag{8.2}$$

Here, p_{it} is the price in period t, q_{it} is the output of Firm i in period t, and Q_t is the total output of all firms. The demand intercept $a_i(t)$ includes the effects of various exogenous variables, including outputs of countries not explicitly included in the model. The slope parameter b (or b_{ij}) is a positive constant.

Firm i has a marginal cost $c_i(t)$ of producing contemporaneous output, q_{it}. This formulation allows the marginal cost to shift with exogenous variables over time. The marginal cost can change over time but is constant with respect to output. The change in output from one period to the next is $u_{it}\tau \equiv q_{it} - q_{it-\tau}$, where τ is the duration of a period and u_{it} is a rate. The cost of changing output is quadratic in the rate of change, $(\theta_{0it} + \theta u_{it}/2)u_{it}\tau$. For most of this chapter, we can set $\tau = 1$, in which case $u_{it} \equiv q_{it} - q_{it}$. The more general formulation with τ is useful for examining the effect on the equilibrium of the duration of a period, and also for considering the relationship between the discrete and continuous time models.

The intercepts of the inverse demand function, a_{it}, the marginal cost function, c_{it}, and the intercept of the marginal adjustment costs, θ_{0it}, can vary across firms and over time. These coefficients are functions of exogenous demand and cost shifters contained in the vector x_t. The empirical model must allow some nonstationarity and heterogeneity across agents in order to fit the data. The slopes of demand and marginal adjustment cost, b and θ, are constant. For most of our discussion, we also assume they are the same for all firms. The stationarity and homogeneity assumptions that b and θ are the same over time and across firms simplify the estimation problem.

As with the previous models, we estimate market power using the necessary conditions to a firm's problem when the firm behaves as if its rivals respond *in the same period* to its current decision. The conjecture is $dQ_{-it}/dq_{it} = v_i$, where Q_{-it} is the aggregate output at time t of all firms other than Firm i. As in Chapter 7, here we also use the conjecture with respect to aggregate industry output: $dQ_t/dq_{it} = \Lambda_i$. In a symmetric equilibrium (where all firms are identical, so that we do not need the i subscript), the two parameters are linearly related: $v + 1 = \Lambda$.

THE STATIC ANALOG

The model is static if $\theta = 0$. Here, the adjustment costs are linear. Future marginal adjustment costs do not depend on the future value of the state, so the future marginal adjustment costs do not depend on the current (or subsequent) investments. With linear adjustment costs, there are no fundamental reasons why decisions in the future depend on the current decision.

If the commodity is homogenous, Firm i's effective marginal revenue curve (the marginal revenue given the degree of market power actually exercised) is

$$MR_i(v_i) = p + (1 + v_i)\, p' q_i = p - (1 + v_i)\, b q_i,$$

where we suppress the subscript t.

Suppose that all firms are identical in the sense that they have identical $\nu = \nu_i$ and marginal costs: $MC = MC_i = c(t) = c_i(t)$. To determine ν, we estimate the demand curve, Equation (8.2), and the equilibrium condition for each firm, $MR_i = MC$. We rewrite this equation as

$$p = c + (1 + \nu)bq_i. \tag{8.3}$$

We obtain an estimate of ν by dividing the estimated coefficient on the q_i term in Equation (8.3) by the estimate of b from the demand curve, Equation (8.2), and then subtract one. The markup between price and marginal cost equals $p - c = (1 + \nu)\, bq_i$, which depends on ν. For example, if $\nu = -1$, marginal revenue equals price ($MR = p$) and there is no markup. If $\nu = n - 1$, marginal revenue is less than price $[MR = p + p'(nq_i) = p + p'Q]$ and the monopoly markup is observed in a symmetric equilibrium. Intermediate solutions, such as the Nash-Cournot equilibrium where $\nu = 0$, are also possible.

THE DYNAMIC MODEL

The dynamic model, $\theta > 0$, is a special case of the model of quasi-fixed inputs described in Chapter 6. Firm i's profit function (excluding adjustment costs) is

$$\pi_i(\mathbf{q}_t, \mathbf{x}_t) = (a_{it} - b\,(q_{it} + Q_{-it}) - c_{it})\, q_{it}.$$

We define $\mathbf{q}_t$ and $\mathbf{u}_t$ as n dimensional column vectors with q_{it} and u_{it} in the ith positions. The state variable is the vector $(\mathbf{q}_{t-1}', \mathbf{x}_t')'$. The vector of control variables for the firms is $\mathbf{u}_t$ and the (discrete) equation of motion is

$$\mathbf{q}_t = \mathbf{q}_{t-\tau} + \mathbf{u}_t \tau.$$

The vector of outputs plays the same role in this model as does the quasi-fixed input (capital) in the model in Chapter 6. The vector of changes in output plays the same role as investment in the earlier model. Here, there is no depreciation in the endogenous state variable. Single-period profits are a quadratic function of the state and control variables, and the equation of motion is linear in these variables. Firms incur nonlinear costs of changing their output levels because of costs associated with changing levels of production or inventory.

At an arbitrary time t, Firm i wants to maximize its expectation of the present discounted value of profits minus adjustment costs,

$$\mathrm{E}_{it} \sum_{t=1}^{\infty} \delta^{(t-1)} \left[(p_{it} - c_{it})\, q_{it} - \left(\theta_{0it} + \frac{\theta u_{it}}{2} \right) u_{it} \right] \tau.$$

Hereafter, we assume that the econometrician knows the discount factor, $\delta = e^{-r\tau}$. For purposes of discussing the model, we make two further assumptions, neither of which is needed for estimation. First, we set $\theta_{0it} = 0$. This assumption means that adjustment costs are positive whenever the change in the (endogenous) state variable (q) is non-zero; adjustment costs are zero when there is no change in this state variable. Second, we suppose that the demand and cost intercepts a_{it} and c_{it} are identical across firms, so we drop the firm index. (We do not use this assumption in estimation because it is important to allow cross-firm heterogeneity in empirical work.) We redefine a_t as the difference between the demand and cost intercepts at time t (rather than the demand intercept, as explained earlier).

With these assumptions and our previous definitions, we rewrite the expression for the present discounted value in matrix notation:

$$\mathrm{E}_i \sum_{t=1}^{\infty} \delta^{t-1} \left(a_t \mathbf{e}_i' \left(\mathbf{q}_{t-\tau} + \mathbf{u}_t \tau\right) - \frac{1}{2} \left(\mathbf{q}_{t-\tau} + \mathbf{u}_t \tau\right)' \mathbf{K}_i \left(\mathbf{q}_{t-\tau} + \mathbf{u}_t \tau\right) - \frac{1}{2} \mathbf{u}_t' \mathbf{S}_i \mathbf{u}_t \right) \tau, \tag{8.4}$$

where $\mathbf{e}_i$ is the ith unit column vector (a vector of zeroes with a one in the ith position); $\mathbf{e}$ is an n-dimensional column vector consisting entirely of ones; $\mathbf{K}_i = b(\mathbf{e}\mathbf{e}_i' + \mathbf{e}_i\mathbf{e}')$ – that is, $\mathbf{K}_i$ is an $n \times n$ dimensional matrix of zeroes with bs on the ith column and the ith row, except for the (i, i) element, which contains $2b$; and $\mathbf{S}_i$ is an $n \times n$ matrix consisting of zeroes except for the (i, i) element, which contains θ.

IMPLICATIONS OF THE LINEAR-QUADRATIC STRUCTURE

The linear-quadratic structure of the game has several important implications. There always exists an equilibrium linear control rule. The intercept and slopes of that control rule can be computed recursively, as described subsequently. These features are important for estimation of the index of market power. In addition to the linear-quadratic structure, we assume subsequently that uncertainty is additive. This additional assumption means that the control rule for the stochastic game is identical to the control rule for the corresponding deterministic game in which all stochastic variables are replaced by their expected values.

In Chapter 6, we used a continuous time model with one state variable to explain why the Markov Perfect equilibrium (MPE) is typically not unique. This non-uniqueness results because the necessary conditions that determine a steady state contain more unknowns than equations. We therefore have a missing boundary condition, and cannot obtain a unique solution to the differential (or difference) equations that determine the equilibrium.

For empirical work or applied theory, it may be reasonable to select the equilibrium obtained by considering the limit of a finite horizon problem as the horizon goes to infinity. Hereafter, we refer to this limiting equilibrium as the *Markov equilibrium*. The value function in the finite horizon linear-quadratic game is quadratic in the endogenous state, and the equilibrium control rule – the function that maps the state into the control – is linear in this state. In studying the infinite horizon problem, we therefore look for a linear control rule and a linear-quadratic value function.

We use time-series observations on firms' output to estimate the industry's actual control rules. We then use these control rules to infer the index of market power, v, under the assumption that firms use either open-loop or Markov strategies. As we previously emphasized, it is not reasonable to think that firms believe that their rivals will respond to their actions *within the same period* – the literal interpretation of the conjectural variations parameter. Instead, this parameter is merely a means of measuring how close the market outcome is to the perfectly competitive, Nash-Cournot, or cartel equilibria. We explained why outcomes other than these three cases are reasonable in Chapters 5 and 6.

To simplify our discussion, we now assume that the demand intercept minus marginal cost is a linear function of the exogenous random variables $\mathbf{x}_t$, and that the equation of motion for these variables is linear with an additive shock:

$$a(t) = \beta' \mathbf{x}_t \quad \text{and} \quad \mathbf{x}_{t+1} = \mathbf{\Phi} \mathbf{x}_t + \mu_t, \tag{8.5}$$

where β (a vector) and $\mathbf{\Phi}$ (a matrix) are constant and μ_t is an *iid* random variable with zero mean. A constant term can be included in the vector $\mathbf{x}_t$.

The linear-quadratic assumptions make it possible to obtain a closed-form solution to the equilibrium rules as a function of the model's parameters (including v). Using this solution and estimates of the demand function and the control rule, we can infer the value of v. In the absence of a closed-form solution, we could use the type of numerical strategy discussed at the end of Chapter 7. The linear-quadratic specification enables us to avoid those complications.

The closed-form solution for the equilibrium control rule – under both the open-loop and Markov assumptions – has properties that are useful for empirical work. The equilibrium level of output in the current period is a linear function of lagged output. That is, the control rule is of the form

$$\mathbf{q}_t = \mathbf{g}_t + \mathbf{G} \mathbf{q}_{t-1} \tag{8.6}$$

for some vector $\mathbf{g}_t$ and a matrix $\mathbf{G}$.

The Recursive Structure of the Solution

The solution to the linear-quadratic problem has a particular recursive structure: we use a subset of the parameters of the model to find the equilibrium matrix $\mathbf{G}$. Using this value of $\mathbf{G}$ and all of the parameters of the model, we solve a second system of equations to obtain the equilibrium value of $\mathbf{g}_t$. This recursive structure has important implications for estimating the parameters of the model.

The equilibrium value of the matrix $\mathbf{G}$ is a function of the demand slope, b; the adjustment parameter, θ; the discount factor, δ; and the index v. (In the more general case, in which ν_i is firm-specific, we replace the scalar ν by a vector $\boldsymbol{\nu}$ whose ith element is ν_i.) That is, we can write

$$\mathbf{G} = \mathbf{F}^k(b, \theta, \delta, \nu), \tag{8.7}$$

where $k =$ *Markov Perfect* or *open loop.* The function $\mathbf{F}^k$ imposes certain restrictions on the form of the matrix **G**. (Later in this chapter we discuss this function in detail. Our objective at this point is to explain the structure of the solution, and its implications for estimation.) We can impose these restrictions in estimating **G**. Given an estimate that satisfies those restrictions, we can invert the function $\mathbf{F}^k$and recover a subset of the parameters $b,\ \theta,\ \delta,\ \nu$.

In particular, if we know δ(as previously assumed), and have an independent estimate of b (obtained by estimating the demand equation), then we can invert $\mathbf{F}^k$ to obtain estimates of the adjustment cost parameter and the market power index (θ and ν) under either the open-loop or the Markov assumption. These are the economically interesting parameters, and they cannot be estimated without using a structural model. For example, in practice, we seldom, if ever, have data on adjustment costs, so we could not estimate the parameter θ using a standard regression. We are able to estimate θ and ν without using the remaining parameters (e.g., the demand and cost intercepts) or the equilibrium condition that determines $\mathbf{g}_t$ due to the recursive structure of the solution to the linear-quadratic game.

The intercept vector, $\mathbf{g}_t$ depends on all of the parameters of the model, including the demand intercept minus the marginal cost, and expectations about future random variables. Given the assumptions in Equation (8.5), the intercept of the control rule is a linear function of the exogenous state, $\mathbf{g}_t = \varphi \boldsymbol{x}_t$; the coefficient vector φ depends on all of the parameters of the model, including β and $\boldsymbol{\Phi}$, in Equation (8.5). That is, we have

$$\mathbf{g}_t = \varphi \boldsymbol{x}_t \quad \text{with} \quad \varphi = \mathbf{f}^k\left(\beta, \boldsymbol{\Phi}, \delta, \nu, \theta; \mathbf{G}\right), \tag{8.8}$$

where $k =$ Markov Perfect or open loop. The function $\mathbf{f}^k$ is determined by the equilibrium conditions to the game. We discuss a possible use of Equation (8.8) in the next subsection. We do not need this equation to estimate the structural parameters θ and ν. We can estimate the vector β by estimating the demand function, and estimate $\boldsymbol{\Phi}$ by time-series estimation of Equation (8.5); we have already discussed estimation of the remaining parameters.

The Principle of Certainty Equivalence

In Chapter 6, we noted that the term open loop does not have exactly the same interpretation in control-theory and in game-theory contexts. In the game-theoretic context, the important aspect of the open-loop equilibrium is the assumption that firms do not anticipate that their rivals will change future decisions as a consequence of current actions (due to changes in the state variable). When making the open-loop assumption (in the estimation process), we are not indicating (necessarily) that agents will not change their future decisions in response to the arrival of new information. Further, we also noted in Chapter 6 that much of the dynamic game theory uses nonstochastic models in which agents do not expect to receive new exogenous information. For empirical work, we need to use a stochastic model.

An attractive feature of the linear-quadratic model (with additive stochastic variables in the equation of motion) is that the equilibrium control rule is the same regardless of whether agents recognize that they will receive new information about the stochastic variables in the future. That is, the optimal control rule for each agent's problem (when they anticipate the arrival of new information about the stochastic variables) is identical to the control rule for the "certainty equivalent" problem. This certainty equivalent problem is obtained by replacing all of the random variables with their expected values and ignoring stochastic issues. In other words, the equilibrium control rule depends on the first moments of the random variables, but not on their higher moments (e.g., variance). This property, which is known as the *Principle of Certainty Equivalence*, holds for a linear-quadratic model in which there are additive random terms in the equation of motion, as assumed in Equation (8.5).[1]

This feature is attractive for empirical work: the open-loop assumption is merely a statement that firms believe they do not affect their rivals' future actions. The open-loop assumption does not imply that firms naïvely think that they would not change their own future decisions after receiving new information.

The Principle of Certainty Equivalence states that the control rule, the solution to Equations (8.7) and (8.8), is independent of the higher moments of the random shock vector, μ_t in Equation (8.5). Firms would use the same control rule whether they believe they can exactly predict future exogenous variables, or whether they recognize that these variables are random. Because these higher moments do not affect the optimal (or equilibrium) control rule, it does not matter what beliefs agents have about the higher moments.

If we want to impose (or test) the hypothesis that firms have rational expectations with respect to the exogenous random variables, we need to estimate the parameters in Equations (8.5) and (8.6), imposing the restrictions implied by equilibrium behavior and contained in Equations (8.7) and (8.8). This estimation problem has been studied extensively in the context of a single-agent linear-quadratic control problem (Hansen and Sargent 1980, Chow 1981). The same types of methods can

[1] If random terms enter the equation of motion multiplicatively (e.g., there is parameter uncertainty), then the control rule is still linear in the state. However, in this case, the control rule depends on both the mean and the variance of the random terms. Therefore, the Principle of Certainty Equivalence does not hold for the linear-quadratic problem with multiplicative disturbances. See Hoel and Karp (2001) for an application of that model.

be used in the linear-quadratic game. If we are not interested in imposing this rational expectations hypothesis, we do not need to estimate Equation (8.5) or impose the restrictions in Equation (8.8).

Our comments on the estimation of this model would still hold if b, θ, and v were not constant, provided they were nonrandom. The only difference is that G becomes nonstationary. Similarly, none of these comments depends on the homogeneity assumptions that b, θ, and v are the same for all firms.

PROPERTIES OF THE EQUILIBRIA

This model, in which we assume that the good is homogeneous and the firms are identical, has four important properties.[2] First, if $v = -1$ or $v = n - 1$, the open-loop and Markov Perfect trajectories, control rules, and equilibria are identical.[3] This result holds because if firms are either price takers or share the market (behave as a cartel) in each period, it does not matter whether they recognize that future values of output are endogenous.

Second, in both the open-loop and Markov Perfect equilibria, output is decreasing in v. If this relation did not hold, the parameter v would be a poor index of market power. Taken together, the first two properties provide a justification for using v as an index of market power: v is monotonically related to the obvious measures of market performance, such as price, output, and the markup.

Third, we can use simulation to show that for $-1 < v < n - 1$ and for given symmetric initial output level q, the outcome in the MPE is more competitive than in the open-loop equilibrium. The greater degree of competition results in higher output, lower prices, greater social welfare, and lower industry profits in the MPE. In particular, this comparison holds at the Nash-Cournot equilibrium, where $v = 0$.

In Chapter 6, we explained how information on whether actions are strategic substitutes or complements can be used to compare steady-state Nash-Cournot outcomes under open-loop and Markov Perfection. In the model we discuss now, actions are strategic substitutes because a higher level of output for one firm lowers the marginal value of output for other firms. Therefore, firms have a strategic incentive to increase their output, in the Markov equilibrium, as a means of discouraging their rivals from choosing a large output in the future. This incentive is absent in the open-loop equilibrium, in which firms believe that their rivals do not respond to changes in the endogenous state. Consequently, the equilibrium output is higher when firms use Markov strategies. The Nash-Cournot MPE level of output is also higher than the open-loop level outside the steady state. This ranking also holds for $v \neq 0$ – that is, for equilibria between the cartel and price-taking equilibria, other than Nash-Cournot.

2 This section is based on Karp and Perloff (1993b).

3 We establish sufficiency analytically, by examining the equilibrium conditions. Simulation results indicate that this condition is also necessary.

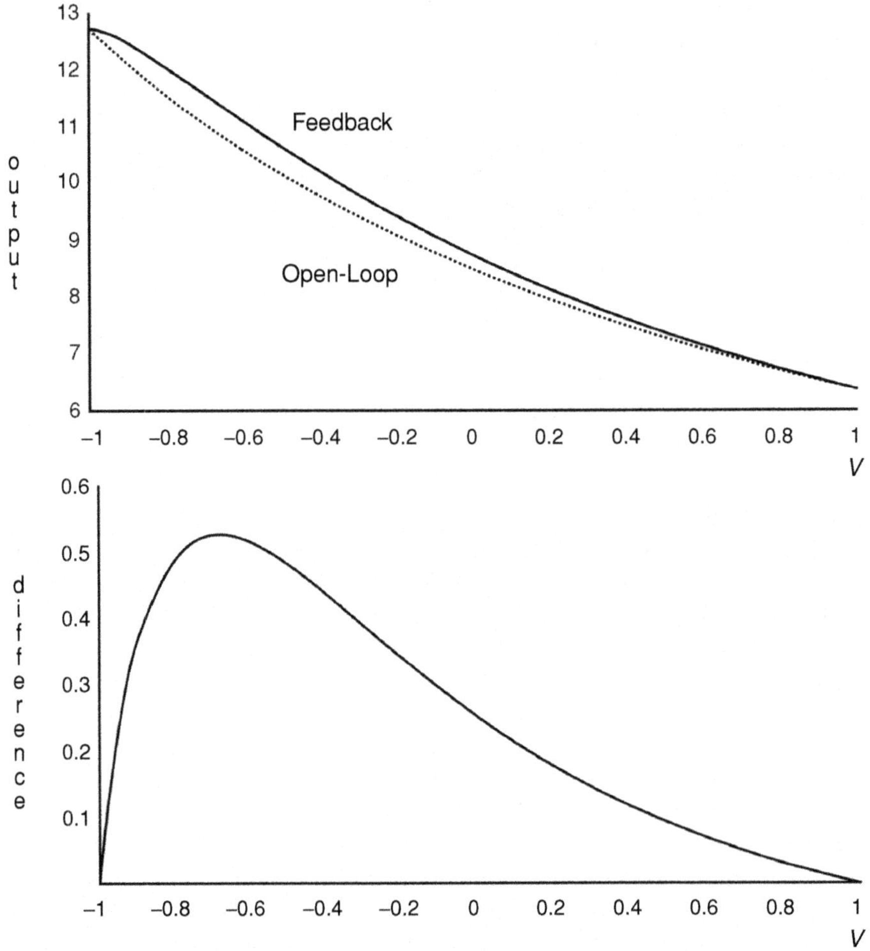

Figure 8.1. Markov Perfect (Feedback) and Open-Loop Steady-State Outputs.

Figure 8.1 compares the two models using parameter values $a = 250$, $b = 10$, $\delta = 0.95$, $\theta = 10$, $\tau = 1$, and $n = 2$. The graph at the top shows the steady-state equilibrium output levels, and the bottom graph shows their difference, as a function of ν. The absolute difference between the open-loop and Markov steady states is greatest when the equilibrium is between Nash-Cournot and price-taking ($\nu \approx -0.7$). The difference in output is less than 10% of aggregate output; at the Nash-Cournot level, the difference is approximately 7% of aggregate output. These results suggest that the distinction between Markov Perfect and open-loop equilibria is not negligible, but it may be less important than other kinds of modeling decisions, such as the choice of functional form.

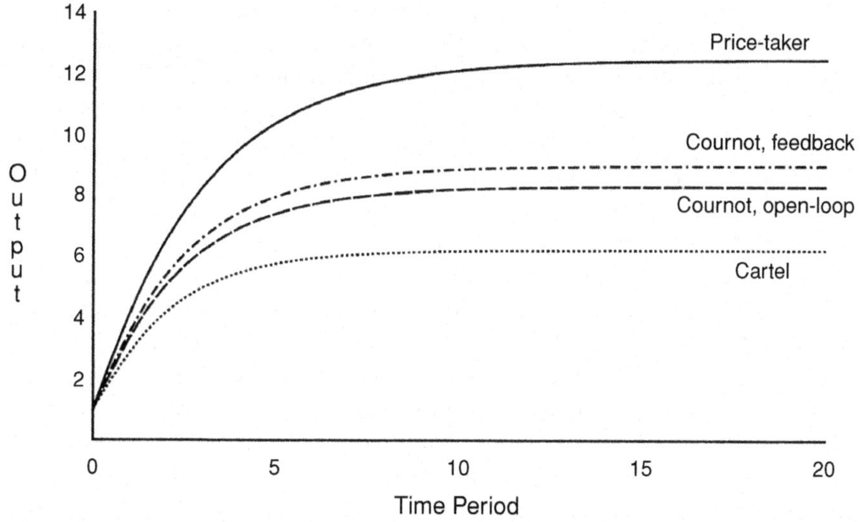

Figure 8.2. Trajectories for Four Models.

For the same parameter values, Figure 8.2 shows the trajectories of the aggregate output under the four leading market structures (price taking, cartel, open-loop Cournot, and Markov Perfect Cournot) from a low initial condition. At least for these parameter values, the level of output is very close to the steady-state level within five and ten years. This simulation suggests that qualitative information about the steady state may be useful because the system is likely to be close to its steady state.

Fourth, for $-1 < \nu < n - 1$, the steady-state equilibrium output depends on τ (the duration of a period) and on θ (the adjustment cost parameter) when firms use Markov strategies; the steady-state output is independent of τ and θ when firms use open-loop strategies. This property implies that the estimated index of market structure depends on the period of adjustment with Markov strategies. Data limitations may determine the duration of a period that the econometrician assumes that firms use, and therefore may affect the estimate of market power.

That the open-loop steady state (but not, of course, the adjustment path to this steady state) is independent of τ and θ can be verified by inspection of the steady-state equilibrium conditions. This conclusion depends on our previous assumption that adjustment costs equal zero when adjustment is zero: at the steady state.

The importance of τ and θ in determining the steady state under Markov strategies is easiest to understand in the case in which firms play Nash-Cournot ($\nu = 0$). Here, firms act under the assumption that rivals respond only in future periods. The strength of the incentive to increase current output as a means of encouraging rivals to lower their future output depends on how quickly rivals are able to respond. When τ is small, rivals respond quickly, so the strategic incentive to increase current output is quite strong, leading to higher equilibrium output. When τ is large, rivals respond only after a considerable lag, so the strategic incentive is lower. This incentive is absent in the open-loop equilibrium. Simulations show that the (positive) difference between the Markov and open-loop steady states is decreasing in τ.

Holding τ fixed at a positive level, we can make the difference in steady states under the open-loop and the Markov assumptions arbitrarily small by making θ small. Thus, this discrete stage model approaches the static model. As the fundamental reason for dynamics (the presence of adjustment costs) becomes unimportant, the difference between the open-loop and Markov equilibria also becomes unimportant.

This conclusion does not hold in the continuous time model, in which Reynolds (1987) shows that the open-loop and Markov steady states are different even in the limiting case, $\theta \to 0$. We can reconcile this result with the conclusions from our discrete time model using simulations. These simulations show that as we move toward the continuous time model by making τ smaller, we need to make adjustment costs less important (decrease θ) in order to keep the difference between Markov and open-loop steady states at a constant level. In considering the continuous time model without adjustment costs, the order in which limits are taken is important. If we first let τ approach 0, we obtain Reynolds' continuous time model. If we then let θ approach 0, we obtain the result that the Markov and open-loop steady states differ. If we begin with the discrete stage model and first let θ approach 0, we obtain the static model. The equilibrium to this model is independent of the duration of a period.

We also used simulations to compare the estimated ν and δ in the open-loop and Markov equilibria. For this experiment, we chose parameter values for the model (including ν and θ) and solved the open-loop equilibrium to obtain the open-loop control rule. Using this control rule and the correct demand parameter b, we used the MPE conditions to estimate ν and θ under the Markov assumption. These estimated values are both greater than the true values (the ones used to generate the open-loop equilibrium).

This result is consistent with the comparison between the Markov and open-loop equilibria for given ν described earlier. For a given ν, the Markov rules lead to more competitive behavior. Suppose we have two industries facing the same demand function, and firms use open-loop strategies in the first market and Markov strategies in the second. In order for the two markets to lead to approximately the same price and quantity series, the second industry must be more collusive, as measured by the index ν. This larger value of ν is needed to offset the fact that Markov strategies are less collusive for a given value of ν.

EQUILIBRIUM CONDITIONS USED FOR ESTIMATION

We now discuss the equilibrium conditions that are used to obtain estimates of the market conduct parameter ν and the cost of adjustment parameter. We start by discussing these conditions under the open loop and then discuss them under the Markov assumptions. Here, we explain in detail the vector function $\mathbf{F}^k$used in Equation (8.7). We will not discuss the equilibrium conditions that determine the intercept of the control rule, $\mathbf{g}_0$ (Equation (8.8)). We do not use these conditions in estimation, because we do not impose or test the hypothesis that firms have rational expectations with respect to the exogenous variables.

In this section, we relax some of the assumptions concerning firm homogeneity used in the previous discussion. In our description of the model, we used a single (possibly firm-specific) parameter, ν_i to denote Firm i's conjecture about the aggregate response of all other firms to Firm i's control ($\nu_i = \mathrm{d}Q_{-it}/\mathrm{d}q_{it}$). However, we see from the control rule, Equation (8.6), that each firm's equilibrium decision depends on the entire vector of lagged sales – not simply on the rivals' aggregate lagged sales. This observation suggests that it might be possible to generate a more general family of equilibria by allowing Firm i to have different conjectures for each of its rivals.

To describe this situation, we define $\nu_{ij} = \mathrm{d}q_{jt}/\mathrm{d}q_{it}$ as Firm i's conjecture of j's response. We define $\mathbf{v}_i$ as an n dimensional column vector with one in the ith position and ν_{ij} elsewhere. This formulation generalizes the model in the previous section. If Firm i's conjecture is the same for all its rivals j – that is, if $\nu_{ij} = \nu_i^*$ for a constant ν_i^* – then we have the same model as described earlier. In this case, $\nu_i^* = \nu/(n-1)$. When ν_{ij} varies over j, Firm i has different conjectures for the outputs of different rivals.

This more general formulation is not useful for estimating the open-loop model because the additional conjectural parameters are not identified. In principle, it appears possible to estimate an additional parameter in the Markov Perfect setting. However, one of our primary objectives is to compare the estimated indices under the open-loop and Markov settings, and this requires that the indices have the same dimension. Therefore, in the empirical section, we use the simpler formulation in which firms have a conjecture about the aggregate response, but not about their rivals' individual responses.

Necessary Conditions for the Open-Loop Equilibrium

We start by stating the equilibrium conditions for the matrix $\mathbf{G}$ in the open-loop equilibrium. Given a value of δ, an estimated matrix $\mathbf{G}$, and demand slope b (and hence $\mathbf{K}_i$), the open-loop parameters $\mathbf{v}_i$ and θ_i satisfy (see the Appendix)

$$\mathbf{K}_i \nu_i = [\mathbf{G}'^{-1}(\mathbf{I}-\mathbf{G})(\mathbf{I}-\delta\mathbf{G})]\mathbf{e}_i\theta_i. \tag{8.9}$$

The derivation of Equation (8.9) does not depend on the assumption that firms are symmetric, but the solution to the equation requires either symmetry or a similar restriction. The matrix $\mathbf{K}_i$ is of rank 2, so in general there are either infinitely many solutions to Equation (8.9) or no solutions.

For example, suppose that Firm i faces the demand function

$$p_{it} = a_{it} - \sum_{j=1}^{n} b_{ij} q_{jt}.$$

Setting $I = 1$, Equation (8.9) can be written

$$\begin{bmatrix} 2b_{11} & b_{12} & . & . & . & b_{1n} \\ b_{12} & 0 & . & . & . & 0 \\ . & . & . & & & . \\ . & . & & . & & . \\ . & . & & & . & . \\ b_{1n} & 0 & . & . & . & 0 \end{bmatrix} \begin{bmatrix} 1 \\ v_{12} \\ . \\ . \\ . \\ v_{1n} \end{bmatrix} = \begin{bmatrix} y_{11} \\ y_{12} \\ . \\ . \\ . \\ y_{1n} \end{bmatrix} \theta_1, \tag{8.10}$$

where the elements y_{1j} are obtained from the right side of Equation (8.9); they are functions of the discount factor δ and the elements of **G**. The existence of a solution to Equation (8.10) (replacing the index 1 by the index i to denote an arbitrary firm) requires that

$$\frac{b_{ij}}{b_{ik}} = \frac{y_{ij}}{y_{ik}}, \quad j,\ k \neq i. \tag{8.11}$$

If Equation (8.11) is satisfied, Equation (8.10) implies that

$$\theta_i = \frac{b_{ij}}{y_{ij}}, \quad j \neq i. \tag{8.12}$$

Given that we have an estimate of the **G** matrix (and therefore can calculate y_{ij}), Equation (8.12) states that θ_i is linear in the estimated demand slope coefficients. If we use Equation (8.12) to eliminate θ_i from Equation (8.10) (again replacing the index 1 by i), we obtain

$$\sum_{j \neq i} \frac{b_{ij}}{b_{ii}} v_{ij} = \frac{y_{ii}\, b_{ik}}{y_{ik}\, b_{ii}} - 2, \quad i = 1, 2 \ldots n; \quad k \neq i. \tag{8.13}$$

This system consists of n equations in $(n-1)n$ unknowns. An additional set of restrictions, such as $v_{ij} = v_i^*$, is needed in order to obtain a unique solution. With this particular restriction, we estimate an aggregate index (or aggregate conjectural variation) for each firm, but we cannot distribute this index over a firm's rivals. In this situation, the generalization that we described at the beginning of this section (replacing a firm-specific aggregate conjectural variation, v_i, with a firm-specific "individual" conjectural variation, v_{ij}) cannot be estimated under the assumption of an open-loop equilibrium.[4]

[4] See Chapter 9 and the Statistical Appendix for other methods that can be used in theses cases and are specifically helpful in the cases in which there are more unknown parameters than data points.

If each firm's output has the same effect on the price of Firm i's commodity – that is, if $b_{ij} = b_{ik}, \forall j, k \neq i$ – and if, in addition, we assume that $v_{ij} = v_i^*$, then (8.11) and (8.13) simplify to

$$1 = \frac{y_{ij}}{y_{ik}}, \forall j, k \neq i, \tag{8.14}$$

$$v_i^* = \frac{(y_{ii} - 2\, y_{ik})}{(n-1)\, y_{ik}}. \tag{8.15}$$

In this case, we can estimate the n^2 elements of **G** subject to the $(n-2)\,n$ restrictions of (8.14) and use (8.15) to infer v_i^*. This approach does not require estimation of the demand-slope parameters, b_{ij} (b if the product is homogenous). The slope parameters are needed only to recover θ_i and to test whether the hypotheses $b_{ij} = b_{ik}$ are reasonable.

In general, it is difficult to impose the restrictions in Equation (8.11). However, these restrictions certainly hold if there is sufficient symmetry in the model and the equilibrium. In particular, suppose that the demand slopes are symmetric (i.e., the demand function is Equation (8.2) instead of Equation (8.1)). Suppose also that each firm has the same equilibrium response to its own lagged quantity and each firm has the same equilibrium response to any rival's lagged quantity. That is, suppose that **G** has the form

$$\mathbf{G} = \begin{bmatrix} g_1 & g_2 & \cdots & g_2 \\ \vdots & g_1 & & \vdots \\ & & \ddots & g_2 \\ g_2 & \cdots & g_2 & g_1 \end{bmatrix}, \tag{8.16}$$

where g_1 and g_2 are constants. If **G** is estimated subject to this restriction, all elements except the ith in the column vector on the right-hand side of Equation (8.9) are equal and the equation has a unique solution.

Necessary Conditions for the Markov Perfect Equilibrium

We want to derive the necessary conditions for the MPE so that we can estimate the vector $\mathbf{v}_i$ and the scalar θ_i.[5] We begin by defining the vectors

$$\mathbf{w}_i = (I - \delta(\mathbf{G}' \otimes \mathbf{G}))^{-1}([\mathbf{G}' \otimes \mathbf{G}'][vec(\mathrm{K}_i)]),$$

$$\mathbf{z}_i = (I - \delta[\mathbf{G}' \otimes \mathbf{G}'])^{-1}[(\mathbf{G}' \otimes \mathbf{G}') - (\mathbf{I} \otimes \mathbf{G}') - (\mathbf{G}' \otimes \mathbf{I}) + \mathbf{I}][vec(\mathbf{e}_i\mathbf{e}_i')].$$

[5] Recall that the ith element of the vector $\mathbf{v}_i$ is one and the jth element is v_i.

The symbol $\otimes$ denotes the Kronecker product. The operator vec($\mathbf{K}$) stacks the columns of the $n \times n$ dimensional matrix $\mathbf{K}$ into a n^2 dimensional column vector. (The first n elements of this vector consist of the first column of $\mathbf{K}$, the second n elements consist of the second column, and so on.) The "inverse vec" operator reverses this process; that is, it creates a $n \times n$ dimensional matrix from a n^2 dimensional column vector. Applying the inverse vec operator to the definitions of $\mathbf{w}_i$ and $\mathbf{z}_i$ produces matrices $\mathbf{W}_i$ and $\mathbf{Z}_i$. By inspection, $\mathbf{W}_i$ is linear in Firm i's demand coefficient(s), which are elements of the matrix $\mathbf{K}_i$. The matrix $\mathbf{Z}_i$ depends only on δ and $\mathbf{G}$. If agents use Markov strategies, $\mathbf{v}_i$ and θ must satisfy

$$\left[\mathbf{K}_i + \delta\mathbf{W}_i + \left(\mathbf{e}_i\mathbf{e}_i' + \delta\mathbf{Z}_i\right)\theta_i\right]\mathbf{v}_i = \overset{\prime-1}{\mathbf{G}}\,\mathbf{e}_i\theta_i \equiv \mathbf{y}_i^*\,\theta_i. \tag{8.17}$$

The complexity of $\mathbf{W}_i$ and $\mathbf{Z}_i$ makes it difficult to analyze Equation (8.17) for the general case. Therefore, we now consider the symmetric case, in which $p_i = a_i - bQ$, and θ and $v_{ij} = v^*$, the same constant for all firms. Here, the left side of Equation (8.17) is of rank 2. Under this symmetry assumption, the estimate of v^* is independent of b – as is the case in the open-loop equilibrium. Because $\mathbf{K}_i$ and $\mathbf{W}_i$ are both linear in the demand slope, we can define the matrix $\mathbf{A}_i$and $\mathbf{B}_i$ such that $b\mathbf{A}_i = \mathbf{K}_i + \delta\mathbf{W}_i$ and $\mathbf{B}_i = \mathbf{e}_i\mathbf{e}'_i + \delta\mathbf{Z}_i$. Note that the matrices $\mathbf{A}_i$ and $\mathbf{B}_i$ depend only on $\delta$and $\mathbf{G}$, a fact that we use subsequently. To recover v^* and θ, we rewrite the ith and the kth ($k \neq i$) equations of the system (8.17) as

$$b\left(A_{ii} + v\sum_{j\neq i} A_{ij}\right) + \theta\left(B_{ii} + v\sum_{j\neq i} B_{ij}\right) = y_{ii}^*\,\theta \tag{8.18}$$

$$b\left(A_{ki} + v\sum_{j\neq i} A_{kj}\right) + \theta\left(B_{ki} + v\sum_{j\neq i} B_{kj}\right) = y_{ik}^*\,\delta, \tag{8.19}$$

where A_{ij}, B_{ij}, and y_{ij}^* are elements of $\mathbf{A}_i$, $\mathbf{B}_i$ and $\mathbf{y}_i^*$. Solving (8.19) gives θ as a linear function of b and a nonlinear function of the scalar v^*. Substituting this function into (8.18) gives a quadratic in v^* that is independent of b (because $\mathbf{A}_i$ and $\mathbf{B}_i$ are independent of b). Therefore, given symmetry, we can estimate v^* using only the assumed value of δ and the estimated value of $\mathbf{G}$.

The fact that estimation of v^* requires solving a quadratic equation (which depends on other parameter estimates) is not surprising, given the structure of the model. Obtaining the optimal control rule in a control problem requires solving a quadratic equation, known as the algebraic Riccati matrix equation. Finding the Markov equilibrium to the dynamic game requires solving a different polynomial, closely related to the Riccati matrix equation. These polynomials (in general) have multiple roots. We select the correct root by using the requirement that the representative agent's decision problem is concave. We also use the transversality condition, which requires that the present value of the shadow value of the state (the levels of output) t periods in the future, converges to 0 as t approaches infinity. An alternative to using the tranversality condition in selecting the correct root is to require that the level of output converges to a steady state; that is, we require that, in equilibrium, the controlled state converges to a finite value.

Our estimation problem is the inverse of this optimization problem and we use the same equilibrium condition (the algebraic Riccati equation for the control problem or its game analog) to obtain parameter estimates. Although there are two solutions to Equations (8.18) and (8.19), we found through extensive simulations that one value is close to the open-loop value and the other is implausible ($\nu^* < -1/(n-1)$ or $\nu^* > 1$). Therefore, in practice, it is easy to choose the correct root.

Additional Restrictions and Testing

It is possible for a value (or values in the asymmetric case) of ν^* to satisfy Equations (8.9) or (8.17) without the implied game being meaningful. Given the solution to Equations (8.9) or (8.17), it is necessary that we check that each player's second-order conditions are satisfied and that system-of-difference equations that determine the stationary equilibrium (the Ricatti difference equation or its game analog) are stable. For the open-loop equilibrium, these tests can be performed by using the results from Chapters 6 and 7 that the open-loop equilibrium can be generated by solving a control problem. It is simply necessary to check whether the control problem that generates the open-loop equilibrium is concave (Karp and Perloff 1993b). For the MPE, we solve the game using the estimated ν^*; this computation is straightforward.

Given sufficient data, we can test whether the equilibrium is open-loop or Markov, in addition to estimating the degree of competitiveness, ν^*. If we assume symmetry so that $\mathbf{G}$ is estimated as in Equation (8.16), we impose exactly the same restrictions in estimating the parameters of demand and the control rule under both open-loop and Markov strategies. To distinguish between the two equilibria, an over-identifying restriction is needed. For example, given information on adjustment costs, it would be possible to estimate jointly a cost function involving θ and the demand function and control rule subject to Equations (8.9) or (8.17). In principle, we could apply methods of non-nested hypothesis testing or, less formally, compare the values of the likelihood functions under the two sets of restrictions.

Unfortunately, a complete set of cost data rarely is available. Most firm-specific cost data are constructed by allocating total cost to a set of categories that do not include a category called *adjustment*. Even if such data existed, it would be surprising if they would enable us to obtain a reliable estimate of θ.

In the absence of cost data, it is, in principle, possible to test open-loop versus Markov behavior by dropping the symmetry assumption. In general, the estimation of b_{ij}, $\mathbf{G}$, ν_i, and θ subject to Equations (8.9) or (8.17) will result in different estimates and different values of the likelihood function. That is, in the absence of symmetry, the two sets of restrictions (8.9) and (8.17) are not equivalent.

We can demonstrate this nonequivalence by means of an example. This example also shows that it is possible to estimate more parameters of the vector ν_i under the Markov assumption; in this sense, the Markov model provides more information than the open-loop model. We noted earlier that it is possible to estimate only a single value of the vector $\boldsymbol{\nu}_i$ (denoted ν_i^*) in the open-loop model. For the example, we let $n = 3$, and we chose an arbitrary $\mathbf{G}$, b_{11}, and b_{12} and then chose b_{13} to satisfy Equation (8.9). By construction, a unique estimate of ν^* and δ satisfies the open-loop restrictions Equation (8.9). However, for these values of $\mathbf{G}$ and b_{1j}, the MPE restrictions constitute three independent equations in θ and ν^*, and (in general) no solution exists. To make these equations consistent, we could, for example, change b_{13}. In that case, the open-loop restrictions would cease to be consistent. Therefore, the value of the likelihood function may be either greater or less under the open-loop formulation. That is, the open-loop equilibrium and MPE are observationally distinct even without cost data. However, to impose the restrictions in Equations (8.9) and (8.17) in the absence of symmetry, we face a more complicated numerical problem.

EMPIRICAL APPLICATIONS

We apply the linear-quadratic methodology to two export markets – coffee (Karp and Perloff 1993) and rice (Karp and Perloff 1989b). In both cases, we concentrate on some of the largest exporting countries and assume that the other countries act as a competitive fringe and treat their output levels as exogenous. In both cases, we assume that the governments of the major exporting countries control exports (rather than production itself). We now briefly describe these two markets.

Coffee

We concentrate on the two largest producers of coffee, Brazil and Colombia. From 1959 until the 1980s, most exporting and importing countries participated in a series of International Coffee Agreements (ICAs). These agreements set quotas for exporting countries, but there is substantial evidence that many countries violate the agreement. During 1974, in the absence of an ICA, Brazil and Colombia attempted to form an explicit producers' cartel; they were later joined by smaller producers.

The institutional arrangements in the coffee market constitute circumstantial evidence of large producers' intent to exert market power. The difficulties of negotiating these agreements, and the failure to comply fully with them, indicate that it is unlikely that producers behaved as monopolists. Thus, the hypothesis that the market structure lies "between" monopoly and competition is plausible.

There are two reasons why it is important to use a dynamic model in attempting to estimate the market structure of coffee. First, when firms change levels of production, they almost certainly incur nonlinear costs. There is a lag of two to five years between planting and the first harvest; a tree produces its maximum output between five to ten years of age, and bears for up to thirty years. This pattern suggests that average costs of adjustment increase with the size of the change. Second, the two largest producers, Brazil and Colombia, maintain substantial stockpiles. Standard inventory models assume that there are costs of adjusting inventories; these costs are often approximated using quadratic functions.

The costs of adjusting exports, therefore, consist of costly adjustment of production or inventories. A more fully specified model would include both stocks and lagged production level as state variables. For simplicity and as an approximation to this more complex model, we treat lag exports as the state variable and interpret the costly adjustment of this variable as consisting of the adjustment costs of production and of inventories.

We examine the period from the 1961–1962 crop year to the 1983–1984 crop year. During that period, Brazil and Colombia's share of total world exports ranged from 32% to 50% and averaged 43%. Brazil's share was, on average, twice that of Colombia.

It is reasonable to treat Brazil and Colombia as single agents because each country centrally controlled exports during the estimation period. The Brazilian Coffee Institute controlled supply and price; supervised grading, packing, and weighing; and set quotas within the country. The Colombian Federation of Coffee Growers bought from small farmers, evaluated, blended, graded, cleaned, and managed the market through prices and taxes.

Coffee export data are from *Coffee: World Coffee Situation* (various years) published by the U.S. Department of Agriculture, Foreign Agriculture Service. The price of coffee is an average of the prices of all coffee traded in the New York market, the major market for coffee. Price data, the world commodity wholesale price index, and world gross domestic product at constant prices are from the International Monetary Fund, *International Financial Statistics* (various years).

Rice

We concentrate on three of the largest rice exporters, China, Pakistan, and Thailand, which accounted for half of all exports for the period 1961–1985. Thailand's share exceeded a third during the latter part of our sample and China's share was that large earlier. China, Pakistan, Thailand, and the United States were responsible for two-thirds of all exports during the last decades of our sample.

We treat the United States as part of the fringe because, unlike the other large exporting countries, the United States does not have a single exporting agency. U.S. firms appeared to act independently. Though the U.S. government intervened often, the nature of the intervention varied substantially over time and did not appear to be motivated by conditions in international markets.

We expect noncompetitive behavior by China, Pakistan, and Thailand for three reasons. First, these countries have large shares and central agencies that handle all their sales. Second, nontariff barriers affect 93% of world rice imports and 76% of exports. Third, the rice export market is thin. There are no large organized exchanges, so that major brokerage houses in the United States, Europe, Singapore, and Hong Kong are able to charge fees as high as 5% to 10%. With other high transaction or search costs and high shipping costs, f. o. b. (freight-on-board) prices may not equalize rapidly.

The nominal rice export prices and quantities are from the United Nations Food and Agriculture Organization (various years). The price of wheat, a substitute, is from the International Wheat Council (various years). A world commodity wholesale price index and gross domestic product indexes are from the International Monetary Fund (various years).

ESTIMATION RESULTS

For both commodities, we use instrumental variables to estimate linear demand curves, Equation (8.2), including prices of various substitutes and time trends; and we estimate the adjustment rule, Equation (8.6). We then use these two sets of equations to obtain estimates of v for coffee and rice. For the demand curves, all prices were deflated by a world commodity wholesale price index. Because the demand-slope coefficients are necessary only to estimate θ but not v, we do not discuss them further here.

We estimate the adjustment equations (8.6) using Zellner's seemingly unrelated equations method. Each country's exports are regressed on its own lagged exports, rival lagged exports, a time trend, and dummies for adverse weather conditions. We included a dummy in the coffee equation for the major freeze in Brazil in 1977–1978 and in the rice equation for bad weather in 1973 that reduced the rice crop substantially.

We impose the cross-equation symmetry constraints that the coefficient on the own lagged exports is equal across equations, as is the coefficient on the other country's lagged exports. That is, $g_{11} = g_{22} \equiv g_1$ and $g_{12} = g_{21} \equiv g_2$, where g_{ij} is the (i, j) element of $\mathbf{G}$. Testing these restrictions, we conclude that for neither commodity can we reject these equality restrictions at the 0.05 level. For both, we can reject that the hypotheses that $g_1 = 0$ or $g_2 = 0$. Table 8.1 shows the coffee adjustment equations.

Classical Estimates

For both commodities, we assume that $\delta = 0.95$ and then use the adjustment equations to infer v^* for both the open-loop and MPE. Hereafter, we drop the superscript "*" on $v^*$and use superscripts to distinguish between estimates under the assumption of either open-loop (OLE) or MPE. The first set of estimates in Table 8.2 is based on standard, classical regressions.

Table 8.1. *Adjustment equations: regression of exports on lagged exports*

	Brazil	Colombia
Constant	12,986.0	6,967.9
	(4.99)[a]	(4.28)
Brazilian freeze 1977–78	−9,980.7	843.7
	(−4.66)	(0.74)
Time trend (1, 2, ...)	22.4	124.8
	(0.30)	(2.59)
Lagged Brazil exports	0.302	−0.192
	(2.27)	(−2.42)
Lagged Colombia exports	−0.192	0.302
	(−2.42)	(2.27)
R^2	0.57	0.74
Durbin-Watson	2.23	1.57
Durbin's h	−0.72	1.34

[a] Figures in parentheses are t-statistics against the null hypothesis that the coefficient equals zero.

For coffee, the classical (subscript c) estimates are $\nu^{OLE} = \varphi_c^{OLE}(\mathbf{G}) = -0.84$, where $\varphi_c^{OLE}(\mathbf{G})$ is the nonlinear function of $\mathbf{G}$ in the open-loop model, Equation (8.15), and $\nu^{MPE} = \varphi_c^{MPE}(\mathbf{G}) = -0.8$, where $\varphi_c^{OLE}(\mathbf{G})$ is the nonlinear function of $\mathbf{G}$ in the Markov model, Equation (8.17). These point estimates of ν appear close to the price-taking level, $-1/(n-1) = -1$. Based on standard errors calculated using Taylor expansions, we cannot reject price-taking ($\nu = -1$), but we can reject Nash-Cournot ($\nu = 0$) or collusive behavior ($\nu = 1$).

For rice, the open-loop and Markov estimates are $\nu^{OLE} = -0.37$ and $\nu^{MPE} = -0.32$, which again are close to the price-taking level of $-0.5(-1/(n-1) = -1/(3-1) = -0.5$ in this case). Based on the Taylor approximated standard errors, we cannot reject price-taking ($\nu = -0.5$) or Nash-Cournot behavior ($\nu = 0$), but can reject collusion ($\nu = 1$).

In order to be consistent with the assumptions of our model, this estimated dynamical system must have three properties:

(i) The system is *stable*: $-1 < g_1 + (n-1)g_2 < 1$ and $-1 < g_1 - g_2 < 1$.
(ii) The *market structure* lies between collusion and price taking: $-1/(n-1) \leq \nu \leq 1$ for both the open-loop and Markov models.
(iii) The *adjustment* parameter in each of the models is positive: $\theta > 0$.

Our classical point estimates of the elements of G and our estimates of ν and θ meet these restrictions.

Table 8.2. *Classical and Bayesian inequality constrained estimates*

	Coffee		Rice	
	ν^{OLE}	ν^{MPE}	ν^{OLE}	ν^{MPE}
Classical estimates ν^k (unrestricted)	−0.84	−0.80	−0.37	−0.32
Standard deviation (Taylor approximation)	0.27	0.31	0.17	0.20
Bayesian inequality constrained estimates[a]				
Quadratic loss ν^k (mean)	−0.65	−0.62	−0.26	−0.21
Standard deviation (σ)	0.35	0.36	0.26	0.27
Precision of the mean of ν^k ($\sigma/\sqrt{T}$)	0.006	0.006	0.004	0.004
Absolute loss ν^k (median)	−0.76	−0.73	−0.35	−0.30
Standard deviation	0.37	0.37	0.28	0.28
Reject because (%) Unstable	0.002	0.002	0.004	0.004
$\delta^k \leq 0$	25.2	23.6	8.2	7.8
$\nu^k \leq -1/n$	24.9	25.4	8.2	8.2
$\nu^k > 1$	1.7	1.2	3.2	3.2
Total rejections $(1 - p)$	26.5	26.5	11.4	11.4
Asymptotic standard error of p: $\sqrt{p(1-p)/T}$	0.007	0.007	0.005	0.005

[a] 5,000 replications (T).

Bayesian Estimates

Rather than estimating the unconstrained system and hoping that the point estimates lie in the desired range as we did using the classical approach, we can impose these three sets of restrictions. Although it would be extremely difficult, if not impossible, to impose or test these inequality restrictions using a classical approach, Geweke (1986, 1988, 1989), Chalfant and White (1988), and Chalfant, Gray, and White (1991) have shown how such inequality restrictions can be imposed and tested using Bayesian techniques.[6]

In this Bayesian approach, a prior is used that is the product of a conventional uninformative distribution and an indicator function that equals one where the inequality constraints are satisfied and zero elsewhere. The posterior distribution is calculated using Monte Carlo numerical integration with importance sampling. Geweke (1986) explains this approach for a single equation. The multi-equation generalization used here is based on Chalfant and White (1988) and Chalfant, Gray, and White (1991). These papers and Kloek and Van Dijk (1978) discuss Monte Carlo integration using importance sampling.

To estimate the probability that the restrictions hold, we calculate the (importance weighted) proportion of Monte Carlo replications satisfying the restrictions.

[6] This can also be done with other IT methods, such as the GME discussed in Chapters 9 and 10 and the Statistical Appendix.

Table 8.3. *The distribution of ν^k based on Bayesian estimates*

Proportion of weight between[a]		Coffee ν^{OLE}	Coffee ν^{MPE}	Rice ν^{OLE}	Rice ν^{MPE}
$-1/n$	0	93.5%	92.8%	88.1%	84.5%
0	1/2	4.2	4.8	9.0	12.4
1/2	1	2.3	2.4	2.9	3.1
$-1/n$	ν_c^k	34.0	35.1	43.6	46.5
ν_c^k	0	59.5	57.7	44.5	38.0
$-1/n$	ν_b^k	67.2	65.5	66.5	64.5
ν_b^k	0	26.3	27.3	21.6	19.9

[a] The classic estimate is ν_c^k, where $k = OLE$ (open-loop) or MPE (Markov Perfect), and ν_b^k is the Bayesian estimate based on a quadratic-loss function. By definition, half the weight lies between $-1/n$ and the absolute loss (median estimators), which are, for coffee, $\nu^{OLE} = -0.76$ and $\nu^{MPE} = -0.73$ and, for rice, $\nu^{OLE} = -0.35$ and $\nu^{MPE} = -0.30$.

The odds that these restrictions hold are as shown in Table 8.2 (based on 5,000 importance-sampling replications). The stability conditions are virtually always met. Because all three sets of conditions hold in approximately three-quarters of the replications for coffee and in seven-eighths for rice, imposing these restrictions seems reasonable. Because the restriction that θ is positive holds in three-quarters of the cases for coffee and nearly 90% for rice, the data indicate that there is dynamic adjustment; that is, the odds in favor of a positive θ are three to one for coffee and nearly nine to one for rice.

Given a quadratic (absolute difference) loss function, estimates of the parameters consistent with the restrictions are obtained by calculating the mean (median) of the coefficient estimates for all replications where the constraints are satisfied (Zellner 1971, pp. 24–5). Indeed, we obtain the full posterior distributions of ν under either the open-loop or Markov assumptions.

Table 8.2 summarizes the results of the classical and the Bayesian estimates. The estimated values of ν based on an absolute difference loss function (medians) are close to the classical point estimates. The estimated ν values based on a quadratic loss function (means) are slightly higher than the classical estimates (0.1 higher for rice and 0.2 for coffee). The standard deviations on the quadratic loss function ν are only slightly greater than the Taylor approximations for the classical estimates.

The Bayesian estimates, which provide an entire posterior distribution for the market structure parameter, ν, can be used to calculate the probability that $\nu^k (k = OLE$ or $k = MPE)$ lies within a certain range. Some of the interesting ranges for both sets of Bayesian estimates are summarized in Table 8.3.

The probability that the market structure lies between price taking and Nash-Cournot exceeds 0.9 for coffee and is only slightly less for rice. Two-thirds of both distributions lie below the mean (quadratic loss) estimates of ν. Under the Markov

Table 8.4. *Simulated exports under various models*

Model (ν)	Brazilian and Colombian Exports (Static or Steady State)	Percentage of Price-taker Output
Static and dynamic price taking ($\nu = -1$)	25,789	100
MPE (ν_c^{OLE})	24,665	96
MPE (ν_c^{MPE})	24,308	94
Open-loop and static models (ν_c^{OLE})	23,868	93
Open-loop and static models (ν_c^{MPE})	23,469	91
MPE (ν_s^{MPE})	22,601	88
MPE (ν_b^{MPE})	22,504	87
Open-loop and static models (ν_s^{OLE})	22,232	86
Open-loop and static models (ν_b^{OLE})	21,948	85
MPE Cournot ($\nu = 0$)	17,557	68
Open-loop and static Cournot ($\nu = 0$)	17,192	67
Static and dynamic collusion ($\nu = 1$)	12,894	50

Note: Exports are in thousands of 60-kilogram bags. The ν_c^k are the classic estimates, the ν_b^k are the Bayesian quadratic loss estimates, and the ν_s^k are the bootstrap estimates, where $k = OLE$ (open-loop) or *MPE* (Markov).

assumption, the posterior odds ratio that the market structure lies between price taking and Nash-Cournot (rather than between Nash-Cournot and collusive) is 12.9 for coffee and 12.6 for rice. That is, the probability that these markets are more competitive than Nash-Cournot is nearly thirteen times as great as the probability that they are less competitive than Nash-Cournot.

Simulations

The estimates have implications for steady-state outputs, as we show using the coffee estimates in Table 8.4. We normalize the data so that each country's steady-state output would be 100 if the two major coffee exporting countries were price takers, 66.67 if the countries played open-loop Nash-Cournot, and 50 if they were a perfect cartel.

The cost of adjustment affects the steady state in the Markov model, as we have already discussed in the properties section. Thus, where costs of adjustment are positive, more is produced in the MPE or feedback steady state than would be produced in a static model with the same ν. In contrast, the open-loop steady state is independent of the adjustment cost parameter. Because the Markov steady state depends on this parameter, the Markov steady state is greater than the open-loop steady state.

We now show how the steady states differ by examining various combinations of open-loop or feedback models with various estimates of ν. Given the classical (c) point estimate for the OLE, $\nu_c^{OLE} = -0.84$, the steady-state output is ninety-three in an open-loop model and ninety-six in a feedback model. Similarly, for the classic Markov Perfect equilibrium (*MPE*) point estimate, $\nu_c^{MPE} = -0.83$, the steady-state output is ninety-one in an open-loop model and ninety-four in the feedback model. Thus, for a given estimate of ν, the feedback model steady-state output is about three percentage points higher than the open-loop steady-state or static output. Moreover, while the estimated market structure is "close" to price taking in the sense that both estimates of ν are close to -1, the steady-state outputs are below the price-taking levels by between 4% and 9% percent, depending on the model and the market structure estimate used.

We now compare the steady states obtained using our various estimators in the corresponding feedback or open-loop model. For the Bayesian quadratic loss estimate based on the open-loop model, $\nu_b^{OLE} = -0.65$, the open-loop output is eighty-five. For the corresponding estimate for the Markov model, $\nu_b^{MPE} = -0.62$, the feedback output is eighty-seven. Thus, although the Bayesian Markov ν is slightly smaller than the open-loop ν, the Markov steady-state output is slightly larger. The results for the bootstrap estimates are similar.

SUMMARY

We use a conjectural variation or a market conduct parameter model to estimate market structure under the assumption that the equilibrium is either open-loop or Markov Perfect. Our formulation requires that (i) the single-period payoff is a quadratic function of the state and the control variables, that (ii) the equation of motion is linear in those variables, and that (iii) agents use linear decision rules. Under these restrictions, we can solve the equilibrium conditions in closed form to obtain the decision rules, which are linear in the state variables. This closed-form solution means that we avoid the complexities associated with estimating Markov equilibria in the dynamic models we discussed in Chapter 7.

This (simplified) equilibrium decision rule is nonlinear in the demand and cost parameters of the model and in the conjectural variation parameter. That parameter can be estimated without specifying whether firms have rational expectations with respect to exogenous state variables (such as demand and cost shifters). If there were data that would enable us to obtain an independent estimate of the adjustment cost parameter, it would be possible to test whether firms use open-loop or Markov policies. In the absence of such data, we can estimate market structure under the assumption that decision rules are open-loop or Markov, and compare the resulting estimates.

We apply this estimation method to the rice and coffee export markets using both a classical and a Bayesian technique in which we impose inequality constraints.

The Bayesian results are generally close to the classical ones. One advantage of the Bayesian approach is that we obtain an empirical approximation to the distribution of the behavior strategy variable, so we can easily calculate the probability that market structure lies in a particular range. For example, we estimate that the steady-state coffee outputs are between 7% and 14% lower than if Brazil and Colombia were pure price takers.

APPENDIX 8A: DERIVATION OF RESTRICTIONS

Because we are only interested in imposing restrictions on the demand slopes and the coefficients on q in the control rule and not on the intercepts of the demand and control systems, we can restrict our attention to the quadratic part of the optimization problems.

The Open-Loop Restrictions

The Lagrangean for the ith player is

$$\sum_{\tau=t}^{T} \delta^{\tau-t}\left[-\frac{1}{2}\mathbf{q}_\tau'\mathbf{K}_i\mathbf{q}_\tau - \frac{1}{2}\mathbf{u}_\tau'\,\mathbf{S}_i\,\mathbf{u}_\tau + \lambda_{i\tau}'\,(\mathbf{q}_{\tau-1} + \mathbf{u}_\tau - \mathbf{q}_\tau)\right].$$

The first-order conditions for $\mathbf{q}_\tau$ and $\mathbf{u}_{i,\tau}$ are

$$-\,\mathbf{K}_i\,\mathbf{q}_\tau - \lambda_{i\tau} + \delta\,\lambda_{i,\tau+1} = \mathbf{0} \tag{8.20}$$

and

$$-\,\mathbf{v}_i'\mathbf{S}_i\mathbf{u}_\tau + \mathbf{v}_i' + \mathbf{v}_i'\lambda_{i\tau} = \mathbf{0}. \tag{8.21}$$

We can show that, at time T, λ_{iT} is a linear function of $\mathbf{q}$, and that if λ_{it} is a linear function of $\mathbf{q}$, then so is $\lambda_{i,t\text{-}1}$. Thus, by induction, we know that $\lambda_{i,\tau} = \mathbf{H}_{i,\tau}\,\mathbf{q}_\tau$, for some matrix $\mathbf{H}_{i,\tau}$. Consequently, if we let $T \to \infty$ so that $\mathbf{H}_{i\tau} \to \mathbf{H}_i$, Equation (8.21) becomes

$$\mathbf{v}_i'\,\mathbf{H}_i\,\mathbf{q}_\tau = \theta_i\,u_{i\tau}, \quad i = 1, \ldots, n, + 1.$$

Next, we stack these conditions to obtain $\mathbf{Eq}_\tau = \mathbf{Su}_\tau$, where the ith row of $\mathbf{E}$ is $\mathbf{v}_i'\mathbf{H}_i$ and the ith row of $\mathbf{S}$ is $\theta_i\mathbf{e}_i'$. With these definitions, we can write the stacked necessary conditions as

$$\mathbf{Eq}_t = \mathbf{S}(\mathbf{q}_t - \mathbf{q}_{t-1})$$

$$\text{or } \mathbf{q}_\tau = \mathbf{Gq}_{\tau-1} \text{ where } \mathbf{G} \equiv (\mathbf{S}-\mathbf{E})^{-1}\mathbf{S}.$$

We use the previous definitions to rewrite Equation (8.20) as

$$\mathbf{0}{=}\mathbf{K}_i\mathbf{q}_t - \mathbf{H}_i\mathbf{q}_t + \delta\mathbf{H}_i\mathbf{q}_{t+1} = (-\mathbf{K}_i - \mathbf{H}_i + \delta\mathbf{H}_i\mathbf{G})\,\mathbf{q}_t.$$

This equation implies that

$$\mathbf{H}_i\,(\mathbf{I} - \delta\mathbf{G}) = -\mathbf{K}_i,$$

which we rewrite as

$$\mathbf{H}_i = -\mathbf{K}_i\,(\mathbf{I} - \delta\mathbf{G})^{-1}. \tag{8.22}$$

From the definition of *G*, we have

$$\mathbf{E} = \mathbf{S}(\mathbf{I} - \mathbf{G}^{-1}). \tag{8.23}$$

We premultiply both sides of Equation (8.23) by $\mathbf{e}_i'$ and use the definition of **E** and Equation (8.22) to obtain that

$$\mathbf{e}_i'\mathbf{E} = \mathbf{v}_i'\mathbf{H}_i = -\mathbf{v}_i'\mathbf{K}_i\,(\mathbf{I} - \delta\mathbf{G})^{-1} = \mathbf{e}_i'\mathbf{S}(\mathbf{I} - \mathbf{G}^{-1}) = \theta_i\mathbf{e}_i'(\mathbf{I} - \mathbf{G}^{-1}). \tag{8.24}$$

From the second and the last equality in Equation (8.24), we learn that

$$-\mathbf{v}_i'\mathbf{K}_i = \theta_i\mathbf{e}_i'(\mathbf{I} - \mathbf{G}^{-1})\,(\mathbf{I} - \delta\mathbf{G}). \tag{8.25}$$

The transpose of Equation (8.25) is

$$\mathbf{K}_i\mathbf{v}_i = -[(\mathbf{I} - \mathbf{G}^{-1})(\mathbf{I} - \delta\mathbf{G})]'\mathbf{e}_i\theta_i. \tag{8.26}$$

By factoring out $G^{-1'}$, we obtain Equation (8.9).

The Markov Perfect Restrictions

For ease of comparison, we use some of the same symbols to express the equilibrium conditions in both the OPE and the MPE (e.g., **H** and **E**). The values of these variables are different in the two equilibria. Again, taking only the quadratic part of the problem, the stationary dynamic programming equation is

$$-\frac{1}{2}\,\mathbf{q}_{t-1}'\,\mathbf{H}_i\,\mathbf{q}_{t-1}$$
$$= \underset{q_{it}}{Max}\left\{-\frac{1}{2}\,\mathbf{q}_t'(\,\mathbf{K}_i + \mathbf{S}_i + \delta\,\mathbf{H}_i\,)\,\mathbf{q}_t + \mathbf{q}_t'\,\mathbf{S}_i\,\mathbf{q}_{t-1} - \frac{1}{2}\mathbf{q}_{t-1}'\,\mathbf{S}_i\,\mathbf{q}_{t-1}\right\}. \tag{8.27}$$

The first-order condition is

$$-\mathbf{v}_i'(\,\mathbf{K}_i + \mathbf{S}_i + \beta\,\mathbf{H}_i\,)\mathbf{q}_t + \mathbf{v}_i'\mathbf{S}_i\mathbf{q}_{t-1} = \mathbf{0}.$$

We stack the $n + 1$ first-order conditions to obtain

$$\mathbf{E}\mathbf{q}_t = \mathbf{S}\mathbf{q}_{t-1}, \tag{8.28}$$

where the *i*th row of **E** is $\mathbf{v}'\,(\mathbf{K}_i + \mathbf{S}_i + \delta\mathbf{H}_i)$ and the *i*th row of **S** is $\theta_i\mathbf{e}_i'$. We rewrite Equation (8.28) as $\mathbf{q}_t = \mathbf{G}\,\mathbf{q}_{t-1}$, where $\mathbf{G} = \mathbf{E}^{-1}\mathbf{S}$. By substituting this rule into the maximized value of Equation (8.27), we obtain

$$\mathbf{H}_i = \mathbf{G}'\,(\mathbf{K}_i + \mathbf{S}_i + \delta\mathbf{H}_i)\,\mathbf{G} - \mathbf{G}'\mathbf{S}_i - \mathbf{S}_i\mathbf{G} + \mathbf{S}_i. \tag{8.29}$$

Next, we apply the vec operation to Equation (8.29) and simplify to obtain vec $\mathbf{H}_i = \mathbf{w}_i + \mathbf{x}_i\theta_i$ where $\mathbf{w}_i$ and $\mathbf{x}_i$ are defined in the text. We then convert the vectors back into a matrix to obtain $\mathbf{H}_i = \mathbf{W}_i + \mathbf{X}_i\theta_i$. Taking the ith row of $\mathbf{EG} = \mathbf{S}$ and using the definition of $\mathbf{E}$, we find that

$$\mathbf{v}_i'\left(\mathbf{K}_i + \mathbf{e}_i\mathbf{e}_i'\theta_i + \delta\left(\mathbf{W}_i + \mathbf{X}_i\theta_i\right)\right)\mathbf{G} = \mathbf{e}_i'\theta_i. \tag{8.30}$$

By rearranging Equation (8.30), we derive Equation (8.17).

PROBLEMS

Note: Answers to problems are available at the back of the book.

8.1 You are asked to use the methods described in this chapter to estimate the degree of market power in a linear-quadratic game. For the purpose of becoming familiar with these methods, it is helpful to use the simplest model, one with a one-dimensional state variable. (In the model in the text, the state vector consists of the lagged quantities, so the dimension of the state vector equals n, the number of players.) We use a discrete-time linear-quadratic version of the sticky price duopoly model discussed in Chapter 7. In order to simplify some calculations, we choose specific parameter values for some variables.

In this model, the current price is

$$p_t = 5 + .5p_{t-1} - (q_{1t} + q_{2t}).$$

The duopolists have constant short-run costs in period t c_{it}, so firm i's single-period profits are

$$(p_t - c_{it})\, q_{it}.$$

Each firm's constant discount factor is 0.9. Assume that firms set current output as a linear function of lagged price.

As discussed in Chapter 7, there are many MPE to the game with this payoff and equation of motion. However, the *linear* equilibrium has three important features: it is the limit of equilibrium to the finite horizon game, as the horizon goes to infinity; it is defined for all values of the state variable (the lagged price); and it is easy to compute. We therefore consider the linear equilibrium.

Suppose that you have estimated the linear control rule

$$q_{it} = \rho_{it} + \sigma p_{t-1}.$$

Use the estimate of σ (which we hereafter treat as known) to obtain a point estimate of an index of market power as a function of σ. What would you conclude about the degree of market power given an estimate $\sigma = 0.15$?

We now describe the steps necessary to obtain the index. The basic idea uses a conjectural variations parameter $\Lambda = dQ/dq$ to nest the competitive, Nash-Cournot, and cartel equilibria (corresponding to $\Lambda = 0, 1, 2$, respectively) as in the text. The goal is to use the equilibrium condition from a firm's dynamic optimization problem to obtain the unknown parameter Λ as a function of the estimated parameter σ.

In this model, as in the model in the text, the costs affect the intercept of the control rule, ρ_{it}, but not the slope, σ. The estimate of Λ does not require information on the costs or the intercept of the control rule. To simplify the calculations, you can ignore costs (set them equal to 0) and treat ρ as a constant, the same for both firms. These simplifications do not affect the index of market power.

Proceed as follows:

a) Write down the firm's Dynamic Programming Equation. Use the "trial solution," a value function that is quadratic in price: $J(p) = \alpha + \beta p - \frac{\gamma}{2} p^2$, and substitute this trial into the DPE. (Because we are dealing with the "representative firm," we omit the firm subscripts here, but in carrying out these calculations it is important to remember that firm i chooses q_i and takes as given $q_{jt} = \rho + \sigma p_{t-1}$.)

b) Write the first-order condition for the firm's maximization problem, using the conjectural variation parameter Λ. Use the (estimated) equilibrium control rule $q_{jt} = \rho + \sigma p_{t-1}$ to eliminate q_{jt}. (An alternative, equivalent approach is to impose symmetry on the first-order condition by setting $Q = 2q$.) Solve the resulting first-order condition to obtain a control rule that gives q as a linear function of the lagged price. The slope of this rule, σ, is a function only of Λ and γ: $\sigma = f(\gamma, \Lambda)$. Find the function $f()$.

c) Because you have an estimate of σ, you need a second equation in order to eliminate γ, thereby obtaining an equation for Λ as a function of σ. This step shows you how to obtain this second equation. Substitute the (estimated) control rule, together with the equation implied by symmetry ($Q = 2q$) into the DPE and equate coefficients of p^2. The resulting equation gives γ as a function of σ: $\gamma = g(\sigma)$. Your job is to find the function $g()$.

d) Solve for Λ using $\sigma = f(g(\sigma), \Lambda)$. Once you have obtained the expression for Λ as a function of σ, evaluate this function at $\sigma = 0.15$ to obtain the estimate of Λ.

As a consistency check for your calculations, ask yourself, "What is the value of σ that is consistent with perfect competition? When I substitute this value into $\sigma = f(g(\sigma), \Lambda)$, does the solution return $\Lambda = 0$, as required?" To answer the first question, remember that for these calculations you set costs equal to zero, so for the firms to earn zero, price must be zero in every period.

A more complicated consistency check requires that you find the values of σ corresponding to the Nash-Cournot and cartel solutions, and check that these two values return $\Lambda = 1$ for the Nash-Cournot equilibrium and $\Lambda = 2$ for the cartel equilibrium, when substituted into $\sigma = f(g(\sigma), \Lambda)$. To perform this check, you need to solve the optimization problem for the industry (the cartel solution) and the dynamic game (for the Nash-Cournot equilibrium). To solve the optimization problem, you need to use the transversality condition (equivalently, the requirement that price converges); to solve the game, you also need to use the second-order condition for maximization of the DPE. These conditions are needed because the equation that determines γ has more than one root. You need to identify the correct root in order to obtain the correct control rule – that is, the correct value of σ (for either the cartel or the Nash-Cournot equilibrium). Once you have those two values, you can confirm that the relation $\sigma = f(g(\sigma), \Lambda)$ returns the "correct" value of Λ – that is, the value corresponding to either the cartel or the Nash-Cournot equilibrium.

NINE

Estimating Strategies: Theory

Rather than only examine market power measures, we can estimate firms' strategies directly.[1] Structure–conduct–performance (SCP) studies (Chapter 2) examine how measures of market power vary with concentration, barriers to entry, and other factors. The static and dynamic models in Chapters 3 through 8 estimate a measure of market power (rather than rely on the measures used in SCP studies) or conjectural variation while remaining agnostic about firms' strategies. One interpretation of these studies is that, out of a set of possible models of strategic behavior, they try to determine the one that is most consistent with the observed data. In this chapter, we take a more direct approach by estimating firms' strategies. Once we have estimates of the firms' strategies, we can determine the equilibria and examine how the equilibria vary with factors that affect strategies.

This model is an extension of the structural models ideas discussed in earlier chapters. The firms' optimization behavior is specified together with all other relevant functions. With these specifications, the model is solved to yield the optimal behavior (strategies). These strategies are then estimated from the observed data. Having estimated the parameters for a specific game, we can then evaluate market power and the way it is affected by those factors that affect demand, cost, and market structure.

We present two methods for estimating oligopoly strategies. In the first, we estimate strategies using only *hard, observable data*, such as observations regarding the factors that affect demand and cost. Our second method is a generalization of the first one, in which we add restrictions from game theory, or *soft data*. The traditional SCP, structural, and reduced-form approaches to examining market power ignore these game-theoretic restrictions.

Firms' action space may be a single decision variable, such as price alone, or multiple decision variables, such as price and level of advertising. As a first step in both approaches taken here, we divide each firm's continuous action space

[1] The material in this chapter and the next one are based on Golan, Karp, and Perloff (1998, 2000).

into a grid (discrete intervals) over these actions. Then, we estimate the vector of probabilities – the mixed or pure strategies – that a firm chooses a given action or cell in the grid.

For example, in the two-decision variables case, we estimate the probability that each firm takes an action α_{kl} in the discrete price-advertising grid:

Advertising Categories							
5	α_{51}	α_{52}	α_{53}	α_{54}	α_{55}	α_{56}	α_{57}
4	α_{41}	α_{42}	α_{43}	α_{44}	α_{45}	α_{46}	α_{47}
3	α_{31}	α_{32}	α_{33}	α_{34}	α_{35}	α_{36}	α_{37}
2	A_{21}	α_{22}	α_{23}	α_{24}	α_{25}	α_{26}	α_{27}
1	α_{11}	α_{12}	α_{13}	α_{14}	α_{15}	α_{16}	α_{17}
	1	2	3	4	5	6	7

Price Categories

In this grid, the price axis is divided into seven segments and the level of advertising axis is divided into five segments, so that the price-advertising grid has thirty-five cells or actions α_{kl}, where k indexes the row, and l the column. For example, if the firm takes action α_{23}, it sets its price in interval 3 and its level of advertising in interval 2.

If the firm chooses a single cell with a probability of one, then it uses a pure strategy; otherwise, it is using a mixed strategy.[2] The advantage of dividing the action space into discrete intervals is first, that we can easily allow for either pure or mixed strategies, and second, that it is consistent with the observed discrete data. If we used a family of continuous probability distributions, we would have difficulty estimating a mass point or a range with exactly zero weight. However, technically, it is possible to do so using our approach. In principle, dividing the space into too small a number of intervals could cause a big loss of information due to the aggregation. However, if one uses a large enough number of discrete intervals (or cells), the method discussed here works well in practice. In that regard, the estimated results are not very sensitive to the number of divisions as long as the different cases span the same set of possible actions and the number of divisions is not too small.

Once we have estimated strategies for the firms, we can describe the equilibria, calculate summary statistics such as the Lerner index of market structure, and

[2] If the underlying game has a continuum of player types, we should refer to distributional strategies (Milgrom and Weber 1986) rather than mixed strategies. Distributional strategies are the equivalence class of the mixed strategies that yield the same behavior. Throughout, we refer to the strategies as mixed for simplicity.

examine how changes in exogenous variables affect strategies. Thus, this approach allows us to answer all three of the questions we posed in Chapter 1.

This method allows us to estimate firms' strategies subject to restrictions implied by game theory and test hypotheses based on these estimated strategies. The restrictions we impose are consistent with a variety of assumptions regarding the information that firms have when making their decisions and with either pure or mixed strategies.

For example, suppose a firm's marginal cost in a period is a random variable observed by the firm but not by the econometrician. Given the realization of its marginal cost, the firm chooses either a pure or a mixed strategy, which results in an action, say a price–advertising pair. The econometrician observes only the firm's action and not the marginal cost. As a consequence, the econometrician cannot distinguish between pure or mixed strategies. If both firms in a market use pure strategies and each observes its rival's marginal cost, each firm can anticipate its rival's action in each period. Alternatively, firms might use pure strategies and know the distribution but not the realization of their rival's cost. Due to the randomness of the marginal cost, it appears to both the rival and the econometrician that a firm is using a mixed strategy. The equilibrium, however, depends on whether firms' private information is correlated.

All of these possibilities – firms have only public information, firms observe each other's private information but the econometrician does not, or each firm knows only that its private information is correlated or uncorrelated with its rival's – lead to restrictions of the same form. For expositional simplicity, we concentrate on the situation in which firms have private information about their own – but not their rivals' – marginal costs (or some other payoff-relevant variable). The private information of any two firms is uncorrelated.

RELATED STUDIES

A small number of earlier studies have estimated mixed or pure strategies based on a game-theoretic model. Earlier studies (Bjorn and Vuong 1985, Bresnahan and Reiss 1991, and Kooreman 1994) examined binary (discrete) action spaces. For example, Bjorn and Vuong and Kooreman estimate mixed strategies in a game involving spouses' joint labor market participation decisions using a Maximum Likelihood (ML) technique. Some more recent studies generalize the earlier binary game models and provide improved econometric techniques for estimating static and dynamic binary games, but are conceptually different from the information-theoretic model that we use. We summarize some of these recent studies. Though in this chapter we develop our method for estimating strategies of a *static* game, we briefly discuss the few studies dealing with estimating dynamic games as well.

Bresnahan and Reiss (1993) showed that the difference between entry and exit thresholds provides information on firms' sunk costs, which determine the market structure and industry dynamics. Bresnahan and Reiss argue that firms are forward-looking. The current entry decision takes the future market structure and (potential) exit policy into account. Hence, the econometrician will not be able to correctly infer the sunk cost from entry and exit behavior using only current-period information.

Tamer (2003) studies a bivariate simultaneous response model with stochastic payoffs for a two-person discrete game. This game may have multiple equilibria and the econometric model may predict more than a single outcome. This type of game has received substantial attention in the applied game literature.[3]

Consider Tamer's discrete game with stochastic payoffs:

		y_2 = 0	y_2 = 1
y_1	0	0 (player 2: 0)	0 (player 2: $\mathbf{x}_2\boldsymbol{\beta}_2 - \mathbf{u}_2$)
	1	$\mathbf{x}_1\boldsymbol{\beta}_1 - \mathbf{u}_1$ (player 2: 0)	$\mathbf{x}_1\boldsymbol{\beta}_1 + \gamma_1 - \mathbf{u}_1$ (player 2: $\mathbf{x}_2\boldsymbol{\beta}_2 + \gamma_2 - \mathbf{u}_2$)

This game maps directly into the econometric model

$$\mathbf{y}_1^* = \mathbf{x}_1\boldsymbol{\beta}_1 + \gamma_1\mathbf{y}_2 + \mathbf{u}_1$$
$$\mathbf{y}_2^* = \mathbf{x}_2\boldsymbol{\beta}_2 + \gamma_2\mathbf{y}_1 + \mathbf{u}_2,$$

where

$$y_j = \begin{cases} 1 & \text{if } y_j^* \geq 0 \\ 0 & \text{otherwise} \end{cases}, \quad j = 1, 2$$

and $\mathbf{x} = (\mathbf{x}_1, \mathbf{x}_2)$ is a vector of K exogenous variables, $\mathbf{u} = (\mathbf{u}_1, \mathbf{u}_2)$ is a random vector of some latent variables with a conditional distribution F_u representing the unobserved profits, and $\boldsymbol{\beta} = (\boldsymbol{\beta}_1, \boldsymbol{\beta}_2, \gamma_1, \gamma_2)$ are the parameters of interest. The parameters γ can be thought of as incremental payoffs (incremental change in utility for a player playing "1" when the other player moves from "0" to "1").

This class of models provides inequality restrictions on the observed moment conditions that are functions of the parameters of interest. This kind of estimation model has been studied widely in econometrics. It builds on the seminal work of Heckman (1978) and was used in the applied game studies of Bresnahan and Reiss (1991) and others.

To avoid multiplicity in such applied game estimation problems, earlier studies either changed the possible outcome space or imposed other (*ad hoc*) restrictions, such as selection mechanisms in regions of multiplicity of solutions, on the model. Tamer relaxes some of these restrictions. He imposes restrictions on the

[3] See Tamer (2003) for more references.

probability of the non-unique outcomes and develops an efficient ML estimator. Tamer's main contribution is distinguishing between "incoherent" models and incomplete models. A model is "coherent" if it has a well-defined reduced form, or equivalently, the model predicts a unique value for the dependent/endogenous variables given the observed sample. An "incomplete" econometric model is one in which the relationship from the observed noisy data to the dependent variable is a correspondence and not a function. Examples include a selection problem in an underlying well-defined economic model, multiple equilibria, and censoring of regressors or outcomes that map into an econometric structure with a non-unique predicted outcome distribution. This incompleteness is usually the result of avoiding imposing strong (often untestable) assumptions. These incomplete models can often be specified in terms of inequality restrictions on regressions. His other contribution is relating that game to a simultaneous equations model with a discrete outcome.

Pakes, Ostrovsky, and Berry (2004) study the players' strategies within the structure of discrete, dynamic games. Their model is constructed within a basic dynamic game of entry and exit. Because the key variables associated with entry and exit of firms (sunk costs and sell-off costs) are usually not observed, the econometrician needs to infer these unobservable variables from the observed data (such as current profits). Earlier studies used a two-period model, which is essentially a static model. Unfortunately, a two-period model cannot be used to study the impact of policy and other macro or environmental changes on the structure of the industry. Pakes, Ostrovsky, and Berry develop a dynamic model of entry and exit. They start by using observed data to consistently estimate entry costs and the continuation values of being in the market or out of the market (e.g., as a consequence of having exited or having never entered). Then they obtain an estimate of the probability of entry or exit conditional on the parameters of the model. Next, they search for that set of values of the model's parameters that make the in-sample prediction for entry and exit as close as possible to the rates observed in the data.[4] They develop an innovative approach to estimate the parameters of discrete dynamic games, using some restrictive assumptions (e.g., assuming a unique equilibrium for a given data generating process). Their model is computationally complex.

Bajari, Hong, and Ryan (2004) study the identification and estimation of discrete, simultaneous-move games of complete information allowing for both multiple and mixed strategy equilibria. They study the strategic decision of firms in spatially separated markets whether to establish a presence on the Internet. They employ the basic game structure of Bresnahan and Reiss (1990, 1991) in which a discrete game is a generalization of a standard discrete-choice model in which utility depends on the actions of the other players. Using recently developed computer algorithms, they develop simulation-based estimators for static, discrete games that allow them

[4] Naturally, different metrics of closeness yield different estimators.

to compute all of the Nash equilibria to the game. They identify the model using relatively weak parametric assumptions: exclusion restrictions on the way covariates enter into the payoff functions and influence the equilibrium selection.

In general, their model is based on the specification of latent utilities and on an equilibrium selection mechanism that determines the probability that a particular equilibrium occurs. Using these basic concepts, they constructed a method of estimating simulated moments. They compute all of the equilibria to discrete games that are included in the publicly available software package Gambit (McKelvy and McLennan 1996). Though their model can be applied to games with flexible specified structure and allows for both pure and mixed strategies, it is computationally complex and at times based on some restrictive assumptions. Their identification strategy is closely related to approaches found in treatment effect and sample selection models. The probability that a particular equilibrium is played is analogous to the "selection equation" and the equation that determines utility to the "treatment equation" (Heckman 1990).

Ciliberto and Tamer (2006) study the market structure of a multiple equilibria airline industry. They estimate the payoff functions of players in static, discrete games with complete information. Building on Bresnahan and Reiss (1991) and Berry (1992), they allow for heterogeneity across players (airlines) without making specific equilibrium selection assumptions. Like the other studies, the basic model is a 2×2 game. To reduce dimensionality, Ciliberto and Tamer estimate four different specifications for the market entry structure.

Berry and Tamer (2006) review and study some of the basic identification problems in empirical studies of both static and dynamic market structures. They emphasize that a realistic study must take into account that entry or exit in oligopoly markets is complicated by the strategic interactions between firms. Consequently, estimates of discrete-choice models need to be modified to account for these strategic interactions. The framework of their study is a binary choice on entering or not with multiple decision makers and strategic interactions. The identifying restriction is that a firm enters the market if entry is profitable. Given a profit function, containing both variable and fixed profits, they can estimate probabilities. They then compare these estimates to observed choices.

Aguirregabiria and Ho (2006) extend Bresnahan and Reiss's (1993) approach. Their model incorporates private information shocks and thus is constructed as a dynamic game of incomplete information. Aguirregabiria and Ho estimate a dynamic oligopoly game of the U.S. airline industry. They study the sources of market power in this industry and evaluate counterfactual policy experiments such as changes in the fees that airports charge airlines. An airline chooses the network of local markets (city-pairs) where it operates and its price in each of these markets. Consumers value larger airline networks. Costs of entry and operation in a city-pair market depend on a company's own network and on the number of (potential) competitors in that market. Entry and exit are determined endogenously in the dynamic model. They use a panel data set with information on quantities, prices, and entry and exit decisions for every airline. First, they estimate the variable profits using information on quantities and prices where the structure of the model provides instruments for estimating the demand parameters. In a second stage, they estimate fixed operating costs and sunk costs in the dynamic game of entry and exit. They use the estimation method of Aguirregabiria and Mira (2007).

Estimating models that are consistent with Nash equilibrium behavior and allow for both pure and mixed strategies is an important empirical problem. Unfortunately, these empirical studies do not fully capture all the implications of the underlying theory. The approach we take in this chapter differs from the aforementioned studies in five important ways. First, they allow each agent a choice of only two possible actions, whereas we allow for a very large number of actions. Second, in order to use a ML approach, most of them assume a specific error distribution and likelihood function, which we do not.[5] Despite the limited number of actions, their ML estimation problems are complex. Third, some of these studies assume that there is no exogenous uncertainty. Fourth, three of the aforementioned studies also discuss dynamic games. Fifth, and most importantly, we use the observed data to estimate the game-theoretic parameters as well as the demand and market parameters simultaneously.

Our problem requires that we include a large number of possible actions to analyze oligopoly behavior and allow for mixed strategies. Doing so using a ML approach would be difficult, if not impossible. Instead, we use the information-theoretic, generalized maximum entropy (GME) estimator. We discuss the GME estimator at length in the Statistical Appendix, where we note that an important advantage of the GME estimator is its computational simplicity. Using GME, we can estimate a model with a large number of possible actions and impose inequality and equality restrictions implied by the equilibrium conditions of the game. In addition to this practical advantage, the GME estimator does not require the same strong, explicit distributional assumptions that are required in the standard ML approach. One can view the GME as a generalized ML approach in which, rather than using zero-moment conditions, one uses stochastic moments.

In the next section, we review mixed strategies. Then we present a game-theoretic model of firms' behavior. In the following section, we describe the GME approach to estimating this game.

MIXED STRATEGIES

Until now, we have concentrated on games with *pure strategies* – each firm chooses an action with certainty – as in the Nash-Cournot game in the prisoners' dilemma game in Chapter 6. However, a firm may employ a *mixed strategy*, in which it chooses between its possible actions with given probabilities.

[5] Bajari, Hong, and Ryan (2004) used computer algorithms to compute all Nash-equilibria within a simulation-based estimator rather than a ML estimator.

To illustrate the concept of a mixed strategy, we use an advertising game. Firms i and j can either choose a low-level (L) or high-level (H) of advertising.[6]

		Firm i	
		L	*H*
Firm j	*L*	0 0	1 0
	H	0 1	−1 −1

By inspection, this game has two Nash equilibria in pure strategies: Firm i chooses L and Firm j chooses H, and Firm i chooses H and Firm j chooses L. The equilibrium in which only Firm i chooses H is Nash because neither firms wants to change its behavior. Given that Firm j chooses L, Firm i does not want to change its level of advertising because, if it were to reduce its level of advertising to L, its payoff would fall from 1 to 0. Similarly, given that Firm i chooses H, Firm j does not want to change its level of advertising because, if it were to increase its level of advertising to H, its payoff would fall from 0 to -1. The reasoning is the same for the other pure-strategy Nash equilibrium.

How do the players know which (if any) pure-strategy Nash equilibrium will result? They do not. In addition, these pure Nash equilibria are unappealing because identical firms use different strategies. However, the firms may use the same strategies if their strategies are mixed. An example of a Nash equilibrium mixed strategy is for both firms to choose H with a probability of one-half – say if a flipped coin lands heads up.

Why would a firm pick a mixed strategy in which its probability of choosing H is one-half? Because the payoff matrix is symmetrical, we can look for an equilibrium in which each firm has the same probability of choosing H. If Firm i uses a mixed strategy, it must be willing to use either of the pure strategies, so it must be indifferent between choosing L or H. Thus, the probability that Firm j chooses H, α, must be such that Firm i's expected profit from choosing L, $E\pi^i_L$, equals its expected profit from choosing H, $E\pi^i_H$:

$$E\pi^i_L = 0(1-\alpha) + 0\alpha = 1(1-\alpha) + (-1)\alpha = E\pi^i_H.$$

[6] This game is similar to the well-known game of *chicken*, in which two lunatics drive toward each other in the middle of a road. As they approach the impact point, each has the option of continuing to drive down the middle of the road or to swerve. Both believe that, if only one driver swerves, that driver loses face (payoff $= 0$) and the other gains in self-esteem (payoff $= 1$). If neither swerves, both are maimed or killed (payoff $= -1$).

Given that $E\pi^i_L = 0$, for the expected profits to be equal, it must be true that $E\pi^i_H = 1(1-\alpha) + (-1)\alpha = 0$ so $\alpha = 1/2$: The firm picks either action with an equal probability.

If both firms use this mixed strategy, each of the four outcomes in the payoff matrix is equally likely. Firm *i* has a one-fourth chance of earning one (upper-right cell), a one-fourth chance of losing one (lower-right cell), and a one-half chance of earning zero (upper-left and lower-left cells). Thus, Firm *i*'s expected profit is $(1 \times 1/4) + (-1 \times 1/4) + (0 \times 1/2) = 0$, as is Firm *j*'s expected profit.

By construction, given that Firm *i* uses this mixed strategy, Firm *j* cannot do better by using a pure strategy. If Firm *j* chooses *H* with certainty, it earns one half the time and loses one the other half, so its expected profit is zero. If it chooses *L* with certainty, it similarly earns an expected profit of zero. Consequently, both firms using a mixed strategy is a Nash equilibrium (in addition to the two pure-strategy Nash equilibria that we previously discussed).

OLIGOPOLY GAME

Our objective is to determine the strategies of oligopolistic firms using time-series data on their decision variables, quantities, and variables that affect cost or demand, such as input prices or seasonal dummies. We assume that two firms, *i* and *j*, play a static game in each period of the sample, and each firm optimizes with respect to all relevant decision variables.

The econometrician observes payoff-relevant public information, such as demand and cost shifters, **z**, but does not observe private information known only to the firms. Firm *i* (and possibly Firm *j*), but not the econometrician, observes Firm *i*'s marginal cost or some other payoff-relevant random variable $\varepsilon^i(t)$ in period $t = 1, \ldots, T$. Where possible, we suppress the time index *t* for notational simplicity. The set of *K* possible realizations $\{\varepsilon_1, \varepsilon_2, \ldots \varepsilon_K\}$ is the same every period for both firms. The distributions are constant over time but may differ across firms. The firms, but not the econometrician, know these distributions and ε^i and ε^j are private, uncorrelated information.

The Strategies and the Game

There are *n* possible actions for each firm at a given time. For example, a firm with one decision variable (price) has *n* possible prices, whereas a firm that optimizes with respect to two decision variables (say, prices and level of advertising) has *n* possible actions or price–advertising pairs. The set of *n* possible outcomes for Firm *i* is $\{x^i_1, x^i_2, \ldots, x^i_n\}$.

We start with the problem in which the random state of nature is private information and that private information is uncorrelated across firms. The profit of Firm *i* in a particular time period is $\pi^i_{rsk}(\mathbf{z}) = \pi^i(x^i_r, x^j_s, \varepsilon^i_k, \mathbf{z})$, where *r* is the action chosen by Firm i and s is the action chosen by Firm j. In State k, Firm i's strategy is $\boldsymbol{\alpha}_k^i(\mathbf{z}) = (\alpha_{k1}^i(\mathbf{z}), \alpha_{k2}^i(\mathbf{z}), \ldots, \alpha_{kn}^i(\mathbf{z}))$, where $\alpha_{kr}^i(\mathbf{z})$ is the probability that Firm i chooses action x_r given private information ε_k^i and public information $\mathbf{z}$. If Firm i uses a pure strategy, $\alpha_{kr}^i(\mathbf{z})$ is one for a particular r and zero otherwise.

Firm j does not observe Firm i's private information, so it does not know the conditional probability $\alpha_{kr}^i(\mathbf{z})$. However, Firm j knows the distribution of Firm i's private information. We assume that firms' beliefs about the unconditional probabilities are correct in equilibrium. This probability is the expectation over Firm i's private information: $\alpha_r^i(\mathbf{z}) = \mathrm{E}_k \alpha_{kr}^i(\mathbf{z})$, where E_k is the expectations operator. Similarly Firm i knows the unconditional probability $\alpha_s^j(\mathbf{z})$ of Firm j.

In State k, Firm i chooses $\boldsymbol{\alpha}_k^i(\mathbf{z})$ to maximize expected profits, $\sum_s \alpha_s^j(\mathbf{z})\,\pi_{rsk}^i(\mathbf{z})$, where the expectation is taken over its rival's actions. If $Y_k^i(\mathbf{z})$ is Firm i's maximum expected profits given ε_k^i and $\mathbf{z}$, then Firm i's expected loss from using action x_r must be less than or equal to $Y_k^i(\mathbf{z})$:

$$L_{rk}^i(\mathbf{z}) \equiv \sum_s \alpha_s^j(\mathbf{z})\pi_{rsk}^i(\mathbf{z}) - Y_k^i(\mathbf{z}) \leq 0. \tag{9.1}$$

If it is optimal for Firm i to use action r with positive probability, the expected loss of using that action must be zero. Hence, optimality requires that

$$L_{rk}^i(\mathbf{z})\alpha_{rk}^i(\mathbf{z}) = 0. \tag{9.2}$$

This last condition is the mixed-strategy equilibrium condition.

The equilibrium to this game may not be unique. If there are multiple equilibria, our estimation method selects the most uniform strategy equilibrium that is consistent with the sample's data.

Econometric Adjustments for the Game

Our objective is to estimate the firms' strategies subject to the constraints (structure) implied by the optimization represented by Equations (9.1) and (9.2). However, we cannot use these constraints directly because they involve the private information ε_k^i. By taking expectations, we eliminate these unobserved variables and obtain empirically usable restrictions.

We define $Y^i(\mathbf{z}) \equiv E_k Y_k^i(\mathbf{z})$ and $\pi_{rs}^i(\mathbf{z}) \equiv E_k \pi_{rsk}^i(\mathbf{z})$. Taking expectations with respect to k of Equations (9.1) and (9.2) and using the previous definitions, we obtain

$$\sum_s \alpha_s^j(\mathbf{z})\pi_{rs}^i(\mathbf{z}) - Y^i(\mathbf{z}) \leq 0 \tag{9.3}$$

$$\left(\sum_s \alpha_s^j(\mathbf{z})\pi_{rs}^i(\mathbf{z}) - Y^i(\mathbf{z})\right)\alpha_r^i(\mathbf{z}) + \delta_r^i(\mathbf{z}) = 0, \tag{9.4}$$

where $\delta_r^i \equiv \text{cov}(L_{rk}^i, \alpha_{rk}^i) \geq 0$. For each Firm $i = 1, 2$, we can estimate the unobservable strategies $\boldsymbol{\alpha}^i(\mathbf{z})$ subject to the conditions implied by Firm i's optimization problem, Equations (9.3) and (9.4).

Firms may use approximately optimal decisions due to bounded rationality, or there may be some measurement errors. Therefore, Equation (9.4) should be treated as a stochastic restriction and include additive errors (with mean zero). However, Equation (9.4) already has an additive function, $\delta(\mathbf{z})$, that we cannot distinguish from the additive error. Thus, $\delta(\mathbf{z})$ is the only "error term" that we include in this equation.

If ε^i and ε^j are correlated or observed by both firms, the restrictions are slightly more complicated. If information is correlated, it would be reasonable to suppose that Firm i's beliefs about j's actions depend on the realization of ε^i, so that α_s^j is replaced by α_{ks}^j. If information is observed by both firms, Firm i's beliefs would also be conditioned on the realization of ε^j. In both cases, we can take expectations with respect to the private information and obtain equations analogous to (9.3) and (9.4). However, with either generalization, we would have an additional additive term in (9.3), say θ, and the definition of δ would be changed. The signs of both θ and δ would be indeterminate. In some of our empirical applications, all the estimated δ are positive, which is consistent with the model in the text where ε^i and ε^j are uncorrelated.

If we tried to estimate the model consisting of Equations (9.3) and (9.4) using traditional techniques, we would run into a number of problems. First, imposing the various equality and inequality restrictions from our game-theoretic model would be very difficult, if not impossible, with standard techniques. Second, because the problem is underdetermined (ill posed) in small samples (there may be more parameters than observations), we would have to impose additional assumptions to make the problem well posed. Third, we have to choose a certain likelihood function and present the game theoretic information via that likelihood, a practically impossible task. To avoid these and other estimation and inference problems, we estimate this class of methods using the information-theoretic GME framework.

THE ESTIMATION MODEL

If we have enough data, we could estimate firms' strategies using ML multinomial logit or probit. However, multinomial logit has four weaknesses. First, it requires an arbitrary distributional assumption. Second, it cannot handle actions that are not observed, which almost always occur – firms rarely choose all possible actions within a sample period. Third, multinomial logit does not perform well with small samples. Fourth, it is difficult to impose equality and inequality restrictions from game theory when using multinomial logit (or probit).

The information-theoretic GME method is superior to multinomial logit on all four grounds. First, multinomial logit is a special case of the GME (hence GME is more flexible and less arbitrary). Second, GME can handle actions that are not observed. Third, GME is more efficient than ML (Golan, Judge, and Perloff 1996 [GJP]). Fourth, it is relatively easy to impose equality and inequality restrictions using GME.

The GME method is discussed at length in the Statistical Appendix. (If you are unfamiliar with GME, you may want to read the Statistical Appendix first.) Our GME method is closely related to the GME multinomial choice approach in GJP and Golan, Judge, and Miller (1996).

Classical Maximum Entropy Formulation for the Multinomial Problem

In this section, we provide a brief intuitive summary of the Maximum Entropy (ME) formulation for the multinomial problem, relate it to the ML-logit model, and extend it to the GME framework (see the Statistical Appendix for details).

We start by describing the ME multinomial model for estimating the strategies α_s and α_r. We then generalize it to the semiparametric, GME method, which allows us to estimate the strategies based on stochastic moments and additional economic theoretic information such as game theoretic restrictions. Consider a random variable $\mathbf{x}$ with possible outcomes x_s, $s = 1, 2, \ldots, n$. Associated with each possible outcome x_s is a positive probability α_s where $\boldsymbol{\alpha}$ is a proper probability distribution: $\sum_s \alpha_s = 1$. We want to estimate the unknown probabilities $\boldsymbol{\alpha}$ given a small number of observed moments of the random variable $\mathbf{x}$. For example, $\mathbf{x}$ has $n = 10$ possible states, and we have estimates of the mean and variance, which we treat as known for this example. Even with this information, we still have more unknowns to be estimated than observations. Therefore, this problem is underdetermined. There are infinitely many $\boldsymbol{\alpha}$s that satisfy these two basic moments and the requirement that $\boldsymbol{\alpha}$ is proper. One way to solve such an underdetermined problem is to decide on a certain criterion that will identify one of the infinitely many $\boldsymbol{\alpha}$s that are consistent with the observed moments. Following the classical ME formulation of Jaynes (1957a,b) and the information theoretic literature, the criterion used here is the *entropy* (see the Statistical Appendix). The *entropy* of the distribution $\boldsymbol{\alpha} = (\alpha_1, \alpha_2, \ldots, \alpha_n)'$, is

$$H^{\alpha}(\alpha) \equiv -\sum_s \alpha_s \log \alpha_s \tag{9.5}$$

with $x \log(x)$ tending to zero as x tends to zero.

To solve our underdetermined problem, we maximize the entropy subject to the available information and the requirement that all probabilities are proper. That is, we maximize Equation (9.5) subject to the two first moments' requirements and the additional requirement that $\boldsymbol{\alpha}$ is a proper probability distribution. The estimated probabilities resulting from maximizing the entropy are intuitively reasonable estimates of the true distribution when we lack any other information.

These are the most uniform (most uninformed) estimated probabilities that are consistent with our information: they satisfy the two first moments.

If $(n-1)L \leq T$, where L is the dimension of **z**, the number of covariates, T is the number of observations, and all categories are observed in the sample, the ML-multinomial logit estimator has a unique solution. Though starting from a different philosophical background, these ME estimates are the same as those from the ML-logit model (see the Statistical Appendix). Consequently, we refer to this estimator as the ME-ML. If $(n-1)L > T$, the ML problem is underdetermined (ill-posed). However, even where the ML problem is ill-posed, the ME estimator provides a unique estimate, whereas the (nonexistent) multinomial logit ML estimator does not exist.

In all real-world applications, we expect our observed moments (or data) to be noisy (stochastic moments). If, in addition to these noisy sample moments, we have some nonsample information about the strategies, such as restrictions from economic theory, we want to incorporate that information into our estimation method. It is not feasible to estimate this problem using ML-multinomial logit because we cannot practically impose the theoretical restrictions. We do not want to use ME because the sample moments may be different than the population moments. Therefore, we use GME, a more flexible estimation method that allows us to treat all observed moments as stochastic and consequently, to include all other economic-theoretic restrictions, such as the first-order conditions resulting from a certain game.

Incorporating the Sample Information

In our game, the firms' decisions are the random variables that correspond to **x** in the previous example. We want to estimate the firms' strategies, which are their probability distributions over their actions. This subsection and the next subsection explain how we incorporate sample and nonsample (theory) information within the GME framework. In general, the sample information includes time-series data of the decision variables, quantities sold, and possibly time series of exogenous variables that affect demand and cost. The game-theoretic restrictions, Equations (9.3) and (9.4) , contain all the nonsample information.

We incorporate the sample information into our GME estimator of the strategies, $\boldsymbol{\alpha}^i$, by maximizing the entropy of $\boldsymbol{\alpha}^i$ subject to the sample's moments. We can use either of two approaches. If we require that the sample's moment restrictions hold exactly (zero moment conditions), we derive the ME-ML estimator when the ML estimate is unique (as described in the previous section). Otherwise, rather than treating the observed moments as pure or noiseless, we view the observed sample's moments as stochastic. We then treat the signal and the noise (in the moments) as two sets of unknowns to be estimated. This problem is always underdetermined, so we use our GME estimator. With this approach, we obtain estimates of the probabilities $\boldsymbol{\alpha}^i$ as a function of the public information, **z**.

We now sketch the GME approach (see the Statistical Appendix for details). In our problem, there are n actions. The variable y^i_{tr} equals one in period t if action r is observed, and zero otherwise. The variable y^i_{tr} is a function of the public information:

$$y^i_{tr} = G\left(\mathbf{z}_t \zeta^i_r\right) + e^i_{tr} = \alpha^i_{tr} + e^i_{tr}, \tag{9.6}$$

for $i = 1, 2$ where y^i_{tr} and $\mathbf{z}_t$ are observed and α^i_{tr}, e^i_{tr}, and ζ^i_r are unknown parameters to be estimated.

By eliminating $\mathbf{e}^i$ from Equation (9.6) and assuming that $G(\bullet)$ is a known cumulative density function (CDF) such as the logistic or the normal, we can estimate this model using maximum likelihood multinomial logit or probit. To avoid having to assume a specific CDF, we follow GJP and Golan, Judge, and Miller (1996) and relate the set of covariates $\mathbf{z}_t$ to the data y^i_{tr} and the unknown α^i_{tr} and e^i_{tr} via the cross moments. Multiplying Equation (9.6) by each covariate variable, z_{t1}, and summing over the observations, we obtain the stochastic sample-moment restrictions:

$$\sum_t y^i_{tr} z_{tl} = \sum_t \alpha^i_{tr} z_{tl} + \sum_t e^i_{tr} z_{tl}, \tag{9.7}$$

for $l = 1, \ldots, L$, which is the number of covariates in $\mathbf{z}$, and $r = 1, \ldots, n$. The basic GME estimator is obtained by maximizing the sum of the entropies corresponding to the strategy probabilities, $\boldsymbol{\alpha}^i$, and the entropy from the noise, $\mathbf{e}^i$, subject to the observed stochastic moments Equation (9.7).

The GME objective is a dual-criteria function that depends on the weighted sum of the entropy measures from both the unknown and unobservable $\boldsymbol{\alpha}^i$ and $\mathbf{e}^i$. By increasing the weight on the $\mathbf{e}^i$ component of entropy, we improve the accuracy of estimation (decrease the mean square errors of the estimates of $\boldsymbol{\alpha}^i$). By increasing the weight on the $\boldsymbol{\alpha}^i$ component of entropy, we improve prediction (correct assignment of observations to price–advertising categories). The ME estimator is a special case of the GME, in which no weight is placed on the noise component, and is similar to maximizing the logistic likelihood function. As a practical matter, our GME objective weighs the $\boldsymbol{\alpha}^i$ and $\mathbf{e}^i$ entropies equally because we lack any theory that suggests other weights.

The elements of $\boldsymbol{\alpha}^i$ are proper probabilities, but the elements of $\mathbf{e}^i$ range over the natural interval $[-1, 1]$ because each observed action y^i_{tr} is either one or zero. Therefore, we follow the reparametrization approach (Golan, Judge, and Miller 1996, and GJP – see the Statistical Appendix) to represent $\mathbf{e}^i$ and $\mathbf{e}^j$ as a set of proper probability distributions. Let $\mathbf{v} = [v_1, v_2, \ldots, v_M]'$ be a support space of dimension $M \geq 2$, that is at uniform intervals, symmetric around zero, and spans the interval $[-1/\sqrt{T},\ 1/\sqrt{T}]$, where T is the number of observations in the sample. Each error term e^i_{tr} is viewed as the expected value of the random (support) variable $\mathbf{v}$ ($e^i_{tr} \equiv \sum_m v_m w^i_{trm}$) with the corresponding unknown weights $\mathbf{w}^i_{tr} = [w^i_{tr1}, w^i_{tr2}, \ldots, w^i_{trM}]'$ that have the properties of probabilities: $0 \leq w^i_{trm} \leq 1$ and $\sum_m w^i_{trm} = 1$. If, for example, $M = 3$, then $\mathbf{v} = (-1/\sqrt{T}, 0, 1/\sqrt{T})'$, and there exists w^i_{tr1}, w^i_{tr2}, and w^i_{tr3} such that each noise component can be written as $e^i_{tr} = -w^i_{tr1}/\sqrt{T} + w^i_{tr3}/\sqrt{T}$. Using this parameterization, we represent the sample information (stochastic moments), Equation (9.7), as

$$\sum_t y^i_{tr}\, z_{tl} = \sum_t \alpha^i_{tr}\, z_{tl} + \sum_t e^i_{tr}\, z_{tl} = \sum_t \alpha^i_{tr}\, z_{tl} + \sum_t \sum_m w^i_{trm}\, v_m\, z^i_{tl}\,. \tag{9.8}$$

Other than M, no subjective information on the distribution of probabilities is assumed. It is sufficient to have two points ($M = 2$) in the support of $\mathbf{v}$, which converts the errors from $[-1, 1]$ into $[0, 1]$ space. This estimation process recovers $M - 1$ moments of the distribution of unknown errors, so a larger M permits the estimation of more moments. Monte-Carlo experiments (GJP; Golan, Judge, and Miller 1996) show a substantial decrease in the mean square error (MSE) of estimates when M increases from two to three. Further increases in M provide smaller incremental improvements. The estimates hardly change if M is increased beyond seven.

Let $\mathbf{w}$ be a vector containing the elements w_{trm}. For notational simplicity, we now drop the firm superscript. If we assume that the actions, $\mathbf{x}$, and the errors, $\mathbf{e}$, are independent, the GME estimation model for each firm is

$$\underset{\alpha,\mathbf{w}}{Max}\; H^{\alpha,\mathbf{w}}(\boldsymbol{\alpha}, \mathbf{w}) \equiv \underset{\alpha,\mathbf{w}}{Max}\left\{-\boldsymbol{\alpha}' \log \boldsymbol{\alpha} - \mathbf{w}' \log \mathbf{w}\right\} \tag{9.9}$$

subject to the GME sample information, Equation (9.8), and the requirement that both $\boldsymbol{\alpha}$ and $\mathbf{w}$ are proper probability distributions.

$$\mathbf{1}'\boldsymbol{\alpha}_t = \mathbf{1}, \tag{9.10}$$

$$\mathbf{1}'\mathbf{w}_{ts} = \mathbf{1}, \tag{9.11}$$

for $s = 1, 2, \ldots, n$ and $t = 1, 2, \ldots, T$.

For simplicity and to be able to compare that model with the basic GME models, in the Statistical Appendix, we develop the detailed solution for the simplest case without the covariates $\mathbf{z}$ and omitting the subscript t. To solve that model, we construct the Lagrangean

$$\begin{aligned}\ell(\boldsymbol{\lambda}, \rho, \beta) = &- \sum_s \alpha_s - \sum_s \sum_m w_{sm} \ln w_{sm} + \sum_s \lambda_s (y_s - \alpha_s - \mathbf{v}'\mathbf{w}_s) \\ &+ \rho(1 - 1'\boldsymbol{\alpha}) + \sum_s \eta_s (1 - \mathbf{1}'\mathbf{w}_s),\end{aligned} \tag{9.12}$$

where $\boldsymbol{\lambda}$, ρ, and $\boldsymbol{\eta}$ are Lagrange multipliers. The GME solutions (for this simple no-covariates model) are

$$\breve{\alpha}_s = \frac{\exp\left(-\breve{\lambda}_s\right)}{\sum_j \exp\left(-\breve{\lambda}_j\right)} \equiv \frac{\exp\left(-\breve{\lambda}_s\right)}{\Omega\left(\breve{\boldsymbol{\lambda}}\right)}, \tag{9.13}$$

$$\breve{w}_{sm} = \frac{\exp\left(-\breve{\lambda}_s v_m\right)}{\sum_m \exp\left(-\breve{\lambda}_s v_m\right)} \equiv \frac{\exp\left(-\breve{\lambda}_s v_m\right)}{\Psi_s\left(\breve{\boldsymbol{\lambda}}\right)}, \tag{9.14}$$

and

$$\breve{\mathbf{e}} = \breve{W}\mathbf{v}. \tag{9.15}$$

Because the Hessian is negative definite, the solution is globally unique. Following Agmon et al. (1979), Golan, Judge, and Miller (1996), and the Statistical Appendix, we can reformulate the GME problem as a concentrated, dual, generalized-likelihood function, which includes the traditional likelihood as a special case:

$$\begin{aligned}
\ell(\boldsymbol{\lambda}) &= -\sum_s \alpha_s(\boldsymbol{\lambda}) \log \alpha_s(\boldsymbol{\lambda}) - \sum_s \sum_m w_{sm}(\boldsymbol{\lambda}) \log w_{sm}(\boldsymbol{\lambda}) \\
&\quad + \sum_s \lambda_s (y_s - \alpha_s - \mathbf{v}'\mathbf{w}_s) \\
&= -\sum_s \alpha_s(\boldsymbol{\lambda})[-\lambda_s - \log \Omega(\boldsymbol{\lambda})] - \sum_s \sum_m w_{sm}(\boldsymbol{\lambda})[-\lambda_s v_m - \log \Psi_s(\boldsymbol{\lambda})] \\
&\quad + \sum_s \lambda_s (y_s - \alpha_s - \mathbf{v}'\mathbf{w}_s) \\
&= \sum_s \lambda_s y_s + \log \Omega(\boldsymbol{\lambda}) + \sum_s [\log \Psi_s(\boldsymbol{\lambda})].
\end{aligned} \tag{9.16}$$

Minimizing Equation (9.16) with respect to $\boldsymbol{\lambda}$ (setting the gradient, $\Delta\ell(\boldsymbol{\lambda}) = \mathbf{y} - \boldsymbol{\alpha} - \mathbf{e}$, equal to zero) yields the same estimates as from the primal formulation. The concentrated (dual) model – the expression after the last equality in Equation (9.16) – is computationally more efficient than the primal because the former involves only the multipliers $\boldsymbol{\lambda}$. The unknown probabilities are functions of $\boldsymbol{\lambda}$: $\alpha_s(\boldsymbol{\lambda})$ and $w_{sm}(\boldsymbol{\lambda})$ given by Equations (9.13)and (9.14). For future use, we note that these functions are independent of the multipliers associated with the adding-up conditions, Equations (9.10) and (9.11). The complexity of the numerical problem increases with the number of moments (the number of elements of the vector $\boldsymbol{\lambda}$); it does not increase with the number of unknown probabilities. This model is the GME multinomial model that includes the ML-logit as a special case. Henceforth we refer to the GME estimator that uses only sample information (or hard data) as the *GME estimator*. As with the ML, when using the GME estimator, we can estimate $\boldsymbol{\alpha}^i$ and $\boldsymbol{\alpha}^j$ separately.

Incorporating the Nonsample, Game-Theoretic Information

We obtain our other estimator, the *GME-Nash* estimator, by adding the game-theoretic restrictions in Equations (9.3) and (9.4) to the GME estimator and estimating $\boldsymbol{\alpha}^i$ and $\boldsymbol{\alpha}^j$ simultaneously. To explain how to implement this estimator, we initially proceed as if we knew the parameters of the profit functions, π^i_{rs}. This assumption allows us to concentrate on the game-theoretic restrictions. We then consider the more realistic case in which we need to estimate the parameters of the profit functions.

To use the GME-Nash estimator, we need to estimate $\boldsymbol{\alpha}^i$ and $\boldsymbol{\alpha}^j$ jointly because both strategy vectors appear in Equation (9.4). Further, we also have to estimate $\boldsymbol{\delta}^i(\mathbf{z})$, $i = 1, 2$, from Equation (9.4). As we discussed earlier, $\boldsymbol{\delta}^i(\mathbf{z})$ is nonzero if the econometrician does not observe firms' private information or if the firms make mistakes in their optimization.

Our first step is to respecify the vector $\boldsymbol{\delta}^i(\mathbf{z})$ of point estimates as a set of proper probability distributions. Let $\mathbf{v}^\delta$ be a vector of dimension $H \geq 2$ with corresponding unknown weights $\boldsymbol{\omega}^\delta$ such that

$$\sum_h \omega^\delta_{rh} = 1, \tag{9.17}$$

$$\sum_h v^\delta_h \omega^\delta_{rh} = \delta_r, \tag{9.18}$$

for $\boldsymbol{\delta} = \boldsymbol{\delta}^i, \boldsymbol{\delta}^j$. The support spaces $\mathbf{v}^\delta$ are defined to be symmetric around zero for all $\boldsymbol{\delta}$s. We do not have natural boundaries for $\boldsymbol{\delta}^i$, so we use the "three-sigma rule" (Pukelsheim 1994, Golan, Judge, and Miller 1996) to choose the limits of these support spaces, where *sigma* is the larger of the empirical standard deviation of the discrete action space of prices or advertising. For example, in the cola problem studied in the next chapter, the largest empirical standard deviation is 26.7, so the support space for $M = 3$ is $\mathbf{v} = (-80.1, 0, 80.1)$.[7]

Next, to simplify notation, we stack the three sets of probability vectors ($\boldsymbol{\alpha}^i$, $\boldsymbol{\alpha}^j$; $\mathbf{w}^i$, $\mathbf{w}^j$ and ω^{δ^i}, ω^{δ^j}) for each firm together. Let

$$\boldsymbol{\alpha} = \begin{pmatrix} \boldsymbol{\alpha}^i \\ \boldsymbol{\alpha}^j \end{pmatrix}, \quad \mathbf{w} = \begin{pmatrix} \mathbf{w}^i \\ \mathbf{w}^j \end{pmatrix} \quad \textit{and} \quad \boldsymbol{\omega} = \begin{pmatrix} \boldsymbol{\omega}^{\delta^i} \\ \boldsymbol{\omega}^{\delta^j} \end{pmatrix}.$$

[7] We calculate the empirical standard deviation as follows. First, we represent the set of possible actions by a finite set of discrete points, which are the midpoints of the intervals of the grid discussed in an earlier section. Second, we transform each data point with a point from this set (the midpoint of the interval in which the data point falls). Third, we calculate the standard deviation of this transformed data.

Following convention, we continue to assume independence between the actions (signal) and the noise. The GME-Nash problem is

$$\underset{\boldsymbol{\alpha},\mathbf{w},\boldsymbol{\omega}}{Max}\ H^{\alpha,w,\varpi}(\boldsymbol{\alpha},\mathbf{w},\boldsymbol{\omega}) \equiv \underset{\boldsymbol{\alpha},\mathbf{w},\boldsymbol{\omega}}{Max}\left\{-\boldsymbol{\alpha}'\log\boldsymbol{\alpha} - \mathbf{w}'\log\mathbf{w} - \boldsymbol{\omega}'\log\boldsymbol{\omega}\right\} \quad (9.19)$$

subject to the empirical stochastic sample's moments conditions (9.8) for each Firm $i = 1, 2$:

$$\begin{aligned}\sum_t y^i_{tr}\, z_{tl} &= \sum_t \alpha^i_{tr}\, z_{tl} + \sum_t e^i_{tr}\, z_{tl}\\ &= \sum_t \alpha^i_{tr}\, z_{tl} + \sum_t\sum_m w^i_{trm}\, v^i_m\, z^i_{tl}\end{aligned} \quad (9.20)$$

and subject to the (reparameterized) necessary economic conditions (9.3) and (9.4) for each Firm $i, j = 1, 2$:

$$\sum_s \alpha^j_s(\mathbf{z})\pi^i_{rs}(\mathbf{z}) - Y^i(\mathbf{z}) \le 0 \quad (9.21)$$

$$\left(\sum_s \alpha^j_s(\mathbf{z})\pi^i_{rs}(\mathbf{z}) - Y^i(\mathbf{z})\right)\alpha^i_r(\mathbf{z}) + \delta^i_r(\mathbf{z}) = 0, \quad (9.22)$$

and subject to the requirement that all the probabilities, $\boldsymbol{\alpha}$, $\mathbf{w}$, and $\boldsymbol{\omega}$ are proper:

$$\mathbf{1}'\boldsymbol{\alpha} = 1, \quad \mathbf{1}'\mathbf{w} = 1, \quad \mathbf{1}'\boldsymbol{\omega} = 1. \quad (9.23)$$

The terms $\boldsymbol{\delta}$ in Equation (9.22) are defined by Equations (9.17) and (9.18). Solving the GME-Nash primal problem (9.19) through (9.23) yields the estimates, $\tilde{\boldsymbol{\alpha}}$, $\tilde{\mathbf{w}}$, and $\tilde{\boldsymbol{\omega}}$.[8]

We now turn to the more realistic case in which we do not know the parameters of the profit functions, but we observe Firm i's output, q^i, and some factor cost variables, $\mathbf{z}_c$. We also assume that Firm i's cost is given by a cost function $C^i(q^i, \mathbf{z}_c; \boldsymbol{\eta}^i)$, where $\boldsymbol{\eta}^i$ is a vector of parameters. Similarly, we assume that the demand for Firm i's product is $q^i(x^i, x^j, \mathbf{z}_d; \boldsymbol{\varphi}^i)$, where $\mathbf{z}_d$ are demand shifters (such as income and a seasonal dummy) and $\boldsymbol{\varphi}^i$ is a vector of parameters to be estimated. We simultaneously estimate the strategies and the parameters of the profit function, which depend on the demand and cost functions. We substitute these functions in the Constraints (9.3) and (9.4), or (9.21) and (9.22), and estimate $\boldsymbol{\eta}^i$ and $\boldsymbol{\varphi}^i$ (for $i = 1, 2$) jointly with the other parameters in the GME-Nash model.

Finally, because we observe demand (but not cost), we have an additional set of data (sample) restrictions in the form of demand equations for each Firm i,

$$\mathbf{q}^i = \mathbf{q}^i\left(x^i, x^j, \mathbf{z}_d; \boldsymbol{\varphi}^i\right) + \mathbf{u}^i,$$

[8] Because we are simultaneously estimating equations for both firms, we could generalize the seemingly unrelated equation approach and add another equation within our GME-Nash model to capture the possible correlations of the errors across equations. To keep notation as simple as possible, we do not include that equation here.

where $\mathbf{u}^i$ is a vector of error terms (with zero means). Once we specify the support spaces for both $\boldsymbol{\varphi}^i$ and $\boldsymbol{\eta}^i$ (and the noise) for both firms ($i = 1, 2$), we estimate these parameters simultaneously with all the other parameters in the GME-Nash model. We perform this estimation by maximizing the sum of all the entropy measures in Equation (9.19) plus the entropy associated with the unknown probabilities representing the demand and cost parameters and their relevant error terms.

Properties of the Estimators

The appendix to this chapter provides conditions under which both the GME and GME-Nash estimators are consistent. These estimators converge to the ML-logit estimator as the sample size increases. However, the estimators differ in efficiency and information content. Because we seldom, if ever, have large data sets when we analyze games, the increased efficiency of the GME-Nash model (relative to the GME and the ML-logit) provides a justification for using it.

Under the null hypothesis that the game-theoretic conditions are consistent with the empirical data, the possible solution space for the GME-Nash estimate of $\boldsymbol{\alpha}$ is a subset of the solution space of the GME estimate of $\boldsymbol{\alpha}$. Under the assumption that a solution to the GME-Nash estimation problem exists for all samples, the GME-Nash estimator is consistent (see the appendix to this chapter for an outline of the proof).

The GME-Nash Estimator: Hypothesis Testing

We can quantify the added information contained in the game-theoretic restrictions by comparing the normalized entropy of $\boldsymbol{\alpha}$ with and without the restrictions. The normalized entropy measure is $S(\boldsymbol{\alpha}) = -(\sum_r \alpha_r \log \alpha_r)/(\log n)$. The normalized entropy measure is $S(\boldsymbol{\alpha}) = 1$ if all outcomes are equally likely (a mixed strategy that is uniform over the action space) and is $S(\boldsymbol{\alpha}) = 0$ if we know which action will be taken with certainty (a pure strategy). The magnitude of the change in the value of the normalized entropy after imposing the game-theoretic restrictions provides a measure of the additional information they contain.

Following the likelihood and the empirical likelihood literature, and their corresponding likelihood ratio test and the empirical likelihood ratio test, we use here an "entropy ratio" (ER) statistic, which has a limiting χ^2 distribution (see Kullback 1959, Gokhale and Kullback 1978, Soofi 1992). We use this statistic to test hypotheses about parameters corresponding to certain covariates, to the strategies, to the game, or about any combination of these three sets of hypotheses.[9]

[9] On the direct relationship between entropy and chi-square see, for example, Golan, Judge and Miller (1996). It is shown that the entropy divergence measure, or cross entropy, and the chi-square are second-order equivalent.

The basic logic of the ER test is that we compare the value of the objective function under different scenarios (restrictions) such as without the moment restrictions and with the moment restrictions. If the value of the objective function of the GME, Equation 9.19, is approximately the same with and without a certain restriction, we can conclude that there is a very high probability that the restrictions contain no additional information relative to the unrestricted case (i.e., the restriction is consistent with the observed data). Two times the difference between the values of the objective functions in two scenarios (restricted and unrestricted) is asymptotically (as the sample size grows) distributed as a χ^2 with degrees of freedom equal the number of constraints imposed.

Conceptually, we can view the different restrictions we test as two types of restrictions: "direct" restrictions (imposed directly on the parameters of interest) and "indirect" restrictions – restrictions that impose a structure on the overall model (and may also introduce new parameters) and indirectly affect the parameters of interest. For example, the restriction $\lambda_1 = 0$ within the GME model (Equation (9.9) subject to (9.8), through (9.11) or its dual formulation) is a direct restriction. The Lagrange multiplier here is the basic parameter of interest (called β_1 in the likelihood literature). Thus, our null hypothesis is $H_0 : \lambda_l = 0$ (vs., say, $H_1 : \lambda_l \neq 0$) and we impose that constraint within the GME model and compare its objective value with the objective value of the unrestricted case. It is equivalent to the hypothesis $H_0 : \beta_l = 0$ (vs. $H_1 : \beta_l \neq 0$) in the ML-Logit. Similarly, under the GME we can impose direct restrictions (hypotheses) on the strategies α: $H_0 : \alpha_s = \alpha_s^0$ vs. $H_1 : \alpha_s \neq \alpha_s^0$ for some fixed value α_s^0.

As a second and more general example, consider comparing the ME and the GME models. Using the same data **z**, under ME, the moment conditions enter as pure (zero moment) conditions ($\sum_t y^i_{tr}\, z_{tl} = \sum_t \alpha^i_{tr}\, z_{tl}$), whereas, under the GME, the moments are viewed as stochastic moments ($\sum_t y^i_{tr}\, z_{tl} = \sum_t \alpha^i_{tr}\, z_{tl} + \sum_t e^i_{tr}\, z_{tl} = \sum_t \alpha^i_{tr}\, z_{tl} + \sum_t \sum_m w^i_{trm}\, v_m\, z^i_{tl}$). Ignoring the firm's index i (because each firm is estimated independently in these models), the entropy objective functions for the ME and GME models are H^α and $H^{\alpha,w}$, respectively. To test the hypothesis that the two models are consistent with each other (and the data), we need to compare these objective functions. To carry out this comparison, we must first ensure that the two different objective functions are comparable. The ME objective function is a function of only the strategies α, whereas the GME objective is a function of both the strategies $\boldsymbol{\alpha}$ and the error probabilities **w**. The maximal possible value of H^α is attained for uniform $\boldsymbol{\alpha}$s, while the maximal possible value of $H^{\alpha,w}$ is achieved for uniform $\boldsymbol{\alpha}$s and uniform **w**s. Accordingly, the maximal value of the objective function under the ME is $log\, \mathrm{n}$ (there are n strategies), whereas under the GME it is $log\, \mathrm{n} + \mathrm{T}\, log\, \mathrm{M}$ (in addition to the n strategies, there are T probability distributions **w** of dimension M each). A test whether the two models are the same requires a special adjustment for these **w**s in the H^α criterion. Without that adjustment, the two criteria are not comparable and a formal test cannot be done. This adjustment is implicitly done in comparing the optimal value of the objective resulting from the GME model ($H^{\alpha,w}$) with that resulting from the GME model where all the **w**s are restricted to be uniform $H^{\alpha,w}$ ($w_{trm} = 1/M$ for all t, r, m). This restricted GME model is equivalent to the ME model. Similarly, we can add the total entropy of the uniform error probabilities ($T \times \log M$) to the ME optimal objective $H^{\alpha *}$ and compare it directly with the GME optimal objective value $H^{\alpha *, w*}$. Doing so allows us to compare the two models directly and provide the same statistic: $2|(H^{\alpha *} + T \times \log M) - H^{\alpha *, w*}|$. Though the main question here is whether the estimated $\boldsymbol{\alpha}$s are the same in both models, the constraints imposed here directly affect the errors (or moment restrictions) and indirectly affect the $\boldsymbol{\alpha}$s (via the **w**s).

Next, consider the more general case of indirect restriction/s. The set of Nash restrictions is an example of such a restriction. These restrictions are not imposed directly on the Lagrange multiplier/s corresponding to a particular covariate z_{tl} or on the strategies $\boldsymbol{\alpha}$. These restrictions impose a certain structure. There are Lagrange multipliers corresponding to each one of these restrictions. Similar to the previous example, we need to compare the optimal values of $H^{\alpha,w,\varpi}$ with that of $H^{\alpha,w}$. Within the GME-Nash model (9.19) through (9.23), if we restrict the set of Lagrange multipliers corresponding to the Nash, or game-theoretic, conditions (9.21) and (9.22) to be exactly zero, this restricted model is equivalent to the simple GME model. If we compare the values of the objective functions of both cases (restricted and nonrestricted), we can evaluate whether the game-theoretic restrictions are consistent with the observed data. The effect of the restrictions on the estimated strategies (an indirect effect) can be evaluated by comparing the two sets of estimated strategies: those resulting from the simple GME, $\tilde{\alpha}^*_{GME}$, and those resulting from the GME-Nash model, $\tilde{\alpha}^*_{GME-Nash}$ ($H_0 : \tilde{\boldsymbol{\alpha}}_{GME\_Nash} = \tilde{\boldsymbol{\alpha}}_{GME}$ vs. $H_1 : \tilde{\boldsymbol{\alpha}}_{GME\_Nash} \neq \tilde{\boldsymbol{\alpha}}_{GME}$). To perform this test, we use the traditional χ^2-test for comparing two discrete distributions.[10]

Suppose that within our GME-Nash model we wish to test whether a certain covariate is extraneous. Our null hypothesis for each firm is $H_0 : \lambda_l = 0$ (vs. $H_1 : \lambda_l \neq 0$). We impose that constraint within the GME-Nash model. The ER statistic for testing our hypothesis is

$$\mathrm{ER} = 2\left|\tilde{H}^{\alpha,w,\varpi}(\lambda_1 = 0) - \tilde{H}^{\alpha,w,\varpi}\right| \to \chi^2_{(2)}, \tag{9.24}$$

where $\tilde{H}$ is the maximal value of the objective function in each case. Under the mild assumptions, stated in the appendix to this chapter (or the assumptions of Owen 1990 and Qin and Lawless 1994), $\mathrm{ER} \to \chi^2_J$ as $T \to \infty$, when the null hypothesis is true and J is the total number of restrictions. The approximate α-level confidence intervals for the estimates are obtained by setting $ER(\,) \leq C_\alpha$, where C_α is chosen

[10] The χ^2-test of the null hypothesis examined whether the two discrete distributions are consistent with one another. Chi-square is calculated by finding the difference between the observed frequencies of both distrubutions, squaring them, dividing each squared term by the corresponding frequency of the based distribution (say the GME-Nash strategies), and taking the sum of the result.

so that $\Pr(\chi_J^2 < C_\alpha) = \alpha$. Similarly, we can test any other hypothesis of the form $\boldsymbol{\alpha} = \boldsymbol{\alpha}_0$ for all, or any subset, of the parameters. We use this ER statistic to test whether the economic and Nash restrictions are consistent with the data. See the Statistical Appendix for details.

Using the same line of reasoning as earlier, each constraint or data point represents additional potential information that may lower the value of the objective function but can never increase it. To simplify notation, let λ^* be the set of all Lagrange multipliers for all the model constraints – the moment conditions, the game-theoretic conditions, and the conditions used to estimate the demand functions – excluding the adding up conditions. Following the derivations of the Statistical Appendix, we use the following "goodness of fit" measure (or "pseudo R^2") for our multinomial estimator:

$$R^* = 1 - \frac{H\left(\tilde{\lambda}^*\right)}{H(\mathbf{0})} = 1 - S\left(\tilde{\lambda}^*\right), \tag{9.25}$$

where $R^* = 0$ implies no informational value of the data set and $R^* = 1$ implies perfect certainty or perfect in-sample prediction. Thus, there is a close relationship between the goodness of fit measure and the normalized entropy measure.[11]

The small-sample approximated variances can be computed in several ways. We briefly discuss a simple approach here. For each equation (say the two sets of demand equations), we calculate

$$\hat{\sigma}_i^2 = \frac{1}{T} \sum_t \tilde{u}_{it}^2, \tag{9.26}$$

where $\tilde{u}_{it} \equiv \sum_j \tilde{w}_{tj}^u v_j^u$ and $\hat{\text{var}}(\phi_k^i) \cong \hat{\sigma}_i^2 (XX)^{-1}$ for each parameter ϕ_k^i and X is the full set of covariates. Similarly, for each set of equations, the relevant $\hat{\sigma}^2$ is estimated.

Because our model is a system of a large number of equations, the elements of the asymptotic variance-covariance matrix for the error terms of the entire system are estimated in the traditional way, taking into account all the data and all the restrictions, Equations (9.3) and (9.4).

SUMMARY

We developed a framework for modeling an oligopolistic game over a discrete action space. This approach allows us to use sample data as well as the game-theoretic first-order conditions to estimate pure or mixed strategies for each of the players. We then formulated three models to solve the firms' strategies. The first is a simple ME-ML logit that cannot incorporate the game-theoretic restrictions into the estimation process. The second is the multinomial GME, which is more efficient

[11] This measure, R^*, is the same as the information index (e.g., Soofi 1992).

than the first model but also did not incorporate the game-theoretic restrictions. The third model is the GME-Nash model that provides a simple framework for a simultaneous estimation of both firms' strategies while taking into account all of the available data and the game-theoretic conditions. We also discuss the relevant test statistics and diagnostics.

In Chapter 10, we use this model in two empirical applications. We also provide detailed simulations to show the behavior of our approach for a small sample.

APPENDIX 9A: PROOF THAT THE GME-NASH ESTIMATOR IS CONSISTENT

We provide the basic steps and logic of the proof that the GME-Nash estimator is consistent. Call the GME-Nash estimates of the strategies $\tilde{\boldsymbol{\alpha}}$, the GME estimates $\breve{\boldsymbol{\alpha}}$, and the ME-ML estimates $\hat{\boldsymbol{\alpha}}$ (see the Statistical Appendix). We make the following assumptions:

Assumption 1: A solution of the GME-Nash estimator $(\tilde{\boldsymbol{\alpha}}, \tilde{\mathbf{w}}, \tilde{\boldsymbol{\omega}})$ exists for any sample size.

Assumption 2: The expected value of each error term is zero, its variance is finite, and the error distribution satisfies the Lindberg condition (Davidson and MacKinnon 1993, p. 135).

Assumption 3: The true value of each unknown parameter is in the interior of its support space.

With these assumptions, we want to show that:

Proposition: Given Assumptions 1–3, and letting *all* the end points of the error support spaces $\mathbf{v}$ and $\mathbf{v}^d$ be normalized by $\sqrt{T}$, $\text{plim}\,(\tilde{\boldsymbol{\alpha}}) = \text{plim}\,(\breve{\boldsymbol{\alpha}}) = \text{plim}\,(\hat{\boldsymbol{\alpha}}) = \boldsymbol{\alpha}$.

This result holds when the profit parameters are known and when these parameters are unknown. According to this proposition, the GME-Nash estimates, $\tilde{\boldsymbol{\alpha}}$, and the GME basic estimates, $\breve{\boldsymbol{\alpha}}$, approach each other and the true strategies as the sample size approaches infinity. That is, all these three estimators are consistent.

Proof:

(*i*) The consistency of the multinomial GME estimator is proved by GJP. Let the end points of the error supports of $\mathbf{v}$, v_1, and v_M be $-1/\sqrt{T}$ and $1/\sqrt{T}$, respectively. As $T \to \infty$, $\Psi_s \to 1$ for all s in the concentrated (dual) GME equation. Thus, $\sum_s \ln \Psi_s(\lambda) \to 0$ and $\text{plim}\, \breve{\boldsymbol{\alpha}}_T = \boldsymbol{\alpha}$.

(*iia*) The GME-Nash with known profit parameters is consistent: by Assumption 1, after we have added the restrictions (9.3) and (9.4), we still have a solution.

(*iib*) The argument in (*iia*) together with Assumption 2 implies that plim $\breve{\boldsymbol{\alpha}}_T = \boldsymbol{\alpha}$.

(*iii*) The GME-Nash with unknown profit parameters is consistent: given Assumption 3, the GME provides consistent estimates of $\boldsymbol{\varphi}$ in the demand equations; plim $\tilde{\boldsymbol{\varphi}}_T = \boldsymbol{\varphi}$. This follows from the consistency of the GME for the linear model. For a detailed proof, see Golan, Judge, and Miller (1996) or Mittelhammer and Cardell (1997). By the argument in (ii), plim $\breve{\boldsymbol{\alpha}}_T = \boldsymbol{\alpha}$. These asymptotic properties can also be established using the empirical likelihood approach (Owen 1990, Qin and Lawless 1994, and Golan and Judge 1996).

PROBLEMS

Note: Answers to problems are available at the back of the book.

9.1 Consider a game consisting of two players and two possible choices.
   A) Construct the basic ML model when no covariates exist.
   B) Construct the ME model and contrast with the ML.
   C) Construct the GME model.
   D) You just received a data set composed of time-series data of the basic covariates affecting the individuals' behavior. Repeat Questions A–C.

9.2 Construct the simple version of Tamer's (2003) model, described in this chapter, as a GME model. (*Hint*: this is a basic censored model discussed in Golan, Judge, and Perloff 1997.)

9.3 Construct the Generalized Cross Entropy (GCE)-Nash model. To do so, assume that you – the econometrician – have some priors on each players' actions (call it $\boldsymbol{\alpha}^{0i}$). Note, that these are the econometrician's priors on $\boldsymbol{\alpha}$ and not additional information each player has. Reconstruct the GME-Nash model taking into account these priors. (Note, to answer this question, you need to look at the Statistical Appendix and study how to incorporate priors within the cross entropy model or within the basic GCE model.)

9.4 Show that it is impossible to incorporate the economic-theoretic (or game-theoretic) conditions, specified in this chapter, within the multinomial-ML and the ME models. (*Hint*: the moment conditions in these models are not stochastic.)

TEN

Estimating Strategies: Case Studies

We now apply the theory developed in Chapter 9 to estimate strategies and market power in airlines and cola markets.[1] First, we estimate the pricing strategies of American Airlines and United Airlines. We assume that the airlines choose only price and that we have a reliable measure of cost. Next, we estimate the strategies of Coca-Cola and Pepsi Cola. This second study is more general than the airlines model in two ways: we assume that the airlines set both price and advertising levels and that the strategies are conditional on exogenous demand and cost variables. Unlike most other studies that estimate strategies, we do not assume that the firms use a single pure strategy, nor do we make the sort of *ad hoc* assumptions used in conjectural variations models.

AIRLINES GAME

We estimate the strategic pricing behavior of American and United Airlines using the maximum entropy-maximum-likelihood multinomial logit (ME-ML),[2] generalized maximum entropy (GME), and GME-Nash approaches and compare the results. After approximating the airlines' continuous action spaces – price – with a discrete grid, we estimate the vector of probabilities – the pure or mixed strategies – that United and American Airlines choose an action within each possible interval in the grid. We then conduct hypothesis tests. Next, we use our estimated strategies to calculate the Lerner index of market structure. Then, we present estimates of the strategies and demand estimates of United and American Airlines as well as detailed statistics and a battery of hypothesis tests. Finally, we describe a number

[1] This chapter is based on Golan, Karp, and Perloff (1998, 2000).

[2] As discussed in Chapter 9, we cannot practically estimate the multinomial logit model when some outcomes are not observed. Consequently, we estimate the maximum entropy-multinomial logit (ME-ML) model developed in Golan, Judge, and Perloff (1996), which is identical to multinomial logit when both models can be estimated.

of sampling experiments that illustrate the small sample properties of our GME estimators.[3]

Airlines Model

We allow for the possibility that American and United provide differentiated services on a given route and assume that the (linear) demand curve facing Firm i is

$$q^i = a^i + b^i p^i + d^i p^j + u^i, \tag{10.1}$$

where $i = 1, 2, i \neq j$, q^i is the quantity sold, p^i is the real price charged, and u^i is an error term with mean zero. We expect the parameters a^i and d^i to be positive and b^i to be negative.[4] In the Statistical Appendix, we showed how to estimate equations like (10.1) using the GME approach. In our model, Equation (10.1) is estimated simultaneously with the other parameters in the GME-Nash model.

The necessary conditions for the game are given by Equations (9.1) and (9.2). If we let Firm i form a prior, β^i_{sk}, about the probability that Firm j will pick action x^i_s when Firm i observes ε^i_k, and we apply the Nash assumption that agents' beliefs about their rival's actions are correct so that $\beta^i_r = \alpha^i_r$, then if firms choose prices, the necessary conditions become

$$\sum_r \beta^i_r \left(p^i_s - c^i\right) q^i_{rs} - Y^i + \theta^i_s \leq 0, \tag{10.2}$$

$$\left[\sum_r \beta^i_r \left(p^i_s - c^i\right) q^i_{rs} - Y^i\right] \left(\alpha^i_s + \mu^i_s\right) + \delta^i_s = 0, \tag{10.3}$$

where the Nash condition $\beta^i_r = \alpha^i_r$ is unchanged. Using the expectations operator E_k, we define $\beta^i_r \equiv \mathrm{E}_k \beta^i_{rk}$, $Y^i \equiv \mathrm{E}_k Y^i_k$, $\alpha^i_s \equiv \mathrm{E}_k \alpha^i_{sk}$, $\pi^i_{rs} \equiv \mathrm{E}_k \pi^i_{rsk}$, and $L^i_s \equiv \mathrm{E}_k L^i_{sk}$. If we let $\theta^i_{sk} \equiv L^i_{sk} - (\sum_r \beta^i_r \pi^i_{rs} - Y^i)$ and take expectations, then we find that $\mathrm{E}_k \theta^i_{sk} = Cov(\beta^i_{rk}, \pi^i_{rsk}) \equiv \theta^i_s$. Thus, $L^i_s \equiv \mathrm{E}_k L^i_{sk} = \sum_r \beta^i_r \pi^i_{rs} - Y^i + \theta^i_s$. Taking expectations with respect to k, we get the previous two equations where $\delta^i_s \equiv \theta^i_s \alpha^i_s + Cov(\theta^i_{sk}, \alpha^i_{sk})$. As before, private, uncorrelated information implies $\theta^i_s = 0$ and $\delta^i_s \geq 0$.

The data set includes price, quantity, and cost data for fifteen quarters (1984:4–1987:4, 1988:2, 1988:4) for various routes between Chicago and other cities.[5] We calculated the airlines marginal costs using the formula in Oum, Zhang, and Zhang

[3] Some of the very recent related game-theoretic studies on entry and exit in the airline industry, such as Ciliberto and Tamer (2006) and Aguirregabiria and Ho (2006), are discussed in Chapter 9.

[4] In our empirical analysis, we experimented with including various additional right-hand-side variables such as measures of income, population, or economic conditions. None of these variables, however, affected the fit of the equation or the parameters a_i, b_i, and d_i substantially.

[5] The data were generously provided by James A. Brander and Anming Zhang. They describe the data in their studies, Brander and Zhang (1990, 1993) and Oum, Zhang, and Zhang (1993).

(1993), and we used the average of these for the values c^i. The nominal data are deflated using the Consumer Price Index.

We restrict our attention to two city pairs, Chicago–Providence and Chicago–Wichita, where United and American Airlines had no (or trivial) competition from other firms during the four years analyzed here. On these two routes, the average marginal cost was lower than observed prices and the estimated demand curves were consistent with economic theory: the demand curves slope down, $b_i < 0$, and the services are substitutes, $d_i > 0$.

We first specify the upper and lower bound of the price space. The lower bound is the lowest observed price for both airlines minus 10% and the upper bound is the highest observed price for both airlines plus 10%. We then divide the price space into twenty equal-size increments. Our decision to divide the price space into twenty intervals is arbitrary, but as long as our grid covers the entire possible price range and has an adequate number of discrete points in it, the basic estimated strategies are relatively insensitive to the number of intervals.

Because we do not know the true demand curve parameters, we estimate simultaneously the linear demand curve and a price-strategic choice model for each firm. We do not estimate c^i because we have a calculated measure of the marginal cost.

Estimates

In the GME-Nash model, the simple correlations between the *actual* and *estimated* quantities in the demand equations are 0.1 for the American Airlines demand equation and 0.2 for the United Airlines equation for the Providence route. The correlations are 0.5 for both airlines for the Wichita equations. The demand coefficients (a_i, b_i, and d_i) for Providence are 1,865.8 (with an asymptotic standard error of 373.4), −12.1 (5.1), 4.7 (1.6) for American Airlines and 1,571.7 (456.2), −10.2 (5.6), 4.8 (6.2) for United Airlines. Given these parameters, the own-demand elasticities at the sample mean are -2.6 for American Airlines and −2.1 for United Airlines. Both airlines have cross-elasticities of 0.95.

In Wichita, the demand coefficients are 637.7 (345.7), −3.7 (4.4), and 2.6 (4.0) for American Airlines, and 810.4 (238.9), −6.2 (2.8), and 3.6 (3.1) for United Airlines. The own-demand elasticities are −1.5 for American Airlines and −2.1 for United Airlines, and the cross-price elasticities are 0.9 in the American equation and 1.2 in the United Airlines equation at the sample mean. For comparison, we estimated these demand curves *separately* using the ordinary least squares method. The estimated values were of the same sign and magnitude as the above GME-Nash estimates that were achieved via simultaneous estimation of the full model.

The estimated strategy parameters, α, are shown in Figure 10.1 for American Airlines and in Figure 10.2 for United Airlines for the Providence route and in Figures 10.3 and 10.4 for Wichita. The ME-ML estimates are the observed frequencies.

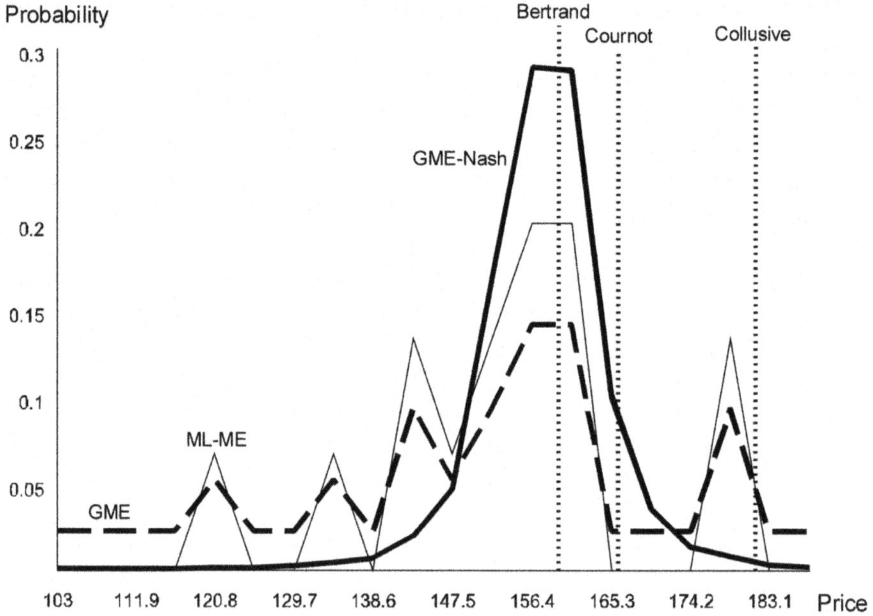

Figure 10.1. Price Strategies of American Airlines, Chicago–Providence.

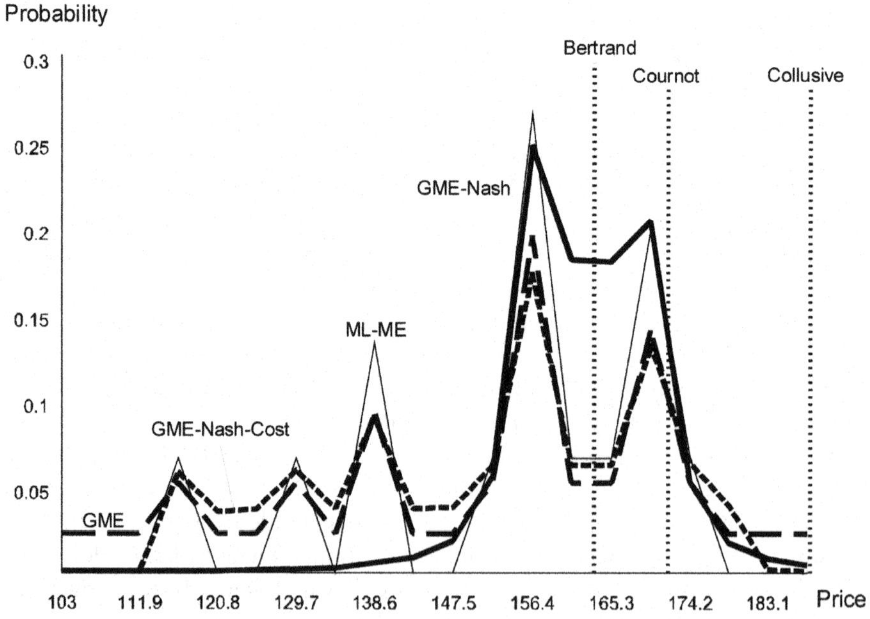

Figure 10.2. Price Strategies of United Airlines, Chicago–Providence.

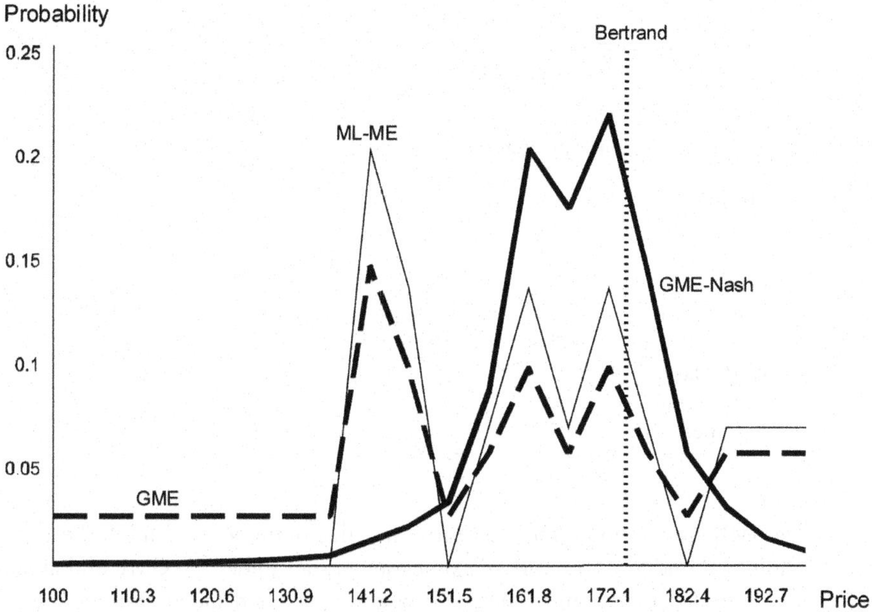

Figure 10.3. Price Strategies of American Airlines, Chicago–Wichita.

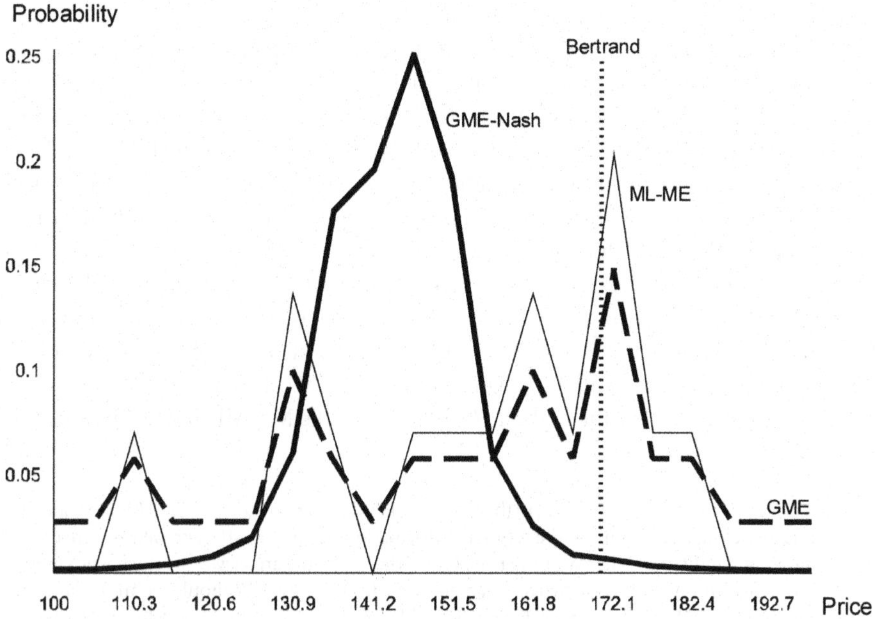

Figure 10.4. Price Strategies of United Airlines, Chicago–Wichita.

Table 10.1. *Normalized entropy and pseudo*-R²

	Providence		Wichita	
	Normalized Entropy, S(α)	Pseudo-R^2	Normalized Entropy S(α)	Pseudo-R^2
ME-ML				
American	0.66	0.34	0.73	0.27
United	0.67	0.33	0.77	0.23
GME				
American	0.90	0.10	0.93	0.07
United	0.90	0.10	0.94	0.06
GME-Nash				
American	0.61	0.39	0.71	0.29
United	0.65	0.35	0.66	0.34

The GME distribution is more uniform than that of the ME-ML model because the moment conditions are more flexible (stochastic) under the GME and allow the estimates to differ from the actual frequency (see the detailed example in the Statistical Appendix). The GME estimator pushes the probability estimates toward uniformity, meaning the estimated strategies are as far away from a pure-strategy solution as allowed by the data. The GME-Nash distribution is smoother than the other two models.

Using the statistics summarized in the previous chapter, the amount of information in our estimates is summarized by the normalized entropy measure $S(\alpha) = -\left(\sum_i \alpha_i \log \alpha_i\right)/(\log n)$, which ranges from zero (no uncertainty) to one (full ignorance). For the game, $S(\boldsymbol{\alpha}) = 1$ if all outcomes are equally likely (a mixed strategy that is uniform over the action space), and $S(\boldsymbol{\alpha}) = 0$ if we know which action will be taken with certainty (a pure strategy). The goodness of fit measure is the pseudo-R^2, which is $1 - S(\boldsymbol{\alpha})$.

Table 10.1 shows the normalized entropy and pseudo-R^2 measures for the three models. For the Providence route, the pseudo-R^2 is 0.34 (American) and 0.33 (United) for the ME-ML estimator, 0.10 for both airlines for the GME model, and 0.39 (American) and 0.35 (United) for the GME-Nash model. That is, the GME-Nash model has the highest R^2 followed by the ME-ML and GME models.[6]

[6] It is not surprising that the GME, in this case, has a lower R^2 than the ME-ML. This is because in this model – a multinomial – the moment information in the ME-ML is viewed as pure (zero-moment conditions) whereas, under the GME, the moments are viewed as stochastic (noisy) moments, implying the estimated strategies for all finite samples should be more uniform than for the ME-ML estimator. Under the GME-Nash model, in addition to the stochastic moment conditions, a specific (stochastic) structure is imposed in terms of the stochastic Nash restrictions, which, in turn, affect the strategies. If this game structure is consistent with the observed data, it may increase the pseudo-R^2.

The same pattern holds for Wichita. Comparing the statistics of the GME and the GME-Nash estimated strategies, we see that the game-theoretical restrictions contain substantial information in the sense that they are consistent with the data, and in addition yield estimated strategies that are significantly different from those resulting from the GME.

The estimated expected rents, $\bar{Y}$, are \$420,000 per quarter for American and \$435,000 for United on the Providence route, and \$435,000 for American and \$449,000 for United on the Wichita route. These rent calculations are based on the assumption that the average cost equals the marginal cost. That is, the rents do not reflect fixed costs. Unless the fixed costs are large, these numbers suggest that the airlines made positive profits during this period. The estimated expected rents are consistent with the magnitudes of the prices and quantities observed.

For both airlines for both cities, the average value of $\bar{\theta}$ is practically zero. The average value of $\bar{\delta}$ is positive. For example, in Providence, only two out of the forty values of $\bar{\delta}$ were negative. This sign pattern is consistent with firms having private, uncorrelated information. This pattern is inconsistent with the hypothesis that firms use mixed strategies despite the absence of exogenous randomness.

Comparing Estimators. How does our approach compare with traditional models and methods?[7] We can calculate the average prices for the Bertrand, Cournot, and collusive models using the estimated demand curves and the marginal costs. The mode of the GME-Nash distribution is closer to the average price based on a standard Bertrand model than to a Cournot or a collusive model; see Figures 10.1 and 10.2 for Providence. The means are too large to appear in Figures 10.3 and 10.4 for Wichita for the Cournot model (\$216 for American and \$185 for United) and the collusive model (\$285 and \$223).

For the purposes of comparison, we also estimated a traditional conjectural variations (CV) model given our heterogeneous demand equations. The CV model consists of four equations: the two demand curves and two optimality (first-order) conditions Equation (3.3).[8]

[7] We cannot directly compare our results with those in Brander and Zhang (1990, 1993) and Oum, Zhang, and Zhang (1993) because they assume that the services of the two airlines are homogeneous, whereas we estimate demand curves based on differentiated services. Moreover, they estimate pure strategy models in two of their papers, whereas we permit mixed or pure strategies. Brander and Zhang (1993) estimate a trigger price equilibrium using a supergame model. If there are punishment periods during the sample, our estimates may show two or more peaks in the distribution of α. However, if the firms are playing a supergame, we should modify our repeated single-period game model accordingly.

[8] When we tried to estimate the four equations simultaneously using standard ML techniques, some of the demand parameters took on theoretically incorrect signs. Consequently, we estimated the demand curves and then estimated the optimality conditions, treating the estimated demand parameters as exact. Both approaches produced similar estimates of the conjectures. Figures 10.5 and 10.6 use the second set of estimates, in which we used the marginal cost in each period to generate a distribution of estimates.

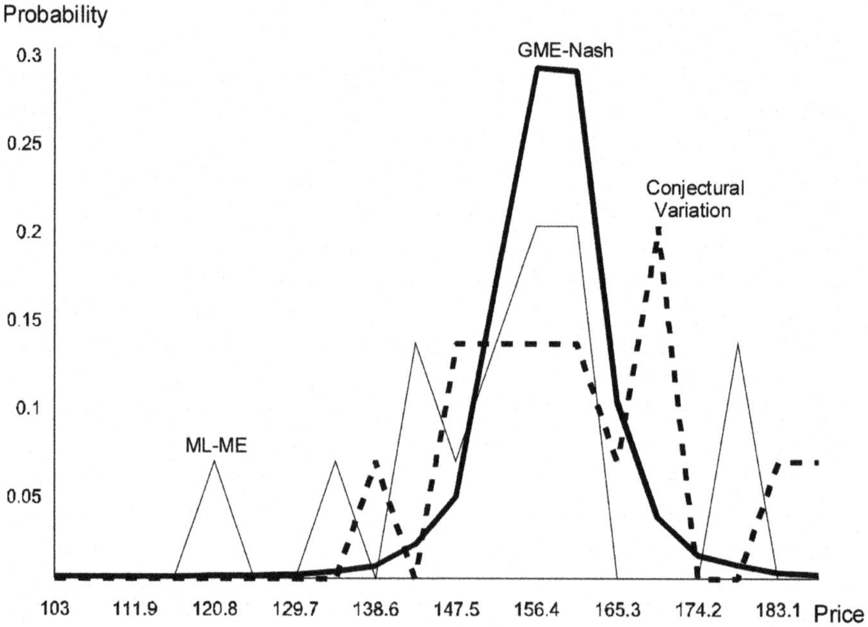

Figure 10.5. Strategy and Conjectural Variation Models for American Airlines, Chicago–Providence.

Figures 10.5 and 10.6 show how the CV distribution compares to the GME-Nash and ME-ML for Providence. We generate a CV distribution by using the GME demand estimates and the estimated CV. The CV distribution has multiple peaks, with its global maximum lower than that of the GME-Nash. The CV distribution is significantly different from the ME-ML for United on the Chicago–Providence route based on a Kolmogorov-Smirnov test.[9] Similarly, for United on the Chicago–Wichita route, the CV distribution differs from the GME-Nash strategy distribution.

The estimated market power of these firms is similar for the different estimators. Table 10.2 shows the expected Lerner index of market power (the difference between price and marginal cost as a percentage of price) for the different estimators. By the way it is estimated, the ME-ML Lerner index is identical to the index based on the observed data. The GME indexes are virtually the same or slightly lower than the ME-ML indexes. The average GME-Nash and CV estimates are virtually identical and slightly higher than the sample-based index.

[9] The Kolmogorov-Smirnov test is a nonparametric test for testing whether two probability distributions are the same. See, for example, Massey, F. J. Jr. (1951) or Johnson and Leone (1964).

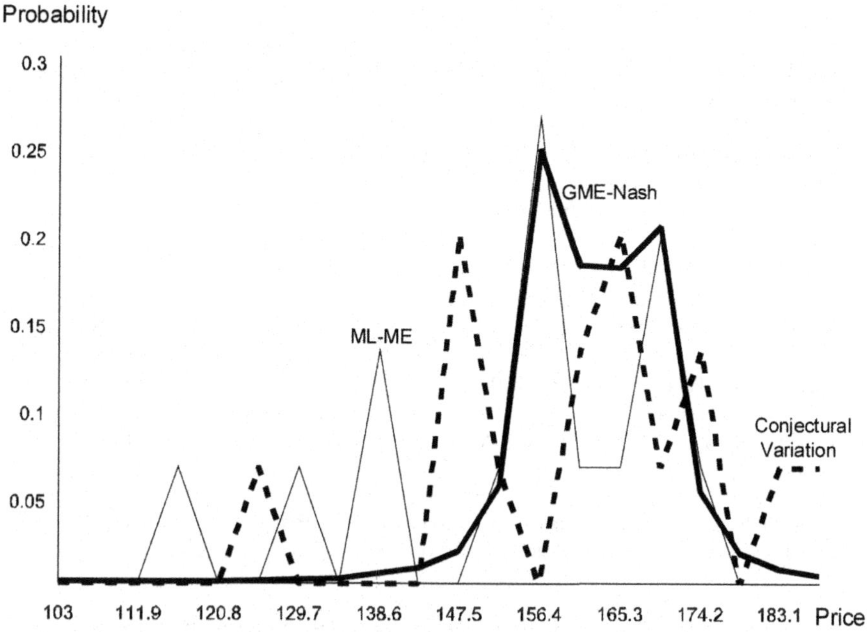

Figure 10.6. Strategy and Conjectural Variation Models for United Airlines, Chicago–Providence.

Using the demand parameters from the GME-Nash model, we also calculated the average Bertrand, Cournot, and collusive Lerner indexes. The average Bertrand index is virtually the same as the average GME-Nash and CV indexes. The Cournot and collusive indexes are much higher.

Hypothesis Tests. Using our estimates and the statistics developed in the Statistical Appendix and in Chapter 9, we can test various market-structure hypotheses. Using

Table 10.2. *Average Lerner indexes, (p −MC)/p*

	Providence		Wichita	
	American	United	American	United
ME-ML: Observed	0.35	0.37	0.62	0.62
GME	0.34	0.35	0.62	0.61
GME-Nash	0.37	0.40	0.64	0.59
Conjectural variation	0.37	0.40	0.65	0.64
Bertrand	0.37	0.40	0.64	0.59
Cournot	0.40	0.43	0.72	0.68
Collusive	0.45	0.48	0.78	0.74

Table 10.3. *Hypothesis tests (entropy-ratio statistics)*

Null hypothesis (degrees of freedom)	Providence	Wichita
Competitive market hypothesis $\sum_i \tilde{\alpha}_i p_i = \overline{MC}$ (2 df)	reject	reject
Distribution of MC = Distribution of prices (14 df)	AA: 0.17 fail to reject UA: 0.12 fail to reject	AA: 21.1 fail to reject UA: 29.2 reject
Distribution of $\tilde{\alpha}$ is the same for both airlines (19 df)	15.0 fail to reject	96.1 reject
Maximizing behavior (121 df)	27.0 fail to reject	40.5 fail to reject
Nash (140 df)	0.0 fail to reject	0.7 fail to reject
Distribution of $\tilde{\alpha}$ is the same for GME and GME-Nash models (19 df)	AA: 79.6 reject UA: 36.4 fail to reject	AA: 55.8 reject UA: 128.0 reject
Distribution of $\tilde{\alpha}$ is the same for ME-ML and GME-Nash models (19 df)	AA: 206.0 reject UA: 308.5 reject	AA: 56.0 reject UA: 128.0 reject

Note: Our hypothesis tests are based on the 0.05 criterion (though the competitive market hypothesis would be rejected at virtually any significance level).

a *standard* χ^2 test,[10] we strongly reject the competitive market hypothesis that the expected price equals the expected marginal cost (first row of Table 10.3).

In contrast, for three of the four cases, and again using the traditional χ^2 test, we do not reject the hypothesis that the distribution of the marginal cost is the same as the distribution of the prices (second row of Table 10.3). That is, the prices and marginal costs "move together," as we expect.

Next, we examine whether the airlines use identical strategies in the GME-Nash model. Using the traditional χ^2 test, we fail to reject (at the 0.05 level) the hypothesis that both airlines have the same strategies in Providence, but we reject this hypothesis in Wichita.

To examine the hypotheses that firms maximize single-period profits and that the Nash restriction holds, we use the entropy-ratio test defined and discussed in Chapter 9 (see also Statistical Appendix). We fail to reject that firms maximize single-period expected profits. We similarly fail to reject that they use Nash equilibrium strategies to maximize single-period expected profits. That is, our Nash restrictions (in the GME-Nash model) are consistent with the data.

Although the data are consistent with our game-theoretical restrictions, these restrictions affect the estimated strategies significantly. Based on a standard χ^2 test of comparing the estimated strategies, we reject the hypothesis in three of four cases that the estimated strategies, $\tilde{\boldsymbol{\alpha}}$, are the same for the GME (which lacks the game-theoretic–Nash restrictions) and the GME-Nash models. Not surprisingly,

[10] Let $\{p_i\}$ be a set of K observed frequencies over K observations. Let the null hypothesis be $H_0 : P = P^0$. Then, $\chi^2_{(K-1)} = \sum_i (1/p_i^0)(p_i - p_i^0)^2$.

we strongly reject the hypothesis that the estimates of the ME-ML model are the same as those for the GME-Nash model. In other words, the additional structure imposed in the GME-Nash model is consistent with the observed data in the sense that the measures of fit (or in-sample predictions) of the two models are practically the same. However the estimated strategies of the two models differ significantly. This is because in the GME-Nash model, the estimated strategies are not only consistent with the hard data; they are fully consistent with the Nash equilibrium conditions.

Sampling and Sensitivity Experiments

We can investigate the small-sample properties of the GME-Nash, GME, and ML models using sampling experiments. In our experimental design, we based the demand equations on the estimated (linear demand) parameters from the Chicago–Wichita route. We assumed that these parameters are the correct (unknown) parameters and we used the linear demand equation (10.1). The random errors, $\mathbf{u}$, in the data generation process were taken from a $N(0,1)$ distribution. We further assumed that Firm i has information ε^i about its marginal cost and that this information is private and uncorrelated (as is consistent with our estimates), so that Firm i's beliefs, β_r^i, do not depend on ε_k^i. The marginal cost for each firm in each period is drawn from the normal distribution $N(60,5)$, which closely approximates the distribution of marginal costs for Wichita. We approximate this continuous distribution using a finite grid and use the probabilities associated with the resulting discrete distribution, ρ_k, to determine the Nash restriction that beliefs are correct in equilibrium. This restriction requires that $\sum_k \alpha_{rk}^j \rho_k = \beta_r^i$. We then generate Nash equilibrium strategies, $\boldsymbol{\alpha}$, using this restriction and the necessary conditions $L_{sk}^i \leq 0$ and $L_{sk}^i \alpha_{sk}^i = 0$. By conducing sensitivity studies, we find that this equilibrium is unique. We use the resulting equilibrium probabilities, $\boldsymbol{\alpha}^*$, to generate samples of actions by drawing a uniform random number on the unit interval and using that to assign an action for each observation. We generate 200 samples for T (the number of observations in each sample) $= 10, 20$, and 40, with n (the number of possible actions for each firm) $= 20$.

The variance of $\boldsymbol{\alpha}$ under the GME is smaller than the variance of $\boldsymbol{\alpha}$ under the ME-ML.[11] Given that the game-theoretic constraints are correct, the possible solution space for the GME-Nash estimate of $\boldsymbol{\alpha}$ is a subset of the solution space of the GME estimate of $\boldsymbol{\alpha}$. Thus, we conjecture that the GME-Nash estimator has a smaller variance than the GME.

The superior finite sample properties of the GME-Nash and GME over the ME-ML are confirmed by our sampling experiments. Table 10.4 reports the empirical mean square error $\text{MSE}(\boldsymbol{\alpha}^i) = \sum_{s,t} (\alpha_{st}^i - \alpha_s^i)^2/200$ (where the index t denotes the sample) and the correlation coefficient between the estimated and true α_s^i for

[11] The proof is analogous to the one given in Golan, Judge, and Perloff (1996).

Table 10.4. *Sample size sampling experiment* (n = *20)*

	$MSE\,(\tilde{\alpha}^1)$	$MSE\,(\tilde{\alpha}^2)$	Correlation, Firm 1	Correlation, Firm 2
$T = 10$				
ME-ML	.285	.145	.68	.79
GME	.137	.068	.66	.77
GME-Nash[a]	.086	.037	.79	.89
GME-Nash[b]	.110	.060	.66	.76
$T = 20$				
ME-ML	.263	.104	.69	.84
GME	.132	.050	.66	.81
GME-Nash[b]	.075	.023	.77	.91
$T = 40$				
ME-ML	.245	.091	.70	.86
GME	.124	.049	.67	.80
GME-Nash[b]	.075	.026	.78	.90

[a] Known demand coefficients.
[b] Unknown demand coefficients.

each of the models. The table shows two sets of results depending on whether the econometrician knows the demand coefficients or has to estimate them. In the latter case, we generate quantities demanded by adding a $N(0,1)$ term to the demand equation.

As we expected, the ME-ML and GME perform better in terms of mean square error (MSE) and correlations as the number of observations increases. However, the GME-Nash performs well (relative to the other estimators) for a small number of observations, and the GME-Nash estimates do not improve as the number of observations increases beyond twenty. The result that the GME-Nash needs only a relatively small number of observations to achieve an estimate with low MSE and high correlation is very attractive if one has relatively few time-series observations. Finally, the GME-Nash estimator yields superior estimates even when the demand coefficients are unknown, without assuming knowledge of the error distributions. Overall, these sampling experiments show the superiority of the GME relative to the ME-ML-Logit and also show that when game (economic) theoretic conditions are known, and are consistent with the data, not only is incorporating these restrictions within the GME approach simple, but it yields an improved set of estimates. This method allows us to estimate pure and mixed strategies.

Airlines Summary

This application of the GME to the airline market shows that we can estimate firms' strategies that are consistent with game theory and the underlying data generation process. The GME-Nash approach outperformed all other standard models. In addition to sampling experiments, the empirical results of analyzing American and United Airlines appear consistent with economic intuition and expectations.

On the basis of our hypothesis tests, we find that the static game-theoretic restrictions are consistent with the data. Nonetheless, these game-theoretic restrictions have bite: the GME estimates of firms' strategies based on these theoretical restrictions differ from those based on the unrestricted model. In the next section, we examine a version of this model in which firms can choose both price and advertising and firms' strategies may vary with observable demand and cost variables.

COLA GAME

We now apply our basic oligopolistic framework for estimating firms' strategies over a discrete action space to estimate the pricing and advertising strategies of Coca-Cola and Pepsi-Cola.[12] This application is more general than the airlines example: firms have two decision variables rather than just one and their strategies are explicitly a function of exogenous variables that affect demand and cost.

Cola Model

We start by applying the game-theoretic model described in Chapter 9 to the cola market. Coca-Cola and Pepsi-Cola's decision variables are price and advertising level. We divide each firm's continuous price-advertising action space into the grid in Chapter 9. Next, we estimate the vector of probabilities – the mixed or pure strategies – that the firms choose an action (a rectangle in the price-advertising grid) conditional on exogenous variables. In the following sections, we test hypotheses and use our strategy estimates to calculate the Lerner index of market structure and to examine the impact of the exogenous variables on the firms' strategies.

Using quarterly data for 1968–1986, we estimate the price and advertising strategies for Coca-Cola and Pepsi-Cola using the GME and GME-Nash approaches. The Coca-Cola Company and Pepsico, Inc. dominate the cola and soft-drink markets.[13] In 1981, for example, Coca-Cola had a 44.4% share of colas and a 27.8% share of the national carbonated soft-drink market (according to the *Beverage Industry Annual* for 1986). The corresponding shares for Pepsi were 34.6% and 21.6%.

[12] This section is based on Golan, Karp, and Perloff (2000). We benefited greatly from George Judge's comments about econometrics and Leo Simon's comments on game theory. We are very grateful to Jean Jacques Laffont, Quang Vuong, and especially Farid Gasmi for generously providing us with the data used in this study and for advice. We received useful suggestions from participants at the "Industrial Organization and Food-Processing Industry" conference at the Institute D'Economie Industrielle at the Université des Sciences Sociales de Toulouse and a number of anonymous referees. We thank Gary Casterline and Dana Keil for substantial help with computer programs.

[13] The data were generously provided to us by Gasmi, Laffont, anad Vuong. The data were obtained from a variety of secondary sources and are described in Gasmi (1988), Gasmi and Vuong (1991), and Gasmi, Laffont, and Vuong (1992).

Using the detailed derivations of Chapter 9, letting $Y^i(\mathbf{z}) \equiv \mathrm{E}_k Y^i_k(\mathbf{z})$ and $\pi^i_{rs}(\mathbf{z}) \equiv \mathrm{E}_k \pi^i_{rsk}(\mathbf{z})$, and taking expectations with respect to k of Equations (9.3) and (9.4), we obtain the restrictions

$$\sum_s \alpha^j_s(\mathbf{z})\pi^i_{rs}(\mathbf{z}) - Y^i(\mathbf{z}) \leq 0, \tag{10.4}$$

$$\left[\sum_s \alpha^j_s(\mathbf{z})\pi^i_{rs}(\mathbf{z}) - Y^i(\mathbf{z})\right] \alpha^i_r(\mathbf{z}) + \delta^i_r(\mathbf{z}) = 0, \tag{10.5}$$

where $\delta^i_r \equiv \mathrm{cov}(L^i_{rk}, \alpha^i_{rk}) \geq 0$. For each Firm i=1, 2 (Coke, Pepsi), we estimate the unobserved strategies $\boldsymbol{\alpha}^i(\mathbf{z})$ subject to the conditions implied by Firm i's optimization problem, Equations (10.4) and (10.5). We treat Equation (10.5) as a stochastic restriction and include additive errors where $\boldsymbol{\delta}(\mathbf{z})$ is the only "error term" that we include in this equation. In our empirical analysis of the cola market, all the estimated $\boldsymbol{\delta}$s are positive, which is consistent with our assumption that ε^i and ε^j are private, uncorrelated information.

To apply this model, we need to specify the demand and cost structures. We use the cola demand equation from Gasmi (1988), Gasmi and Vuong (1991), and Gasmi, Laffont, and Vuong (1992):

$$q^i_t = \phi^i_0 + \phi^i_1 p^i_t + \phi^i_2 p^j_t + \phi^i_3 \left(A^i_t\right)^{1/2} + \phi^i_4 \left(A^j_t\right)^{1/2} + \phi^i_5 D + \phi^i_6 I + u^i, \tag{10.6}$$

where $i = 1, 2,\ i \neq j$; q^i is the quantity sold, p^i is the real price charged, A^i is the real advertising by Firm i, D is a seasonal dummy ($D = 1$ for warm-weather quarters 2 and 3 and 0 for the others), I is income, and u^i is an error term. We expect that ϕ^i_1 is negative and that ϕ^i_2 and ϕ^i_3 are positive. We reparameterize the coefficients in Equation (10.6) so that they can be estimated along with the other coefficients within the GME-Nash model.

We assume that the marginal and average cost of Firm i is $c^i = \eta^i_0 + \eta^i_1 \times$ real price of sugar $+\eta^i_2 \times$ real unit cost of labor in the nondurable manufacturing sector $+\eta^i_3 \times$ real yield on a Moody's AAA corporate bond, where η_0, η_1, η_2, $\eta_3 \geq 0$.[14]

Following Gasmi, Laffont, and Vuong, we choose a demand curve that does not include lagged values of the decision variables (prices and advertising) or lagged functions of those variables (lagged quantity). This restrictive functional form is necessary given our economic model in which firms play a repeated (static) game and both price and advertising are decision variables. Were the demand curve to depend on lagged values of decision variables, firms would realize that choices today influence profits in the future and hence would not act as though they were playing a repeated static game.

[14] The previous cola studies did not include a constant term. Moreover, some of them used separate interest rates for the two companies. Because the correlation between these two interest rate measures is 0.99, we use only one.

It would be possible to alter our model to allow for lagged advertising by assuming that the firms' only decision variable is price and that advertising is only a demand shifter (like income). Though this approach would lead to a much simpler estimation problem than the one we examine, we believe that the only reasonable view is that advertising is a decision variable.

Another approach we could have taken would be to include lagged sales (arguing that consumers develop brand loyalties) and then estimated a dynamic oligopoly model such as Roberts and Samuelson (1988), Karp and Perloff (1989b, 1993a, 1993b, 1996), and Erickson (1992) – see Chapters 6 through 8. Erickson, for example, estimates a game in which Coke and Pepsi's current market shares depend on the lagged market share in addition to current advertising, so that a stock effect exists. In principle, our estimation methods can be applied to dynamic games, although the problem becomes much more demanding due to data and computational limitations.

Estimates

We arbitrarily divide the range of possible prices into seven intervals and the range of possible advertising levels into five intervals (see the grid in Chapter 9). Within the sample, the prices range between \$10.886 (thousands/millions of cases) and \$17.790 for Coca-Cola and between \$6.646 and \$9.521 for Pepsi-Cola. This difference in price levels between the companies is apparently due to the greater use of Coke syrup at fountains. Advertising expenditures range between \$5.726 (thousands) and \$71.966 for Coca-Cola and from \$7.058 to \$50.814 for Pepsi-Cola. Thus, each firm has thirty-five possible actions in each period.

Our estimated results are relatively insensitive to increasing or decreasing the number of divisions along the price or advertising axes as long as we cover the full range of possibilities. If we substantially reduce the number of possible actions, we estimate strategy distributions that are always single peaked (unlike the double-peaked mixed strategies for Pepsi). That is, we observe the standard smoothing effect from reducing the number of categories in a histogram. Smoothing aside, our estimates did not vary greatly as we experimented with more or less finely divided action spaces. For example, the strategy mode still occurs at the same area of price-advertising space.

To estimate the GME-Nash model, we imposed sign restrictions from economic theory on both the cost (all cost coefficients are non-negative) and demand parameters (demand falls with a firm's own price and rises with the other firm's price and its own advertising) as well as the set of game-theoretic restrictions.[15]

[15] We imposed these restrictions every fifth quarter starting with the third quarter. By only imposing the restrictions in about one-fifth of the periods, we greatly reduced the size of the estimation problem. We examined the sensitivity of our results to this assumption. We compared the estimate here, where we imposed the theoretical restrictions on every fifth period

The estimated Coca-Cola demand coefficients are $\phi_0 = 4.549, \phi_1 = -1.079$, $\phi_2 = 2.137$, $\phi_3 = 0.741$, $\phi_4 = -0.232$, $\phi_5 = 7.730$, and $\phi_6 = 0.737$. The corresponding estimated demand coefficients for Pepsi-Cola are 20.021, −1.596, 0.582, 0.808, −0.211, 5.592, and 2.056. The correlation coefficients between observed quantities and those predicted by the demand equation are 0.93 for Coke and 0.94 for Pepsi.

For the GME-Nash, the estimated cost parameters are $\eta_0 = 13.482$, $\eta_1 = \eta_2 = 0$ (due to the theoretical restriction that the coefficient be non-negative), and $\eta_3 = 13.482$ for Coca-Cola. The corresponding cost coefficients for Pepsi-Cola are 7.251, 0, 0, and 0.

Table 10.5 shows the GME estimates of Coca-Cola's coefficients for the set of exogenous variables, **z** (the other tables for Pepsi and for the GME-Nash results are similar). Due to an arbitrary normalization convention, the GME (and GME-Nash) estimates have the opposite sign of the coefficients that would be produced by the comparable ML multinomial logit approach.

From the estimated coefficients, we can calculate the strategy probabilities, $\boldsymbol{\alpha}$ for each period. We show the estimates for the first quarter of 1977, near the midpoint of the sample, for Coca-Cola in Figures 10.7 (GME) and 10.9 (GME-Nash) and for Pepsi-Cola in Figures 10.8 (GME) and 10.10 (GME-Nash).

As we expected, the GME probability estimates are more uniform (reflect greater entropy) than the GME-Nash estimates for both firms. These figures illustrate that the game-theoretic conditions contain additional information beyond that in the data alone. If this theoretical information is true, it improves our estimates.

The corresponding marginal distributions for price and advertising strategies for both the GME and GME-Nash models are shown in Figures 10.11 and 10.13 for Coke and in Figures 10.12 and 10.14 for Pepsi. The results show that GME-Nash marginal distributions put more weight on the category with the greatest probability than do the GME marginal distributions.

This pattern is repeated in virtually all periods. We can compare the different estimators empirically using the normalized entropy (information) measure, $S(\tilde{\boldsymbol{\alpha}})$. The normalized entropy measures for the GME, 0.66 (Coke) and 0.73 (Pepsi), are closer to one (the upper bound of entropy corresponding to full ignorance) than are the corresponding GME-Nash measures, 0.31 and 0.41. These numbers show the extent to which the game theoretic restrictions bind: they measure the amount of additional information contained in the restrictions. Similarly, the pseudo-R^2, which is the expected value of $1 - S(\bullet)$ for both firms, is 0.31 for the GME model and 0.64 for the GME-Nash model.

(the frequency) starting with the third quarter, to one with the same frequency, in which we started with the second or fourth quarter, and found that the results were virtually identical. We also found that our estimates were not very sensitive to reducing the frequency. Note, however, that with today's more powerful computers, it is easy to impose the restrictions on all the observations and to work with much larger data sets.

Table 10.5. *GME estimates of coefficients for Coca-Cola*

Price	Advertising	Constant	Seasonal dummy	Income	Price of sugar	Wage	Bond rate
1	2	−46.738	1.851	0.832	1.207	49.393	−0.077
1	3	−43.588	−1.188	0.822	0.295	49.534	−0.115
1	4	1.441	0.017	−0.013	−0.098	−0.955	0.002
1	5	1.428	0.017	−0.013	−0.098	−0.940	0.002
2	1	77.525	0.834	−1.384	−0.041	−90.107	−0.052
2	2	10.040	0.896	−0.274	0.823	−11.263	−0.275
2	3	−20.309	−1.695	0.586	1.785	11.465	−0.396
2	4	51.699	−0.287	−0.860	−0.441	−60.512	−0.277
2	5	33.840	−1.141	−0.769	−0.266	−30.543	−0.024
3	1	1.428	0.017	−0.013	−0.098	−0.940	0.002
3	2	9.887	1.542	−0.196	−0.841	−12.846	−0.021
3	3	−13.102	−0.128	0.203	1.646	7.332	0.109
3	4	−61.368	−1.401	1.070	2.526	65.273	0.420
3	5	−0.719	−0.671	−0.190	1.200	5.090	0.357
4	1	21.993	0.756	−0.262	−2.909	−23.202	−0.168
4	2	−19.817	2.187	0.354	−2.500	25.788	−0.034
4	3	−5.802	0.697	−0.110	−0.903	11.068	0.291
4	4	59.688	−1.339	−1.201	−2.096	−59.023	0.281
4	5	1.428	0.017	−0.013	−0.098	−0.941	0.002
5	1	1.441	0.017	−0.013	−0.098	−0.955	0.002
5	2	1.425	0.017	−0.013	−0.098	−0.938	0.002
5	3	−22.607	−1.331	0.543	−0.379	23.203	−0.110
5	4	1.452	0.017	−0.013	−0.099	−0.966	0.002
5	5	1.462	0.017	−0.014	−0.099	−0.977	0.002
6	1	1.433	0.017	−0.013	−0.098	−0.947	0.002
6	2	1.438	0.017	−0.013	−0.098	−0.952	0.002
6	3	1.418	0.017	−0.013	−0.098	−0.930	0.002
6	4	−23.977	−1.188	0.479	0.901	24.449	0.037
6	5	1.453	0.017	−0.013	−0.099	−0.968	0.002
7	1	1.420	0.017	−0.013	−0.098	−0.932	0.002
7	2	−29.797	1.311	0.546	1.344	29.438	0.026
7	3	1.453	0.017	−0.013	−0.099	−0.968	0.002
7	4	1.418	0.017	−0.013	−0.098	−0.930	0.002
7	5	1.457	0.017	−0.013	−0.099	−0.972	0.002

Note: The first two columns show the price and advertising categories. The coefficients in the missing first row are normalized to zero.

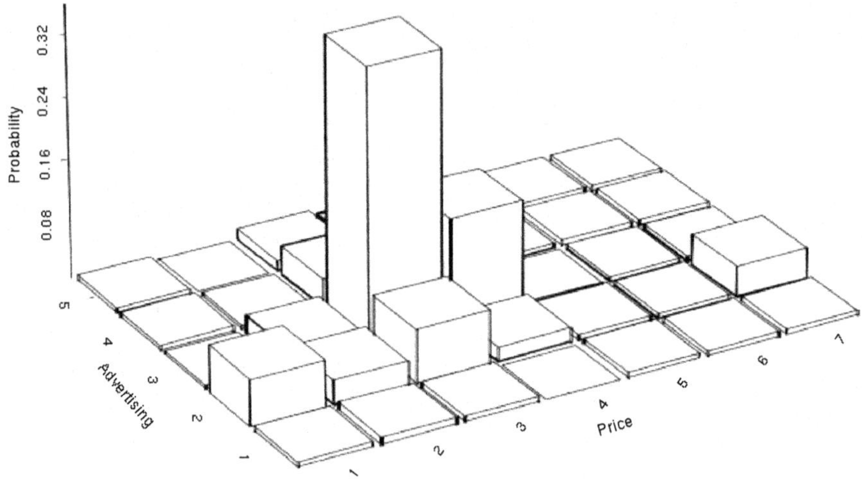

Figure 10.7. GME Estimates of Coke's Strategies (First Quarter 1977).

The GME-Nash model is flexible enough to allow for both pure and mixed strategies. Out of the seventy-six periods of the sample, each firm has only three periods during which it uses a pure strategy.

Basic Statistics and Tests of the Cola Market

We now test whether our theory is consistent with the firms' behavior (data), using a variety of tests (see the Statistical Appendix, Chapter 9, Kullback 1959,

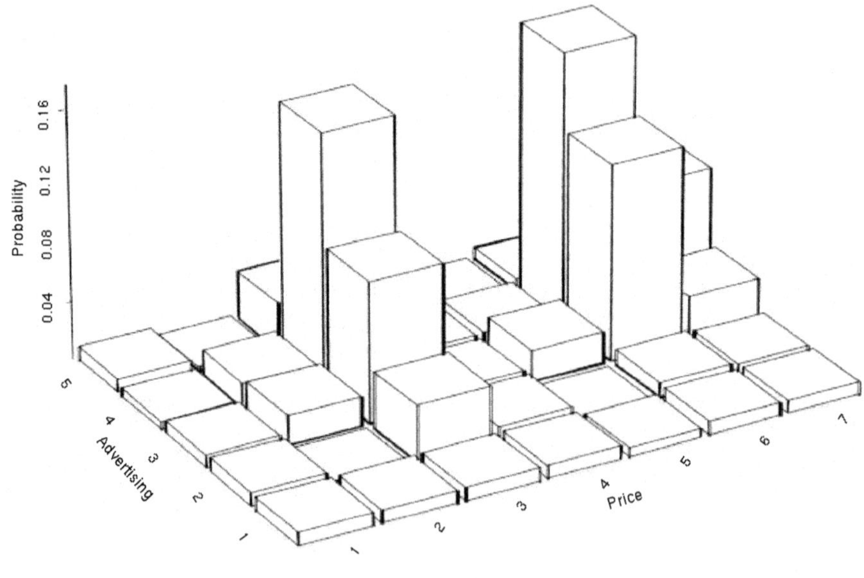

Figure 10.8. GME Estimates of Pepsi's Strategies (First Quarter 1977).

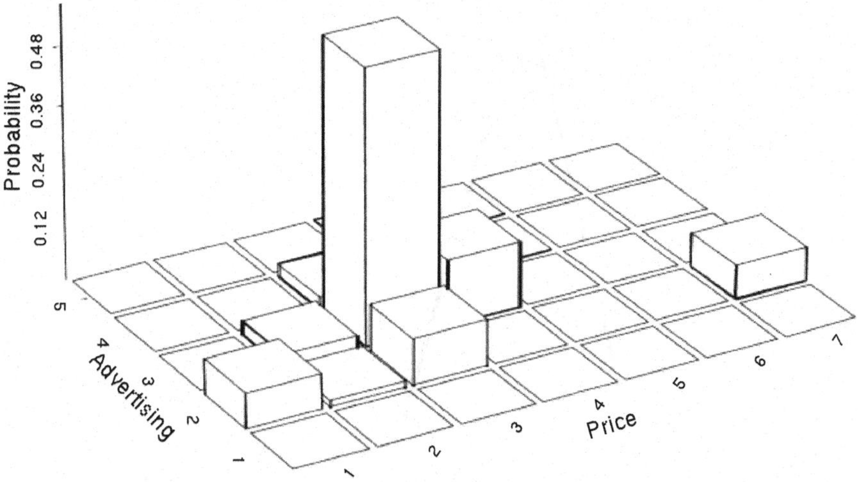

Figure 10.9. GME-Nash Estimates of Coke's Strategies (First Quarter 1977).

and Gokhale and Kullback 1978). The entropy-ratio test statistic is $[2H(GME) - 2H(GME\text{-}Nash)] = 359.38 < \chi^2_{(1,050)}$, where $H(\bullet)$ is the optimal value of the objective function. Thus, we conclude that the economic theory represented by the set of conditions (10.4) and (10.5) is *consistent* with the data.

We now compare the strategies (estimated $\boldsymbol{\alpha}$) of the GME and GME-Nash models using first the χ^2 tests and then the Kolmogorov-Smirnov (KS) tests. These test results are for a 0.05 significance level. As there are seven support points for the

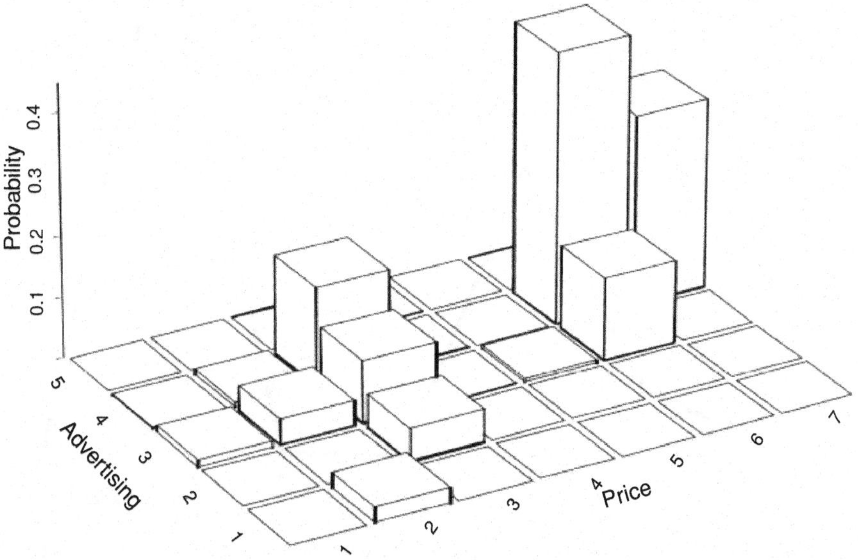

Figure 10.10. GME-Nash Estimates of Pepsi's Strategies (First Quarter 1977).

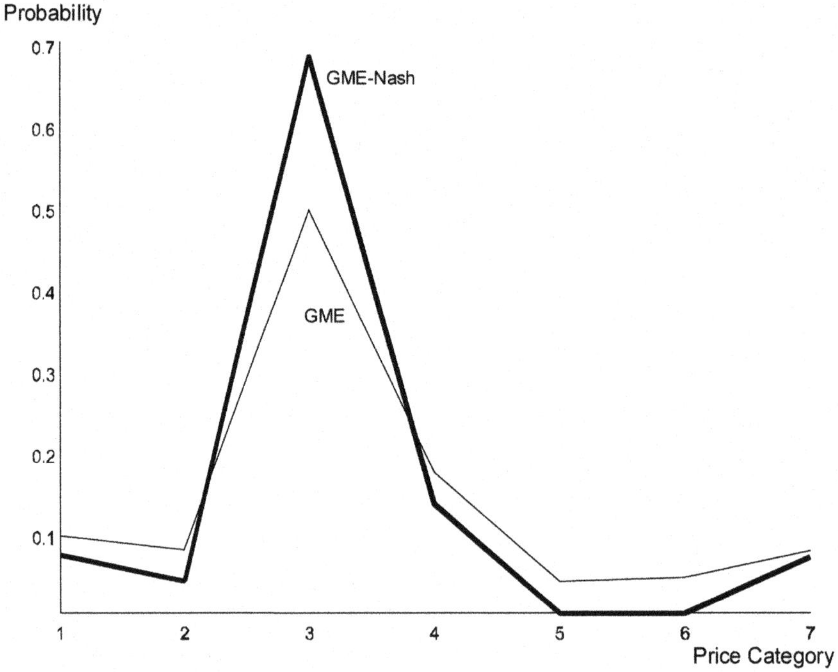

Figure 10.11. GME and GME-Nash Marginal Pricing Strategy Distributions for Coke (First Quarter 1977).

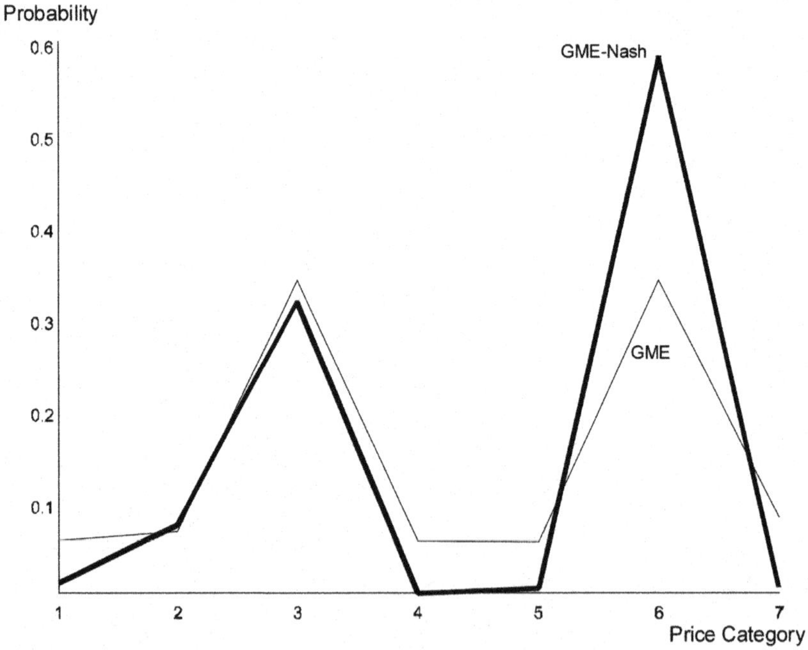

Figure 10.12. GME and GME-Nash Marginal Pricing Strategy Distributions for Pepsi (First Quarter 1977).

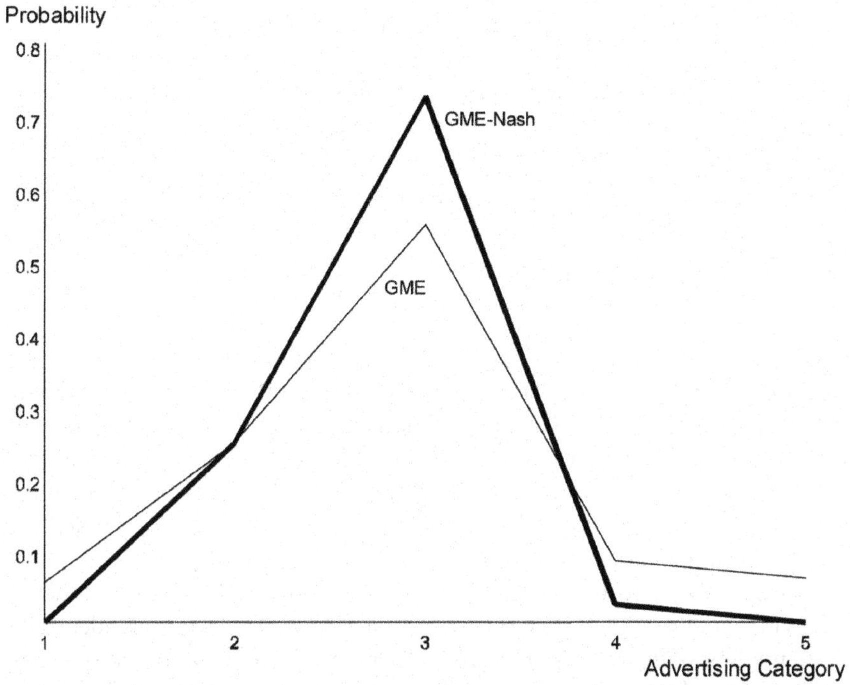

Figure 10.13. GME and GME-Nash Marginal Advertising Strategy Distributions for Coke (First Quarter 1977).

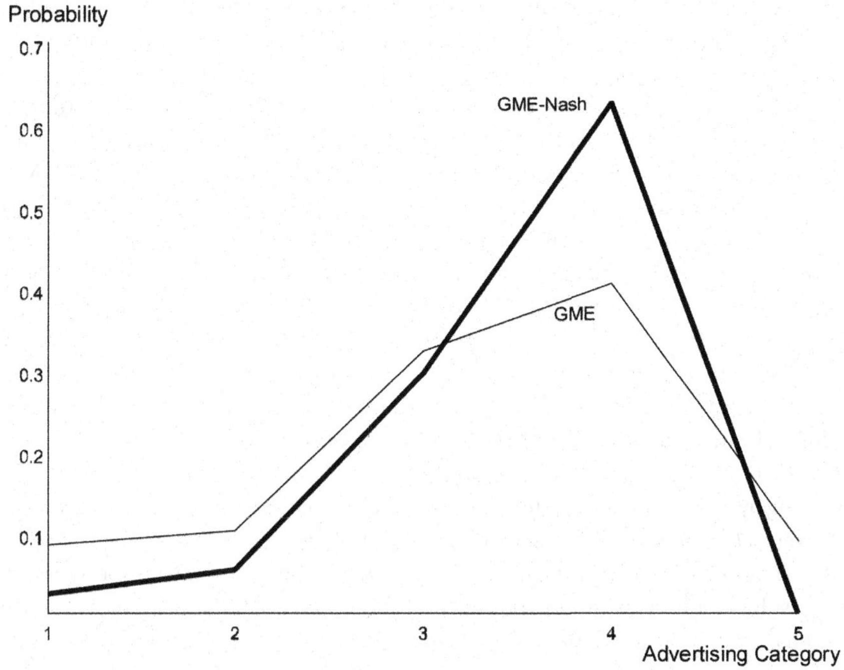

Figure 10.14. GME and GME-Nash Marginal Advertising Strategy Distributions for Pepsi (First Quarter 1977).

Table 10.6. *Percentage of categories correctly predicted*

	GME		GME-Nash	
	Price	Advertising	Price	Advertising
Coke	70	68	55	63
Pepsi	61	33	54	32

price strategy and five for the advertising strategy, there are $(7 - 1) \times (5 - 1) = 24$ degrees of freedom. On the basis of a χ^2 test, we reject the null hypothesis that the GME and GME-Nash estimated strategies are identical in thirty-four periods (out of the seventy-six total periods) for Coke and in twenty-five periods for Pepsi. Thus, we conclude that the profit-maximizing, Nash restrictions are consistent with the data and contain useful information, so that imposing these restrictions affects our estimates of the strategies.

Next, we compare the strategies of the two firms for the GME-NASH model. We reject the null hypothesis that the two sets of estimated strategies are identical in seventy-four of the seventy-six periods. That is, the firms use *different* strategies.

For example, by comparing Figures 10.9 and 10.10, we see that Coke and Pepsi had very different strategy distributions in the middle of the sample. Coke had a single-modal strategy distribution with most weight on a moderate price-moderately intense advertising strategy, whereas Pepsi had a bimodal distribution with the most weight on a high price-intensive advertising strategy (though the scaling of the two companies' prices differs).

We obtain similar results using the KS test to examine whether the estimated GME and GME-Nash distributions differ systematically. On the basis of a KS test at a 5% significance level, we cannot reject the hypothesis that the GME and GME-Nash strategies and marginal strategies (with respect to either prices or advertising), averaged over all periods, are identical. The estimates from ML multinomial logit (or ME model), for the entire sample (ignoring the covariates $\mathbf{z}$), are the same as the empirical distribution (the frequencies) of the actions. We cannot reject the hypothesis that the ML-ME estimate is the same as the average of the GME and GME-Nash estimates based on KS tests. However, if we examine the hypothesis that the distributions are the same period by period, we can reject the hypothesis for Coke in sixty-six and for Pepsi in sixty-two of seventy-six periods.

Next, we investigate the significance of the individual covariates (income, price of sugar, wage, and bond rate). That is, we test whether the estimated coefficient is zero (H_0: $z_1 = 0$ vs. H_1: $z_1 \neq 0$). The χ^2 test-statistic values are 54.41, 34.38, 78.07, and 56.51 for income, price of sugar, wage, and bond rate, respectively. As a result, we reject the null hypothesis for *all* the covariates at the $\alpha = 0.01$ level. Thus, though the factor prices do not greatly affect the marginal costs of the firms, they do affect the strategies the firms use.

These estimators fit the data reasonably well, as Table 10.6 shows for both the GME model and the GME-Nash model. For example, the GME-Nash estimator

Table 10.7. *Lerner indexes*

	GME-Nash	Gasmi-Laffont-Vuong Model 1
Coke	0.24	0.42
Pepsi	0.27	0.45

correctly predicted which of the seven price categories Coke chose in 55% of the periods. Moreover, the model missed by more than one category in only 11 percent of the periods (this fact is not shown in the table). The GME predictions are, in each case, more accurate than those of the GME-Nash: for example, Coke's price category is correctly predicted in 70% of the periods by the GME model and only 55% by the GME-Nash. Based on our Monte Carlo simulations, such as those presented in the previous section, the GME-Nash can predict better than the GME. One explanation for this improved prediction in the sampling experiments is that the data were generated using the correct (stochastic) game-theoretic conditions.

Lerner Measures of Market Power

As before, we used our estimates to calculate the Lerner index. Recall that this index ranges between zero (competition) and one (monopoly). In the cola case, we use our estimates to calculate the *expected* Lerner index, $E[(p^i - c^i)/p^i] = \sum_r \alpha_r^i[(p_r^i - c^i)/p_r^i]$, where c^i is our estimate of Firm i's marginal cost and r indexes Firm i's action space. We suppress the dependence of all functions on the public information, **z**, and hold **z** constant for purposes of this discussion. Appendix 10A provides the detailed derivation of the expected Lerner index.

Table 10.7 shows that the average adjusted Lerner index is 0.24 for Coke and 0.27 for Pepsi. To compare our results with those of Gasmi, Laffont, and Vuong (1992), we also calculated the Lerner index for the Bertrand-Nash model using their (Model 1) ML estimates of a Bertrand-Nash equilibrium (see Gasmi, Laffont, and Vuong estimates of Model 1). Averaged over the sample, the index for Coke is 0.42 and for Pepsi is 0.45. Thus, the GME-Nash estimates indicate that firms have less market power than do ML estimates of a Bertrand-Nash equilibrium. These differences in the Lerner indexes are largely due to differences in the estimates of costs. Our GME-Nash cost estimates are substantially higher than their ML-Bertrand estimates.

Effects of the Exogenous Variables

Using our estimated models, we can calculate the effect on the strategy probabilities, $\boldsymbol{\alpha}$, of a marginal change in each of the exogenous **z** variables using the same approach as is used with logit and probit models. Table 10.8 shows the average strategy elasticities using the GME-Nash estimates (the percentage change in

Table 10.8. *Strategy elasticities*

	Categories						
	1	2	3	4	5	6	7
Interest rate							
Coke price	.000	.000	.000	.001	−2.920	2.998	−.192
Pepsi price	.000	.000	−.003	.003	.000	.000	.000
Coke advertising	.262	.000	−.005	−1.266	3.767		
Pepsi advertising	−.004	.000	.000	.000	.003		
Income							
Coke price	.000	.000	−.000	.015	−87.737	64.180	15.077
Pepsi price	.000	.000	−.165	.204	.000	.001	.000
Coke advertising	10.825	.000	.635	−32.756	75.448		
Pepsi advertising	−.265	.000	.000	.000	.155		

expected action divided by the percentage change in a **z** variable).[16] Some of these elasticities are large in absolute value because the corresponding probabilities are close to zero.

By inspecting Table 10.8, we see that an increase in income, which shifts out demand, increases the probability that Coke and, to a lesser extent, Pepsi, charge higher prices. The elasticity of Coke's expected price with respect to income is 0.154 and the corresponding elasticity for Pepsi is 0.0013.

An increase in income spreads a unit cost of advertising over a greater volume of sales, so we expect higher income to shift the distribution for advertising to the right. Pepsi's advertising strategy does shift to the right, but more probability weight is shifted to both tails for Coke. The elasticity of expected advertising with respect to income is −0.097 for Coke and 0.03 for Pepsi.

We can calculate similar elasticities with respect to the other exogenous variables. According to our estimates, the corporate bond rate does not directly affect Pepsi's costs, and it has a negligible effect on Pepsi's strategy. Despite the absence of a direct effect (via costs), the bond rate might indirectly affect Pepsi's strategy, possibly because Pepsi thinks that it alters Coke's strategy. Coke's costs increase with the interest rate. An increase in the interest rate changes the mix of Coke's probabilities of charging a high price. An increase in the interest rate shifts more weight to the tails of Coke's advertising strategy. The elasticities with respect to the corporate

16 First, we calculate the derivatives of probabilities and average them over the fifty-nine periods in which we do not impose the game-theoretic constraints. Then, we average the probabilities for these periods. Using these averages, we sum over categories to compute the marginal effects of the averages, and use the results to calculate the elasticities of the marginal effects. By using the periods in which we do not impose the constraints, we are able to use an explicit formula for probabilities when calculating the derivatives. Had we used the periods in which the game-theoretic constraints are imposed, we would have had to calculate the derivatives of a system of seventy implicit equations.

bond rate are 0.004 for Coke's expected price, 0.032 for Coke's expected advertising, 0.004 for Pepsi's expected price, and 0.0005 for Pepsi's expected advertising. Thus, for changes in either income or bond rates, Coke responds more than does Pepsi.

Cola Summary

We applied our two methods for estimating the strategies of Coke and Pepsi, where the firms' actions are price–advertising pairs. Both methods used are free of parametric assumptions about distributions and *ad hoc* specifications such as those used in conjectural-variations models. Unlike previous studies of oligopoly behavior that only allowed for pure strategies, we allow for both pure and mixed strategies.

The first and simplest approach is to use the GME to estimate the strategies for each firm using only sample information (hard data). This method is more flexible and efficient than the standard maximum-likelihood (ML) multinomial logit estimator. Both the traditional ML and the GME estimators ignore restrictions imposed by economic theory and some information about demand and costs.

The second method used is the GME-Nash approach. Here, we estimate both firms' strategies consistent with the underlying data generation process or the sample's moments (hard data) and the restrictions implied by game theory.

The statistical tests show that the profit-maximizing, Nash restrictions are consistent with the data. These restrictions contain significant information that alters our estimates of the firms' strategies. Once we estimate the strategies as well as all other demand and cost coefficients, we use these estimates to study the impact of changes in the exogenous variables, such as income or factor prices, on the firms' strategies.

Our GME and GME-Nash approaches for estimating games can be applied to many problems in addition to oligopoly, such as wars and joint decisions by husbands and wives. To do so only requires replacing profits with an appropriate alternative criterion.

SUMMARY

Combining data with game-theoretic restrictions, we estimated the mixed strategies of leading firms in the airlines and cola markets. We assumed that firms have only one decision variable – price – in the airline model, and that they choose two – price and advertising – in the cola model. We used a battery of tests to examine hypotheses about the games and the market structures analyzed and contrasted our results to those from models that do not employ game-theoretic restrictions. Using Monte Carlo simulations, we contrasted our methods with traditional structural models. We find that our game-theoretic method is easy to implement, is statistically robust, and can be used to model a large class of economic models in which one wishes to incorporate the economic theory directly into the estimation process. By using a game-theoretic approach that allows for mixed strategies, one need not make conjectural variation or other pure strategy assumptions.

APPENDIX 10A: EXPECTED LERNER MEASURE

In addition to knowing firms' strategies, we are typically interested in determining how much market power they exercise. Given our estimates of firms' strategies and costs, we can calculate the market equilibrium, and hence the amount of market power. Our expected Lerner index is $E[(p^i - c^i)/p^i] = \sum_r \alpha_r[(p_r - c^i)/p_r]$, where c^i is our estimate of Firm i's marginal cost and r indexes the action space. We suppress the dependence of all functions on the public information, $\mathbf{z}$, and hold $\mathbf{z}$ constant for purposes of this discussion. In the absence of private information (and with no fixed cost such as advertising), the estimate of a firm's expected profit is positive if and only if the estimate of the expected Lerner index is positive. If there is private information, however, our estimate of the expected Lerner index can be negative even though our estimate of expected profits is positive.

In the cola game, Firm i's expected profit, conditional upon using its price, p_r^i, and advertising, A_r^i, is $\sum_s \alpha_s^j \pi_{rs}^i = \sum_s \alpha_s^j (p_r^i - c^i) q(p_r^i, p_s^j, A_r^i, A_s^j) - A_r^i$, where $q(\bullet)$ is Firm i's demand function and r indexes Firm i's action space while s indexes Firm j's. Taking expectations with respect to Firm j's actions, we can rewrite Firm i's expected profit as $(p_r^i - c^i) Q(p_r^i, A_r^i) - A_r^i$, where $Q(p_r^i, A_r^i) \equiv \sum_s \alpha_s^j q(p_r^i, p_s^j, A_r^i, A_s^j)$ is the expected quantity demanded from Firm i conditional upon taking action r, where it chooses p_r^i and A_r^i. Using these expressions in Equation (10.5) and rearranging terms, we find that

$$\left[\left(p_r^i - c^i\right) Q\left(p_r^i, A_r^i\right) - A_r^i - Y^i\right] \alpha_r^i + \delta_r^i = 0. \tag{10.7}$$

By dividing both sides of Equation (10.7) by a probability α_r^i that is strictly positive, we find that the expected Lerner index, Ξ_r^i, for Firm i given it takes action r is

$$\Xi_r^i \equiv \frac{p_r^i - c^i}{p_r^i} = \frac{Y^i + A_r^i - \delta_r^i / \alpha_r^i}{p_r^i \, Q\left(p_r^i, A_r^i\right)}. \tag{10.8}$$

As we discussed in the chapter, with private uncorrelated information, $\delta_r^i > 0$. If it is optimal to use action r with positive probability for all realizations of private information ε_k^i, the loss $L_{rk}^i = 0$ for all k, and $\delta_r^i \equiv \text{cov}(L_{rk}^i, \alpha_{rk}^i) = 0$. However, if there are some ε_k^i for which it is not optimal to use action r, then $\delta_r^i > 0$. Thus, Equation (10.8) shows that expected profits, Y^i, and the expected Lerner index can have opposite signs.

Suppose, for example, that there is no advertising, $A_r^i = 0$, or other fixed costs, and that the market is very competitive so that expected profits, Y^i, are zero. It may still be the case that it is optimal to use action r (that is, $\alpha_r^i > 0$) for some states, ε_k^i, and that for some other ε_k^i, it is not optimal to use action r, so $\delta_r^i > 0$. Given $A_r^i = Y^i = 0$, the Lerner index is never positive for any action, so the expected Lerner index is strictly negative. If we perturb the game so that equilibrium expected profits become slightly positive, then – assuming that the mixed strategies vary continuously – we could observe positive expected profits and a negative expected

Lerner index. Indeed, in our estimates, we observe negative Lerner indexes for some periods.

Thus, this Lerner index may be a misleading measure of market power. It is contaminated by the econometrician's lack of knowledge about private information. The reason that we estimate negative values in some periods is that our estimate of δ_r^i, the term that incorporates private information of firms, is positive. From the viewpoint of Firm i, $\delta_r^i = 0$, so if that firm calculated its own Lerner index, it would obtain a positive value where we estimate a negative one.

We can avoid this problem by using an adjusted Lerner index, Ξ^{i*}, that purges the original Lerner index of this private-information effect. By taking expectations over the actions r, we obtain

$$\Xi^{i*} = \sum_r \left[\alpha_r^i \, \Xi_r^i + \frac{\delta_r^i}{p_r^i \, Q\left(p_r^i, A_r^i\right)} \right].$$

This adjusted Lerner index is unit free and has the same sign as expected profit if there are no fixed costs such as advertising.[17]

PROBLEMS

Note: Answers to problems are available at the back of the book.

10.1 In the GME-Nash airlines model, how would you test the joint hypothesis that all the demand parameters (Equation 10.1) have the expected signs (H_0: $a^i > 0$, $b^i < 0$, $d^i > 0$; $i = 1, 2$)?

10.2 For the cola model, describe a way to calculate (simulate) the impact of a joint 10% decrease in the real price of sugar together with a 15% increase in wages.

10.3 Describe briefly the necessary changes to the airline model if, rather than using a linear demand function, you use a nonlinear function (but the same right-hand-side variables).

[17] We can only calculate this adjusted measure reported in the text for the periods in which we impose the game-theoretic restrictions because we have estimates of δ^i for only those periods. The corresponding unadjusted Lerner indexes are −0.09 for Coke and 0.10 for Pepsi (these averages are the same for the entire sample and for just those quarters in which the restrictions were imposed).

STATISTICAL APPENDIX

New Econometric Methods[1]

We provide a self-contained discussion of modern econometric methods useful in analyzing applied industrial-organization problems such as determining firms' market power, the effect of factors underlying this power, and the strategies used by firms. We develop and summarize each method in enough detail that a reader can apply these methods without having to search through other texts.

We concentrate on information-theoretic (IT) methods. These methods are well-suited for problems in which we lack information about the exact objective function and the data generation process, we have relatively few observations or the data are excessively aggregated, and we want to impose constraints from economic theory. If we have few observations and we do not know the underlying data generation process, the traditional maximum-likelihood (ML) approach may be inappropriate. Within the IT methods, we describe in greatest detail the maximum entropy (ME) and generalized maximum entropy (GME) methods, which are used in Chapters 9 and 10.

We start by introducing the concept of entropy and discuss several estimation techniques base on maximizing entropy. Finally, we turn to three other closely related models: empirical likelihood (EL), generalized method of moments (GMM), and the Bayesian method of moments (BMOM). Though we mostly use the GME method to analyze problems discussed in the text, the other IT methods presented in this appendix are suitable for analyzing many of these problems.

ESTIMATING ILL-POSED PROBLEMS

We are interested in problems in which there are more unknown parameters to be estimated than we have observed moments from the data. These problems are underdetermined in the sense that there are infinitely many solutions (distributions) that satisfy the observed moments. For example, consider the following

[1] We thank Alastair Hall for his comments on an earlier version of this chapter.

problem.[2] We know the empirical mean value (first moment) of one million tosses of a six-sided die. With that information, we wish to predict the probability that in the next throw of the die we will observe the value 1, 2, 3, 4, 5, or 6. We also know that the probability is proper (sum of the probabilities is one). Thus, in that case, there are six values to predict (six unknown values) and two observed (known) values: the mean and the sum of the probabilities. As such, there are more unknowns than knowns, meaning there are infinitely many proper probability distributions that satisfy the observed mean. Such a problem is called an underdetermined problem. So how can we handle such problems? One method is to use an information criterion to choose one of the infinitely many proper distributions that are consistent with the observed data.

Information

We want a measure of the amount of information within a data set. Let $\mathcal{A} = \{a_1, a_2, \ldots, a_M\}$ be a finite set and $\boldsymbol{p}$ be a proper probability mass function on $\mathcal{A}$. We want to measure the uncertainty or informational content of the data $\mathcal{A}$ that is implied by $\mathbf{p}$.

One measure of the amount of information needed to fully characterize all of the elements of this set consisting of K discrete elements is Hartley's formula, $I(\mathcal{A}_K) = \log_2 K$. Building on Hartley's formula, Shannon (1948) developed his better-known information criterion, called entropy:

$$H(\mathbf{p}) = -\sum_{k=1}^{K} p_k \log p_k, \tag{A.1}$$

where $x \log(x)$ tends to zero as x tends to zero. This information criterion measures the uncertainty or informational content of the data $\mathcal{A}$ that is implied by $\mathbf{p}$. The entropy measure $H(\mathbf{p})$ reaches a maximum when $p_1 = p_2 = \cdots = p_K = 1/K$. The entropy $H(\mathbf{p})$ reaches its minimal value of zero when one of the p_k's, say p_j, equals one and the rest of the p_k's $(k \neq j)$ are zero. Thus, the entropy is a continuous function of $\mathbf{p}$ from a state of perfect certainty, $H(\mathbf{p}) = 0$, to a state of complete ignorance, $H(\mathbf{p}) = \log(K)$ for $p_k = 1/K$ for all $k = 1, 2, 3, \ldots, K$. Entropy, $H(\mathbf{p})$, is a function of the probability distribution $\mathbf{p}$ representing the data $\mathcal{A}$. For example, if $\mathbf{y}$ is a random variable with possible distinct realizations $y_1, y_2, \ldots, y_K$ with probabilities $p_1, p_2, \ldots, p_K$, the entropy $H(\mathbf{p})$ does not depend on the values $y_1, y_2, \ldots, y_K$ of $\mathbf{y}$ but rather depends on $\mathbf{p}$.[3]

[2] This classical example is taken from Jaynes's famous Brandeis lectures (1963).

[3] For a continuous random variable $\mathbf{y}$, the (differential) entropy of a continuous density is $H(\mathbf{y}) \equiv -\int p(y) \log p(y) dy$. For a further detailed and clear discussion of the entropy concept and of information theory, see Cover and Thomas (1991) and Soofi (1994).

If, in addition, some prior information **q**, defined on $\mathcal{A}$, exists, the cross-entropy or divergence (Kullback-Leibler 1951) measure is

$$I(\mathbf{p};\mathbf{q}) = \sum_{k=1}^{K} p_k \log(p_k/q_k), \tag{A.2}$$

where, if **q** is uniform, $I(\mathbf{p};\mathbf{q})$ simplifies to $H(\mathbf{p})$. This measure reflects the gain in information with respect to $\mathcal{A}$ resulting from the additional knowledge in **p** relative to **q**. As with $H(\mathbf{p})$, $I(\mathbf{p};\mathbf{q})$ is an information-theoretic distance of **p** from **q** (see Gokhale and Kullback 1978). For example, if Ben believes the random drawing is governed by **q** (for example, $q_k = 1/K$ for all $k = 1, 2, \ldots, K$) while Maureen knows the true probability **p** (which is different from uniform), then $I(\mathbf{p};\mathbf{q})$ measures how much less informed Ben is relative to Maureen about the possible outcome. Similarly, $I(\mathbf{p};\mathbf{q})$ measures the gain in information when Ben learns that Maureen is correct – the true distribution is **p**, rather than **q**. Equivalently, $I(\mathbf{p};\mathbf{q})$ represents Ben's loss of information when he uses **q**. For more details on this measure, see Cover and Thomas (1991).

Maximum Entropy Principle

We can use the entropy measure (or the related cross-entropy measure) to choose one of the infinitely many proper distributions that are consistent with the observed data. This approach, now known as the ME principle, was initially proposed by Jaynes (1957a, b). Jaynes recognized that the entropy objective could be used as a foundation for estimating the unknown and unobserved distribution from a small number of moments of a distribution.

Suppose that we observe the first T moments of an unknown K-dimensional $(K > T - 1)$ distribution **p** corresponding to the K-dimensional random variable **x**. For example, in the linear case, these T moments are $y_t = \sum_k x_{tk} p_k$. If X is the $T \times K$ design matrix and the observed moments are **y**, we can write the problem as

$$\mathbf{y} = X\mathbf{p}, \text{ or } \mathbf{y} - X\mathbf{p} = \mathbf{0},$$

where **p** is a K-dimensional proper probability distribution. Given the T nonstochastic (pure) moments **y**, our objective is to estimate the K-dimensional, unknown distribution **p**. The ME formulation is

$$ME = \begin{cases} \hat{\mathbf{p}} = \arg\max \left\{ -\sum_k p_k \log p_k \right\} \\ \text{s.t.} \mathbf{y} - X\mathbf{p} = 0;\ \sum_k p_k = 1 \end{cases}. \tag{A.3}$$

Similarly, the cross-entropy (CE) formulation when prior information is used is

$$CE = \begin{cases} \tilde{\mathbf{p}} = \arg\min \left\{ \sum_k p_k \log (p_k/q_k) \right\} \\ \text{s.t.}\mathbf{y} - X\mathbf{p} = 0; \sum_k p_k = 1 \end{cases}. \tag{A.4}$$

Note that under the ME formulation we maximize the entropy, whereas under the CE formulation we minimize the entropy difference between **p** and **q**. The two procedures are similar in the sense that the ME (A.3) can be viewed as the CE (A.4) with uniform **q**s.

The exact CE solution of this model, where $\boldsymbol{\lambda}$ are the Lagrange multipliers corresponding to the T moments, is

$$\tilde{p}_k = \frac{q_k \exp\left(\sum_{t=1}^{T} \tilde{\lambda}_t x_{tk}\right)}{\sum_k q_k \exp\left(\sum_{t=1}^{T} \tilde{\lambda}_t x_{tk}\right)} \equiv \frac{q_k \exp\left(\sum_{t=1}^{T} \tilde{\lambda}_t x_{tk}\right)}{\Omega}, \tag{A.5}$$

where $\Omega(\tilde{\lambda}) \equiv \sum_k q_k \exp(\sum_{t=1}^{T} \tilde{\lambda}_t x_{tk})$. The dual (or concentrated) CE counterpart is

$$\begin{aligned} \underset{\mathbf{p}\in P}{Min}\, I\,(\mathbf{p}, \mathbf{q}) &= \underset{\lambda\in D}{Max}\{\lambda'\mathbf{y} - \log \Omega\,(\lambda)\} \\ &= \underset{\lambda\in D}{Max}\left\{ \sum_t y_t \lambda_t - \log\left[\sum_k q_k \exp\left(\sum_{t=1}^{T} \lambda_t x_{tk} \right) \right] \right\}. \end{aligned} \tag{A.6}$$

To derive the dual formulation, we constructed the Lagrangean for Equation (A.4) and solved for the first-order conditions (with respect to the **p**s), which yields the estimated **p**s as a function of the Lagrange multipliers $\boldsymbol{\lambda}$, Equation (A.5). Substituting this function into the objective in the Lagrangean yields the dual formulation, Equation (A.6).

GENERALIZED MAXIMUM ENTROPY MODEL

One problem with the ME approach is that the observed moments are viewed as pure (noiseless) moments. We can generalize this approach using the GME method. Here, we show how to estimate the unknown parameters of the traditional linear regression model. Consider the linear regression model with T observations and K explanatory variables,

$$\mathbf{y} = X\boldsymbol{\beta} + \mathbf{u}, \tag{A.7}$$

where $\mathbf{y}$ is a T-dimensional vector of an observed random variable, X is a $T \times K$ matrix of exogenous variables, $\boldsymbol{\beta}$ is a K-dimensional vector of the unknown parameters that we want to recover from the data,[4] and $\mathbf{u}$ is a T-dimensional vector of the unobserved and unobservable random errors. In line with tradition, we assume that the set of true (unknown) parameters is bounded: $\boldsymbol{\beta} \in B$ where B is a convex set.

Rather than search for the point estimates $\boldsymbol{\beta}$, we view each β_k as the mean value of some well-defined random variable $\mathbf{z}$. We also view the unobserved error vector $\boldsymbol{\varepsilon}$ as another set of unknowns and, similar to the signal vector $\boldsymbol{\beta}$, we treat each u_t as the mean value of some random variable $\mathbf{v}$. Our objective is to estimate simultaneously the full distribution for each β_k and each u_t with minimal distributional assumptions. We now formulate this model.

We assume that each (k) element of $\boldsymbol{\beta}$ is bounded below by z_k and above by $\bar{z}_k$:

$$B = \{\boldsymbol{\beta} \in \Re^K \,|\, \beta_k \in (\underline{z}_k, \bar{z}_k),\ k = 1, 2, \ldots, K\}. \tag{A.8}$$

Let $\mathbf{z}_k$ be an M-dimensional vector $\mathbf{z}_k \equiv (\underline{\mathbf{z}}_k, \ldots, \bar{\mathbf{z}}_k)' = (z_{kl}, \ldots, z_{kM})'$ for all $k = 1, 2, 3, \ldots, K$, and Z is a $K \times M$ matrix consisting of the individual M-dimensional vectors $\mathbf{z}_k$ and the elements z_{km}. Instead of searching directly for the point estimates β_k, we view β_k as the expected value over some reference set. Let $\mathbf{p}_k$ be an M-dimensional proper probability distribution defined on the set $\mathbf{z}_k$ such that

$$\beta_k = \sum_m p_{km} z_{km} \equiv E_{\mathbf{p}_k}[\mathbf{z}_k] \text{ or } \boldsymbol{\beta} = E_P[Z]. \tag{A.9}$$

In this formulation, the observed data, $\mathbf{y}$, are viewed as the mean process Z with a probability distribution P that is defined on the $\mathbf{z}_k$s. Thus, the econometrician chooses the support space $\mathbf{z}_k$, and then uses the data to estimate the Ps, which, in turn, yield the point estimates of $\boldsymbol{\beta}$.

Similarly, we assume that $\mathbf{u} \in V$ where V is a convex set that is *symmetric around zero*. As we did with the $\boldsymbol{\beta}$s above, we redefine each error term as

$$u_t = \sum_j w_{tj} v_j \equiv E_{w_t}[\mathbf{v}] \text{ or } \mathbf{u} = E_W[V]. \tag{A.10}$$

We view the observed errors as elements taken as random draws from a certain distribution with probability weights $\{w_{tj}\}$. The dimension of the matrices V and W is $T \times J$.

Having reformulated $\boldsymbol{\beta}$ and $\mathbf{u}$, we rewrite the linear model (A.7) as

$$y_t = \sum_{k=1}^{K} \sum_{m=1}^{M} z_{km} p_{km} x_{tk} + \sum_j v_j w_{tj}, \text{ or } \mathbf{y} = X E_P[Z] + E_W[V]. \tag{A.11}$$

[4] These parameters are analogous to those we could obtain by the traditional least squares solution for that model: $\boldsymbol{\beta}_{LS} = \left(X'X\right)^{-1} X'\mathbf{y}$.

The GME estimation method is

$$GME = \begin{cases} \hat{\mathbf{p}} = \underset{\mathbf{p},\mathbf{w}}{\arg\max} \left\{ -\sum_k \sum_m p_{km} \log p_{km} - \sum_t \sum_j w_{tj} \log w_{tj} \right\} \\ \text{s.t.} \\ y_t = \sum_{k=1}^{K} \sum_{m=1}^{M} z_{km} p_{km} x_{tk} + \sum_j v_j w_{tj} \ (or\ \mathbf{y} = X E_P[Z] + E_W[V]), \\ \sum_m p_{km} = 1, \sum_j w_{tj} = 1. \end{cases} \tag{A.12}$$

The estimated probabilities for the signal vector $\boldsymbol{\beta}$ are

$$\hat{p}_{km} = \frac{\exp\left(-z_{km} \sum_t \hat{\lambda}_t x_{tk}\right)}{\sum_m \exp\left(-z_{km} \sum_t \hat{\lambda}_t x_{tk}\right)} \equiv \frac{\exp\left(-z_{km} \sum_t \hat{\lambda}_t x_{tk}\right)}{\Omega_k(\hat{\boldsymbol{\lambda}})}, \tag{A.13}$$

where $\boldsymbol{\lambda}$ are the T Lagrange multipliers associated with the T moments (but not with the adding up restrictions). The estimated probabilities for the noise vector ε are

$$\hat{w}_{tj} = \frac{\exp(-\hat{\lambda}_t v_j)}{\sum_j \exp(-\hat{\lambda}_t v_j)} \equiv \frac{\exp(-\hat{\lambda}_t v_j)}{\Psi_t(\hat{\lambda})}. \tag{A.14}$$

Having estimated the two sets of probabilities $\hat{P}$ and $\hat{W}$, we proceed to calculate the estimated values of $\boldsymbol{\beta}$ and $\mathbf{u}$:

$$\hat{\beta}_k \equiv \sum_m z_{km} \hat{p}_{km} \tag{A.15}$$

and

$$\hat{u}_t \equiv \sum_j v_j \hat{w}_{tj}. \tag{A.16}$$

As with the ME, we can transform the primal optimization GME model (A.12) into a dual, concentrated model that is a function of the Lagrange multipliers $\boldsymbol{\lambda}$:

$$\begin{aligned} \underset{p \in P, w \in W}{Max} \quad H(P, W) &= \underset{\lambda \in D}{Min} \left\{ \sum_t y_t \lambda_t + \sum_\mathrm{k} \log \Omega_\mathrm{k}(\lambda) + \sum_t \log \Psi_t(\lambda) \right\} \\ &= \underset{\lambda \in D}{Min} \left\{ \sum_t y_t \lambda_t + \sum_\mathrm{k} \log \left[\sum_m \exp\left(-z_{km} \sum_t \lambda_t x_{tk}\right) \right] \right. \\ &\quad \left. + \sum_t \log \left[\sum_j \exp(-\lambda_t v_j) \right] \right\}. \end{aligned} \tag{A.17}$$

We solve the concentrated model by minimizing with respect to $\boldsymbol{\lambda}$, to obtain the optimal $\boldsymbol{\lambda}$. We then use the optimal $\boldsymbol{\lambda}$ to obtain the Ps via Equation (A.13), with which we estimate the set of βs using Equation (A.15). The Hessian matrix of the GME problem is negative definite for $P, W \gg 0$ and thus satisfies the sufficient condition for a unique global minimum (Golan, Judge, and Miller 1996).[5]

The GME minimizes the joint entropy distance between the data and the state of complete ignorance (the uniform distribution). It is a dual-loss function that assigns equal weights to prediction and precision.[6] Equivalently, it can be viewed as a shrinkage estimator that simultaneously shrinks the data to the priors (uniform distributions).

Extensions

We can impose either equality or inequality restrictions on the GME model by including them as additional constraints within the optimization model, Equation (A.12). We use this approach in Chapters 9 and 10, where we impose both types of constraints to estimate firms' strategies.

We can similarly incorporate information to correct for the statistical nature of the data (see Golan, Judge, and Miller 1996). For example, we can adjust for first-order autocorrelation in the data: $u_t = \rho u_{t-1} + \varpi_t$, where ρ is the autocorrelation coefficient with $\rho \in (-1, 1)$ and ϖ is a vector of independently and identically distributed errors with mean zero. We can incorporate that additional set of restrictions in model (A.12) so that if there is first-order autocorrelation in the data, our model will capture it; however, we do not force that correlation to exist and bias the estimates in the absence of autocorrelation. The GME with first-order autocorrelation version of (A.12) is:

$$
\begin{aligned}
&\underset{\{\mathbf{p},\mathbf{w},\rho\}}{Max} \left\{ -\sum_{k,m} p_{km} \log p_{km} - \sum_{tj} w_{tj} \log w_{tj} \right\} \\
&s.t. \\
&y_t = \sum_{k=1}^{K} \sum_{m=1}^{M} z_{km} p_{km} x_{tk} + u_t \quad (or\ \mathbf{y} = X E_P[Z] + \mathbf{u}) \\
&u_t = \varpi_t = \sum_j w_{tj} v_m \ for\ t = 1 \\
&u_t = \rho u_{t-1} + \varpi_t = \rho u_{t-1} + \sum_j w_{tj} v_j \ for\ t = 2, 3, \ldots, T \\
&\sum_m p_{km} = 1; \sum_j w_{tj} = 1.
\end{aligned}
\tag{A.18}
$$

[5] Here, the GME is expressed in terms of discrete and bounded support spaces. For specification of continuous and unbounded supports see Golan and Gzyl (2002, 2004).

[6] The objective function puts equal weights on the **p** and **w** entropies. If one prefers, one could use unequal weights. See Golan, Judge, and Perloff (1996) for a discussion of why unequal weights might be used and the implications for estimation.

Inference and Diagnostics

There are a number of basic statistics and diagnostics available for the GME. These statistics are part of the output provided in SAS, LIMDEP, SHAZAM, and other software that include the GME procedure.

Because the GME is an IT method, we start with the information measures known as the normalized entropy measures (Golan, Judge, and Miller 1996). These measures quantify the relative informational content in the data. For each variable k, the entropy measure is a continuous function from zero to $\log(M)$. For convenience in making comparisons, we normalize it to the zero-one interval. The normalized entropy measure, $S(\cdot)$, for the GME model is

$$S(\hat{\mathbf{p}}) = \frac{-\sum_{k,m} \hat{p}_{km} \log \hat{p}_{km}}{K \log M}, \tag{A.19}$$

where $S(\hat{\mathbf{p}}) \in [0,\ 1]$.

Similarly, we can use the same measure to evaluate the information in each of the variables $k = 1, 2, \ldots, K$:

$$S(\hat{\mathbf{p}}_k) = \frac{-\sum_{m} \hat{p}_{km} \log \hat{p}_{km}}{\log M}. \tag{A.20}$$

These variable-specific information measures reflect the relative contribution (of explaining the dependent variable) of each of the independent variables.

The asymptotic variance of the GME model is

$$Var(\hat{\beta}) = \frac{\sigma^2(\hat{\beta})}{\varpi^2(\hat{\beta})}(X'X)^{-1}, \tag{A.21}$$

where

$$\sigma^2(\hat{\beta}) \equiv \frac{1}{T}\sum_i \hat{\lambda}_i^2 \tag{A.22}$$

and

$$\varpi^2(\hat{\beta}) \equiv \left[\frac{1}{T}\sum_i \left(\sum_j v_{ij}^2 \hat{w}_{ij} - \left(\sum_j v_{ij}\hat{w}_{ij}\right)^2\right)^{-1}\right]^2. \tag{A.23}$$

The entropy ratio (ER) test – which is similar in logic to the likelihood ratio test or to the empirical likelihood test – measures the entropy discrepancy between the constrained (say, $\boldsymbol{\beta} = \boldsymbol{\beta}_0$) and the unconstrained ($\hat{\boldsymbol{\beta}}$) models:

$$\mathrm{ER} = \frac{2\varpi^2(\hat{\beta})}{\sigma^2(\hat{\beta})}\left|H_U(\hat{\beta}) - H_R(\beta = \beta_0)\right| \cong 2\left|H_U(\hat{\beta}) - H_R(\beta = \beta_0)\right|, \tag{A.24}$$

where H_R is the maximized dual objective function (defined in Equation (A.17)) under the restriction, and H_U is the value of the dual without the restriction. For example, the entropy-ratio statistic for testing the null hypothesis that all values of $\boldsymbol{\beta}$ are $\mathbf{0}$ is

$$\mathrm{ER}(\boldsymbol{\beta} = \mathbf{0}) \equiv 2H_R(\boldsymbol{\beta} = 0) - 2H_U(\hat{\boldsymbol{\beta}}). \tag{A.25}$$

Under certain regularity conditions (see, for example, Owen 1990, Qin and Lawless 1994, or Golan and Gzyl 2004), $\mathrm{ER}(\boldsymbol{\beta} = \mathbf{0}) \rightarrow \chi^2_K$ as $T \rightarrow \infty$, when the restriction is true and K is the number of restrictions. The approximate α-level confidence interval for the estimates is obtained by setting $\mathrm{ER}(\bullet) \leq C_\alpha$, where C_α is chosen so that $\Pr(\chi^2_K < C_\alpha) = \alpha$ where C_α is the critical value of the χ^2_K statistic (with K degrees of freedom) at a significance level of α. Similarly, we can test any other hypothesis of the form H_0: $\boldsymbol{\beta} = \boldsymbol{\beta}_0$ for all, or any subset, of the parameters.

A goodness of fit measure for the GME estimator is

$$R^* = 1 - \frac{H_U(\hat{\boldsymbol{\beta}})}{H_R(\boldsymbol{\beta} = \mathbf{0})}, \tag{A.26}$$

where $R^* = 0$ implies no informational value of the dataset, and $R^* = 1$ implies perfect certainty or perfect in-sample prediction.[7]

We can use the Wald test to examine hypotheses about possible convex combinations of $\boldsymbol{\beta}$. For the null hypothesis H_0: $L\boldsymbol{\beta} = c$, where L is a set of linearly independent combinations of some, or all, of the $\boldsymbol{\beta}$s and c is a specific value (such as zero), the Wald statistic is

$$WT = (L\boldsymbol{\beta} - c)'(L(Var(\hat{\boldsymbol{\beta}}))L')^{-1}(L\boldsymbol{\beta} - c), \tag{A.27}$$

which, under H_0, has a central χ^2 with degrees of freedom equal to Rank(L). All of these tests can be performed directly on the Lagrange multipliers $\boldsymbol{\lambda}$, which determine $\boldsymbol{\beta}$ in the GME framework.

Empirical Examples for the Linear Model

We use two empirical examples to illustrate the difference between least squares and the GME model for the linear model. The first example is a well-known linear model of beer demand (see Griffiths et. al. 1993, p. 372 for a discussion and data). Consider the logarithmic linear model

$$\log(\mathbf{q}) = \beta_1 + \beta_2 \log(\mathbf{p}_B) + \beta_3 \log(\mathbf{p}_L) + \beta_4 \log(\mathbf{p}_R) + \beta_5 \log(\mathbf{I}) + \mathbf{u}, \tag{A.28}$$

[7] This measure, R^*, is the same as the information index of Soofi (1992) and is directly related to the normalized entropy measure (Golan, Judge, and Miller 1996).

Table A.1. *A linear model of beer demand (estimated standard errors in parentheses)*

Coefficient	OLS	GME
β_1	−3.24	−3.01
	(3.743)	(3.46)
β_2	−1.02	−1.01
	(0.239)	(0.221)
β_3	−0.58	−0.57
	(0.560)	(0.518)
β_4	0.21	0.21
	(0.08)	(0.0737)
β_5	0.92	0.90
	(0.416)	(0.384)
R^2	0.798	0.768
SSE	0.0899	0.1030
MSE	0.0036	0.0034

Source: Data are from Griffiths et al. (1993, p. 372).

where $\mathbf{q}$ is the quantity of beer demanded, $\mathbf{p}_B$ is the price of beer, $\mathbf{p}_L$ is the price of liquor (a substitute), $\mathbf{p}_R$ is the prices of all other goods and services, and $\mathbf{I}$ is income.

For the GME model, we arbitrarily use the support space: $\mathbf{z} = (-100, -50, 0, 50, 100)$ for each of the five coefficients. For the errors' supports, we set the support at three empirical standard deviations of the dependent variable. By investigating the original data, we find that there is a high level of multicollinearity – the condition number is 1,098 – so the least squares estimates may be unstable. The results are presented in Table A.1 with estimated standard errors in parentheses. Finally, for a fair comparison, we also estimated the restricted least squares model where we restricted all estimated parameters to be in the range [-100, 100]. In this example, the restricted least squares yielded estimates similar to those of the nonrestricted case. Finally, we note that the GME and ordinary least squares (OLS) results in Table A.1 are very close.

In our second example, we compare OLS and GME estimates of an airline cost function based on panel data of six U.S. airlines for fifteen time periods (Greene 2003, Chap. 13). The estimated cost function is

$$\log(\cos t_{it}) = \beta_1 + \beta_2 \log(\text{output}_{it}) + \beta_3 \log(\text{fuelprice}_{it}) + \beta_4(\text{loadfactor}_{it}) + u_{it}, \tag{A.29}$$

where output is measured in "revenue passenger miles" and load factor is the capacity utilization measured in average rate at which seats on the airline's planes are filled. A number of models are estimated (without fixed effects, with firms' fixed effects, and with time fixed effects). For the GME, we use a support space of $\mathbf{z} = (-500, -250, 0, 250, 500)'$ for each parameter β_k, and $\mathbf{v} = (-3\sigma_y, \ 0, \ 3\sigma_y)$ for each error term, where σ_y is the sample's (dependent variable) standard deviation. Following Greene's analysis, we provide results for different model specifications in Table A.2. In the last case, involving both time and firm fixed effects, we include an intercept term and restrict the sum of the fixed effects (for both time and firm) to be zero. To measure the degree of collinearity in the data, we calculate the condition level for each specification. The *no effect* model (which has no firm or time effect dummies) has a condition number of forty-six (low to moderate collinearity). The *firm effect* model has a condition number of eighty-seven (moderate collinearity). The *time effect* model has a very high level of collinearity (condition number of 957), whereas the *firm and time fixed effects* model has practically perfect collinearity (condition number of eight digits). Highly collinear models may yield least squares estimates that are highly unstable. The main reason for showing this example is to demonstrate the simplicity and applicability of the GME and that it may yield different results than the least squares. Looking at the estimates for the highly collinear case (Table A.2, bottom rows of OLS and GME) illustrates the substantial difference between these two methods.

Discrete Choice Problem

In Chapters 9 and 10, we want to estimate a multinomial discrete choice problem. Consider an experiment consisting of T trials. In each experiment, a binary random variable, $y_{i1}, \ldots, y_{Tj}$, is observed, where y_{ij} (for $i = 1, 2, \ldots, T$) takes on one of the J unordered categories $j = 1, 2, \ldots, J$. In each trial i, one of the J categories is observed in the form of a binary variable y_{ij} that equals unity if alternative j is observed and zero otherwise. Let the probability of alternative (choice) j, on trial i, be $p_{ij} = Prob(y_{ij} = 1)$ and assume the p_{ij} are related to a set of explanatory variables (the individuals' characteristics), X, via the nonlinear model

$$p_{ij} \equiv Prob(y_{ij} = 1 | \mathbf{x}_i, \boldsymbol{\beta}_j) = F(\mathbf{x}_i' \boldsymbol{\beta}_j) > 0, \tag{A.30}$$

for all i and j where $\boldsymbol{\beta}_j$ is a $(K \times 1)$ vector of unknowns, $\mathbf{x}_i'$ is a $(1 \times K)$ vector of covariates, and F($\bullet$) is a function linking the probabilities p_{ij} with the (linear structure) covariates $\mathbf{x}_i' \boldsymbol{\beta}_j$ such that $\sum_j F(\mathbf{x}_i' \boldsymbol{\beta}_j) = 1$.

Maximum Likelihood Approach Traditionally, researchers have used ML techniques to estimate discrete choice models. A likelihood function is specified where the specification depends on the researcher's assumptions (beliefs) of the underlying data generation process.

Table A.2. *Airlines cost equations with firm and time effects (estimated standard errors in parentheses)*

Specification and estimation method	β_1 Constant term	β_2 Log output	β_3 Log fuel price	β_4 Load factor	R^2	SSE	MSE	
No Effects								
OLS	9.517	0.883	0.454	−1.628	0.988	1.335	0.016	
	(0.229)	(0.013)	(0.020)	(0.345)				
GME	9.518	0.890	0.455	−1.612	0.988	1.351	0.015	
	(0.224)	(0.013)	(0.020)	(0.338)				
Firm Effects								
OLS		0.919	0.417	−1.070	0.999	0.293	0.004	
		(.0299)	(.0152)	(.2017)				
c_1 . . . . c_6:	9.706	9.665	9.497	9.891	9.730	9.793		
GME		0.899	0.425	−1.045	0.993	0.844	0.009	
		(0.028)	(0.014)	(0.191)				
c_1 . . . . c_6:	9.657	9.617	9.439	9.830	9.659	9.715		
Time Effects								
OLS		0.868	−0.484	−1.954	0.999	1.088	0.015	
		(.01541)	(.36411)	(.44238)				
t_1 . . . . t_8:	20.496	20.578	20.656	20.741	21.200	21.411	21.503	21.654
t_9 . . . . t_{15}:	21.829	22.114	22.465	22.651	22.616	22.552	22.537	

GME		0.876	0.478	−2.026	0.989	1.241	0.014	
		(0.014)	(0.341)	(0.415)				
$t_1 \ldots t_8$:	9.335	9.376	9.425	9.495	9.429	9.373	9.391	9.400
$t_9 \ldots t_{15}$:	9.500	9.424	9.345	9.375	9.408	9.410	9.4441	
Firm and Time Effects								
OLS	12.667	0.817	0.169	−0.883	0.998	0.177	0.003	
	(2.081)	(.032)	(.163)	(.262)				
$c_1 \ldots c_6$:	0.128	0.065	−0.189	0.134	−0.093	−0.046		
$t_1 \ldots t_8$:	−0.374	−0.319	−0.277	−0.223	−0.154	0.108	−0.077	−0.021
$t_9 \ldots t_{15}$:	0.047	0.092	0.207	0.285	0.301	0.300	0.319	
GME	0.000	0.846	1.142	−0.794	0.963	4.269	0.047	
	(0.000)	(0.0369)	(0.7341)	(0.3037)				
$c_1 \ldots c_6$:	0.098	0.035	−0.194	0.163	−0.056	0.001		
$t_1 \ldots t_8$:	0.792	0.769	0.838	0.829	0.335	0.142	0.082	−0.002
$t_9 \ldots t_{15}$:	−0.049	−0.394	−0.686	−0.755	−0.698	−0.626	−0.557	

Notes: The c_i ($I = 1, 2, \ldots, 6$) capture firm-fixed effects and the t_j ($j = 1, 2, \ldots, 15$) reflect time-fixed effects. The reported coefficients do not correspond to the column heads.

Source: Data are from the attached CD for Greene (2000, Chapter 14).

The likelihood function is

$$L = \prod_{j=1}^{J} p_{1j}^{y_{1j}} p_{2j}^{y_{2j}} \dots p_{Tj}^{y_{Tj}}. \tag{A.31}$$

and the log-likelihood function is

$$\log(L) \equiv \ell = \sum_i \sum_j y_{ij} \log p_{ij}. \tag{A.32}$$

Next, the researcher chooses a reasonable distributional form for $\mathbf{p}$. To maintain generality, for a large J, it is possible but not practical to choose the normal distribution (probit). A more practical distribution for large J is the logistic (exponential) distribution. For the logit given the X matrix, after normalizing $\boldsymbol{\beta}_{1k} = \mathbf{0}$, we have for $j = 2, \dots, J$ that

$$p_{ij} = \frac{\exp\left(\sum_k \beta_{jk} x_{ik}\right)}{\sum_j \exp\left(\sum_k \beta_{jk} x_{ik}\right)} \equiv \frac{\exp\left(\sum_k \beta_{jk} x_{ik}\right)}{1 + \sum_{j=2}^{J} \exp\left(\sum_k \beta_{jk} x_{ik}\right)} \equiv \frac{\exp\left(\sum_k \beta_{jk} x_{ik}\right)}{\Omega_i(\beta)} \tag{A.33}$$

and, for $j = 1$,

$$p_{i1} = \frac{1}{1 + \sum_{j=2}^{J} \exp\left(\sum_k \beta_{jk} x_{ik}\right)} \equiv \frac{1}{\Omega_i(\beta)}. \tag{A.34}$$

Substituting Equation (A.33) into (A.32), we obtain

$$\begin{aligned} \ell &= \sum_{ij} y_{ij} \log \left[\frac{\exp\left(\sum_k \beta_{jk} x_{ik}\right)}{1 + \sum_{j=2}^{J} \exp\left(\sum_k \beta_{jk} x_{ik}\right)} \right] \\ &= \sum_i \sum_j \sum_k y_{ij} \beta_{jk} x_{ik} - \sum_i \sum_j y_{ij} \log \Omega_i(\boldsymbol{\beta}) \\ &= \sum_i \sum_j \sum_k y_{ij} \beta_{jk} x_{ik} - \sum_i \log \Omega_i(\boldsymbol{\beta}), \end{aligned} \tag{A.35}$$

which is the ML multinomial logit.[8] For $J = 2$ and $\boldsymbol{\beta}_{1k} = \mathbf{0}$, Equation (A.35) reduces to the conventional binomial ML-logit model.

GME Approach Instead of using a ML approach, we can use a GME method to analyze discrete choice models (Golan, Judge, and Perloff 1996). Imposing a parametric structure through the choice of distributional form for $\mathbf{p}$ is a strong assumption. In practice, the underlying distribution is rarely, if ever, known. For that reason,

[8] The index j disappears from the most right-hand side term of the bottom equality because the sum over the categories for each individual i is exactly one.

we wish to use an estimator for which such a strong assumption is not required. Moreover, we wish to search for an estimator that is based on a *minimum* set of assumptions. Consequently, we do not assume a specific $F(\bullet)$ or a likelihood function. We view the data as noisy so that the constraints (the data) do not hold exactly (stochastic moments). We reformulate the model as

$$y_{ij} = F(\mathbf{x}_i \boldsymbol{\beta}_j) + u_{ij} = p_{ij} + u_{ij},$$

where the p_{ij} are the unknown multinomial probabilities and the u_{ij} are the *natural* noise components for each individual (observation) and are contained to lie within $[-1, 1]$ for each observation. In that formulation, the observed data (moments) are viewed as stochastic.

To incorporate the covariates (individuals' characteristics), we pre-multiply the data by the set of covariates X (a $T \times K$ matrix of observed characteristics) to get the stochastic moments

$$\sum_i y_{ij} x_{ik} = \sum_i x_{ik} p_{ij} + \sum_i x_{ik} u_{ij}, \tag{A.36}$$

where there are $T \times (J - 1)$ unknown probabilities, but only $K \times J$ data points (constraints). Consequently, regardless of the number of observations, there are infinitely many solutions to this underdetermined (ill-posed) problem. In other words, there are infinitely many sets of proper probabilities $\mathbf{p}_j$ that satisfy the observed stochastic moments in Equation (A.36). To solve this problem, we have to (a) incorporate some prior knowledge, or constraints, on the solution, or (b) specify a certain criterion to choose among the infinitely many solutions, or (c) use both approaches.

To formulate the GME-multinomial model, we start by defining the entropy measure for $\mathbf{p}$: $H(\mathbf{p}) = -\sum_{ij} p_{ij} \log p_{ij}$, where $x \log(x)$ approaches zero as x approaches zero. As we illustrated above, this entropy measure can be extended to cover the unknown disturbances u_{ij} in Equation (A.36) by representing the uncertainty of each u_{ij} as a finite and discrete random variable with $S \geq 2$ possible outcomes. That is, the unknown disturbances are represented by an S-dimensional support space $\mathbf{v}$ and an S-dimensional vector of weights, $\mathbf{w}$. Thus, each error component is redefined as $u_{ij} \equiv \sum_s v_s w_{ijs}$ with $\sum_s w_{ijs} = 1$ where the S-dimensional errors' support is $\mathbf{v} = (-1/\sqrt{T}, \ldots, 0, \ldots 1/\sqrt{T})'$ for each u_{ij}. Under this formulation, the S-dimensional vector of weights (proper probabilities) $\mathbf{w}$ converts the errors from the $[-1, 1]$ interval into a set of TS proper probability distributions. We define an extended entropy measure $H(\mathbf{p}, \mathbf{w}) = -\sum_{ij} p_{ij} \log p_{ij} - \sum_{ijs} w_{ijs} \log w_{ijs}$, which extends $H(\mathbf{p})$ to incorporate the unknown w_{ijs}, which represent the disturbances u_{ij}. The full set of unknowns $(\mathbf{p}, \mathbf{w})$ can be recovered by maximizing $H(\mathbf{p}, \mathbf{w})$ subject to the data and the requirement that both $\{\mathbf{p}\}$ and $\{\mathbf{w}\}$ are proper probabilities. Specifically, our objective is to

$$\underset{\{\mathbf{p},\mathbf{w}\}}{\text{Max}} \left\{ H(\mathbf{p}, \mathbf{w}) = -\sum_{i,j} p_{ij} \log p_{ij} - \sum_{i,j,s} w_{ijs} \log w_{ijs} \right\} \tag{A.37}$$

subject to the KJ stochastic moments

$$\sum_i y_{ij} x_{ik} = \sum_i x_{ik} p_{ij} + \sum_{is} x_{ik} w_{ijs} v_s \tag{A.38}$$

and the requirements that all probabilities are proper,

$$\sum_j p_{ij} = 1 \quad \text{and} \quad \sum_s w_{ijs} = 1. \tag{A.39}$$

The GME estimator is the solution to the previous optimization problem where

$$\hat{p}_{ij} = \frac{\exp\left(-\sum_k \hat{\lambda}_{kj} x_{ik}\right)}{1 + \sum_{j=2}^{J} \exp\left(\sum_k \hat{\lambda}_{kj} x_{ik}\right)} \equiv \frac{\exp\left(-\sum_k \hat{\lambda}_{kj} x_{ik}\right)}{\Omega_i(\hat{\lambda})} \tag{A.40}$$

and

$$\hat{w}_{ijs} = \frac{\exp\left(-\sum_k x_{ik} \hat{\lambda}_{jk} v_s\right)}{\sum_s \exp\left(-\sum_k x_{ik} \hat{\lambda}_{jk} v_s\right)} \equiv \frac{\exp\left(-\sum_k x_{ik} \hat{\lambda}_{jk} v_s\right)}{\Psi_{ij}(\hat{\lambda})}. \tag{A.41}$$

The GME minimizes the joint entropy distance between the data and the state of complete ignorance (the uniform distribution).

As was discussed before for the linear ME and GME models, given the basic GME model in its primal form, it is possible to reformulate the model as a dual unconstrained or "concentrated" problem. For completeness of presentation, we provide a detailed discussion of this reformulation. (Readers who are familiar with that transformation may skip the rest of this section.) This reformulation has two advantages. First, it is computationally superior. Second, it allows us to compare the aforementioned entropy-based formulation (GME) with the ML-type estimators. With this dual formulation, the foundation for the statistical properties necessary for estimating and evaluating the discrete choice model is developed.

Starting with the Lagrangean of model Equations (A.37)–(A.39) and substituting the posterior, or post-data, Equations (A.40) and (A.41) for **p** and **w** in $H(\mathbf{p}, \mathbf{w})$ and ignoring the last term of the Lagrangean (because the posteriors already satisfy the normalizations, or the requirements of proper distributions, Equations (A.39)) yields the unconstrained (or generalized log-likelihood) model

$$\begin{aligned} L(\lambda) &= -\sum_{ijk} y_{ij} x_{ik} \lambda_{kj} + \sum_i \log\left[\sum_j \exp\left(-\sum_k \lambda_{kj} x_{ik}\right)\right] \\ &\quad + \sum_{ij} \log\left[\sum_s \exp\left(-v_s \sum_k \lambda_{kj} x_{ik}\right)\right] \\ &= -\sum_{ijk} y_{ij} x_{ik} \lambda_{kj} + \sum_i \log \Omega_i + \sum_{ij} \log \Psi_{ij}. \end{aligned} \tag{A.42}$$

Minimizing the *dual, unconstrained* (*concentrated*) model $L(\boldsymbol{\lambda})$ with respect to $\boldsymbol{\lambda}$, we obtain the optimal value $\hat{\lambda}$. We then use $\hat{\lambda}$ to obtain estimates $\hat{p}_{ij}$ from Equation (A.40). It is computationally much more efficient to use the dual objective, Equation (A.42), rather than the primal approach. For example, a 10-covariate binomial problem with 100 observations may take about 5,000 iterations with the basic primal model, whereas the dual model typically takes no more than 30 iterations. Because there are exponent functions in the dual approach, a normalization of the data may be required. A simple normalization is to divide each element of X by $\max\{X_{ik}\}$.

The first two components of the dual unconstrained model, Equation (A.42), are the same as the conventional ML-logit model in Equation (A.35).[9] Thus, the ML-logit is a special case of the GME estimator. Specifically, as $T \rightarrow \infty$ and $\mathbf{v} \rightarrow \mathbf{0}$, the GME approaches the ML-logit. The information matrix and covariance matrix for the GME is therefore similar in structure to the one for the ML. With small data sets, these two estimators yield different estimates. Further, sampling experiments indicate that the covariance elements in general, and the variances in specific, are always lower than those for the ML-logit model, so that the GME produces more stable estimates (Golan, Judge, and Perloff 1996, Golan, Judge, and Miller 1996). In Chapters 9 and 10, we use this method for analyzing empirical games.

EMPIRICAL LIKELIHOOD, GENERALIZED METHOD OF MOMENTS, AND BAYESIAN METHOD OF MOMENTS MODELS

Among econometricians who want to analyze data with minimum assumptions or to avoid specifying a likelihood function, the EL and GMM, which extends the traditional method of moments, as well as the BMOM are increasingly popular. All of these are information theoretic estimation methods. In general, if we try to avoid distributional assumptions, or assumptions on the likelihood function, all problems become underdetermined (ill-posed) and we need to use a certain criterion to choose among the many solutions (sets of estimates) that are consistent with our observed data. The common feature of the methods within the class of IT estimation methods is their entropy-type criterion. This criterion is called entropy of order α (or higher-order entropy) and is more familiar to econometricians as the Cressie-Read criterion.

The discrete Shannon entropy function can be generalized to higher-order entropy measures. For a proper probability distribution, Renyi (1970) defined the generalized entropy measure as

$$H_{\alpha}^{R}(\mathbf{p}) = \frac{1}{1-\alpha} \log \sum_{k} p_{k}^{\alpha}. \tag{A.43}$$

[9] Note that in the ML-Logit model, we follow tradition and call the parameters $\boldsymbol{\beta}$, so $\boldsymbol{\beta}_{ML} \equiv -\boldsymbol{\lambda}_{ME}$.

The Shannon measure is a special case of this measure in which $\alpha \to 1$. Similarly, the Renyi cross entropy (between two distributions p and q) of order α is

$$I_\alpha^R(\mathbf{x}|\mathbf{y}) = I_\alpha^R(\mathbf{p}, \mathbf{q}) = \frac{1}{1-\alpha} \log \sum_k \frac{p_k^\alpha}{q_k^{\alpha-1}}, \tag{A.44}$$

which is equal to the traditional cross-entropy measure as $\alpha \to 1$.

Building on Renyi's work, and independent of his work, a number of other generalizations were developed during the 1980s by Cressie and Read (1984) and Tsallis (1988). The cross-entropy version of the Tsallis measure is

$$I_\alpha^T(\mathbf{x}|\mathbf{y}) = I_\alpha^T(\mathbf{p}, \mathbf{q}) = \frac{1}{1-\alpha} \left(\sum_k \frac{p_k^\alpha}{q_k^{\alpha-1}} - 1 \right), \tag{A.45}$$

and the commonly used Cressi-Read measure is

$$I_\alpha^{CR}(\mathbf{x}|\mathbf{y}) = I_\alpha^{CR}(\mathbf{p}, \mathbf{q}) = \frac{1}{\alpha(1+\alpha)} \sum_k p_k \left[\left(\frac{p_k}{q_k} \right)^\alpha - 1 \right]. \tag{A.46}$$

See Golan (2002) for detailed discussion and comparisons of these measures. In general, the Tsallis and Renyi measures of order $(\alpha + 1)$ are similar to that of Cressi-Read measure of order α:

$$I_{\alpha+1}^R(\mathbf{p}, \mathbf{q}) = -\frac{1}{\alpha} \log \left[1 - \alpha I_{\alpha+1}^T(\mathbf{p}, \mathbf{q}) \right] = -\frac{1}{\alpha} \log \left[1 + \alpha(\alpha+1) I_\alpha^{CR}(\mathbf{p}, \mathbf{q}) \right], \tag{A.47}$$

where the traditional cross-entropy measure is a special case of the above for $\alpha \to 0$. All of the aforementioned measures are commonly known as *α-entropies* (Golan 2002).

Though all of these IT methods are related via criterion (A.47), they differ in the way the observed data enter into the optimization and the prespecified α. For example, under the GME, the optimization is done with respect to each data point, or with respect to stochastic moments and $\alpha \to 0$, whereas in the EL and the GMM, the empirical pure moments enter into the optimization, whereas in the EL, $\alpha \to -1$, Equation (A.47).

The relationship of this criterion to entropy and other IT measures, such as the GMM, is discussed in Kitamura and Stutzer (1997), Imbens et al. (1998), Mittlehammer, Judge, and Miller (2000, Chapters 12–13), and Golan (2002).

Empirical Likelihood Formulation

We now briefly discuss the EL approach for the linear model with a $T \times K$ design matrix X and the T observed moments $\mathbf{y}$:

$$\mathbf{y} = X\mathbf{p} \quad \text{or} \quad \mathbf{y} - X\mathbf{p} = \mathbf{0},$$

where **p** is a K-dimensional proper probability distribution and $K > T$. Given the T (pure, i.e., nonstochastic) moments **y**, our objective is to estimate the K-dimensional, unknown distribution **p**. Let **y** be a K-dimensional random vector characterized by an unknown K-dimensional distribution **p** with a vector of unknown parameters θ and $g_t(y_k;\theta)$ represents the T moments of the distribution **p**. For example, if $T = 2$, $g_t(y_k;\theta)$ may be $\sum_k p_k y_k = \theta_1$ and $\sum_k p_k y_k^2 = \theta_2$. Similarly if **y** is a function of a set of covariates X, $\mathbf{y} = f(X)$, these two moments can be expressed accordingly. The T (pure) moments can be expressed as

$$\sum_k p_k g_t(y_k;\theta) = 0,$$

where θ is an unknown parameter (or a vector of parameters). Because $K > T$, we use an approach similar to the ME, where we replace the Shannon entropy criterion with the EL criterion. The EL criterion is the multinomial or multiplicity factor: $\prod_{k=1}^{K} p_k$ or $\sum_{k=1}^{K} \log(p_k)$ or $\frac{1}{K}\sum_{k=1}^{K} \log(p_k)$, which is Equation (A.47) where $\alpha \to -1$.

Following Owen (1990, 1991, 2001), DiCiccio, Hall, and Romano (1991), and Qin and Lawless (1994), the EL approach for choosing the probability distribution **p** is

$$\operatorname*{Max}_{\mathbf{p}} \frac{1}{K}\sum_{k=1}^{K} \log p_k \tag{A.48}$$

subject to the structural and general constraints

$$\sum_k p_k g_t(y_k;\theta) = 0, \tag{A.49}$$

$$\sum_k p_k = 1, \tag{A.50}$$

$$p_k \geq 0. \tag{A.51}$$

The corresponding Lagrangean and first-order conditions with respect to **p** are

$$L_{EL} = \frac{1}{K}\sum_k \log p_k - \sum_t \lambda_t \left[\sum_k p_k g_t(y_k,\theta)\right] + \eta\left(1 - \sum_k p_k\right) \tag{A.52}$$

$$\frac{\partial L}{\partial p_k} = \frac{1}{K}\frac{1}{p_k} - \sum_t \lambda_t g_t(y_k,\theta) - \eta = 0, \tag{A.53}$$

from which it follows that

$$\sum_k p_k \frac{\partial L}{\partial p_k} = \frac{1}{K}K - \eta = 0, \tag{A.54}$$

so $\eta = 1$. The resulting optimal estimated weights (probabilities) are

$$\hat{p}_k = K^{-1}\left[\sum_t \hat{\lambda}_t g_t(y_k;\theta) + 1\right]^{-1}. \tag{A.55}$$

If we substitute the linear version for the general moment constraints (A.49), we get

$$\hat{p}_k = K^{-1}\left[\sum_t \hat{\lambda}_t x_{tk} + 1\right]^{-1}. \tag{A.56}$$

For the pure moment problem, the sole difference between these two approaches (the ME and the EL) is the choice of the objective function.

The EL model for the linear regression model (A.7) is

$$\begin{aligned}
&\ell(\boldsymbol{\beta},\theta;\mathbf{y}) \equiv \underset{\mathbf{p},\boldsymbol{\beta}}{\text{Max}}\left\{\sum_{i=1}^{T} \log p_i\right\}\\
&\text{s.t.}\\
&\sum_{i=1}^{T} p_i \mathbf{x}_i \left(y_i - \sum_k x_{ik}\beta_k\right) = \mathbf{0}\\
&\sum_{i=1}^{T} p_i = 1; \quad p_i \geq 0.
\end{aligned} \tag{A.57}$$

When $p_i = 1/T$ for all $i = 1, \ldots, T$ (uniform), the EL solution is equivalent to the least squares solution. If the Xs are correlated with the $\mathbf{u}$, we can use a set of instruments S that are correlated with X but not with $\mathbf{u}$. In that case, rather than using the moments $X'X$ and $X'\mathbf{y}$ in the linear equation, as is done in (A.57), we are using the instruments for the moments $S'X$ and $S'\mathbf{y}$:

$$\begin{aligned}
&\ell(\boldsymbol{\beta},\theta;\mathbf{y}) \equiv \underset{\mathbf{p},\boldsymbol{\beta}}{\text{Max}}\left\{\sum_{i=1}^{T} \log p_i\right\}\\
&\text{s.t.}\\
&\sum_{i=1}^{T} p_i \mathbf{s}_i \left(y_i - \sum_k x_{ik}\beta_k\right) = \mathbf{0}\\
&\sum_{i=1}^{T} p_i = 1; \quad p_i \geq 0.
\end{aligned} \tag{A.58}$$

If all probabilities are uniform ($p_i = 1/T$ for all $i = 1, \ldots, T$), the EL solution is equivalent to the traditional instrumental variable (IV) solution: $\hat{\boldsymbol{\beta}}_{IV} = (S'X)^{-1} S'\mathbf{y}$. For more details, including examples and test statistics, see Owen (2001), Qin and Lawless (1994), and Mittelhammer, Judge, and Miller (2001, Chap. 12). For more recent work on the generalized empirical likelihood and its relationship to EL and the higher-order entropy (Cressie Read function), see Smith (1997 and 2004).

Generalized Method of Moments

The GMM encompasses a large number of estimators providing a very general framework for statistical inference.[10] The GMM is computationally friendly and offers a relatively simple framework for investigating linear, nonlinear, and dynamic models without a pre-specified likelihood function. Unlike some of the previous models we discussed, the GMM is used when the number of observed moments is larger than the number of unknown parameters to be estimated – an overdetermined system of equations. In this case, we can consistently estimate the unknown parameters using only a subset of the observed moments. However, doing so is not efficient, as we do not use all of the available information. The GMM framework allows us to incorporate all of the observed moments while giving a certain weight for each of these moments.

GMM is well-suited for a particular class of problems. There are three possible relationships between the number of unknown parameters and the number of data points, or moment restrictions:

1. The dimension of the population moment condition is *smaller* than the dimension of the parameter vector θ_0: $M < J$ (underidentified or underdetermined).
2. The dimension of the population moment condition *equals* the dimension of the parameter vector θ_0: $M = J$ (perfectly identified).
3. The dimension of the population moment condition is *larger* than the dimension of the parameter θ_0: $M > J$ (overidentified).

When the model is underdetermined (Case 1), there are more unknown coefficients to estimate than known data points. The ME, GME, and EL are well-suited to deal with this problem. In the perfectly identified model (Case 2), the basic method of moments provides a good estimation rule. The overidentified model (Case 3) poses a different type of problem because we need only $M = J$ data points to get a unique solution to the estimation problem. But what moments should we use? How can we arbitrarily choose $M < J$ moments? GMM is particularly well-suited to provide a good estimation rule for such problems.[11] It utilizes all the $M > J$ moments by giving some weight to each moment $m = 1, 2, \ldots, M$ based on the empirical informational content in that moment.

Assume that the observed data of some economic model satisfy certain moment conditions. Let **y** be an M-dimensional vector of observed variables, say $y = f(X)$,

[10] For a detailed discussion and review of this method, see the *Journal of Econometrics* special issue on IEE (107, 1–2, 2002), Owen (2001), Smith (1997), and Hall (2004).

[11] The EL as well as the GME can also be applied to the overidentified cases. The problem discussed here is defined as overidentified if the number of observed moments is greater than the number of unknown parameters. But if we do not want to assume a likelihood function or an underlying distribution, and we wish to also estimate the natural weight for each observation (rather than assume all data points have the same weight), this problem is also underdetermined.

and $\boldsymbol{\theta}_0$ be a J-dimensional vector of unknown parameters satisfying the set of population moments

$$E[f(y_i, \boldsymbol{\theta}_0)] = \mathbf{0}. \tag{A.59}$$

The objective is to estimate $\boldsymbol{\theta}_0$. The GMM gives the researcher a means of incorporating the information in Equation (A.59), together with the sample information on $\mathbf{y}$, to obtain an estimate of the vector $\boldsymbol{\theta}_0$.

Consider an example in which we observe three moments ($m = 1, 2, 3$) and we want to estimate two parameters. To get consistent estimates, we can use the first two moments (1 and 2), or the last two (2 and 3), or the first and the last (1 and 3). As expected, each of these three choices (submodels) will yield different estimated values. Further, none of these cases uses all of the observed information. A good and efficient estimation rule should utilize all of the observed information.

To do so, we need to give a certain weight for each of these three pieces of information (the three moments). These weights are functions of the "realized" noise in each moment. The larger the noise level in a certain observation (or moment) relative to the other data points, the smaller its weight (relative to others) should be in the estimation procedure. For simplicity, let us assume that we know the noise-to-signal ratio associated with each one of the three observed moments. The second moment has twice as high noise-to-signal ratio as the first moment, whereas the third moment has twice as high noise-to-signal ratio as the second moment. In that case, the weights (normalized to sum up to one) these three moments receive in the estimation should be approximately 0.57, 0.28, and 0.14 for $m = 1$, 2, and 3, respectively. Using these weights allows us to utilize all of the observed information efficiently.

More generally, suppose that we observe a sample $\{y_i : i = 1, 2, \dots, N\}$ from which we wish to estimate the unknown J-dimensional vector $\boldsymbol{\theta}$ that has a true (but unknown) value, $\boldsymbol{\theta}_0$. As before, $\mathrm{E}[f(y_i, \theta_0)] = \mathbf{0}$ is the set of M population moments; $f_N(\theta)$ is the corresponding sample moments, $f_N(y_i, \theta) = N^{-1}\sum_{i=1}^{N} f(y_i, \theta)$; and $u_i = (y_{i,} \boldsymbol{\theta}_0)$ are the GMM disturbances. The objective (or criterion) function

$$Q_N \equiv f_N(\boldsymbol{\theta})' A_N f_N(\boldsymbol{\theta}), \tag{A.60}$$

where A_N is a sequence of positive semi-definite matrices converging to the nonstochastic positive matrix A. The matrices A_N and A are the weight (or distance) matrices.

The GMM estimation rule is

$$\hat{\theta}_N = \arg\min_{\theta} Q_N(\boldsymbol{\theta}). \tag{A.61}$$

Thus, the GMM is a quadratic optimization similar in logic to minimizing the sum of errors squares except that the information is weighted by its relative noise. In the least squares approach, the weights are taken to be uniform. In some applications of least squares, such as weighted least squares (which is used where the data are heteroskedastic), the information is also weighted by the relative noise of each observed data point. Thus, weighted least squares is a special case of the GMM. We turn now to some examples.

Linear Example. Consider the following example of the traditional linear regression Equation (A.7) with $M > J$ valid instruments S (where S is an $N \times M$ matrix), where the moment conditions are

$$\mathrm{E}(\mathbf{s}_i, u_i) \equiv \mathrm{E}[\mathbf{s}_i(y_i - \mathbf{x}_i'\boldsymbol{\beta}_0)] = \mathbf{0} \tag{A.62}$$

and the sample moments are

$$f_N(\boldsymbol{\beta}) = N^{-1}\sum_{i=1}^{N} \mathbf{s}_i(y_i - \mathbf{x}_i'\boldsymbol{\beta}) = N^{-1}(S'\mathbf{y} - S'X\boldsymbol{\beta}). \tag{A.63}$$

Next, we need to choose the weighting matrix A. One possibility is to choose weights based on the moments of the instruments:

$$A_N \equiv \left(N^{-1}\sum_{i=1}^{N} \mathbf{s}_i\mathbf{s}_i'\right)^{-1} = N(S'S)^{-1}. \tag{A.64}$$

We also assume that $N^{-1}S'S$ converges in probability to the constant matrix A (weak law of large numbers). The objective (criterion) function (A.60) becomes

$$Q_N(\boldsymbol{\beta}) \equiv N^{-1}(S'\mathbf{y} - S'X\boldsymbol{\beta})'(S'S)^{-1}(S'\mathbf{y} - S'X\boldsymbol{\beta}). \tag{A.65}$$

Maximizing with respect to $\boldsymbol{\beta}$ yields the first-order conditions

$$\frac{\partial Q_N(\boldsymbol{\beta})}{\partial \boldsymbol{\beta}} = N^{-1}2X'S(S'S)^{-1}(S'\mathbf{y} - S'X\hat{\boldsymbol{\beta}}_N) = \mathbf{0}. \tag{A.66}$$

Thus,

$$\hat{\boldsymbol{\beta}}_N = [X'S(S'S)^{-1}S'X]^{-1}[X'S(S'S)^{-1}S'\mathbf{y}]. \tag{A.67}$$

We see that Equation (A.67) is of the same form as the traditional instrumental variable or two-stage least squares estimator for the case in which there are more instruments than regressors.

Unlike in the GME method, in the EL and GMM approaches, the parameter vector is treated as a constant and the probabilities relate to the data. In the GME approach, the errors' probability relates directly to the data and, instead of estimating the parameter vector directly, we estimate the full distribution of each of the parameters (within a reference space).

Discussion. In the perfectly identified case, the GMM estimator does not depend on the choice of the distance matrix A (or A_N). However, when there are more moment conditions than unknown parameters, there are overidentifying restrictions. Here, we obtain a different GMM estimator for each choice of the weight matrix A. Whenever possible, we should choose a weight matrix that yields an asymptotically efficient GMM estimator. The estimator is efficient if A equals the inverse of the long-run covariance of the sample's moments (or the long run covariance matrix of the GMM disturbance $\mathbf{u}_i$):

$$A = V^{-1} = \left[\lim_{j \to \infty} \sum_{-j}^{j} E(\mathbf{u}_i \mathbf{u}'_{i-j}) \right]^{-1}. \tag{A.68}$$

If V_N is a consistent estimator of V, then $A_N = V_N^{-1}$ is a "perfect" weight matrix that should be used to obtain θ_N in Equation (A.61). An estimator that uses such a matrix, A_N, is known as an optimal and efficient GMM estimator. However, with real data and possibly general covariance structures (for example, one with heteroskedastic errors), one needs to use a two-step or iterated estimation approach in which the two-step GMM is asymptotically equivalent to the EL method. In general, depending on the choice of the weight matrix, there are different GMM estimators. For a good review of such models, see Mátyás (1998) and Hall (2004).

The direct connection between the GMM framework and information-theoretic estimators is discussed in Kitamura and Stutzer (1997), Imbens, Spady, and Johnson (1998), and Mittelhammer, Judge, and Miller (2000). In all these estimation models, the observed moment conditions are used to form unbiased estimating functions for the unknown parameters. For example, the EL or entropy-type estimation in that case can be represented as

$$\hat{\boldsymbol{\beta}} = \underset{\boldsymbol{\beta},\, \mathbf{p}}{\arg\max} \left[f(\mathbf{p}) \text{ s.t.} \sum_{i=1}^{N} p_i \mathbf{s}'_i [y_i - X' \boldsymbol{\beta}] = 0 \text{ and } \sum_{i=1}^{N} p_i = 1 \right], \tag{A.69}$$

where $f(\mathbf{p})$ can be the empirical likelihood objective (A.48) or the entropy objective (A.1) and $\mathbf{s}$ is a vector of instruments.[12]

To conclude, the GMM estimator is a good way to analyze data using minimal assumptions on the likelihood structure. But one should keep in mind that the weight matrix needs to be chosen, approximated or estimated, appropriate instruments (strong or weak) need to be identified, and the overidentified set of restrictions needs to be specified.[13] Luckily, much work has been done on these issues lately and all common software can handle variations of the GMM methods and the necessary inferential statistics.

Bayesian Method of Moments

The IT methods are closely related to Zellner's seminal BMOM approach (Zellner 1996, 1997; Zellner and Tobias 2001). As with the GME (and the generalized cross

[12] If we use X rather than S (where X can be used as an instrument for itself), the EL and the GMM yield coefficient estimates that are the same as the least squares estimates. For example, using the GMM in analyzing the data in Table A.1 and A.2, we get the same estimates but different standard errors for the GMM case.

[13] See Hall (2005) for discussion of weak and strong instruments.

entropy), EL, and GMM methods, the objective behind the BMOM method is to estimate the unknown parameters with minimum assumptions on the likelihood function. As stated by Zellner (1997, p. 86), "The BMOM approach is particularly useful when there is difficulty in formulating an appropriate likelihood function. Without a likelihood function, it is not possible to pursue traditional likelihood and Bayesian approaches to estimation and testing. Using a few simple assumptions, the BMOM approach permits calculation of post-data means, variances and other moments of parameters and future observations."

The basic idea behind Zellner's BMOM is to avoid a likelihood function. This is done by maximizing the differential (Shannon) entropy subject to the empirical moments of the data. This yields the most conservative (closest to uniform) post-data density. In that way, the BMOM uses only assumptions on the realized error terms that are used to derive the post-data density.

If $(X'X)^{-1}$ exists, then the least squares solution to Equation (A.7) is $\hat{\boldsymbol{\beta}}_{LS} = (X'X)^{-1}X'\mathbf{y}$, which is the post-data mean with respect to the (yet) unknown distribution (likelihood). This assumption is equivalent to assuming that $X'\,\mathrm{E}[\mathbf{u}|Data] = \mathbf{0}$; that is, the columns of X are orthogonal to the $N \times 1$ vector $\mathrm{E}[\mathbf{u}|Data]$. Zellner applies the classical ME with the two first empirical moments as constraints. Then, the maximum entropy density for $\boldsymbol{\beta}$, satisfying these two constraints (and the requirement that it is a proper density) is

$$g(\hat{\boldsymbol{\beta}}|Data) \sim N(\hat{\beta}, (X'X)^{-1}\sigma^2),$$

which is the BMOM post-data density that yields $\hat{\boldsymbol{\beta}}$, which is the same as the least squares estimates under the two side conditions used here. If more side conditions are used, the density function $g(.)$ will not be normal. The BMOM produces the post-data density from which one can compute the vector of point estimates $\hat{\boldsymbol{\beta}}$ of the unconstrained problem, Equation (A.7).

SUMMARY

In this appendix, we provide a self-contained review of the various estimation methods that are useful for analyzing applied industrial organization problems. We pay particular attention to the class of IT methods; and, within that class, we concentrate on the GME approach. These methods in general and the GME in particular are well suited for analyzing applied problems in which the available information and data are incomplete, noisy, and at times highly correlated, and where the researcher is uncertain about the underlying process generating the observed data. Further, additional economic theoretical information may be incorporated directly into the estimation procedure.

Bibliography

Agmon, Noam, Yoram Alhassid, and Raphael D. Levine. 1979. "An Algorithm for Finding the Distribution of Maximal Entropy." *Journal of Computational Physics* 30:250–9.

Aguirregabiria, Victor, and Chun-Yu Ho. 2006. "A Dynamic Oligopoly Game of the US Airline Industry: Estimation and Policy Experiment." University of Toronto Working paper.

Aguirregabiria, Victor, and Pedro Mira. 2002. "Swapping the Nested Fixed Point Algorithm: A Class of Estimators for Discrete (Markov) Decision Models." *Econometrica* 70:1519–43.

Aguirregabiria, Victor, and Pedro Mira. 2007. "Sequential Estimation of Dynamic Discrete Games." *Econometrica* (forthcoming).

Allenby, Greg M., and Peter E. Rossi. 1991. "Quality Perceptions and Asymmetric Switching between Brands." *Marketing Science* 10:185–204.

Anderson, Patricia M. 1993. "Linear Adjustment Costs and Seasonal Labor Demand: Evidence from Retail Trade Firms." *The Quarterly Journal of Economics* 108:1015–42.

Anderson, Simon P., André de Palma, and Jacques-François Thisse. 1992. *Discrete Choice Theory of Product Differentiation.* (Cambridge, Mass.: MIT Press).

Applebaum, Elie. 1979. "Testing Price-Taking Behavior." *Journal of Econometrics* 9:283–99.

Applebaum, Elie. 1982. "The Estimation of the Degree of Oligopoly Power." *Journal of Econometrics* 19:287–99.

Ashenfelter, Orley, and Daniel Sullivan. 1987. "Nonparametric Tests of Market Structure: An Application to the Cigarette Industry." *The Journal of Industrial Economics* 35:483–98.

Athey, Susan, Kyle Bagwell, and Chris Sanchirico. 2004. "Collusion and Price Rigidity." *Review of Economic Studies* 71:317–49.

Azzam, Azzeddine M., and Emilio Pagoulatos. 1990. "Testing Oligopolistic and Oligopsonistic Behaviour: An Application to the US Meat-Packing Industry." *Journal of Agricultural Economics* 41:362–9.

Bain, Joe S. 1951. "Relation of Profit Rate to Industry Concentration: American Manufacturing, 1936–1940." *Quarterly Journal of Economics* 65:293–324.

Bain, Joe S. 1956. *Barriers to New Competition.* (Cambridge, Mass.: Harvard University Press).

Bajari, Patrick, C. Lanier Benkard, and Jonathan Levin. 2004. "Estimating Dynamic Models of Imperfect Competition." NBER: Working Paper 10450.

Bajari, Patrick, Han Hong, and Stephen Ryan. 2004. "Identification and Estimation of Discrete Games of Complete Information." NBER: Technical Working Paper 301.

Baker, Jonathan B., and Timothy F. Bresnahan. 1985. "The Gains from Merger or Collusion in Product-Differentiated Industries." *Journal of Industrial Economics* 33:427–44.

Baker, Jonathan B., and Timothy F. Bresnahan. 1988. "Estimating the Elasticity of Demand Facing a Single Firm." *International Journal of Industrial Organization* 6:283–300.

Benston, George J. 1985. "The Validity of Profits-Structure Studies with Particular Reference to the FTC's Line-of-Business Data." *American Economic Review* 75:37–67.

Berndt, Ernst R., and David O. Wood. 1986. "Energy Price Shocks and Productivity Growth in U.S. and UK Manufacturing." *Oxford Review of Economic Policy* 2:1–31.

Berry, Steven. 1992. "Estimation of a Model of Entry in the Airline Industry." *Econometrica* 60:889–917.

Berry, Steven. 1994. "Estimating Discrete-Choice Models of Product Differentiation." *Rand Journal of Economics* 25:242–62.

Berry, Steven, James Levinsohn, and Ariel Pakes. 1995. "Automobile Prices in Market Equilibrium." *Econometrica* 63:841–90.

Berry, Steven, and Elie Tamer. 2006. "Identification in Models of Oligopoly Entry." World Congress Meeting of the Econometric Society Working Paper.

Bhuyan, Sanjib, and Rigoberto A. Lopez. 1997. "Oligopoly Power in the Food and Tobacco Industries." *American Journal of Agricultural Economics* 79:1035–43.

Bjorn, Paul A., and Vuong, Quang H. 1985. "Simultaneous Equations Models for Dummy Endogenous Variables: A Game Theoretic Formulation with an Application to Labor Force Participation." California Institute of Technology: Working Paper 537.

Bradburd, Ralph M., and Mead A. Over, Jr. 1982. "Organizational Costs. 'Sticky Equilibria', and Critical Levels of Concentration." *Review of Economics and Statistics* 64:50–8.

Brander, James A., and Anming Zhang. 1990. "Market Conduct in the Airline Industry: An Empirical Investigation." *Rand Journal of Economics* 21:567–83.

Brander, James A., and Anming Zhang. 1993. "Dynamic Oligopoly in the Airline Industry." *International Journal of Industrial Organization* 11:407–35.

Bresnahan, Timothy F. 1981a. "Departures from Marginal-Cost Pricing in the American Automobile Industry." *Journal of Econometrics* 17:201–27.

Bresnahan, Timothy. 1981b. "Duopoly Models with Consistent Conjectures." *American Economic Review* 71:934–45.

Bresnahan, Timothy F. 1982. "The Oligopoly Solution Concept Is Identified." *Economics Letters* 10:87–92.

Bresnahan, Timothy F. 1987. "Competition and Collusion in the American Automobile Oligopoly: The 1955 Price War." *Journal of Industrial Economics* 35:457–82.

Bresnahan, Timothy F. 1989. "Empirical Studies of Industries with Market Power." In Richard Schmalensee and Robert D. Willig, eds., *The Handbook of Industrial Organization*, pp. 1011–57 (Amsterdam: North-Holland).

Bresnahan, Timothy, and Peter C. Reiss. 1987. "Do Entry Conditions Vary Across Markets?" *Brookings Papers on Economic Activity: Microeconomics* 3:833–71.

Bresnahan, Timothy, and Peter C. Reiss. 1990. "Entry in Monopoly Markets." *Review of Economic Studies* 57:531–53.

Bresnahan, Timothy F., and Peter C. Reiss. 1991. "Empirical Models of Discrete Games." *Journal of Econometrics* 48:57–81.

Bresnahan, Timothy, and Peter C. Reiss. 1993. "Measuring the Importance of Sunk Costs." *Annales D'Economie et de Statistique* 31:181–217.

Bresnahan, Timothy F., and Richard Schmalensee. 1987. "The Empirical Renaissance in Industrial Economics: An Overview." *Journal of Industrial Economics* 35:371–7.

Brozen, Yale. 1971. "Bain's Concentration and Rates of Return Revisited." *Journal of Law and Economics* 14:351–69.

Buhr, Brian L., and Hanho Kim. 1997. "Dynamic Adjustment in Vertically Linked Markets: The Case of the U.S. Beef Industry." *American Journal of Agricultural Economics* 79:126–38.

Bulow, Jeremy I., and Paul Pfleiderer. 1983. "A Note on the Effect of Cost Changes on Prices." *Journal of Political Economy* 91:182–5.

Buschena, David E., and Jeffrey M. Perloff. 1991. "The Creation of Dominant Firm Market Power in the Coconut Oil Export Market." *American Journal of Agricultural Economics* 73:1000–8.

Carlton, Dennis W., and Jeffrey M. Perloff. 2005. *Modern Industrial Organization*, 4th Edition. (Boston: Pearson Addison-Wesley).

Caves, Richard E., and Masu Uekasa. 1976. *Industrial Organization in Japan.* (Washington, DC: Brookings Institution).

Chalfant, James A., and Kenneth J. White. 1988. "Estimation and Testing in Demand Systems with Concavity Constraints." University of California, Department of Agricultural and Resource Economics, Berkeley: Working Paper No. 454.

Chalfant, James A., Richard S. Gray, and Kenneth J. White. 1991. "Evaluating Prior Beliefs in a Demand System: The Case of Meats Demand in Canada." *American Journal of Agricultural Economics* 73:276–490.

Chamberlain, Gary. 1982. "Multivariate Regression Models for Panel Data." *Journal of Econometrics* 18:5–46.

Chamberlin, Edward H. 1933. *The Theory of Monopolistic Competition.* (Cambridge, Mass.: Harvard University Press).

Chow, Gregory. 1981. *Econometric Analysis by Control Methods.* (New York: John Wiley and Sons, Inc.).

Ciliberto, Federico, and Elie Tamer. 2006. "Market Structure and Multiple Equilbria in Airline Markets." University of Virginia Working paper.

Clay, Karen, and Werner Troesken. 2003. "Further Tests of Static Oligopoly Models: Whiskey, 1882–1898." *Journal of Industrial Economics* 51:151–66.

Collins, Norman R., and Lee E. Preston. 1969. "Price-Cost Margins and Industry Structure." *The Review of Economics and Statistics* 51:271–86.

Comanor, William S., and Thomas A. Wilson. 1967. "Advertising, Market Structure, and Performance." *The Review of Economics and Statistics* 49:423–40.

Connolly, Robert A., and Stephen Schwartz. 1985. "The Intertemporal Behavior of Economic Profits." *International Journal of Industrial Organization* 3:379–400.

Corts, Kenneth S. 1999. "Conduct Parameters and the Measurement of Market Power." *Journal of Econometrics* 88:227–50.

Cotterill, Ronald. 1986. "Market Power in the Retail Food Industry: Evidence from Vermont." *Review of Economics and Statistics* 68:379–86.

Cover, Thomas M., and Joy A. Thomas. 1991. *Elements of Information Theory.* (New York: John Wiley & Sons).

Cowling, Keith, and Michael Waterson. 1976. "Price-Cost Margins and Market Structure." *Economica* 43:267–74.

Cressie, Noel A., and Timothy R. C. Read. 1984. "Multinomial Goodness-of-fit Tests." *Journal of the Royal Statistical Society B* 46:440–64.

Csiszár, Imre. 1991. "Why Least Squares and Maximum Entropy? An Axiomatic Approach to Inference for Linear Inverse Problems." *The Annals of Statistics* 19:2032–66.

Cubbin, John, and Paul Geroski. 1987. "The Convergence of Profits in the Long Run: Inter-firm and Inter-industry Comparisons." *The Journal of Industrial Economics* 35:427–42.

Davidson, Russell, and James G. MacKinnon. 1993. *Estimation and Inference in Econometrics.* (New York: Oxford University Press).

Deaton, Angus, and Muellbauer, John N. 1980. *Economics and Consumer Behavior.* (New York: Cambridge University Press).

Demsetz, Harold. 1973. "Industry Structure, Market Rivalry, and Public Policy." *Journal of Law and Economics* 16:1–9.

Denekere, Raymond, and Michael Rothschild. 1986. "Monopolistic Competition and Preference Diversity." *Review of Economic Studies* 59:361–73.

Denzau, Arthur T., Patrick Gibbons, and Edward Greenberg. 1989. "Bayesian Estimation of Proportions with a Cross-Entropy Prior." *Communications in Statistics-Theory and Methods* 18:1843–61.

Deodhar, Satish Y., and Ian M. Sheldon. 1995. "Is Foreign Trade (Im)perfectly Competitive?: An Analysis of the German Market for Banana Imports." *Journal of Agricultural Economics* 46:336–48.

DiCiccio, Thomas J., Peter Hall, and Joseph P. Romano. 1991. Empirical Likelihood Is Bartlett-Correctable." *The Annals of Statistics* 19:1053–61.

Dixit, Avinash K., and Joseph E. Stiglitz. 1977. "Monopolistic Competition and Optimum Product Diversity." *American Economic Review* 67:297–308.

Domowitz, Ian, Glenn R. Hubbard, and Bruce C. Petersen. 1986. "Business Cycles and the Relationship Between Concentration and Price-Cost Margins." *The Rand Journal of Economics* 17:1–17.

Domowitz, Ian, Glenn R. Hubbard, and Bruce C. Petersen. 1987. "Oligopoly Supergames: Some Empirical Evidence on Prices and Margins." *Journal of Industrial Economics* 35:379–98.

Domowitz, Ian, Glenn R. Hubbard, and Bruce C. Petersen. 1988. "Market Structure and Cyclical Fluctuations in U.S. Manufacturing." *Review of Economics and Statistics* 70:55–66.

Doraszelski, Ulrich, and Kenneth Judd. 2005. "Avoiding the Curse of Dimensionality in Dynamic Stochastic Games." Harvard Institute of Economic Research, Working Paper No. 2059.

Driskill, Robert. 2002. "A Proposal for a Selection Criterion in a Class of Dynamic Rational Expectations Models with Multiple Equilibria." Vanderbilt University, Department of Economics Working Paper.

Driskill, Robert, and Stephen McCafferty. 1989. "Dynamic Duopoly with Adjustment Costs: A Differential Game Approach." *Journal of Economic Theory* 49:324–38.

Dunne, Timothy, Mark Roberts, and Larry Samuelson. 1988. "Patterns of Firm Entry and Exit in U.S. Manufacturing Industries." *Rand Journal of Economics* 19:495–515.

Durham, Catherine A., and Richard J. Sexton. 1992. "Oligopsony Potential in Agriculture: Residual Supply Estimation in California's Processing Tomato Market." *American Journal of Agricultural Economics* 74:962–72.

Dutta, Prajit K., and Rangarajan K. Sundaram. 1993. "How Different Can Strategic Models Be?" *Journal of Economic Theory* 60:42–61.

Encoau, David, and Paul A. Geroski. 1984. "Price Dynamics and Competition in Five Countries." University of Southampton Working Paper No. 8414.

Epstein, Larry G. 1981. "Duality Theory and Functional Forms for Dynamic Factor Demands." *Review of Economic Studies* 48:81–95.

Epstein, Larry G., and Michael G. S. Denny. 1983. "The Multivariate Flexible Accelerator Model: Its Empirical Restrictions and an Application to U.S. Manufacturing." *Econometrica* 51:647–74.

Erickson, Gary M. 1992. "Closed Loop Duopoly Advertising Strategies." *Management Science* 38:1732–48.

Fernandez-Cornejo, Jorge, Conrado Gempesaw, Joachim Elterich, and Spiro Stefanou. 1992. "Dynamic Measures of Scope and Scale Economies: An Application to German Agriculture." *American Journal of Agricultural Economics* 74:329–42.

Fershtman, Chaim. 1987. "Identification of Classes of Differential Games for which the Open-Loop Is a Degenerated Feedback Nash Equilibrium." *Journal of Optimization Theory and Applications* 55:217–31.

Fershtman, Chaim, and Morton Kamien. 1987. "Dynamic Duopolistic Competition with Sticky Prices." *Econometrica* 55:1151–64.

Fershtman, Chaim, and Eitan Muller. 1986. "Capital Investments and Price Agreements in Semicollusive Markets." *The Rand Journal of Economics* 17:214–26.

Fisher, Franklin M. 1987. "On the Misuse of the Profit-Sales Ratio to Infer Monopoly Power." *The Rand Journal of Economics,* 18:384–96.

Fisher, Franklin M., and John J. McGowan. 1983. "On the Misuse of Accounting Rates of Return to Infer Monopoly Profits." *American Economic Review* 73:82–97.

Fraumeni, Barbara M., and Dale W. Jorgenson. 1980. "Rates of Return by Industrial Sector in the United States, 1948–1976." *American Economic Review* 70:326–30.

Freeman, Richard B. 1983. "Unionism, Price-Cost Margins and the Return on Capital." National Bureau of Economic Research: Working Paper No. 1164.

Fudenberg, Drew, and Jean Tirole. 1993. *Game Theory.* (Cambridge, Mass.: MIT Press).

Gasmi, Farhid. 1988. *Econometrics of Duopolistic Games in Prices and Advertising: The Case of the U.S. Soft Drink Industry.* Ph.D. diss., California Institute of Technology.

Gasmi, Farhid, Jean Jacques Laffont, and Quang H. Vuong. 1992. "Econometric Analysis of Collusive Behavior in a Soft-Drink Market." *Journal of Economics & Management Strategy* 1:277–311.

Gasmi, Farid, and Quang H. Vuong. 1991. "An Econometric Analysis of Some Duopolistic Games in Prices and Advertising." In George F. Rhodes, Jr., ed., *Advances in Econometrics,* 9, pp. 225–54 (Greenwich, Conn.: JAI Press Inc.).

Gatsios, Constantine, and Larry Karp. 1992. "How Anti-Merger Laws Can Reduce Investment, Help Producers, and Hurt Consumers." *Journal of Industrial Economics* 40:339–48.

Gelfand, Matthew D., and Pablo T. Spiller. 1987. "Entry Barriers and Multiproduct Oligopolies: Do They Forebear or Spoil." *International Journal of Industrial Organization* 5:101–13.

Genesove, David, and Wallace Mullin. 1998. "Testing Static Oligopoly Models: Conduct and Cost in the Sugar Industry, 1890–1914." *The Rand Journal of Economics* 29:355–77.

Geroski, Paul A. 1981. "Specification and Testing the Profits-Concentration Relationship: Some Experiments for the United Kingdom." *Economica* 48:279–88.

Geroski, P. A., L. Phlips, and A. Ulph. 1985. "Oligopoly, Competition and Welfare: Some Recent Developments." *Journal of Industrial Economics* 33:369–87.

Geweke, John F. 1986. "Exact Inference in the Inequality Constrained Normal Linear-Regression Model." *Journal of Applied Econometrics* 1:127–41.

Geweke, John F. 1988. "Antithetic Acceleration of Monte Carlo Integration in Bayesian Inference." *Journal of Econometrics* 38:73–89.

Geweke, John F. 1989. "Bayesian Inference in Econometric Models Using Monte Carlo Integration." *Econometrica* 57:1317–39.

Gokhale, Dattaprabhakar V., and Kullback, Solomon. 1978. *The Information in Contingency Tables.* (New York: Marcel Dekker).

Golan, Amos. 2002. "Information and Entropy Econometrics – Editor's View." *Journal of Econometrics* 107:1–15.

Golan, Amos, and Henryk Gzyl. 2002. "A Generalized Maxentropic Inversion Procedure for Noisy Data." *Applied Mathematics and Computation* 127:249–60.

Golan, Amos, and George G. Judge. 1996. "A Maximum Entropy Approach to Empirical Likelihood: Estimation and Inference." University of California, Berkeley: Working paper presented at the 1997 Summer Meetings of the North America Econometric Society.

Golan, Amos, George G. Judge, and Douglas Miller. 1996. *Maximum Entropy Econometrics: Robust Estimation with Limited Data.* (New York: John Wiley & Sons).

Golan, Amos, George G. Judge, and Jeffrey M. Perloff. 1996a. "Recovering Information from Multinomial Response Data." *Journal of the American Statistical Association* 91:841–53.

Golan, Amos, George G. Judge, and Jeffrey M. Perloff. 1996b. "Estimating the Size Distribution of Firms Using Government Summary Statistics." *Journal of Industrial Economics* 44:69–80.

Golan, Amos, George G. Judge, and Jeffrey M. Perloff. 1997. "Estimation and Inference with Censored and Ordered Multinomial Response Data." *Journal of Econometrics* 79:23–51.

Golan, Amos, Larry S. Karp, and Jeffrey M. Perloff. 1998. "Estimating a Mixed Strategy: United and American Airlines." Working paper (are.berkeley.edu/~perloff/PDF/air.pdf).

Golan, Amos, Larry S. Karp, and Jeffrey M. Perloff. 2000. "Estimating Coke and Pepsi's Price and Advertising Strategies." *Journal of Business & Economic Statistics* 18:398–409.

Golan, Amos, and Henryk Gzyl. 2004. "Priors and Information Theoretic Estimation." American University: Working Paper.

Goldberg, Pinelopi Koujianou. 1995. "Product Differentiation and Oligopoly in International Markets: The Case of the U.S. Automobile Industry." *Econometrica* 63:891–951.

Gollop, Frank M., and Mark J. Roberts. 1979. "Firm Interdependence in Oligopolistic Markets." *Journal of Econometrics* 16:617–45.

Green, Edward J., and Robert H. Porter. 1984. "Noncooperative Collusion under Imperfect Price Information." *Econometrica* 52:87–100.

Green, Richard, and Julian M. Alston. 1990. "Elasticities in AIDS Models." *American Journal of Agricultural Economics* 72:442–4.

Greene, William H. 2000. *Econometric Analysis*, 4th Edition. (Upper Saddle River, NJ: Prentice Hall).

Griffiths, William E., R. Carter Hill, and George Judge. 1990. *Learning and Practicing Econometrics.* (New York: Wiley).

Hajivassiliou, Vassilis A. 1989. "Measurement Errors in Switching Regression Models with Applications to Price-Fixing Behavior." Cowles Foundation for Research in Economics: Working Paper.

Hajivassiliou, V., and Paul Ruud. 1994. "Classical Estimation Methods for LDV Models Using Simulation." In R. Engel and D. McFadden, eds., *Handbook of Econometrics*, IV, pp. 2383–441 (Amsterdam: Elsevier Science Publishers B.V.).

Hall, Alastair. 2005. *Generalized Method of Moments.* (Oxford: Oxford University Press).

Hall, Robert E. 1988. "The Relationship Between Price and Marginal Cost in U.S. Industry." *Journal of Political Economy* 96:921–47.

Hall, Robert E. 2002. "Industry Dynamics with Adjustment Costs." NBER: Working Paper Series 8849.

Haltiwanger, John, and Joseph E. Harrington, Jr. 1991. "The Impact of Cyclical Demand Movements on Collusive Behavior." *Rand Journal of Economics* 22:89–106.

Hansen, Lars Peter, Dennis Epple, and William Roberds. 1985. "Linear-Quadratic Duopoly Models Of Resource Depletion." In *Energy, Foresight and Strategy*, Thomas J. Sargent, ed. (Washington, D.C.: Resources for the Future), pp. 101–42.

Hansen, Lars Peter, and Thomas J. Sargent. 1980. "Formulating and Estimating Dynamic Linear Rational Expectations Models." *Journal of Economic Dynamics and Control* 2:7–46.

Hansen, Lars Peter, and Kenneth J. Singleton. 1982. "Generalized Instrumental Variables Estimation of Nonlinear Rational Expectations Models." *Econometrica* 50:1269–86.

Hart, Peter E., and Eleanor Morgan. 1977. "Market Structure and Economic Performance in the United Kingdom." *Journal of Industrial Economics* 25:177–93.

Hausman, Jerry. 1997. "Valuation of New Goods Under Perfect and Imperfect Competition." In T. Bresnahan and R. Gordon, eds., *The Economics of New Goods* (Chicago: University of Chicago Press, National Bureau of Economic Research: *Studies in Income and Wealth* 58:209–37).

Hausman, Jerry A., and Gregory K. Leonard. 2004. "The Competitive Effects of a New Product Introduction: A Case Study." *Journal of Industrial Economics* 50:237–63.

Hausman, Jerry A., and Gregory K. Leonard. 2005. "Using Merger Simulation Models: Testing the Underlying Assumptions." *International Journal of Industrial Organization* 23:693–8.

Hausman, Jerry A., Gregory K. Leonard, and J. Douglas Zona. 1994. "Competitive Analysis with Differentiated Products." *Annales d'Economie et de Statistique* 34:159–80.

Hayashi, Fumio, and Tohru Inoue. 1991. "The Relation Between Firm Growth and Q with Multiple Capital Goods: Theory and Evidence from Panel Data on Japanese Firms." *Econometrica* 59:731–53.

Heckman, James. 1978. "Dummy Endogenous Variables in Simultaneous Equation System." *Econometrica* 46:931–60.

Heckman, James. 1990. "Varieties of Selection Bias." *American Economic Review* 80:313–18.

Hendricks, Kenneth, and R. Preston McAfee. 2005. "A Theory of Bilateral Oligopoly." Working paper.

Hoel, Michael, and Larry S. Karp. 2001. "Taxes and Quotas for a Stock Pollutant with Multiplicative Uncertainty." *Journal of Public Economics* 82:91–114.

Hotelling, Harold. 1929. "Stability in Competition." *Economic Journal* 39:41–57.

Hotz, V. Joseph, and Robert A. Miller. 1993. "Conditional Choice Probabilities and the Estimation of Dynamic Models." *Review of Economic Studies* 60:265–89.

Hyde, Charles E., and Jeffrey M. Perloff. 1994. "Can Monopsony Power be Estimated?" *American Journal of Agricultural Economics* 76:1151–5.

Hyde, Charles E., and Jeffrey M. Perloff. 1995. "Can Market Power be Estimated?" *Review of Industrial Organization* 10:465–85.

Hyde, Charles E., and Jeffrey M. Perloff. 1998. "Multimarket Market Power Estimation: The Australian Retail Meat Sector." *Applied Economics* 30:1169–76.

Imbens, Guido W., Phillip Johnson, and Richard H. Spady. 1998. "Information-Theoretic Approaches to Inference in Moment Condition Models." *Econometrica* 66:333–57.

Iwata. Gyoichi. 1974. "Measurement of Conjectural Variations in Oligopoly." *Econometrica* 42:947–66.

Jaynes, Edwin T. 1957a. "Information Theory and Statistical Mechanics." *Physics Review* 106:620–30.

Jaynes, Edwin T. 1957b. "Information Theory and Statistical Mechanics II." *Physics Review* 108:171–90.

Johnson, Norman L., and Fred C. Leone. 1964. *Statistics and Experiment Design*, Vol. 1. (New York: John Wiley & Sons). *Journal of Econometrics*, 2002, 107:1–2.

Judd, Kenneth. 1999. *Numerical Methods in Economics.* (Cambridge, Mass.: MIT Press).

Jun, Byoung, and Xavier Vives. 2004. "Strategic Incentives in Dynamic Duopoly." *Journal of Economic Theory* 28:249–81.

Just, Richard E., and Wen S. Chern. 1980. "Tomatoes, Technology, and Oligopsony." *Bell Journal of Economics and Management Science* 11:584–602.

Kadiyali, Vrinda, Naufel Vilcassim, and Pradeep Chintagunta. 1998. "Product Line Extensions and Competitive Market Interactions: An Empirical Analysis." *Journal of Econometrics* 89:339–63.

Kamien, Morton, and Nancy Schwartz. 1983. "Conjectural Variations." *Canadian Journal of Economics* 16:191–211.

Kamien, Morton, and Nancy Schwartz. 1991. *Dynamic Optimization the Calculus of Variations and Optimal Control in Economics and Management*, 2nd edition. (New York: North Holland).

Kandori, Michihiro. 1991. "Correlated Demand Shocks and Price Wars During Booms." *Review of Economic Studies* 58:171–80.

Karp, Larry S. 1992. "Social Welfare in a Common Property Oligopoly." *International Economic Review* 33:353–72.

Karp, Larry, and In Ho Lee. 2003. "Time Consistent Policies." *Journal of Economic Theory* 112:353–64.

Karp, Larry S., and Jeffrey M. Perloff. 1989a. "Estimating Market Structure and Tax Incidence: The Japanese Television Market." *Journal of Industrial Economics* 37:225–39.

Karp, Larry S., and Jeffrey M. Perloff. 1989b. "Dynamic Oligopoly in the Rice Export Market." *Review of Economics and Statistics* 71:462–70.

Karp, Larry S., and Jeffrey M. Perloff. 1993a. "A Dynamic Model in the Coffee Export Market." *American Journal of Agricultural Economics* 75:448–57.

Karp, Larry S., and Jeffrey M. Perloff. 1993b. "Open-Loop and Feedback Models of Dynamic Oligopoly." *International Journal of Industrial Organization* 11:386–9.

Karp, Larry S., and Jeffrey M. Perloff. 1993c. "Dynamic Models of Oligopoly in Agricultural Export Markets." In Ronald W. Cotterill, ed., *Competitive Strategy Analysis in the Food System*, pp. 113–34 (Boulder, Colo.: Westview Press).

Karp, Larry S., and Jeffrey M. Perloff. 1996. "Dynamic Models of Oligopoly in Rice and Coffee Export Markets." In David Martimort, ed., *Agricultural Markets: Mechanisms, Failures, and Regulation* (Amsterdam: Elsevier), pp. 171–204.

Kim, Dae-Wook, and Christopher R. Knittel. 2004. "Biases in Static Oligopoly Models? *Evidence from the California Electricity Market.*" NBER: Working Paper 10895 (http://www.nber.org/papers/w10895).

Kitamura, Yuichi, and Michael Stutzer. 1997. "An Information-theoretic Alternative to Generalized Method of Moment Estimation." *Econometrica* 66:861–74.

Kloek, Tuen, and Herman K. van Dijk. 1978. "Bayesian Estimates of Equation System Parameters: An Application of Integration by Monte Carlo." *Econometrica* 46:1–19.

Kooreman, Peter. 1994. "Estimation of Econometric Models of Some Discrete Games." *Journal of Applied Econometrics* 9:255–68.

Kullback, Solomon. 1959. *Information Theory and Statistics.* (New York: John Wiley & Sons).

Kwoka, John E., Jr. 1979. "The Effect of Market Share Distribution on Industry Performance." *Review of Economics and Statistics* 61:101–9.

Kwoka, John E., Jr., and David Ravenscraft. 1986. "Cooperation vs. Rivalry: Price-Cost Margins by Line of Business." *Economica* 53:351–63.

LaFrance, Jeffrey T. 1990. "Incomplete Demand Systems and Semilogarithmic Demand Models." *Australian Journal of Agricultural Economics* 34:118–31.

LaFrance, Jeffrey T. 2004. "Integrability of the Linear Approximate Almost Ideal Demand System." *Economics Letters* 84:297–303.

Lamm, R. McFall, Jr. 1981. "Prices and Concentration in the Food Retailing Industry." *Journal of Industrial Economics* 30:67–78.

Lapham, Beverly, and Roger Ware. 1994. "Markov Puppy Dogs and Related Animals." *International Journal of Industrial Organization* 12:569–93.

Lau, Lawrence J. 1982. "On Identifying the Degree of Competitiveness from Industry Price and Output Data." *Economics Letters* 10:93–9.

Lee, Lung-Fei. 1992. "On Efficiency of Methods of Simulated Moments and Maximum Simulated Maximum Estimator of Discrete Response Models." *Econometrica* 8:518–52.

Lee, Lung-Fei, and Robert H. Porter. 1984. "Switching Regression Models with Imperfect Sample Selection Information with an Application on Cartel Stability." *Econometrica* 52:391–418.

Levine, Rafi D. 1980. "An Information Theoretical Approach to Inversion Problems." *Journal of Physics A* 13:91–108.

Liebowitz, Stanley J. 1982. "What Do Census Price-Cost Margins Measure?" *Journal of Law and Economics* 25:231–46.

Lopez, Ramon E. 1984. "Measuring Oligopoly Power and Production Responses of the Canadian Food Processing Industry." *Journal of Agricultural Economics* 35:219–30.

Lopez, Rigoberto A., and Daniel Dorsainvil. 1990. "An Analysis of Pricing in the Haitian Coffee Market." *Journal of Development Economics* 25:93–105.

Love, H. Alan, and E. Murniningtyas. 1992. "Market Power of Government Agencies." *American Journal of Agricultural Economics* 74:546–55.

Luh, Yir Hueih, and Spiro E. Stefanou. 1991. "Productivity Growth in U.S. Agriculture under Dynamic Adjustment." *American Journal of Agricultural Economics* 73:1116–25.

Lustgarten, Steven H., and Stavros B. Thomadakis. 1980. "Valuation Response to New Information: A Test of Resource Mobility and Market Structure." *Journal of Political Economy* 88:977–93.

Mann, Michael. 1966. "Seller Concentration, Barriers to Entry, and Rates of Return in Thirty Industries, 1950–1960." *The Review of Economics and Statistics* 48:290–307.

Marvel, Howard. 1978. "Competition and Price Levels in the Retail Gasoline Market." *Review of Economics and Statistics* 60:252–8.

Mason, Edward S. 1939. "Price and Production Policies of Large-Scale Enterprise." *American Economic Review* 29 suppl.:61–74.

Mason, Edward S. 1949. "The Current State of the Monopoly Problem in the United States." *Harvard Law Review* 62:1265–85.

Massey, Frank J., Jr. 1951. "The Kolmogorov-Smirnov Test for Goodness of Fit." *Journal of the American Statistical Association* 46:68–78.

Matsushima, Hitoshi. 2004. "Repeated Games with Private Monitoring: Two Players." *Econometrica* 72:823–52.

Matyas, Laszlo L. 1999. *Generalized Method of Moments Estimation.* (Cambridge, UK: Cambridge University Press).

McFadden, Daniel. 1989. "A Method of Simulated Moments for Estimation of Discrete Choice Models without Numerical Integration." *Econometrica* 57:995–1026.

McFadden, Daniel, and Kenneth E. Train. 2000. "Mixed MFL Models for Discrete Response." *Journal of Applied Econometrics* 15:447–70.

McKelvey, Richard D., and Andrew McLennan. 1996. "The Computation of Equilibrium in Finite Games." In H. Amman, D. A. Kendrick, and J. Rust, eds., *The Handbook of Computational Economics*, Vol. I (Amsterdam: Elsevier), pp. 87–142.

Milgrom, Paul R., and Robert J. Weber. 1986. "Distributional Strategies for Games with Incomplete Information." *Mathematics of Operations Research* 10:619–31.

Miller, Douglas J. 1994. *Entropy and Information Recovery in Linear Economic Models.* Ph.D. thesis, University of California, Berkeley.

Miranda, Mario J., and Paul L. Fackler. 2002. *Applied Computational Economics and Finance.* (Cambridge, Mass.: MIT Press).

Mittelhammer, Ronald C., and Scott N. Cardell. 1997. "On the Consistency and Asymptotic Normality of the Data-Constrained GME Estimator in the GLM." Washington State University: Working paper.

Mittelhammer, Ronald C., George G. Judge, and Douglas Miller. 2000. *Econometric Foundations.* (Cambridge, UK: Cambridge University Press).

Miwa, Yoshiro. 1996. *Firms and Industrial Organization in Japan.* (New York: New York University Press).

Mueller, Dennis C. 1985. *Profits in the Long Run.* (Cambridge, UK: Cambridge University Press).

Nevo, Aviv. 1998. "Identification of the Oligopoly Solution Concept in a Differentiated-Products Industry." *Economics Letters* 59:391–5.

Nevo, Aviv. 2000a. "Mergers with Differentiated Products: The Case of the Ready-to-Eat Cereal Industry." *Rand Journal of Economics* 31:395–421.

Nevo, Aviv. 2000b. "A Practitioner's Guide to Estimation of Random-Coefficients Logit Models of Demand." *Journal of Economics and Management Strategy* 9:513–48.

Nevo, Aviv. 2001. "Measuring Market Power in the Ready-to-Eat Cereal Industry." *Econometrica* 69:307–42.

Newey Whitney, and Richard J. Smith, 2002. "Higher order properties of GMM and Generalized empirical likelihood estimators." MIT, Department of Economics, *Working paper*.

Oum, Tae Hoon, Anming Zhang, and Yimin Zhang. 1993. "Inter-firm Rivalry and Firm Specific Price Elasticities in Deregulated Airline Markets." *Journal of Transport Economics and Policy* 27:171–92.

Owen, Art B. 1990. "Empirical Likelihood Ratio Confidence Regions." *The Annals of Statistics* 18:90–120.

Owen, Art B. 1991. "Empirical Likelihood for Linear Models." *The Annals of Statistics* 19:1725–47.

Owen, Art B. 2001. *Empirical Likelihood.* (New York: Chapman & Hall/CRC).

Pakes, Ariel, and Paul McGuire. 1994. "Computing Markov-Perfect Nash Equilibria: Numerical Implications of a Dynamic Differentiated Product Model." *Rand Journal of Economics* 25:555–89.

Pakes, Ariel, Michael Ostrovsky, and Steve Berry. 2004. "Simple Estimators for the Parameters of Discrete Dynamic Games (with Entry/Exit Samples)." NBER: Working Paper 10506.

Pindyck, Robert. 1985. "The Measurement of Monopoly Power in Dynamic Markets." *Journal of Law and Economics* 28:193–222.

Peltzman, Sam. 1977. "The Gains and Losses from Industrial Concentration." *Journal of Law and Economics* 20:229–63.

Perloff, Jeffrey M. 1992. "Econometric Analysis of Imperfect Competition and Implications for Trade Research." In Ian M. Sheldon and Dennis R. Henderson, eds., *Industrial Organization and International Trade: Methodological Foundations for International Food and Agricultural Market Research.* NC-194 Research Monograph Number 1.

Perloff, Jeffrey M., and Steven C. Salop. 1985. "Equilibrium with Product Differentiation." *Review of Economic Studies* 52:107–20.

Perloff, Jeffrey M., and Edward Z. Shen. 2001. "*Collinearity in Linear Structural Models of Market Power.*" Working paper (are.Berkeley.EDU/~perloff/PDF/linear.pdf).

Perloff, Jeffrey M., and Michael B. Ward. 1998. "A Flexible, Nonparametric Approach to Estimating Market Power." Working paper.

Perloff, Jeffrey M., and Michael B. Ward. 2003. "*Welfare, Market Power, and Price Effects of Product Diversity: Canned Juices.*" Working paper (are.berkeley.edu/~perloff/PDF/welfare.pdf).

Pindyck, Robert, and Julio Rotemberg. 1983. "Dynamic Factor Demands and the Effects of Energy Price Shocks." *American Economic Review* 73:1066–79.

Pinske, Joris, Margaret E. Slade, and Craig Brett. 2002. "Spatial Price Competition: A Semiparametric Approach." *Econometrica* 70:1111–53.

Porter, Robert. 1983. "A Study of Cartel Stability: The Joint Executive Committee 1980–1986." *The Bell Journal of Economics* 14:301–14.

Pryor, Frederic L. 1972. "An International Comparison of Concentration Ratios." *Review of Economics and Statistics* 54:130–40.

Pukelsheim, Friedrich. 1994. "The Three Sigma Rule." *American Statistician* 48:88–91.

Qin, Jing, and Jerry Lawless. 1994. "Empirical Likelihood and General Estimating Equations." *The Annals of Statistics* 22:300–25.

Reiss, Peter C., and Frank A. Wolak. 2007. "Structural Econometric Modeling: Rationales and Examples from Industrial Organization." In J. J. Heckman and E. E. Leamer, eds., *Handbook of Econometrics*, vol. 6 (Amsterdam: Elsevier).

Renyi, Alfred. 1961. "On Measures of Information and Entropy." In *Proceedings of the Fourth Berkeley Symposium on Mathematics, Statistics and Probability*, 1960, vol. I, p. 547.

Renyi, Alfred. 1970. *Probability Theory.* (Amsterdam: North-Holland).

Reynolds, Stanley. 1987. "Capacity Investment, Preemption and Commitment." *International Economic Review* 28:69–88.

Rob, Rafael. 1991. "Learning and Capacity Expansion under Demand Uncertainty." *Review of Economic Studies* 58:655–75.

Roberts, Mark J., and Larry Samuelson. 1988. "An Empirical Model of Dynamic Nonprice Competition in an Oligopolistic Industry." *Rand Journal of Economics* 19:200–20.

Roeger, Werner. 1995. "Can Imperfect Competition Explain the Difference between Primal and Dual Productivity Measures? Estimates for U.S. Manufacturing." *Journal of Political Economy* 103:316–30.

Rosse, James N. 1970. "Estimating Cost Function Parameters Without Using Cost Data: Illustrated Methodology." *Econometrica* 38:256–75.

Rotemberg, Julio, and Garth Saloner. 1986. "A Supergame-Theoretic Model of Price Wars During Booms." *American Economic Review* 76:390–407.

Ruback, Richard S., and Martin B. Zimmerman. 1984. "Unionization and Profitability: Evidence from the Capital Market." *Journal of Political Economy* 92:1134–57.

Rust, John. 1987. "Optimal Replacement of GMC Bus Engines: An Empirical Model of Harold Zurcher." *Econometrica* 87: 999–1033.

Rust, John. 1994. "Structural Estimation of Markov Decision Processes." In Daniel L. McFadden, ed., *Handbook of Econometrics*, vol. 4, pp. 3081–143 (Amsterdam: Elsevier Science).

Salinger, Michael A. 1984. "Tobin's *q*, Unionization, and the Concentration-Profits Relationship." *The Rand Journal of Economics* 15:159–70.

Schmalensee, Richard. 1987. "Collusion versus Differential Efficiency: Testing Alternative Hypotheses." *The Journal of Industrial Economics* 35:399–425.

Schmalensee, Richard. 1989. "Inter-Industry Studies of Structure and Performance." In Richard Schmalensee and Robert Willig, eds., *Handbook of Industrial Organization*, pp. 951–1009 (New York: North Holland).

Schroeter, John R., and Azzedine Azzam. 1987. "Marketing Margins, Power, and Risk." *American Journal of Agricultural Economics* 73:990–9.

Shannon, Claude E. 1948. "A Mathematical Theory of Communication." *Bell System Technical Journal* 27:379–423.

Shapiro, Matthew. 1987. "Measuring Market Power in U.S. Industry." National Bureau of Economic Research: Working Paper No. 2212.

Shen, Edward Z., and Jeffrey M. Perloff. 2001. "Maximum Entropy and Bayesian Approaches to the Ratio Problem." *Journal of Econometrics* 104:289–313.

Shore, John E., and Johnson, Rodney W. 1980. "Axiomatic Derivation of the Principle of Maximum Entropy and the Principle of Minimum Cross-Entropy." *IEEE Transactions on Information Theory*, IT-26, 26–37.

Skilling, John. 1989. "The Axioms of Maximum Entropy." In J. Skilling, ed., *Maximum Entropy and Bayesian Methods in Science and Engineering* (Dordrecht: Kluwer Academic), pp. 173–87.

Slade, Margaret E. 1986. "Conjectures, Firm Characteristics, and Market Structure." *International Journal of Industrial Organization* 4:347–69.

Slade, Margaret. 1987. "Interfirm Rivalry in a Repeated Game: An Empirical Test of Tacit Collusion." *Journal of Industrial Economics* 35:499–516.

Slade, Margaret. 1989. "Price Wars in Price-Setting Supergames." *Economica* 56:295–310.

Slade, Margaret. 1992. "Vancouver's Gasoline-Price Wars: An Empirical Exercise in Uncovering Supergame Strategies." *Review of Economic Studies* 59:257–76.

Slade, Margaret. 1994. "What Does an Oligopoly Maximize?" *Journal of Industrial Economics* 41:45–61.

Slade, Margaret. 1995. "Empirical Games: The Oligopoly Case." *Canadian Journal of Economics* 28:368–402.

Slade, Margaret. 1998. "Beer and the Tie: Did Divestiture of Brewer-Owned Public Houses Lead to Higher Beer Prices?" *The Economic Journal* 108:565–602.

Smith, Richard J. 1997. "Alternative Semi Parametric Likelihood Approaches to GMM Estimations." *Economic Journal* 107:503–10.

Smith, Richard J. 2004. "GEL Criteria for Moment Condition Models." University of Warwick Working paper.

Soofi, Ehsan S. 1992. "A Generalizable Formulation of Conditional Logit with Diagnostics." *Journal of the American Statistical Association* 87:812–16.

Soofi, Ehsan S. 1994. "Capturing the Intangible Concept of Information." *Journal of the American Statistical Association* 89:1243–54.

Spiller, Pablo T., and Ewardo Favaro. 1984. "The Effects of Entry Regulation or Oligopolistic Interaction: The Uruguayan Banking Sector." *The Rand Journal of Economics* 15:244–54.

Steen, Frode, and Kjell G. Salvanes. 1999. "Testing for Market Power Using a Dynamic Oligopoly Model." *International Journal of Industrial Organization* 17:147–77.

Stigler, George J. 1963. *Capital and Rates of Return in Manufacturing Industries.* (Princeton: Princeton University Press).

Stigler, George J. 1964. "A Theory of Oligopoly." *Journal of Political Economy* 72:44–61.

Stigler, George J. 1968. *The Organization of Industry.* (Homewood, Ill.: Richard D. Irwin).

Stone, John R. N. 1953. *The Measurement of Consumers' Expenditure and Behavior in the United Kingdom, 1920–38.* (Cambridge, UK: Cambridge University Press).

Sullivan, Daniel. 1985. "Testing Hypotheses About Firm Behavior in the Cigarette Industry." *Journal of Political Economy* 93:586–98.

Sumner, Daniel A. 1981. "Measurement of Monopoly Behavior: An Application to the Cigarette Industry." *Journal of Political Economy* 89:1010–19.

Suslow, Valerie. 1986. "Estimating Monopoly Behavior with Competitive Recycling: An Application to Alcoa." *The Rand Journal of Economics* 17:389–403.

Suslow, Valerie. 1998. "Cartel Contract Duration: Empirical Evidence from International Cartels." Working paper.
Sutton, John. 1989. "Endogenous Sunk Costs and the Structure of Advertising Intensive Industries." *European Economic Review* 33:335–44.
Sutton, John. 1991. *Sunk Costs and Market Structure.* (Cambridge, Mass.: MIT Press).
Sutton, John. 1998. *Technology and Market Structure: Theory and History.* (Cambridge and London: MIT Press).
Tamer, Elie. 2003. "Incomplete Simultaneous Discrete Response Model with Multiple Equilibria." *Review of Economic Studies* 70:147–67.
Tobin, James. 1969. "A General Equilibrium Approach to Monetary Theory." *Journal of Money, Credit, and Banking* 1:15–29.
Town, Robert. 1991. "Price Wars and Demand Fluctuations: A Reexamination of the Joint Executive Committee." U.S. Department of Justice, Antitrust Division: Discussion Paper EAG91-5.
Train, Kenneth E. 1998. "Recreation Demand Models with Taste Differences Over People." *Land Economics* 74:230–9.
Tsallis, Constantino. 1988. "Possible Generalization of Boltzmann-Gibbs Statistics." *Journal of Statistical Physics* 52:479–87.
Tsutsui, Shunichi, and Kazuo Mino. 1990. "Nonlinear Strategies in Dynamic Duopolistic Competition with Sticky Prices." *Journal of Economic Theory* 52:136–61.
von Neumann, John, and Oskar Morgenstern. 1944. *Theory of Games and Economic Behavior.* (Princeton: Princeton University Press).
Voos, Paula B., and Lawrence R. Mishel. 1986. "The Union Impact on Profits: Evidence from Industry Price-Cost Margin Data." *Journal of Labor Economics* 4:105–33.
Vuong, Q. H. 1989. "Likelihood Ratio Tests for Model Selection and Non-Nested Hypotheses." *Econometrica* 57:307–33.
Wallace, Donald H. 1937. *Market Control in the Aluminum Industry.* (Cambridge, Mass.: Harvard University Press).
Wann, Joyce J., and Richard J. Sexton. 1992. "Imperfect Competition in Multiproduct Food Industries with an Application to Pear Processing." *American Journal of Agricultural Economics* 74:980–90.
Weiher, Jesse C., Robin C. Sickles, and Jeffrey M. Perloff. 2002. "Market Power in the US Airline Industry." In Daniel J. Slottje, ed., *Measuring Market Power, Contributions to Economic Analysis,* Vol. 255 (Amsterdam: Elsevier), pp. 309–23.
Weiss, Leonard W. 1974. "The Concentration-Profits Relationship and Antitrust." In Harvey J. Goldschmid, H. Michael Mann, and J. Fred Weston, eds., *Industrial Concentration: The New Learning* (Boston: Little, Brown).
Werden, Gregory J., and Luke M. Froeb. 1994. "The Effects of Mergers in Differentiated Products Industries: Logit Demand and Merger Policy." *Journal of Law, Economics, & Organization* 10:407–26.
White, Lawrence J. 2003. "*Aggregate Concentration in the Global Economy: Issues and Evidence.*" Working paper (papers.ssrn.com/sol3/papers.cfm?abstract_id=446920).
White, Lawrence. 1976. "Searching for the Critical Industrial Concentration Ratio." In Stephen Goldfeld and Richard E. Quandt, *Studies in Non-Linear Estimation* (Cambridge, Mass.: Ballinger).
Williamson, Oliver E. 1975. *Markets and Hierarchies: Analysis and Antitrust Implications.* (New York: The Free Press).
Xie, Danyang. 1997. "On Time Consistency: A Technical Issue in Stackelberg Differential Games." *Journal of Economic Theory* 76:412–30.

Zellner, Arnold. 1978. "Estimator of Functions of Population Means and Regression Coefficients Including Structural Coefficients: A Minimum Expected Loss Approach." *Journal of Econometrics* 8:127–58.

Zellner, Arnold. 1991. "Bayesian Methods and Entropy in Economics and Econometrics." In Grandy, W. T., Jr. and L. H. Schick, eds., *Maximum Entropy and Bayesian Methods* (Amsterdam: Kluwer), pp. 17–31.

Zellner, Arnold. 1996. "Bayesian Method of Moments/Instrumental Variables (BMOM/IV) Analysis of Mean and Regression Models." In Jack C. Lee, Wesley O. Johnson, and Arnold Zellner, eds., *Prediction and Modeling Honoring Seymour Geisser* (Berlin: Springer-Verlag).

Zellner, Arnold. 1997. "The Bayesian Method of Moments (BMOM): Theory and Applications." In *Advances in Econometrics* (Vol. 11), eds. Thomas B. Fomby and R. Carter Hill, 85–105 (JAI Press).

Zellner, Arnold, and Justin Tobias. 2001. "Further Results on the Bayesian Method of Moments Analysis of Multiple Regression Model." *International Economic Review* 42:121–40.

Answers

2.1 We can proceed as we did to derive Equation (2.3) using Equation (2.2). Substituting $m_i = AVC_i + (r + \delta)p_K K_i/Q_i$ into $L_i = (p - m_i)/p = s_i/\varepsilon$, we find that $(p - m_i)/p = s_i/\varepsilon + (r + \delta)p_K K_i/(p_i Q_i)$. If we weight this expression by s_i and sum over i, we obtain a variant of Cowling and Waterson's (1976) equation:

$$\sum_i s_i \frac{p - AVC_i}{p} = -\sum_i \frac{s_i^2}{\varepsilon} + (r + \delta) \sum_i s_i \frac{p_K K_i}{pq_i}$$

$$= -\frac{HHI}{\varepsilon} + (r + \delta) \sum_i s_i \frac{p_K K_i}{pq_i}.$$

That is, weighted average price–cost margin for the industry depends on the HHI/ε and the quantity share-weighted rental value of capital divided by the value of output.

2.2 Firm i maximizes its profit by an appropriate choice of output, q_i:

$$\max_{q_i} \pi_i = p\left(a - b\sum_{j=i}^{n} q_j\right) q_i - mq_i - F.$$

In equilibrium, all the identical firms produce q, so total output is nq. Each firm's profit is $\pi_i = (a - bnq)q - mq - F$.

Using the Cournot assumption, profit maximizing implies $MR = MC$, or $a - b(n + 1)q = m$. Free entry implies $p = AC$, or $a - bnq = m + F/q$. Substituting the free-entry condition into the profit-maximizing condition to eliminate m, we find that

$$a - b(n + 1)q = a - bnq - \frac{F}{q}1.$$

By rearranging this last expression, we find that the equilibrium quantity is $q = \sqrt{F/b}$. The equilibrium number of firms is

$$n = \frac{a - m}{b\sqrt{F/b}} - 1.$$

The equilibrium price is $p = m + b\sqrt{F/b}$.

Thus, as F increases, $\mathrm{d}q/\mathrm{d}F = 1/[2\sqrt{Fb}] > 0$, $\mathrm{d}p/\mathrm{d}F = b/[2\sqrt{Fb}] > 0$, and $\mathrm{d}n/\mathrm{d}F = -(a - m)/[2F\sqrt{bF}] < 0$. Similarly, we can show that the profitability measure, $p/m = 1 + b\sqrt{F/b}/m$, increases, and that the concentration measure, $C4 = 4/n$, increases. Thus, profitability and concentration both rise because a change in another factor, fixed cost, causes both to rise.

2.3 Sutton shows that for any given market size, equilibrium market concentration is higher, the more competitive the market. The reason for the result is that tough competition leads to a low price, which discourages entry. Traditional SCP empirical studies compare profitability and structure measures across industries without controlling for competitiveness. Thus, the estimated coefficients may reflect an average of relationships if there is a mixture of different levels of competitiveness across the industries.

3.1 The first-order condition for Firm i is $p(Q) + p_Q(Q)q_i(1 + v_i) = MC_i(q_i) = c_i'(q_i)$. Summing across these equations and dividing by n, we obtain

$$p(Q) + \sum_1^n \frac{(1 + v_i)q_i}{nQ} p_Q(Q)Q = \sum_1^n \frac{MC_i(q_i)}{n},$$

or

$$p(Q) + \bar{\lambda} p_Q(Q)Q = \overline{MC},$$

where $\bar{\lambda} = \frac{1}{n}\sum_i (1 + v_i)\frac{q_i}{Q}$ is the average conjecture – each firm's conjecture weighted by its market share – and $\overline{MC}$ is the average marginal cost. Some econometricians have described this last condition as the average first-order condition for a market. Using algebra, we find that $\bar{\lambda} = [(\overline{MC} - p(Q)]/[p_Q(Q)Q]$. If all the v_i are identical, then all the market shares are equal, so that it is reasonable to treat $\bar{\lambda}$ as a constant, as we did in Equation (3.6). If the conjectures vary across firms, then the market shares vary. Thus, if firms enter and exit the market over time, the average value, $\bar{\lambda}$, will vary over time.

3.2 Given that the inverse demand function is linear, $p = a - bQ = a - bnq$, each of the identical firms makes a profit of $\pi_i = (a - bQ)q_i - mq_i - F$. Firm i's first-order condition for profit maximization is

$$(a - bQ) - b[1 + v_i]q_i - m = 0.$$

In the symmetric equilibrium in which each firm has the same conjecture, v, and the same cost function, each firm's equilibrium output is q (so $Q = nq$) and its optimality equation is $MR - MC = 0$, or

$$a - bq[n + 1 + v] - m = 0.$$

Using algebra, we find that the equilibrium quantity is

$$q = \frac{a - m}{b[n + 1 + \nu]}.$$

If the market is oligopolistic such that n is fixed, then a change in marginal cost causes quantity to change by

$$\frac{\mathrm{d}q}{\mathrm{d}m} = \frac{-1}{b[n + 1 + \nu]}.$$

Thus, $\mathrm{d}Q/\mathrm{d}m = \mathrm{d}(nq)/\mathrm{d}m = -n/\{b[n + 1 + \nu]\}$, and

$$\frac{\mathrm{d}p}{\mathrm{d}Q}\frac{\mathrm{d}Q}{\mathrm{d}m} = \frac{n}{n + 1 + \nu}.$$

For example, if $\nu = 0$ (Cournot), then $\mathrm{d}p/\mathrm{d}m$ (abusing notation slightly) is $n/(n + 1)$. For any $\nu > -1$ (competitive/Bertrand), price rises less than in proportion to marginal cost.

Now, instead, suppose that the market is monopolistically competitive so that n is determined by entry. The monopolistic competition free-entry condition implies that firms exit or enter until $p = AC$ or

$$a - bnq = m + \frac{F}{q}.$$

Solving this equation and the first-order condition for m and equating, we find that

$$a - bq[n + 1 + \nu] = a - bnq - \frac{F}{q},$$

or

$$q = \sqrt{\frac{F}{b(1 + \nu)}}.$$

Thus, the monopolistically competitive equilibrium output is not a function of m, so $\mathrm{d}q/\mathrm{d}m = 0$. From the first-order condition, we have that

$$n = \frac{a - m}{bq} - 1 - \nu.$$

Differentiating with respect to m (and remembering that $\mathrm{d}q/\mathrm{d}m = 0$), we find that

$$\frac{\mathrm{d}n}{\mathrm{d}m} = \frac{-1}{bq} < 0.$$

Therefore, $\mathrm{d}Q/\mathrm{d}m = \mathrm{d}(nq)/\mathrm{d}m = -1/b$, and

$$\frac{\mathrm{d}p}{\mathrm{d}Q}\frac{\mathrm{d}Q}{\mathrm{d}m} = (-b)\left[-\frac{1}{b}\right] = 1.$$

Thus, given that $\nu > -1$, price moves proportionally with marginal cost if the market is monopolistically competitive, but price rises less than proportionally if the market is oligopolistic. Consequently, even if we know that the market demand curve is linear and firms are identical, we cannot distinguish between competition and Cournot without knowing whether the number of firms is fixed (oligopoly) or if the number of firms is determined by endogenous entry (monopolistic competition).

3.3 For an answer, see http://are.berkeley.edu/~perloff/PDF/linear.pdf.

4.1 Using the follower's first-order conditions, Equation (3.12), we know that $q_1 p' = p - m$. Similarly, using the leader's first-order condition, Equation (3.15), we know that $q_2 p'[1 + \nu] = p - m$, where ν is the Stackelberg leaders' conjecture about the follower. Equating the right-hand sides of these equations and simplifying, we find that $\nu = q_1/q_2 - 1$. Thus, we can estimate ν using only information about observed output levels. For example, in the linear case, $q_1/q_2 = {}^1/_2$, so that $\nu = -{}^1/_2$.

4.2 Given that the conditional indirect utility for good i is $\tilde{V}_i = X_i\beta - p_i + \varepsilon_i$, the probability that a consumer chooses good i over any of the other n goods is

$$
\begin{aligned}
&\Pr\left\{\tilde{V}_i > \tilde{V}_1, \tilde{V}_i > \tilde{V}_2, \ldots, \tilde{V}_i > \tilde{V}_n\right\}, \text{ or}\\
&\Pr\{(X_i - X_1)\beta + p_1 - p_i + \varepsilon_i > \varepsilon_1, \ldots, (X_i - X_n)\beta\\
&\quad + p_n - p_i + \varepsilon_i > \varepsilon_i > \varepsilon_n\}, \text{ or}\\
&\Pi_j F([X_i - X_j]\beta + p_j - p_i + \varepsilon_i),
\end{aligned}
$$

where F is a cumulative density function. By inspection, $\partial F/\partial p_j > 0$, so the probability that a consumer purchases this good (the good's share) rises as the price of another good increases (Perloff and Ward 2003).

4.3 From the optimality equations, we know that the Lerner markups, Equation (4.32), are a function of cross-price elasticities $\hat{L} = -(E')^{-1}S$, where the relevant elasticity of demand for the item is a weighted average of its own price elasticity and the cross-price elasticities of the other items the firm makes. The matrix E has negative own-price elasticities on the diagonal and positive cross-price elasticities – all items are substitutes – off the diagonal. Thus, if one firm acquires another firm and all its brands or items, it now faces a new, multiproduct elasticity. By placing this new elasticity in Equation (4.32), we can calculate the new prices and Lerner markups.

What effect does the merger have on the elasticity of an item? As the firm lowers the price of one item, it gains sales from that item due to the negative own-price elasticity but it cannibalizes sales from its other items. Consequently, the multiproduct elasticity for an item is less elastic than is the own-price elasticity. Thus, if the firm goes from having one product to acquiring additional items through a merger, the demand for any given item becomes less elastic, if we evaluate at the initial prices. However, if the firm goes from having several products to a larger number, the shares of its products change, so the effect on the multiproduct elasticity is ambiguous. Similarly, if prices change after the merger, the effect on the elasticity will be ambiguous.

5.1 (a) Under cooperation, each firm sells $a/[2(1+b)]$, or (equivalently) sets its price equal to $a/2$. Profits under cooperation equal $a^2/[4(1+b)]$ and profits in the symmetric Nash-Cournot equilibrium equal $a^2/(2+b)^2$. If one firm cheats when the other firm is selling the cooperative quantity, the cheater gains $a^2(2+b)^2/[16(1+b)^2]$. Cooperation can be sustained if and only if

$$\delta \geq \frac{(2+b)^2}{8+8b+b^2}.$$

(b) The price and payoff under cooperation are given in the answer above. Single-period profits under Bertrand competition equal $(1-b)a^2/[(1+b)(b-2)^2]$. If one firm cheats when its rival sets the cooperative price, the single-period payoff of the cheater is $a^2(b-2)^2/[16(1+b^2)]$. Cooperation can be sustained if and only if

$$\delta \geq \frac{4-4b+b^2}{b^2-8b+8}.$$

(c) For this example, it is easier to sustain cooperation when cheating is followed by Cournot competition. That is, the critical discount factor, above which cooperation can be sustained, is lower when the threat is reversion to Cournot competition (compared with when the threat is reversion to Bertrand competition):

$$\frac{4-4b+b^2}{b^2-8b+8} - \frac{(2+b)^2}{8+8b+b^2} = \frac{8b^3}{(b^2-8b+8)(8+8b+b^2)} > 0.$$

This result may seem surprising, because the Bertrand profits are lower than the Cournot profits, so the threat of reversion to Bertrand competition is more serious than is the threat of reversion to Cournot competition. However, the temptation to cheat is also greater when the rival uses the cooperative price level, compared with when the rival uses the cooperative quantity level. In this example, the greater temptation to cheat (under Bertrand) is more powerful than is the greater punishment.

(d) For this example, the critical discount factor (under either of the two games) is increasing in b. Greater competition in the product market makes it harder to sustain cooperation. Again, this result may seem surprising because single-period profits in (either) noncooperative equilibrium (Cournot or Bertrand) are smaller when b is larger, so larger b increases the punishment. However the cooperative level of profits also decreases with b and the single-period benefit from cheating increases with b.

5.2 (a) The collusive level of output in a symmetric equilibrium is $a_i/4$ and each firm's expectation of single-period profits under collusion (when the current state is not known) equals

$$\frac{1}{8}\left(\mu a_H^2 + (1-\mu)a_L^2\right).$$

The present discounted value of these profits is

$$\frac{1}{8(1-\delta)}\left(\mu a_H^2 + (1-\mu)a_L^2\right).$$

(b) The Nash-Cournot level of output is $a_i/3$ and each firm's expectation of profits under the Nash-Cournot equilibrium (when the current state is not known) equals

$$\frac{1}{9}\left(\mu a_H^2 + (1-\mu)a_L^2\right).$$

Divide this quantity by $1-\delta$ to obtain the present discounted value of the stream of profits.

(c) The cost of cheating is the present value of the difference between the streams of payoff under cooperation and cheating:

$$C^{cartel} = \frac{\delta}{1-\delta}\left(\frac{1}{8}-\frac{1}{9}\right)\left(\mu a_H^2 + (1-\mu)a_L^2\right).$$

(d) The single-period payoff from cheating in state a_i is $9a_i^2/64$, so the single-period net benefit from cheating in that state is $(9-8)a_i^2/64$. A firm wants to cooperate in the high state, given its belief that cheating causes reversion to the noncooperative Nash-Cournot equilibrium, if and only if

$$\delta \geq 9\frac{a_h^2}{(9+8\mu)a_h^2 + (1-\mu)8a_l^2}.$$

A firm wants to cooperate in the low state, given its belief that cheating causes reversion to the noncooperative Nash-Cournot equilibrium, if and only if

$$\delta \geq 9\frac{a_l^2}{(17-8\mu)a_l^2 + 8\mu a_h^2}.$$

(e) Collusion can be sustained iff the inequality described earlier is satisfied in both states of nature. Because the right-hand side of the inequality is greater in state $i = H$, collusion requires

$$\delta \geq 9\frac{a_H^2}{(9+8\mu)a_H^2 + (1-\mu)8a_L^2}.$$

(f) Using the last inequality and the parameter values given in the problem, the minimum discount rate is $\delta = 0.643$. If profits in the high state equal χ, output in the high state is

$$y = \frac{1}{2}(5 + \sqrt{25 - 2\chi})$$

When a firm expects its rival to use the level of output y in the high state, if the firm cheats, its single-period maximum payoff is

$$\frac{1}{16}(-15 + \sqrt{25 - 2\chi})^2$$

so the single-period net benefit of cheating is

$$\frac{1}{16}(-15 + \sqrt{25 - 2\chi})^2 - \chi = \frac{1}{8}(125 - 15\sqrt{25 - 2\chi} - 9\chi).$$

The present discounted value of the cost of cheating is

$$C \equiv \frac{\delta}{1 - \delta}\left(\mu\chi + (1 - \mu)\frac{a_L^2}{8} - \left(\frac{1}{9}\left(\mu a_H^2 + (1 - \mu)a_L^2\right)\right)\right).$$

The first two terms in large brackets equal the expected single-period payoff under cooperation, and the last two terms equal the expected single-period payoff in the Nash-Cournot equilibrium. Using the parameter values given in the problem and setting the single-period net benefit of cheating in the high state equal to the cost of cheating yields two solutions, $\chi = 10.8$ and $\chi = 12.393$. The second solution is the highest level of profits that can be sustained in a high demand state. Thus, in the high state, the firms obtain 99% of the cartel level of profits: 12.393 rather than 12.5. Substituting $\chi = 12.393$ into the expression for y gives per-firm output in the high state $y = 2.73$, with the price 4.54. To complete the solution, it is necessary to verify that when the cooperative phase involves full collusion in the low state, and production at y in the high state, firms do not want to cheat in the low state.

(g) When costs are serially correlated, the problem becomes more complicated because now the cost of cheating depends on the current state. We can start, as above, by assuming that in the cooperative phase firms produce at the fully collusive level in both states of nature. With this assumption, we can compute the present discounted expected value of the cost of cheating given that the state is currently high, and the cost of cheating given that the state is currently low. The benefit of cheating is the same as in part (d). Using the cost and the benefit of cheating, we obtain two inequalities (one for the high state and one for the low state) involving the discount factor; each inequality must be satisfied for our assumption (that full cooperation can be sustained) to be correct. If either inequality does not hold, we can calculate equilibrium outcomes, given specific parameter values, using a variation of the approach in part (f). That approach required guessing a particular type of solution – full cooperation in the low state and partial cooperation in the high state. In general, there may be many equilibria (e.g., partial cooperation in both states).

5.3 Find the level of firm output that maximizes industry profit. This level is $q^m = 1.3125$. Next, find the Nash-Cournot level of expected profit. This profit equals 3.0625. The present value of receiving this profit for five periods is

$$V = 3.0625 \sum_{j=0}^{j=1} (0.8)^j = 10.295.$$

Let ε equal the demand shock. Given that a firm sell output q and that its rival sells output 1.3125, the price falls below the critical level p^c if and only if $\varepsilon \leq -3.6875 + q + p^c$. Given the support of the uniform distribution, the probability of this occurrence is $\rho = 2(-3.6875 + q + p^c)$ (assuming that this value is between zero and one – a conjecture that we confirm at the end of the exercise).

Substituting the values just given into the DPE given in the text and simplifying, we have

$$J = \max_q \{5.5 - (q + 1.3125)q + \delta((1 - \rho)J + \rho(V + \delta^5 J))\}.$$

The first-order condition to this problem is $q = 10.205 - 0.53786J$. Setting this value equal to 1.3125 (the level that we have assumed to be the equilibrium level) implies that $J = 16.533$. Substituting this value into the maximized DPE and solving for the critical price gives $p^c = 2.4807$. Substituting this value, and $q = 1.3125$, into the expression for ρ gives $\rho = 0.2114$.

Thus, the probability of a price war occurring in this example is 0.2114. Beginning in a cooperative phase, the expected present discounted value of a firm's problem is $J = 16.533$.

6.1 (a) Because the product is homogeneous, revenue depends only on total sales (not on the distribution of sales). Because firms are identical prior to the investment decision, investment has the same effect on their costs. Under second-stage cooperation, industry profits from sales (excluding investment costs) equal forty regardless of whether one or both firms invest. Therefore, average (equals marginal) production costs must be constant.

In order to confirm this claim, let the cost function for a firm be $c(q, I)$ where $I = 0$ indicates that a firm has not made the investment, and $I = 1$ indicates that the firm has made the investment. Let $Q = q_i + q_j$ be aggregate sales. If both firms have invested, the second-period maximum joint profits are

$$40 = \max_Q \left(p(Q)(Q) - 2c\left(\frac{Q}{2}, 1\right)\right).$$

If only one firm has invested, the second-period maximum joint profits are

$$40 = \max_{q_i, q_j}(p(q_i + q_j)(q_i + q_j) - c(q_i, 1) - c(q_j, 0)).$$

The assumption that average costs are constant implies that maximum industry profit is the same regardless of whether a single firm or both firms have invested. Therefore, (i) if both firms invested, sales (and therefore profit) can be evenly distributed between the two, and (ii) if a single firm invested, that firm should produce the entire quantity (and thus receive all of the industry profits). Thus, constant average costs are sufficient to obtain the payoff structure given in the problem.

To show that constant average costs are necessary (to obtain the payoff structure in the problem), suppose to the contrary that average costs are not constant. If average costs are strictly increasing, costs can be reduced by dividing a fixed quantity between two firms, rather than producing that quantity in a single firm. In that case, the maximum of industry profit is higher when both firms invest. If average costs are strictly decreasing, total costs are lower if a single firm produces the entire quantity, rather than allocating the quantity between two firms. In that case, it would not be possible to achieve maximum industry profits by splitting production (and profits). (Instead, a side payment would be required to split industry profits.)

(b) Under second-stage cooperation, the symmetric equilibrium decision is

$$\textit{invest}\begin{Bmatrix} \text{with probability } 1 \quad \text{if } x < 20 \\ \text{with probability } p = 5 - \dfrac{x}{5} \quad \text{if } 20 < x < 25 \\ \text{with probability } 0 \quad \text{if } 25 < x \end{Bmatrix}.$$

Each firm's expected payoff is

$$\begin{Bmatrix} 20 - x \quad \text{if } x < 20 \\ -60 + 3x \quad \text{if } 20 < x < 25 \\ 15 \quad \text{if } 25 < x \end{Bmatrix}.$$

Under second-stage noncooperation, the symmetric equilibrium decision is

$$\textit{invest}\begin{Bmatrix} \text{with probability } 1 \quad \text{if } x < 11 \\ \text{with probability } p = \dfrac{18 - x}{7} \quad \text{if } 11 < x < 18 \\ \text{with probability } 0 \quad \text{if } 18 < x \end{Bmatrix}.$$

Each firm's expected payoff is

$$\begin{Bmatrix} 15 - x \quad \text{if } x < 11 \\ \dfrac{8x - 60}{7} \quad \text{if } 11 < x < 18 \\ 12 \quad \text{if } 18 < x \end{Bmatrix}.$$

(c) Profits are higher when firms do not cooperate in the second stage if and only if

$$13.33 < x < 24.$$

When investment costs are very low, with high probability (possibly equal to one) firms invest in both of the games (partial cooperation and zero cooperation). Because the first-period actions are the same (with high probability) in the two games, total profits are higher under second-period cooperation. When investment costs are very high, with high probability (possibly equal to one) firms do not invest under both scenarios. Because the first-period actions are the same (with high probability), total profits are again higher under second-period cooperation. Thus, if investment costs are sufficiently high or sufficiently low, expected payoffs are higher under partial cooperation (the first game).

Investment always confers an advantage to a firm in the second period (i.e., ignoring the cost of investment) because the investment lowers the firm's production costs and gives it a larger market share, other things equal. For an intermediate range of investment costs, first-period actions are different (with high probability) in the two scenarios. For the intermediate range of investment costs, firms are more likely to invest under second-period cooperation because the advantage of investment is much greater (compared to the scenario without second-period cooperation). However, for this range of investment costs, it is not efficient to make the investment.

(d) If firms could cooperate on both investment and output, a reasonable outcome is for only one firm to make the investment (in view of the answer to part a). Profits could be split, or the firm that invests might obtain all the profits, with that firm being chosen by the toss of a fair coin.

6.2 To find the subgame perfect equilibrium, we need to find the optimal Firm 1 action and the resulting payoff in each "subgame"; that is, at each node that is reached as a result of the first-period decisions. The following table shows this payoff structure:

Firm 1 \ *Firm 2*	*U*	*D*
U	3 5	5 2
D	0 1	0 1

For example, if Firm 1 chooses *U* in the first period and Firm 2 chooses *D* in the first period, then in the resulting second-period equilibrium Firm 1 chooses *D*, and the payoff pair is (2, 5). The equilibrium for this normal-form game is for Firm 1 to choose *U* in the first period, Firm 2 to choose *D*, and then for Firm 1 to chose *D* in the second period.

In an open-loop equilibrium, Firm 1 chooses *U* in both stages, and Firm 2 chooses *U* in the first stage. The resulting payoff pair is (5, 3). It is straightforward to confirm that these actions are a noncooperative Nash equilibrium. The equilibrium is time consistent because in the second period, Firm 1 wants to choose *U*, given that both firms chose *U* in the first period – that is, given that the game is on the equilibrium trajectory.

However, this open-loop equilibrium is not subgame perfect. If Firm 2 chooses *D* in the first period (i.e., if the game is "off the equilibrium trajectory"), Firm 1's optimal second-period decision is *D*, which is not the continuation of its open-loop trajectory of actions (*U*). In this case, the subgame perfect equilibrium outcome is for Firm 2 to choose *D* in the first period, and for Firm 1 to choose *U* and *D* in the first and second period, respectively.

It helps to write the game in "normal form"; that is, to write a payoff matrix, instead of the game tree in the problem. In an open-loop equilibrium, both players choose all controls at time 0. In this case, the set of actions and the payoffs are

Firm 2

Firm 1	*U*	*D*
U, U	5, 3	0, 0
U, D	0, 6	2, 5
D, D	0, 1	1, 6
D, U	1, 0	0, 1

Firm 1's payoff is the first element in the pair in each entry of the table, and Firm 2's payoff is the second element. From this payoff matrix, it should be clear that the unique Nash equilibrium is for Firm 1 to choose *U*, *U* and for Firm 2 to choose *U*.

One interpretation of the open-loop Nash equilibrium is that firms simultaneously commit to all of their actions. Since Firm 2 moves only in the first period, commitment does not increase its set of feasible actions. However, Firm 1 does benefit from commitment because this commitment discourages Firm 2 from choosing D in the first period. In this case, Firm 1's ability to make a commitment means that it avoids a subgame (the one labeled 1:3) that is unattractive for it.

6.3 (a) Substituting the linear inverse demand function in the first-order condition, Equation (6.8), and solving for μ implies $\mu = (p - q)/\alpha$. Differentiate this equation with respect to time and use Equation (6.9) to eliminate $\dot{\mu}$. (In taking the time derivative, recall that $q = q(p)$ so $\dot{q} = \frac{dq}{dp}\dot{p} = m\alpha(1 - 2q - p)$.) Rearranging the resulting equation implies that

$$m = \frac{-\alpha + 2\alpha p + rp - rq}{\alpha(3q - 1)} \equiv g(q, p) = \frac{-v + 2vp + p - q}{v(3q - 1)}. \quad (*)$$

(b) The condition $g(p, \frac{1-p}{2}) > -0.5$ implies

$$\frac{1}{3} < p < \frac{0.5 + 2v}{1.5 + 4v}. \quad (**)$$

To confirm this inequality, use the expression (*) for g (which is equal to m) from part (a). Evaluate m at a steady state, where $q = (1 - p)/2$. You now have an expression for m (evaluated at the steady state) that depends on p but not on q. This expression is

$$m \equiv g(q, p) = \frac{-v + 2vp + p - q}{v(3q - 1)} = -\frac{3p - 1 - 2v + 4vp}{v(3p - 1)}.$$

First, "guess" that $p > 1/3$ so that the denominator of the last expression is positive. Show that in this case equation (**) is satisfied. Now confirm your "guess." Suppose to the contrary that $p > 1/3$ is false. Show that this hypothesis and equation (*) contradicts the stability requirement, $m > -0.5$.

(c) As $v \to \infty$ (the speed of adjustment becomes large relative to the discount rate), the maximum stable price (in the differentiable MPE) approaches the monopoly level. If price adjusts very rapidly, price declines rapidly when firms increase their sales, so there is a high cost of increasing output. If firms are extremely patient, they are willing to sacrifice short-term gains for long-term profits. At the other extreme, as $v \to 0$, the maximum stable price (in the differentiable MPE) approaches the static Nash-Cournot level.

(d) Setting $m = 0$ in the steady-state condition $g(p, [1 - p]/2) = 0$ gives the open-loop, steady-state price $p = (1 + 2v)/(3 + 4v)$. The open-loop steady state is lower than the *maximum* stable steady state in the MPE.

Therefore, there are some MPE steady states that involve greater cooperation than the open-loop equilibrium.

7.1 (a) Firm i's problem is

$$\max_{\{e_{it}\}} \sum_{t=0}^{\infty} \delta^t \left(\pi(e_{it}) - \tau_{it} e_{it}\right)$$
$$\text{subject to } \tau_{t+1} = \tau_t + \alpha(e_t - \overline{e}),\ \tau_0 \text{ given.}$$

The firm's control variable is emission, and the state variable is the tax.

(b) The firm could take the tax trajectory as given (corresponding to price-taking); it could recognize that the tax is endogenous, and take its rival's trajectory of control variables as given (corresponding to Nash-Cournot); or the two firms could coordinate their emissions to reduce the tax (corresponding to cartel).

(c) To nest these three cases, suppose that when Firm i solves its optimization problem, it uses the "conjecture" $de_{jt}/de_{it} = \nu$.

(d) To obtain the Euler equation, begin with the DPE for Firm i:

$$J(\tau) = \max_{e_i}(\pi(e_i) - \tau e_i + \delta J(\tau + \alpha(e_i + e_j - \overline{e}))).$$

The first-order condition is

$$\pi_e(e_{it}) - \tau_t + (1+\nu)\alpha\delta J_\tau(\tau_{t+1}),$$

which implies that

$$J_\tau(\tau_{t+1}) = -\frac{(\pi_e(e_{it}) - \tau_t)}{(1+\nu)\alpha\delta}.$$

Using the open-loop assumption (i.e., the rival's future emissions level is independent of the future values of the state variable), the envelope condition is

$$J_\tau(\tau_t) = (-e_{it} + \delta J_\tau(\tau_{t+1})).$$

Advancing this equation by one period and using the first-order condition to eliminate the shadow values, we have

$$-\frac{(\pi_e(e_{it}) - \tau_t)}{(1+\nu)\alpha\delta} = -\left(e_{it+1} + \frac{(\pi_e(e_{it+1}) - \tau_{t+1})}{(1+\nu)\alpha}\right)$$

or

$$-(\pi_e(e_{it}) - \tau_t) + \delta\left((1+\nu)\alpha e_{it+1} + (\pi_e(e_{it+1}) - \tau_{t+1})\right) = 0.$$

The stochastic version of this equation can be estimated using the Method of Moments.

(e) In a symmetric steady state, $\tau_t = \tau_{t+1} = \tau^*$ and $e_{it} = \overline{e}/2$. The last equation implies that

$$\pi_e(e_{it}) = 1 - e_{it} = 1 - \frac{\overline{e}}{2}.$$

Substituting these results into the Euler equation implies

$$-\left(1 - \frac{\overline{e}}{2} - \tau^*\right) + \delta\left((1+\nu)\alpha\frac{\overline{e}}{2} + \left(1 - \frac{\overline{e}}{2} - \tau^*\right)\right) = 0.$$

This equation can be solved to give the steady-state tax as a function of the parameters of the problem, including ν:

$$\tau^* = 1 - \frac{\overline{e}}{2}\left(1 + \frac{\delta(1+\nu)\alpha}{1-\delta}\right).$$

The steady-state Euler equation says that the marginal benefit of increasing emissions in the current period should equal the marginal cost of the reduction needed in the subsequent period, to return the tax to its steady state.

7.2 (a) The firm's first-order condition is the same as in the open-loop model, but in taking the derivative of the DPE with respect to the state, it is necessary to take into account the fact that the rival firm's (Firm j) decision is a function of the state, and moreover the rival firm's decision does not maximize Firm i's objective. Therefore, equation (*) is replaced by

$$J_\tau(\tau_t) = (-e_{it} + \delta J_\tau(\tau_{t+1})(1 + \alpha m_t)),$$

where m_t ($m_t = \mathrm{d}e_{jt}(\tau_t)/\mathrm{d}\tau_t$.

Advancing this equation by one period and substituting in the first-order condition to eliminate the shadow value leads to the equation

$$-\frac{(\pi_e(e_{it}) - \tau_t)}{(1+\nu)\alpha\delta} = -\left(e_{it+1} + \frac{(\pi_e(e_{it+1}) - \tau_{t+1})}{(1+\nu)\alpha}(1 + \alpha m_t)\right),$$

which implies that

$$-(\pi_e(e_{it}) - \tau_t) + \delta((1+\nu)\alpha e_{it+1} + (\pi_e(e_{it+1}) - \tau_{t+1})(1 + \alpha m_t)) = 0. \qquad (**)$$

(b) The stochastic version of the Euler equation (**) cannot be estimated using standard methods, such as the Method of Moments, because it contains the unknown function $\mathrm{d}e_{jt}(\tau_t)/\mathrm{d}\tau_t$. Methods of the type described in the text can be used to estimate the model. One possibility is to choose a flexible function form for the control rule, $\tilde{e}_{jt}(\tau_t;\beta)$, where β is a vector of parameters to be estimated, and $\tilde{e}()$ is the functional form chosen by the econometrician. Substituting this function, and $\mathrm{d}\tilde{e}/\mathrm{d}\tau_t = m_t$, into the stochastic version of (**) results in a familiar estimation problem, that of finding the unknown parameters β and ν. Of course, the parameter estimates are conditioned on the econometrician's choice of functional form for the control rule. Because it is very unlikely that the econometrician chooses the correct (equilibrium) functional form, it is important that the form used be flexible.

(c) Specializing by setting $\nu = 0$, using the quadratic form of profits, and evaluating (**) at a symmetric steady state, imply

$$-\left(1-\frac{\overline{e}}{2}-\tau*\right)+\delta\left((1+\nu)\,\alpha\frac{\overline{e}}{2}+\left(1-\frac{\overline{e}}{2}-\tau*\right)(1+\alpha m*)\right)=0, \tag{***}$$

where m^* is the steady-state value of the derivative of the control rule. The steady-state condition is a single equation with two unknowns, so it does not have a unique solution (unlike the corresponding equation in the open-loop model). We encountered the analogous situation in the continuous-time sticky price model. At this level of generality, all that we can say is that in order for the steady state to be asymptotically stable, it must be the case that

$$\frac{d\tau_{t+1}}{d\tau_t}=1+2\alpha m^*$$

be less than one in absolute value, which implies that $-1/\alpha < m^* < 0$. Substituting this inequality into equation (***) tells us the range of steady-state taxes that is consistent with an asymptotically stable, symmetric differentiable MPE.

8.1 (a and b) Substitute the quadratic function into the DPE, take the first-order condition, and then impose symmetry (as described in the problem). As a result of these steps, you obtain the control rule:

$$q_t = \sigma p_{t-1} + \rho,$$
$$\sigma = f(\gamma,\Lambda) \equiv .25\left(\frac{10+9\Lambda\gamma}{10+5\Lambda+9\Lambda\gamma}\right).$$

The "constant" ρ in the control rule depends on parameters of the model (such as the costs), but not on lagged price, and this constant is not needed in order to identify Λ.

(c) If you substitute the control rule $q_t = \sigma p_{t-1} + \rho$ into the DPE and equate coefficients of p^2, you obtain the expression

$$\gamma = g(\sigma) \equiv -40\sigma\left(\frac{-1+4\sigma}{-31-72\sigma+144\sigma^2}\right).$$

(d) Use the last two equations to solve for Λ to obtain the desired result:

$$\Lambda = 0.5\frac{-52\sigma-432\sigma^2+576\sigma^3+31}{\sigma\left(49+144\sigma^2-72\sigma\right)}.$$

If your estimate of the slope of the control rule is $\sigma = 0.15$, then the estimate of the Λ is $\Lambda = 1.24$, implying that the equilibrium is somewhat more collusive than Nash-Cournot ($\Lambda = 1$) but less collusive than the cartel ($\Lambda = 2$).

To conduct a "consistency check," note that under perfect competition, profits are zero in each period, which implies that price must also be zero. (Recall the simplifying assumption that costs are constant, which are normalized to zero; equivalently, the parameter that we call the demand intercept is really the demand intercept minus the cost.) Substitute the control rule into the equation of motion for price to obtain

$$p_t = 5 + .5p_{t-1} - 2(\rho + \sigma p_{t-1}) = 5 - 2\rho + (.5 - 2\sigma)\, p_{t-1}.$$

This equation implies that a necessary condition of the current price to be equal to zero, regardless of the lagged price, is $\sigma = .25$. Substituting this value into the equation for Λ returns $\Lambda = 0$. [It is a bit more work (and was not requested) to find the equilibrium values of σ under the cartel and Nash-Cournot equilibria, but these values are, respectively, $\sigma = 0.11705$ and $\sigma = 0.16366$.

9.1 We solve for each firm independently (though interaction across firms can be added relatively easily). Let n_{is} be the number of times the outcome $y_{is} = 1$ is observed, out of a total of T observations. The observed frequency in the sample is $n^*_{is} = n_{is}/T$. For each firm, the observed frequency is used to estimate the strategies (probabilities) $\boldsymbol{\alpha}^i$.

(a) For the multinomial logit (ML), we use the logistic (exponential) distribution, which is

$$\alpha_{is} = \frac{\exp(\beta_{is})}{\sum_s \exp(\beta_{is})} \equiv \frac{\exp(\beta_{is})}{\Omega_i} \text{ for each firm } i.$$

Substituting this expression into the likelihood function and taking log yields the log likelihood for the ML-Logit (see Statistical Appendix A.31–A.35 for details) for each firm $i = 1, 2$:

$$\begin{aligned} \ell^i \equiv log(L) &= \sum_s n^*_{is}\beta_{is} - log\left[\sum_s \exp(\beta_{is})\right] \\ &= \sum_s n^*_{is}\beta_{is} - log\,\Omega_i(\boldsymbol{\beta}_i). \end{aligned}$$

Solving with respect to β yields the desired solution.

(b) If one uses ME, the problem is

$$ME = \left\{ \begin{array}{l} \hat{\boldsymbol{\alpha}}_i = argmax\left\{-\sum_s \alpha_{is}\, log\, \alpha_{is}\right\} \\ \text{s.t. } n^*_{is} = \alpha_{is};\ \sum_s \alpha_{is} = 1 \end{array} \right. .$$

We can reformulate this problem as a Lagrangean:

$$L^i(\boldsymbol{\lambda}, \boldsymbol{\eta}) = -\sum_s \alpha_{is} \log \alpha_{is} + \sum_s \lambda_{is}(n^*_{is} - \alpha_{is}) + \eta_i \left(1 - \sum_s \alpha_{is}\right).$$

The solution is:

$$\hat{\alpha}_{is} = \frac{\exp(-\hat{\lambda}_{is})}{\sum_s \exp(-\hat{\lambda}_{is})} \equiv \frac{\exp(-\hat{\lambda}_{is})}{\Omega_i(\hat{\boldsymbol{\lambda}}_i)}.$$

The dual problem is

$$\begin{aligned} L^i(\boldsymbol{\lambda}) &= -\sum_s \alpha_{is} \log \alpha_{is} + \sum_s \lambda_{is}(n^*_{is} - \alpha_{is}) \\ &= -\sum_s \alpha_{is}(\boldsymbol{\lambda}_i)[-\lambda_{is} - \log \Omega_i(\boldsymbol{\lambda}_i)] + \sum_s \lambda_{is}(n^*_{is} - \alpha_{is}) \\ &= \sum_s \lambda_{is} n^*_{is} + \log \Omega_i(\boldsymbol{\lambda}_i). \end{aligned}$$

The relationship between the ML-Logit and the ME is that $\boldsymbol{\beta} = -\boldsymbol{\lambda}$. (See the Statistical Appendix and Golan, Judge, and Miller 1996.)

(c) Finally, if one uses the GME, the moments are stochastic (unlike in the ME-ML approaches): $n^*_{is} = \alpha_{is} + e_{is}$ *for* $e_{is} \in [-1, 1]$. To formulate a solution, one defines a support space for $\boldsymbol{e}$:$\mathbf{v} = [v_1, v_2, v_3, \ldots, v_M]'$ and a vector of weights $\mathbf{w} = [w_1, w_2, w_3, \ldots, w_M]'$ where $\mathbf{v}$ and $\mathbf{w}$ are M-dimensional vectors where $M \geq 2$. Thus, $e_{is} \equiv \sum_m w_{ism} v_{sm}$ and $\sum_m w_{ism} = 1$. The errors' support is symmetric around zero and is the same for each firm or player. We can now rewrite the stochastic moments as $n^*_{is} = \alpha_{is} + e_{is} = \alpha_{is} + \sum_m w_{ism} v_{sm}$. The GME model is

$$GME = \begin{cases} \hat{\boldsymbol{\alpha}}_i\,(GME) = \operatorname{argmax}\left\{-\sum_s \alpha_{is} \log \alpha_{is} - \sum_{s,m} w_{ism} \log w_{ism}\right\} \\ \text{s.t. } n^*_{is} = \alpha_{is} + \sum_m w_{ism} v_{sm}; \sum_s \alpha_{is} = 1; \sum_m w_{ism} = 1 \end{cases}.$$

The Lagrangean is

$$\begin{aligned} L^i(\boldsymbol{\lambda}, \boldsymbol{\eta}, \boldsymbol{\mu}) = &-\sum_s \alpha_{is} \log \alpha_{is} - \sum_{s,m} w_{ism} \log w_{ism} \\ &+ \sum_s \lambda_{is}\left(n^*_{is} - \alpha_{is} - \sum_m v_{sm} w_{ism}\right) \\ &+ \eta_i\left(1 - \sum_s \alpha_{is}\right) + \sum_s \mu_{is}\left(1 - \sum_m w_{ism}\right). \end{aligned}$$

The solution is

$$\hat{\alpha}_{is}(GME) = \frac{\exp(-\hat{\lambda}_{is})}{\sum_s \exp(-\hat{\lambda}_{is})} \equiv \frac{\exp(-\hat{\lambda}_{is})}{\Omega_i(\hat{\boldsymbol{\lambda}}_i)},$$

$$\hat{w}_{ism}(GME) = \frac{\exp(-\hat{\lambda}_{is} v_m)}{\sum_m \exp(-\hat{\lambda}_{is} v_m)} \equiv \frac{\exp(-\hat{\lambda}_{is} v_m)}{\Psi_{is}(\hat{\boldsymbol{\lambda}}_i)}.$$

The corresponding dual problem is: $L^i(\boldsymbol{\lambda}) = \sum_s \lambda_{is} n^*_{is} + \log \Omega_i(\boldsymbol{\lambda}_i) + \sum_s \log \Psi_{is}(\boldsymbol{\lambda}_i)$. (See the Statistical Appendix for more details.)[1]

(d) For each firm i, we observe the outcome y_{its} and the covariates x_{itk}. We assume the strategies are fixed across time periods. (The construction of the time-dependent model, contingent on the Xs, is immediate. Just follow the derivation before and add a time dimension for the αs. However, keep in mind that it is a different game.) The stochastic moments are

$$\sum_t x_{itx} y_{its} = \sum_t x_{itx}\alpha_{is} + \sum_t x_{itx} e_{its} = \sum_t x_{itx}\alpha_{is} + \sum_{t,m} x_{itx} v_{sm} w_{ism}.$$

Thus, the new problem is

$$GME = \begin{cases} \hat{\boldsymbol{\alpha}}_i\,(GME) = argmax\left\{-\sum_s \alpha_{is} \log \alpha_{is} - \sum_{s,m} w_{ism} \log w_{ism}\right\} \\ \text{s.t.} \sum_t x_{itx} y_{its} = \sum_t x_{itx}\alpha_{is} + \sum_{t,m} x_{itx} v_{sm} w_{ism}; \sum_s \alpha_{is} = 1; \sum_m w_{ism} = 1. \end{cases}$$

The solution is

$$\hat{\alpha}_{is}(GME) = \frac{\exp\left(-\sum_{tk} x_{tik}\hat{\lambda}_{iks}\right)}{\sum_s \exp\left(-\sum_{tk} x_{tik}\hat{\lambda}_{iks}\right)} \equiv \frac{\exp\left(-\sum_{tk} x_{tik}\hat{\lambda}_{iks}\right)}{\Omega_i\left(\hat{\boldsymbol{\lambda}}_i\right)}.$$

To get the estimated errors ($\hat{e}_{its}$) and the dual, just follow previous steps.

9.2 The econometric model of Tamer (2003) is

$$\begin{aligned} \mathbf{y}_1^* &= \mathbf{x}_1\boldsymbol{\beta}_1 + \gamma_1\mathbf{y}_2 + \mathbf{u}_1 \\ \mathbf{y}_2^* &= \mathbf{x}_2\boldsymbol{\beta}_2 + \gamma_2\mathbf{y}_1 + \mathbf{u}_2 \end{aligned} \quad \text{where } y_j = \begin{cases} 1 & \text{if } y_j^* \le 0 \\ 0 & \text{otherwise,} \end{cases} \quad j = 1, 2,$$

and $\mathbf{x} = (\mathbf{x}_1, \mathbf{x}_2)$ is a vector of K exogenous variables, $\mathbf{u} = (\mathbf{u}_1, \mathbf{u}_2)$ is a random vector of some latent variables with a conditional distribution F_u representing the unobserved profits, and $\boldsymbol{\beta} = (\boldsymbol{\beta}_1, \boldsymbol{\beta}_2, \gamma_1, \gamma_2)$ are the parameters of interest.

This model may be viewed as a member of the class of censored models. To apply the GME model, we need to specify a support space for each of the signal parameters $\boldsymbol{\beta}$ and for the two sets of error terms $\mathbf{u}$. We then respecify the previous equations in terms of the probabilities associated with each

[1] These answers for the ME and GME used discrete, finite support spaces. It is possible to specify infinitely large supports and continuous densities (see, for example, Golan and Gzyl 2002, 2004).

parameter and their corresponding support spaces. Finally, we maximize the joint entropies of all parameters (signal and noise) subject to the two sets of reformulated equations and the conditions that all probabilities are proper (sum up to one). See Statistical Appendix for more details on the GME for the basic linear model. See Golan, Judge, and Perloff (1997) for an exact GME specification for this problem (and more examples).

9.3 The GME-Nash model (see Equations 9.19–9.23 and text) is:

$$\underset{\boldsymbol{\alpha},\mathbf{w},\boldsymbol{\omega}}{max}\ H(\boldsymbol{\alpha}, \mathbf{w}, \boldsymbol{\omega}) = -\boldsymbol{\alpha}' \log \boldsymbol{\alpha} - \mathbf{w}' \log \mathbf{w} - \boldsymbol{\omega}' \log \boldsymbol{\omega}$$

subject to

(A) the sample's stochastic moments conditions for each Firm i $(i = 1, 2)$:

$$\sum_t y^i_{tr}\, z_{tl} = \sum_t \alpha^i_{tr}\, z_{tl} + \sum_t e^i_{tr}\, z_{tl}$$
$$= \sum_t \alpha^i_{tr}\, z_{tl} + \sum_t \sum_m w^i_{trm}\, v^i_m\, z^i_{tl},$$

(B) the (reparameterized) necessary economic conditions for each Firm i $(i = 1, 2)$:

$$\sum_s \alpha^j_s(\mathbf{z})\, \pi^i_{rs}(\mathbf{z}) - Y^i(\mathbf{z}) \le 0$$

$$\left(\sum_s \alpha^j_s(\mathbf{z})\, \pi^i_{rs}(\mathbf{z}) - Y^i(\mathbf{z})\right) \alpha^i_r(\mathbf{z}) + \delta^i_r(\mathbf{z}) = 0,$$

(C) the requirement that all the probabilities, $\boldsymbol{\alpha}, \mathbf{w}$, and $\boldsymbol{\omega}$, are proper (sum to 1):

$$\mathbf{1}'\boldsymbol{\alpha} = \mathbf{1},\ \mathbf{1}'\mathbf{w} = \mathbf{1},\ \mathbf{1}'\boldsymbol{\omega} = \mathbf{1}.$$

Unlike with the GME, under the GCE formulation, we can incorporate priors. Let $\boldsymbol{\alpha}^{0i}$ be the strategy priors for each player i. To formulate the GCE-Nash, we substitute the entropy objective function (9.19) with the entropy divergence measure

$$I(\boldsymbol{\alpha}, \mathbf{w}, \boldsymbol{\omega};\ \boldsymbol{\alpha}^0, \mathbf{w}^0, \boldsymbol{\omega}^0) = \boldsymbol{\alpha}'\, log(\boldsymbol{\alpha}/\boldsymbol{\alpha}^0) + \mathbf{w}'\, log(\mathbf{w}/\mathbf{w}^0)$$
$$+ \boldsymbol{\omega}'\, log(\boldsymbol{\omega}/\boldsymbol{\omega}^0),$$

where, in addition to $\boldsymbol{\alpha}^{0i}$, we also allow for priors for all the other parameters and the error terms. In more explicit notations, the first term on the right hand side of $I(\bullet)$ is $\sum_{i,s} \alpha_{is}\, log\left(\alpha_{is}/\alpha^0_{is}\right)$, whereas in the GME, $H(\bullet)$, it is $-\sum_{i,s} \alpha_{is}\, log\, \alpha_{is}$. We need to specify the errors' supports to be symmetric about zero and, unless specific information is known to the researcher, the errors' priors, $\mathbf{w}^0$, should be uniform. The GCE is

$$\underset{\boldsymbol{\alpha},\mathbf{w},\boldsymbol{\omega}}{min}\ I(\boldsymbol{\alpha}, \mathbf{w}, \boldsymbol{\omega};\ \boldsymbol{\alpha}^0, \mathbf{w}^0, \boldsymbol{\omega}^0) = \boldsymbol{\alpha}' \log(\boldsymbol{\alpha}/\boldsymbol{\alpha}^0) + \mathbf{w}' \log(\mathbf{w}/\mathbf{w}^0)$$
$$+ \boldsymbol{\omega}' \log(\boldsymbol{\omega}/\boldsymbol{\omega}^0)$$

subject to the exact same (A–C) sets of restrictions as in the GME model (Equations 9.20–9.23).

As we did with the GME, to solve this model, we construct the Lagrangean and solve for $\boldsymbol{\alpha}$, $\mathbf{w}$, $\boldsymbol{\omega}$ and the Lagrange multipliers. Note that here we minimize rather than maximize as we did with the GME. If all priors are uniform, the GCE solution is equivalent to the GME solution.

9.4 Here, we provide the basic logic behind a formal proof. Both the ML and the ME treat the observed data as pure moments and provide a unique solution. Incorporating the game-theoretic conditions as additional constraints in these models results in an infeasible solution for all real data. By treating these moment conditions as stochastic, there is an additional "freedom" that allows us to incorporate all these additional restrictions (information) in the optimization procedure directly. (Note, to incorporate these game-theoretic restrictions within an ML method, one would have to represent these conditions in terms of the observed moments within the likelihood. Doing so is practically impossible for these types of problems.)

10.1 The following is one approach to testing joint hypothesis for parameters in the Airline GME-Nash model. Consider the null hypothesis H_0: $a^i > 0$, $b^i < 0$, $d^i > 0$, for $i = 1, 2$, and compare it to the alternative H_1: a^i, b^i, d^i are free for $i = 1, 2$.

To test the null hypothesis, we use the Entropy Ratio (ER) statistic (other statistics could be used as well). To compute the ER statistic, we run the original specification of the Airline GME-Nash model, which we call the *unrestricted* model. Next, we rerun the same model with the H_0 restrictions, which we call the *restricted* model. The ER statistic is two times the (absolute value) difference in the objective values of the unrestricted and restricted models. Under the null, it is approximately distributed as a $\chi^2_{(K)}$ where K is the number of degrees of freedom. In this case, K is the number of additional constraints in the restricted model (three parameters for two firms for a total of six restrictions). Thus, we decide whether to reject the null hypothesis by comparing the ER test statistic against $\chi^2_{(6)}$.

10.2 To evaluate the impact of a joint 10% decrease in the real price of sugar, together with a 15% increase in wages in the cola market, we compare the original predicted values with the updated predicted values using the original set of estimated parameters. Specifically, we estimate the full GME-Nash model and save all of the estimated parameters. Next, we decrease the real price of sugar by 10% and increase wages by 15% for all observations of both firms. Now, using the estimated parameters (Lagrange multipliers as well as demand and cost parameters), we recalculate the strategies with the revised data. We compare the new strategies with the original estimated strategies to estimate the impact of these changes.

10.3 We can use a nonlinear demand in the Airline GME-Nash model. First, we substitute for the linear demand function 10.1 a nonlinear function. (For example, $q_i = a_i + b_{1i} p_i + b_{2i} p_i^2 + d_{1i} p_j + d_{2i} p_j^2 + m_i p_i p_j + u_i$.) Second, we substitute this new equation into the optimal economic equations (10.2–10.3). Third, we define a support space for all the new parameters (e.g., b_{2i}, d_{2i}, and m_i). Fourth, we define a set of proper probabilities corresponding to these support spaces. Fifth, we specify the GME-Nash model with the new nonlinear demand. (We must incorporate the probabilities associated with each one of the new demand parameters in the objective function [the entropy function] and write the demand function in terms of its corresponding probabilities and supports.) Finally, we solve that model as we did in the chapter.

Index

adjustment cost estimation, 115
AdPT model. *See* Anderson/de Palma/Thisse (AdPT) model
advertising decisions
  in dynamic model approach, 10
  as market fundamental, 7
advertising effects
  as fundamental sources of dynamics, 116
  on oligopoly models, 148
advertising model (RS based)
  assumptions, 163–164
  consumer goodwill in, 163
  envelope theorem, 165
  estimation objectives, 163
  Euler equation in, 165–166
  hybrid form, 168–170
  MPE in, 166–168
  open-loop equilibrium in, 164–166
aggregate conjectural variation, as interpretation of λ, 45–47
aggregation bias, 31–32
Agmon, Noam, 226
Aguirregabiria, Victor
  dynamic oligopoly game, 216–217
  dynamic programming equations, 158–159
  MPE estimation, 178
AIDS demand system. *See* almost ideal demand system (AIDS)
airline industry. *See also* estimating strategies, airline case
  dynamic games in, 216–217
  marginal cost measures, 29–30, 236–237
  market structure study, 216
almost ideal demand system (AIDS), 78. *See also* linear approximate version of the almost ideal demand system (LA/AIDS) model
American Airlines. *See* estimating strategies, airline case
Anderson/de Palma/Thisse (AdPT) model, 84–85
Anderson, Patricia M., 115
Anderson, Simon P., 83
Ashenfelter, Orley, 53–54
asymptotic distribution estimators, 88–89
Athey, Susan, 104
AVC margin. *See* price–average variable cost (AVC) margin

Bain, Joe S.
  market power measurement, 3
  rates of return and industry structure, 25–26
  SCP approach, 13
Bajari, Patrick
  MPE estimation, 170, 173, 177
  simultaneous move games, 215–216
Baker, Jonathan B., 75, 77
barriers to entry
  and profitability, 25, 26, 34
  and rates of return, 26
  structural factors in performance, 24–25
  and structure-to-performance relationship, 26
Bayesian estimates
  export market structure estimation, 205–206
  inequality restrictions in, 202–203
  in linear-quadratic models, 202–204
  of market power parameters, 51
  Monte Carlo integration, 202
Bayesian firms, 106
Bayesian method of moments (BMOM) model, 286–287

Berry, Steven
market power estimation, 90
payoff functions in discrete games, 216
players' strategies in dynamic games, 215
strategic interactions, 216
Bertrand competition model, described, 35
Bertrand equilibrium
Bertrand-Nash equilibrium, ML estimates of, 257
Bjorn, Paul A., 213
book value, 15, 17–18
Bradburd, Ralph M., 32
brand diversity, 86
Bresnahan, Timothy
differentiated-product demand systems, 77
discrete games with stochastic payoffs, 214–215
entry and exit thresholds, 213–214
identification of parameter λ, 47–48
market power identification, 50
payoff functions in discrete games, 216
residual demand approach, 75, 77
simultaneous move games, 215–216
sunk costs in dynamic games, 216–217
use of conduct parameters, 43
Brozen, Yale, 26
Buhr, Brian L., 115
Bureau of Census
data limitations, 31
publications of, 20

C4/C8/C20/C50 concentration ratios. *See* concentration measures; concentration statistics
capital-output ratios
and AVC margins, 27
and concentration measures, 26–27
capital valuation, 15
Cardell, Scott N., 234
cartel equilibrium
in dynamic programming equations, 151
in linear-quadratic structures, 186
cartel model
Bertrand equilibrium in, 35
competition in, 36
equilibrium market concentration in, 36
industry concentration levels, 39
and market size increases, 38–39
and output decisions, 171
and railroad industry (U.S.), 103–104
in recessions/depressions, 104
in repeated games, 98
cartel prices
cheating, cost/benefit of, 100–102
and demand function estimation, 97–98
vs. equilibrium prices, 100
firm behavior and, 98
and output decisions, 120
cartel profits
and investment incentive, 120
and optimization problems, 123–124
and output decisions, 120
cartel solutions
in cooperative phase, 8
in Euler equations, 153–154
certainty equivalence principle, in linear-quadratic models, 187–188, 189
Chalfant, James A., 202–203
Chamberlin model, 86
cheating, cost/benefit of, 100–102
Chern, Wen S., 43
chicken, game of, 218
Ciliberto, Federico, 216
Clay, Karen, 60
Cobb-Douglas model
in oligopoly simulation effectiveness, 60–62
in structural model effectiveness, 62–64, 71
Coca-Cola. *See* estimating strategies, cola case
coffee export markets. *See* market structure estimation, coffee exports
cola demand equation, 248–249. *See also* estimating strategies, cola case
Collins, Norman R., 27
Comanor, William S., 30
commodity export markets. *See* market structure estimation, coffee exports; market structure estimation, rice exports
competition
in cartel model, 36
and firm share, 23
Hall's reduced-form model as test for, 65–69
price-to-marginal cost relationship, 54–55
and quality, 37–38
and tax incidence, 51–53
concentration and competition, 39–40
concentration measures
in airline industry, 29
buyer/seller impact on prices, 23
and capital-output ratios, 26–27
definition/classification considerations, 22
described, 20
geographic/international, 21, 22–23, 30–31
HHI, 20
import/export bias, 23, 30–31
industry performance effects on, 32
and price changes, 32
problems with, 22–23, 31–34

profitability considerations, 22, 33
and rates of return, 25–26
concentration-profit relationship, 30
concentration statistics
described, 20–21
global trends, 21
manufacturing sector, 21
U.S. trends, 21
conduct parameters, and market structure nesting, 43
conjectural variation
in dynamic games, 135–136
in estimating strategies, airline case, 241–242
and MPE, 135–136
in static model approach, 5
Connolly, Robert A., 33
consistency assumptions, in GME-Nash estimator, 233
consumers
behavior, and quality, 37–38
goodwill of, 163
representative model, 86
satisfaction of, 33
switching costs of, 116–117
continuous strategies, 8–9. *See also* repeated games, continuous strategies
continuous time models
Markov and open-loop steady states in, 192
multiplicity in, 128
control variable estimates, dynamic programming equation, 160
cooperation breakdown
and punishment phase, 102–103
in repeated games, 102–104
cooperative behavior
empirical implications (in dynamic games), 137, 139
in repeated games, continuous strategies, 104–105
in repeated games, trigger strategies, 99–104
cooperative phase
cartel solutions in, 8
in dynamic model approach, 8–9
Corts, K. S., 47
cost margins
and Lerner index, 28
price-average, 27–28
price-marginal, 28–30
Cotterill, Ronald, 34
Cournot model
HHI in, 20
oligopoly, 35
in SCP approach, 4
in static model approach, 5
Cover, Thomas M., 264–265
Cowling, Keith, 4
Cressie, Noel A., 280
Cressie-Read criterion
higher-order entropy, 280
in IT methods, 279–280
cross-entropy (CE) measure. *See* maximum entropy (ME) principle
Cubbin, John, 34
cumulative density functions, 224
"curse of dimensionality," in dynamic programming equations, 160

de Palma, André, 83
Deaton, Angus, 78
debt ratios, 16–17
decision variables
in dynamic games, 119
empirical implications, 138
demand curve rotation, 50
demand elasticity
and Lerner index, 89–90
structure-to-performance relationship, 31
demand function estimation, 97–98
demand shocks, 101–102
demand system estimates, 7
Deneckere, Raymond, 86
Denny, Michael G. S., 115
Deodhar, Satish Y., 182
depreciation measurement, 15–16
derivation approaches, in Euler equations, 153–154, 179
DiCiccio, Thomas J., 281
differentiable Markov Perfect strategies, 127–128
differential games. *See* dynamic games
differentiated-product demand systems, 77
differentiated-product structural models
advantages of, 91
approaches to, 74–75
estimation and hypothesis tests, 74
neoclassical demand system, 77–83, 91
overview, 74–75
problems with, 91
random parameter model, 83–90, 91
residual demand approach, 75–77, 91
discrete games
examples of, 147–149
payoff functions in, 216
stochastic payoffs in, 214–215
dominant firm (airline), defined, 29
dominant pair (airlines), defined, 29

Domowitz, Ian, 28
Driskill, Robert
  equilibrium selection approach, 132
  production in dynamic games, 117
Dutta, Prajit K., 126–127
dynamic decision, defined, 118
dynamic duality, in MPE estimation, 173
dynamic estimation models
  empirical implications, 98–99
  equilibrium, continuous strategies, 109
  equilibrium, trigger strategies, 109
  repeated games, continuous strategies, 104–108
  repeated games, trigger strategies, 99–104
  strategic/fundamental reasons for, 93–94
  supergames, 94–98
dynamic games
  adjustment cost inputs, 115
  in airline industry, 216–217
  conjectural variation in, 135–136
  differentiable Markov Perfect strategies, 127–128
  empirical implications, 136–140
  fundamental reasons for, 114–117
  Lerner index in, 113
  MPE and conjectural variation, 135–136
  open-loop decision rules in, 121–125
  open-loop interpretations, 140–141
  open-loop vs. Markov equilibria, 132–135
  overview, 113–114
  players' strategies in, 215
  production in, 117
  quasi-fixed inputs in, 117–121
  sticky price models, 128–132
  subgame perfection and Markov strategies, 121–125
dynamic games, estimation
  in advertising model (RS based), 163–170, 179
  discrete-time examples, 147–149
  in MPE, 170–178
  in sticky price model, 10, 149–162
dynamic model approach. *See also* market structure estimation, coffee exports; market structure estimation, rice exports
  advertising decisions in, 10
  competitive behavior in, 7–8
  continuous strategies in, 8–9
  cooperative phase in, 8–9
  equilibrium in, 8
  fundamental considerations in, 9
  fundamental vs. strategic decisions, 7–8
  game theory concepts in, 8
  linear-quadratic models, 11
  Markov equilibria, 10
  Markov strategies, 9–10
  misspecification in, 9
  oligopoly strategy estimation, 11–12
  parameter estimation, 10–11
  punishment strategies in, 8–9
  vs. static model approach, 7
  static vs. dynamic decisions by firms, 9
  subgame strategies, 8
  supergames in, 8
  time consistency in, 9–10
dynamic oligopoly game, 216–217
dynamic oligopoly model
  estimation of, 147–148
  lagged sales in, 249
  in sticky price models, 162
dynamic programming equation
  cartel equilibrium in, 151
  control variable estimates, 160
  "curse of dimensionality" in, 160
  discrete choice problem, 158–159
  estimation use in, 158–162
  loss function evaluations, 161
  optimization errors in, 161
  parameter estimation, 159
  solution approximation, 160
  in sticky price models, 151–152
dynamic programming methods, 160

econometric adjustments, 220–221
econometric methods (modern)
  as assessment tools, 263
  Bayesian method of moments (BMOM) model, 286–287
  EL formulation, 280–282
  GME model, 266–279
  GMM, 283–285
  GMM estimator in, 285–286
  and industrial organization research, 263
  information measurement, 264–265
  IT methods, 279–280, 287
  maximum entropy (ME) principle, 265–266
  in under-determined problems, 263–264
economic market (for products), 22
economic news effects, 27
effective marginal revenue function, 43
EL formulation. *See* empirical likelihood (EL) formulation
empirical comparisons, of market power models, 69–70
empirical implications (in dynamic games)

cooperative behavior and, 137, 139
decision variables, 138
equilibrium assumptions, 136–137
open-loop vs. Markov equilibria, 137–138, 139–140
quasi-fixed inputs, 138
empirical likelihood (EL) formulation, 281
Lagrangean construction in, 281–282
in linear models, 280–281, 282
in modern econometric methods, 280–282
Encoau, David, 30–31
entry and exit thresholds, 213–214
envelope theorem
in advertising models (RS based), 165
in open-loop equilibrium, 165
Epstein, Larry G., 115
equilibrium assumptions, in dynamic games, 136–137
equilibrium calculations, in dynamic games, 123
equilibrium condition requirements
in MPE, 195–197
in open-loop equilibrium, 193–195
restrictions and testing, 197–198
in subgames, 8
equilibrium market concentration, in cartel model, 36
equilibrium prices, vs. cartel prices, 100
equilibrium properties, in linear-quadratic models, 189–192
equilibrium selection approach, 132
Erickson, Gary M., 249
estimating strategies
game-theoretic restrictions in, 227–229, 259
GME techniques, 221–222
ME formulation in, 222–223
optimal behavior, 211
estimating strategies, airline case
case description, 12, 237–241
conjectural variation in, 241–242
estimator comparisons, 241–243
game theoretic consistency, 246–247
GME model vs. ME-ML model, 240–241, 242, 246
GME-Nash model estimates, 237–241
hypothesis tests, 243–245
model assumptions and conditions, 236–237
sampling/sensitivity experiments, 245–246
estimating strategies, cola case, 247–259
advertising effects, 249
bond rate effects, 258–259
case description, 12, 247, 259
cola demand equation, 248–249
exogenous variable effects, 257–259
GME-Nash model in, 249–257
income effects, 258
Lerner index in, 257, 260–261
model assumptions and conditions, 247–249
model estimates, 249–252
test statistics, 252–257
estimation method
in Hall's reduced-form approach, 58
in industrial organization research, 287
estimation objectives, advertising model (RS based), 163
estimation results, in linear-quadratic models, 200–205
estimation strategies
decision variables, 211–212
empirical study problems, 217
mixed strategies in, 217–219
ML multinomial logit/probit, 221
in oligopolies, 211
oligopoly game in, 219–221, 232–233
restrictions and information sources, 213
sample information, incorporation of, 223–227
studies and literature, 213–217
estimation strategy studies
discrete games with stochastic payoffs, 214–215
dynamic oligopoly model, 216–217
empirical study problems, 217
entry and exit thresholds, 213–214
ML approach, 213, 217
payoff functions in discrete games, 216
players' strategies in dynamic games, 215
simultaneous move games, 215–216
strategic interactions, 216
Euler equation
in advertising models (RS based), 165–166
and cartel solutions, 153–154
derivation approaches, 153–154, 179
estimation model, 154–155, 178–179
hybrid form, 168–170, 179
in MPE, 168
special case usage, 152–153
in sticky price models, 10
excess profit, 19
exogenous measures (of structures), defined, 22
explanatory variables, bias elimination considerations, 32

export markets, 198–200. *See also* market structure estimation, coffee exports; market structure estimation, rice exports

Fackler, Paul L., 160
Favaro, Edgardo, 75
Fernandez-Cornejo, Jorge, 115
Fershtman, Chaim, 119
firm behavior, and cartel prices, 98
firm share estimation, with GME estimator, 23
Folk theorem, of supergames, 96
Fraumeni, Barbara M., 25
Freeman, Richard B., 30
Froeb, Luke M.
  in dynamic programming equation, 159
  merger effects on price, 42
Fudenberg, Drew, 126
full marginal cost, defined, 113
fundamental effect, defined, 118
fundamental sources of dynamics
  advertising effects, 116
  consumer switching costs, 116–117
  demand inputs, 116–117
  investment level decisions, 115
  market power estimation, 51
  and market structure, 115–116
  production inputs, 114–116
  results in repeated game models, 104
  variable input costs, 114

game-theoretic restrictions, in estimating strategies, 227–229, 259
game theory
  in dynamic model approach, 8
  and market growth, 34–37
Gasmi, Farid
  approach to continuous λ, 51
  cola demand equation, 248–249
  ML estimates of Bertrand-Nash equilibrium, 257
  neoclassical demand system estimates, 82
Gatsios, Constantine, 120
Gelfand, Matthew D., 75
generalized entropy measures
  Cressie-Read criterion, 280
  probability distributions, 279–280
generalized-likelihood function, 226
generalized maximum entropy (GME) estimator
  in estimation strategies, 217, 221–222
  firm share estimation with, 23
  sample information, incorporation of, 223–227
generalized maximum entropy (GME) model, 266–279
  as concentrated model, 268–269, 278–279
  in discrete choice model analysis, 276–279
  entropy ratio statistic in, 270–271
  error terms in, 267
  estimation method in, 268
  extensions of, 269
  goodness-of-fit measures in, 271
  least square estimates in, 271–273
  in linear models, 271–273
  ML approach in, 273–276
  multinomial choice method, 222
  multinomial discrete choice problem in, 273–279
  normalized entropy measures in, 270
  parameter estimation, 266–267
  test statistics and diagnostics, 270–271
  utility of, 269
  Wald test (WT), 271
generalized method of moments (GMM)
  econometric methods (modern), 283–286
  estimation rule in, 284–285
  and information-theoretic measures, 280
  linear example of, 285
  moment restrictions in, 283–284
  utility of, 283
  weight matrix choice in, 285–286
Genesove, David, 60
geometric approximation, in LA/AIDS model, 78
Geroski, Paul A.
  international concentration ratios, 30–31
  SCP-based research, 34
Geweke, John F., 202–203
global concentration measures, 21
GME estimator. *See* generalized maximum entropy (GME) estimator
GME model. *See* generalized maximum entropy (GME) model
GME-Nash estimator. *See also* generalized maximum entropy (GME) model
  consistency assumptions, 233
  consistency proof, 233–234
  in estimation strategies, 227–229
  implementation of, 227–228
  profit function parameters in, 228–229
  proof, 234
  properties of, 229

GME-Nash estimator, hypothesis testing
  approximated variance computation, 232
  direct vs. indirect restrictions on, 230–231
  entropy ratio statistic in, 229–230
  extraneous covariate tests in, 231–232
  normalized entropy in, 229
GME techniques. *See* generalized maximum entropy (GME) estimator
GMM. *See* generalized method of moments (GMM)
Golan, Amos
  cumulative density functions, 224
  generalized entropy measures, 280
  generalized likelihood functions, 226
  GME multinomial choice method, 222
  GME-Nash estimator proof, 233–234
  GME techniques, 23
  GMM, 280
  summary statistics and firm shares, 23–24
Goldberg, Pinelopi Koujianou, 90
Gollop, Frank M., 82
goodwill, in advertising model (RS based), 163
Gray, Richard S., 202–203
Green, Edward J.
  cooperation breakdown in repeated games, 102–104
  estimation in repeated game models, 99
  results in repeated games models, 103, 104
Greene, William H., 273

Hajivassiliou, Vassilis, A.
  asymptotic distribution estimators, 88–89
  repeated game model results, 104
Hall, Alistair, 285–286
Hall, Peter, 281
Hall, Robert E.
  adjustment cost estimation, 115
  nonparametric model approach, 53
  reduced-form approach, 55–58
  reduced-form oligopsony model, 58, 59
Hall's reduced-form approach
  competitive market test, 65–69
  described, 55–58
  estimation method, 58
  instrument test for competition, 56, 66–67, 69–70
  in market power models, 71–72
  and oligopsony market power, 58
  oligopsony model, 59
Haltiwanger, John, 101–102
Hansen, Lars Peter
  Euler equation estimation, 155
  nonrenewable resources in dynamic games, 123
Harrington, Joseph E. Jr., 101–102
Hausman, Jerry A.
  differentiated product demand systems, 77
  merger effects on price, 42
  multi-level demand specifications, 77
  neoclassical demand system instruments, 81–82
Hayashi, Fumio, 115
Heckman, James, 214–215
Herfindahl-Hirschman Index (*HHI*)
  described, 20
  in industrial organization research, 24
  in SPC models, 4
Ho, Chun-Yu, 216–217
Hong, Han, 215–216
Hotelling model, 86
Hubbard, Glenn R., 28
hybrid form
  advertising model (RS based), 168–170
  Euler equation, 168–170, 179
Hyde, Charles E., 79
hypothesis tests. *See also* GME-Nash estimator, hypothesis testing; Stackelberg leader hypothesis
  in differentiated-product structural models, 74
  estimating strategies, airline case, 243–245
  market power models, 50–51
  in neoclassical demand systems, 82–83

identification of parameter λ, 47, 48
Imbens, Guido W.
  GMM, 280
  IT estimators, 286
import/export bias, concentration measures in, 30–31
incomplete transversality conditions, 131
indirect effects, defined, 118
industrial organization research
  econometric methods (modern) in, 263
  estimation methods in, 287
  HHI in, 24
  SCP approach, 13
industries (individual), structure-to-performance relationship in, 31
industry concentration levels, cartel model, 39
industry performance, and barriers to entry, 24–25
inflation adjustment, and rate of return, 17
information measurement, 264–265

information-theoretic (IT) estimators
  and GMM framework, 286
  and oligopoly strategies, 11–12
information-theoretic (IT) methods
  econometric methods (modern), 279–280, 287
  suitability of, 263
Inoue, Tohru, 115
instrument test for competition, in Hall's reduced-form approach, 56
International Coffee Agreements (ICAs), 198–199
interpretation of λ. *See* λ, interpretation of
investment decisions
  and cartel profits, 120
  in dynamic games, 120
  as fundamental sources of dynamics, 115
IT methods. *See* information-theoretic (IT) methods

Jaynes, Edwin T.
  ME formulation, 222
  ME principle, 265
Johnson, Phillip, 286
Jorgenson, Dale W., 25
Judd, Kenneth, 160
Judge, George G., 226
  cumulative density functions, 224
  EL formulation, 282
  GME multinomial choice method, 222
  GME-Nash estimator, 233–234
  GME techniques, 23
  GMM, 280
  IT estimators, 286
  summary statistics and firm shares, 23–24
Jun, Byoung, 133
Just-Bresnahan-Lau approach, 50
Just-Chern-Bresnahan-Lau model, 58–59
Just, Richard E.
  market power identification, 50
  use of conduct parameters, 43

Kalman filter, 106
Kandori, Michihiro, 101–102
Karp, Larry
  dynamic oligopoly model, 249
  investment decisions in dynamic games, 120
  linear-quadratic models, 182
Kim, Dae-Wook, 60
Kim, Hanho, 115
Kitamura, Yuichi
  GMM, 280
  IT estimators, 286
Kloek, Tuen, 202
Knittel, Christopher R., 60
Kolmogorov-Smirnov test, 23
Kooreman, Peter, 213
Kwoka, John E. Jr.
  AVC margins, 28, 30
  competition and firm share, 23
  market share and profits, 33

λ
  approach to continuous, 51
  as conduct parameter, 43
  as continuous variable, 51
λ, interpretation of
  conjectural variation in, 45–47
  in Lerner index, 45
LA/AIDS model. *See* linear approximate version of the almost ideal demand system (LA/AIDS) model
Laffont, Jean Jacques
  cola demand equation, 248–249
  ML estimates of Bertrand-Nash equilibrium, 257
Lagrangean construction
  in EL formulation, 281–282
  in GME models, 268–269
  in ME principle, 266
Lamm, R. McFall Jr., 34
Lapham, Beverly, 133
Lau, Lawrence J.
  identification of parameter λ, 47
  market power identification, 50
  use of conduct parameters, 43
Lawless, Jerry, 281, 282
Lee, Lung-Fei
  asymptotic distribution estimators, 88–89
  repeated game model variations, 103
Leonard, Gregory K.
  merger effects on price, 42
  multi-level demand specifications, 77
Lerner index. *See also* price–cost margins
  and cost margins, 28
  defined, 2
  and demand elasticity, 89–90
  in dynamic games, 113
  in estimating strategies, cola case, 257, 260–261
  interpretation of λ in, 45
  market power measurements and, 2, 4
  private-information effects, 261
  and rates of return, 18
leverage, and rates of return, 16
linear approximate version of the almost ideal demand system (LA/AIDS) model

budget-share equation in, 78
conditions in, 79
constant returns to scale in, 79
demand curve slopes in, 79–80
elasticities of demand in, 79
equilibrium in continuous strategies, 79
geometric approximation in, 78
incomplete demand system estimation, 78
optimality equation in, 80
linear-quadratic models
assumptions and definitions, 182–183
certainty equivalence principle, 187–188, 189
dynamic model, 184–185
equilibrium comparison with, 11
equilibrium properties, 189–192
estimation problems in, 188–189
and export markets, 198–200
Karp/Perloff approach, 182
market power estimation with, 11, 181
MPE condition requirements, 195–197
MPE restrictions in, 207–208
open-loop equilibrium condition requirements, 193–195
open-loop restrictions in, 206–207
open-loop vs. Markov equilibria, 181–182, 205
static analog in, 183–184
and stochastic variables, 188
structural implications of, 185–187
linear-quadratic models, estimation results
Bayesian estimates, 202–204
classical estimates, 200–201
equilibrium conditions for, 192–198
simulations, 204–205
linear-quadratic structure, implications
closed-form solution in, 186
control rules in, 185, 186
Markov equilibrium in, 185–186
recursive structure, 186–187
linear random utility model
AdPT model, 83, 84–85
optimal pricing strategies, 85–86
PS model, 83–85
long-run profits, 33
loss function evaluation
dynamic programming equation, 161
in MPE estimation, 177
lower bound, defined, 36–37
Luh, Yir Hueih, 115
Lustgarten, Steven H.
economic news effects, 27
price–cost margins, 30
Mann, Michael, 26
manufacturing sector
concentration ratio trends, 21
value added in, 21
marginal cost measures, 29–30, 236–237. *See also* price–marginal cost margins
marginal revenue function, 43
market fundamental, advertising decisions as, 7
market performance measures, 14. *See also* price–cost margins; rate of return; Tobin's q
market power
defined, 1
degree exercised by firms, 1–2
in dynamic games, 93–94, 113–114
in estimated demand systems, 89–90
estimation of, 2
identification of parameter λ, 80–81
measurement of, 3
and product differentiation, 74
research applications, 1
static model approaches, 2
variation across industries, 2
market power estimation
in differentiated goods markets, 90
Lerner index in, 2
linear-quadratic models, 11, 181
and open-loop interpretations, 141
in open-loop vs. Markov equilibria, 181–182
ratio estimation problems, 51
market power models
demand curve rotation in, 50
estimation and hypothesis tests, 50–51
function form choice, 49–50
identification of parameter λ, 47–50
non-parametric approach, 42
oligopsony, 58–59
market power models, effectiveness of
cost evidence, 60
empirical comparisons, 69–70
Hall's reduced-form approach, 65–69, 71–72
oligopoly simulations, 60–62
structural models, 62–64, 71–72
market power models, structural approach
estimation and hypothesis tests, 50–51
identification of parameter λ, 47–50
illustration of (typical), 43–45
interpretations of λ in, 45–47
and market power of firms, 42
tax incidence, 51–53
textile market example (U.S.), 44–45

market share and profits, 33
Market Share Reporter, 23
market size increases, and cartel model, 38–39
market structure
  airline industry study, 216
  and fundamental sources of dynamics, 115–116
market structure estimation, coffee exports
  Bayesian estimates, 202–204, 205–206
  classical estimates, 200–201
  dynamic models, 198–199
  estimation results, 200
  simulations, 204–205
market structure estimation, rice exports
  Bayesian estimates, 202–204, 205–206
  classical estimates, 200–201
  estimation results, 200–205
  model assumptions, 199–200
  simulations, 204–205
market structure measures. *See also* structure-to-performance relationship
  barriers to entry, 24–25
  concentration measure problems, 22–23
  concentration ratios, 20
  concentration statistics, 20–21
  firm size distribution, 20
  summary statistic biases, 23–24
  unionization, 25
Markov Perfect equilibria estimation
  dynamic duality in, 173
  empirical limitations, 178
  general function forms, 173
  inequality equation example, 174–177
  linearity assumption, 174, 177–178
  loss functions under, 177
  market structure evaluation, 172–173
  and optimization problems, 171, 172
  parameter estimation, 170–171, 179
  profit function parameters in, 170
  stage estimates, 178
Markov Perfect equilibrium (MPE)
  in advertising models (RS based), 166–168
  and conjectural variation, 135–136
  consistent conjectural equilibria, 141
  in dynamic model approaches, 10
  equilibrium condition requirements in, 195–197
  equilibrium response, 135
  Euler equation under, 168
  incomplete transversality condition, 141
  MPE continuum, 141–142
  multiplicity of, 126–127
  as Pareto superior MPE support, 126
Markov Perfect restrictions, in linear-quadratic models, 207–208
Markov strategies
  defined, 9, 119
  dynamic model approach, 9–10
  investment and cooperative states, 126
  renewable resources in dynamic games, 126–127
  smooth strategies in, 127–128
  subgame perfection in, 126
  switching regressions, limitations of, 127
Marvel, Howard, 34
Mason, Edward S., 3, 13
Matsushima, Hitoshi, 104
Mátyás, Laszlo, L, 285–286
maximum entropy-maximum likelihood (ME-ML) models, in estimating strategies (airlines), 240–241
maximum entropy (ME) formulation
  entropy criterion, 222
  in multinomial problems, 222–223
maximum entropy (ME) principle
  distribution estimation, 265
  Lagrangean construction in, 266
  in modern econometric methods, 265–266
maximum likelihood (ML) approach
  in estimation strategies, 213, 217
  Lerner index calculation, 257
  multinomial logit/probit in, 221
McCafferty, Stephen, 117
McFadden, Daniel, 88
McGuire, Paul, 173
ME formulation. *See* maximum entropy (ME) formulation
ME-ML model. *See* maximum entropy-maximum likelihood (ME-ML) models
ME principle. *See* maximum entropy (ME) principle
merger effects on price, 42
Miller, Douglas, 226
  cumulative density functions, 224
  EL formulation, 282
  GME multinomial choice method, 222
  GME-Nash estimator proof, 234
  GMM, 280
  IT estimators, 286
Mino, Kazuo
  continuous time models, 128
  incomplete transversality conditions, 131
Mira, Pedro
  dynamic programming equation, 158–159
  MPE estimation, 178

Miranda, Mario J., 160
Mishel, Lawrence R., 30
Mittelhammer, Ronald
  EL formulation, 282
  GME-Nash estimator proof, 234
  GMM, 280
  IT estimators, 286
mixed logit. *See* random parameter model
mixed strategies
  equilibria evaluation in, 218–219
  in estimation strategies, 217–219
  illustration of, 217–218
ML approach. *See* maximum likelihood (ML) approach
modern static studies, vs. SCP approach, 70–71
monopoly profits, and rate of return, 17–18
MPE. *See* Markov Perfect equilibrium (MPE)
Muellbauer, John N., 78
Mueller, Dennis C., 33
Muller, Eitan, 119
Mullin, Wallace, 60
multi-level demand specifications, 77
multinomial discrete choice problem
  in GME model, 273–279
  ML approach in, 273–276
multiproduct elasticity, defined, 90

Nash equilibrium, in repeated games, continuous strategies, 105–106
Nash-in-advertising equilibrium
  endogenous state variable changes, 179
  vs. open-loop Nash equilibrium, 164
  in RS model, 163
neoclassical demand system
  differentiated-product structural models, 91
  estimates in, 80–81, 82
  hypothesis tests, 82–83
  instrument use in, 80–81
  LA/AIDS model example, 78–80
  market power determination with, 77
  multi-level demand specifications, 77–78
  parameter identification, 80–81
neoclassical demand system estimates
  continuous parameters in, 82
  exogenous variables in, 81–82
neoclassical demand system instruments, 81–82
Nevo, Aviv
  market power estimation, 90
  merger effects on price, 42
  neoclassical demand system estimates, 80–82
news effects, economic, 27
nominal rate of return, 17
nonparametric model approach
  comparative statistics experiment, 53–55
  as competitive behavior test, 53, 54
  Hall's reduced-form approach, 55–58
nonrenewable resources, in dynamic games, 123
normalized entropy measures, in GME model, 270

oligopoly game (in estimating strategies)
  assumptions/objectives, 219
  econometric adjustments, 220–221
  modeling framework, 232–233
  strategic alternatives (formulas), 219–220
oligopoly models
  advertising effects on, 148
  strategy estimation in, 11–12
oligopoly simulations, 60–62
oligopsony market power models
  Hall's reduced-form oligopsony model, 59
  and reduced-form models, 58
  structural model approach, 58–59
open-loop decision rules
  defined, 122
  in dynamic games, 121–125
  dynamics in, 123
  equilibria in, 122–125
  optimization problem solutions in, 124
  reduced-form profit function in, 121–122
  and subgame perfection, 125
  time consistency of, 122–123
open-loop equilibrium
  advertising model (RS based), 164–166
  condition requirements, 193–195
  envelope theorem, 165
  in game-theoretic contexts, 187–188
  and stochastic variables, 188
open-loop interpretations
  in deterministic settings, 140
  in empirical dynamic oligopolies, 140
  information availability, 140–141
  and market power estimation, 141
  open-loop vs. Markov equilibria, 141
  in stochastic settings, 140
open-loop restrictions, in linear-quadratic models, 206–207
open-loop strategies, defined, 9

open-loop vs. Markov equilibria
  in commodity export models, 200–201
  comparison of, 147
  continuous time model example, 133–134
  in dynamic games, 132–135, 137–138, 139–140
  linear equilibrium, 133
  in linear-quadratic models, 205
  market power estimation in, 181–182
  MPE selection, 132–133
  rival behavior in, 132, 133
  strategic complements/substitutes, 133, 134–135, 189–192
optimal pricing strategies, multiproduct, 85–86
optimization errors, in dynamic programming equation, 161
optimization problems
  and cartel profits, 123–124
  and MPE estimation, 171, 172
Ostrovsky, Michael, 215
Oum, Tae Hoon, 236–237
output decisions, and cartel model, 171
Over, Mead A. Jr., 32
Owen, Art B., 281, 282

Pakes, Ariel
  MPE estimation, 170, 173
  players' strategies in dynamic games, 215
parameter estimation
  in Bayesian firms, 106
  in dynamic model approach, 10–11
  in generalized maximum entropy model, 266–267
  in MPE, 170–171, 179
payoff functions, in discrete games, 216
payoff-relevant variables, 119
Pepsi-Cola. *See* estimating strategies, cola case
perceived marginal revenue function, 43
Perloff, Jeffrey M.
  brand diversity in spatial models, 86
  cumulative density functions, 224
  dynamic oligopoly model, 249
  GME multinomial choice method, 222
  GME-Nash estimator proof, 233–234
  GME techniques, 23
  LA/AIDS model, 79
  linear-quadratic models, 182
  linear random utility model, 83
  market power estimation, 51
  summary statistics and firm shares, 23–24
Perloff/Salop (PS) model, in linear random utility models, 83–85
Petersen, Bruce C., 28
Pindyck, Robert
  adjustment cost estimation, 115
  market power in dynamic games, 113–114
Pinske, Joris, 90
players' strategies, in dynamic games, 215
Porter, Robert H.
  cooperation breakdown in repeated games, 102–104
  estimation in repeated game models, 99
  results in repeated game models, 104
  variation in repeated game models, 103
Preston, Lee E., 27
price–average variable cost (AVC) margin
  at firm level, 28
  and industry concentration, 28
  and industry growth, 30
  industry structure proxy, 27
  vs. price-marginal cost margin, 18–19
  regression (typical), 27–28
price–cost margins
  and advertising–sales ratios, 30
  defined, 14
  described, 18–19
  efficiency vs. competition, 28
  explanatory variables in, 30
  and increased buyer concentration, 30
  and industry concentration, 4
  and industry structure, 27–30
  and Lerner index, 18
  union effects on, 30
price–marginal cost margins
  in airline industry, 29–30
  vs. AVC margin, 18–19
  described, 28–30
price-theory models vs. SCP approach, 13
price-to-marginal cost relationship, and competition, 54–55
prisoners' dilemma, in supergames, 97–98
private-information effects, Lerner index in, 261
product differentiation, and market power, 74
production inputs, and fundamental sources of dynamics, 114–116
profit function parameters, in GME-Nash estimator, 228–229
profitability
  and barriers to entry, 25, 34
  concentration measure considerations, 22, 33
PS model. *See* Perloff/Salop (PS) model
punishment phase
  and cooperation breakdown, 102–103

in repeated games, 106–107
in supergames, 97–98
punishment strategies, in dynamic model approach, 8–9

Qin, Jing, 281, 282
quality, and endogenous sunk costs, 37–38
quasi-fixed inputs in dynamic games
cooperative outcomes, 120
example, 117–121
output decisions, 120
technology decisions, 119

railroad industry (U.S.), cartel model of, 103–104
random demand shifters, in sticky price model estimations, 157–158
random-parameter logit (RPL) model
and logit generalization, 87–88
substitution patterns in, 88
random parameter model
differentiated-product structural models, 91
estimation of, 86–89
linear random utility model, 83–86
market power in, 89–90
rate of return
and advertising spending, 16, 26
and barriers to entry, 26
calculation difficulties, 15–18
and capital valuation, 15
and concentration measures, 25–26
conceptual approach, 14–15
and debt ratios, 16–17
defined, 14
and depreciation measurement, 15–16
differences in firms, 25
and highly leveraged firms, 16
and industry structure, 25–26
and inflation adjustment, 17
and Lerner index, 18
and monopoly profits, 17–18
and price–cost margins, 18–19
and R&D spending, 16, 26
real rate of return, 17
and risk adjustment, 16
and structural variables, 26
and tax rate calculations, 18
and Tobin's *q*, 19
Ravenscraft, David
AVC margins, 28, 30
market share and profits, 33
Read, Timothy R.C., 280
real rate of return, 17
recursive structure, of linear-quadratic model, 186–187
reduced-form models. *See* Hall's reduced-form approach; nonparametric model approach
reduced-form oligopsony model, 59
Reiss, Peter C.
discrete games with stochastic payoffs, 214–215
entry and exit thresholds, 213–214
payoff functions in discrete games, 216
simultaneous move games, 215–216
structural model derivation, 51
sunk costs in dynamic games, 216–217
Renyi, Alfred, 279–280
repeated game models
cheating, cost/benefit of, 99–102
estimates in, 99
research findings, 104
results, 104
repeated games. *See also* dynamic estimation models
cartel model in, 98
cooperation breakdown in, 102–104
estimating models, 104
model results, 104
model variations, 103
Nash equilibrium in, 105–106
repeated games, continuous strategies
cooperative behavior in, 104–105
Nash equilibrium in, 105–106
price-setting game model, 104
punishment phase, 106–107
tacit collusion estimation in, 106–108
repeated games, trigger strategies
cheating, cost/benefit of, 100–102
cooperative behavior in, 99–104
estimation models in, 99
residual demand approach, differentiated-product structural models, 75–77, 91
Reynolds, Stanley
continuous time models, 192
production in dynamic games, 117
rice export markets. *See* market structure estimation, rice exports
risk adjustment, and rate of return, 16
Roberts, Mark J.
dynamic oligopoly model, 249
neoclassical demand system estimates, 82
RS model, 147, 149, 163, 168–170, 182
Romano, Joseph P., 281

Rotemberg, Julio
  adjustment cost estimation, 115
  cooperation breakdown, 102–103
  estimation in repeated game models, 99
  repeated game model results, 104
  repeated game models, 99–102
  results in repeated game models, 104
Rothschild, Michael, 86
RPL model. *See* random-parameter logit (RPL) model
RS model. *See also* advertising model (RS based)
  data and assumptions in, 149
  open-loop equilibrium in, 147
RS model simplification, 168–170
Ruback, Richard S., 30
Rust, John, 158–159
Ruud, Paul, 88–89
Ryan, Stephen, 215–216

Salinger, Michael A.
  concentration–profit relationship, 30
  structural variables and rates of return, 26
Saloner, Garth
  cooperation breakdown, 102–103
  estimation in repeated game models, 99
  repeated game models, 99–102
  results in repeated game models, 104
Salop, Steven C.
  brand diversity in spatial models, 86
  linear random utility model, 83
Salvanes, Kjell G., 162
Samuelson, Larry
  dynamic oligopoly model, 249
  RS model, 147, 149, 163, 168–170, 182
Schmalensee, Richard
  performance measures, 33
  SCP-based research, 34
Schwartz, Stephen, 33
SCP approach. *See* structure–conduct–performance (SCP) approach
SCP paradigm. *See* structure–conduct–performance (SCP) approach
shadow values, defined, 151
Shannon, Claude E., 264
Shannon entropy function
  and EL criterion, 280–281
  IT methods, 279–280
Sheldon, Ian M., 182
Shen, Edward A., 51
simultaneity bias problem, 33
simultaneous move games, estimation strategy studies, 215–216
Singleton, Kenneth J., 155
Slade, Margaret E.
  equilibrium calculations in dynamic games, 123
  merger effects on price, 42
  repeated games, continuous strategies, 104, 106–108
  residual demand approach, 75
Solow residual, 56
Solow, Robert, 56
Spady, Richard H., 286
spatial model, 86
Spiller, Pablo T., 75
Stackelberg equilibrium rules, and open-loop strategies, 141
Stackelberg leader hypothesis
  and profit maximization, 82–83
  test difficulties, 91
static analog, in linear-quadratic models, 183–184
static decision, defined, 118
static model approach
  assumptions and estimates, 5–6
  conjectural variation in, 5
  Cournot models in, 5
  demand system estimates, 7
  firm-level studies, 6–7
  industry-level data studies, 5–6
  market power explanations in, 5
  optimality estimation in, 5
Steen, Frode, 162
Stefanou, Spiro E., 115
sticky price model
  equilibrium conditions in, 130–132
  equilibrium selection, 132
  estimation of, 10
  example of, 128–129
  Markov assumption in, 129
  MPE vs. differential games, 131–132
  open-loop equilibria in, 129
  static problem sequence in, 162
sticky price model, estimation in
  data and assumptions, 149
  demand assumption, 156–157
  demand function, 149–150
  demand uncertainty, 150
  dynamic oligopoly model example, 162
  dynamic programming equation, 151–152, 158–162
  Euler equation, 152–154
  general model equation, 155–156
  random demand shifters, 157–158

Stigler, George J.
long-run profits, 33
price-theory models vs. SCP approach, 13
stochastic games. *See* dynamic games
Stone, John R. N., 78
straight-line depreciation, 15–16
strategic complements, defined, 133
strategic interactions, estimation strategy studies, 216
strategic substitutes, defined, 133
strategies (firm), defined, 1
structural approach. *See* market power models, structural approach
structural models
Cobb-Douglas model in, 71
derivation approaches, 51
reliability of, 60
structure–conduct–performance (SCP) approach
background of, 3–5
and buyer/seller conduct, 3
conceptual problems with, 32–34
criticisms of, 3, 13
defined, 13
and differentiated-product structural models, 74
empirical research, 39–40
industrial organization research, 13
industry comparisons, 13
market power causes, 2, 4–5
microeconomic analysis in, 13
modern approach/theory, 34
vs. modern static studies, 70–71
Nash-Cournot equilibrium quantities in, 4
Nash equilibrium in, 3
Nash-in-quantities assumption in, 4
recent research, 34
study flaws, 31–32
study stages of, 13–14
theoretical model example, 3–5
structure-to-performance relationship
and advertising spending, 26
and barriers to entry, 26, 34
and capital-output ratios, 26–27
conceptual problems with, 32–34
consumer satisfaction in, 33
demand elasticity effects, 31
and economic news, 27
in individual industries, 31
international studies, 30–31
measurement/statistical problems with, 31–32
price–cost margins, 27–30
and R&D spending, 26
and rates of return, 25–26, 27
Stutzer, Michael
GMM, 280
IT estimators, 286
subgame perfection and Markov strategies in dynamic games, 121–125
history dependent strategies and, 125
investment and cooperative states, 126
MPE in, 126
multiplicity of MPE, 126–127
open-loop equilibria in, 125
subgame strategies, described, 8
substitution patterns, complexity of, 88
Sullivan, Daniel A., 53–54
summary statistic biases
and data availability, 24
overview, 23–24
summary statistics, and firm shares, 23–24
Sumner, Daniel, 53–54
sunk cost
endogenous, 37–39
exogenous, 35–37
supergames
decision rules in, 94, 95–96
described, 8
equilibrium vs. subgame perfect equilibrium, 95–96, 108–109
Folk theorem of, 96
game history/past values in, 94
Nash equilibrium in, 94
outcomes/firm actions in, 94–95
prisoners' dilemma example, 97–98
punishment phase, 97–98
subgames in, 95
supply substitutes, 22
Suslow, Valerie
repeated game model results, 104
residual demand approach, 75
Sutton, John
concentration and competition, 39–40
game-theory and market growth, 34–37
international concentration ratios, 30
SCP-based research, 34
vertical differentiation, 38–39
symmetric equilibria, in static game models, 148

Tamer, Elie
discrete games with stochastic payoffs, 214–215
payoff functions in discrete games, 216
strategic interactions, 216

tax incidence, and market structure, 51–53
tax rate calculations, and rate of return, 18
Thisse, Jacques-François, 83
Thomadakis, Stavros B., 27
Thomas, Joy A., 264–265
time-consistency
  in dynamic model approaches, 9–10
  and equilibrium, 9–10
Tirole, Jean, 126
Tobin's *q*
  calculation considerations, 19
  defined, 14, 19
  described, 19
Train, Kenneth E., 88
trigger strategies. *See* repeated games, trigger strategies
Troesken, Werner, 60
Tsallis, Constantino, 280
Tsallis measure, 280
Tsutsui, Shunichi
  continuous time models, 128
  incomplete transversality conditions, 131

unionization
  effects of, 25
  and profitability, 30
United Airlines. *See* estimating strategies, airline case
unrelated equations method, 200
useful life (of assets), 15–16

value added, in manufacturing sector, 21
Van Dijk, Herman K., 202
vertical differentiation
  defined, 38
  product quality ranking in, 38–39
Vives, Xavier, 133
Voos, Paula B., 30
Vuong, Quang H.
  approach to continuous λ, 51
  cola demand equation, 248–249
  ML approach, 213
  ML estimates of Bertrand-Nash equilibrium, 257

Wald test (WT), in generalized maximum entropy model, 271
Ware, Roger, 133
Waterson, Michael, 4
Weiher, Jesse C., 29
Weiss, Leonard W.
  simultaneity bias problem, 33
  structural variables and rates of return, 26
Werden, Gregory J., 42
White, Kenneth J., 202–203
White, Lawrence J.
  concentration measures, 32
  global concentration measures, 21
Wilson, Thomas A., 30
Wolak, Frank A., 51

Zellner, Arnold
  Bayesian method of moments (BMOM) model, 286–287
  market power estimation, 51
  unrelated equations method, 200
Zhang, Anming, 236–237
Zhang, Yimin, 236–237
Zimmerman, Martin B., 30